Teaching in Post-Compulsory Education

1303
£2

D0530726

Also available from Continuum:

Teaching in Further Education 6th Edition – Curzon
Reflective Teaching in Further and Adult Education – Hillier
Widening Participation in Post-Compulsory Education – Thomas
Continuum Guide to Teaching in Higher Education – Martinez-Pons
Teaching and Learning in Higher Education – Evans and Abbott

Teaching in Post-Compulsory Education

Learning, Skills and Standards

Fred Fawbert
with contributions by
Alison Barton, Lyn Butcher, Janet Hobley, Yvonne Hutton, Karen Lowe,
Margaret Postance, Tricia Semeraz

continuum
LONDON • NEW YORK

Continuum
The Tower Building   15 East 26th Street
11 York Road   New York
London SE1 7NX   NY 10010

© Fred Fawbert 2003

All rights reserved. No part of this publication may be reproduced or transmitted in any form or by any means, electronic or mechanical, including photocopying, recording, or any information storage or retrieval system, without prior permission in writing from the publishers.

British Library Cataloguing-in-Publication Data
A catalogue record for this book is available from the British Library.

ISBN: 0 8264 5594 8 (hardback) 0 8264 5595 6 (paperback)

Typeset by YHT Ltd, London
Printed and bound in Great Britain by MPG Limited, Bodmin

CONTENTS

ACKNOWLEDGEMENTS

THE AUTHORS

At the time of writing, we were all teachers on the University of Central Lancashire Certificate in Education/PGCE (Post-Compulsory) programme delivered by a network of partner colleges in the north-west of England.

In putting this book together, we have all drawn on our many years of practice in teacher education. As one of the first programmes in the country to implement the FENTO Standards for professional development in Further Education, we felt that our experience may benefit our colleagues in other teacher education programmes and their students. Our intentions have been twofold. We wished to provide new and intending teachers in the post-compulsory sector with a useful structure to help them relate practice and theory to the national Standards and to present this in the form of a guide to the many other informative publications. To this end we have attempted to acknowledge all our sources and we apologize for those we may have missed.

Alison Barton	Yvonne Hutton
Lyn Butcher	Karen Lowe
Fred Fawbert*	Margaret Postance
Janet Hobley	Tricia Semeraz

* Dr Fred Fawbert was the Programme Director of the UCLAN Cert Ed/PGCE at the time of writing and wishes to acknowledge the contribution of his colleagues who found time to write their chapters while working full-time within the highly pressurized context of Further Education.

Our sincere thanks to Kathryn Ecclestone for her Foreword to this book. Dr Ecclestone is currently seconded part-time from the University of Newcastle School of Education to the Cambridge-based Teaching and Learning Research Project, where she is supporting work within the FE/Post-16 Sector. Kathryn was one of the first external examiners of the UCLAN Cert Ed/PGCE and we are pleased she has remained such a good friend of the programme.

TIPCET (Teachers in Post-Compulsory Education and Training) was originally formed among members of the UCLAN network of partner colleges as a forum to discuss all aspects of provision in the sector. We have developed our website *tipcet.com* to continue the debate electronically and nationally. This site also contains additional materials, which we have developed to support each of the chapters in this book. Although there is a small fee to pay when you become a member, you may wish first of all to explore the contents of the site before joining. We are confident that all teachers, trainers and support workers in PCET will find something of value and we do hope that you will decide to join us and contribute your views to current national debates.

Finally, we would like to receive feedback from any readers on the effectiveness or otherwise of this book. We would also welcome recommendations about the sort of materials you would like to see added to our website *tipcet.com*. Please email: *fredfawbert@tipcet.com*

FOREWORD

Starting a new job in post-16 teaching is daunting enough, whether you are working part-time or full-time. Participants in a post-16 teacher training course might be full-time lecturers in a further education college, adult education centre or in workplace training. Others of you will be part-time, doing a few hours in different institutions.

Not only is the day-to-day teaching complicated but you are working under the full glare of the political spotlight that now shines over the whole post-16 education and training sector. Policy-makers in government, and their many intermediaries in the Learning and Skills Councils, inspectorates, awarding and qualification bodies, are more interested in the processes and outcomes of post-16 teaching, learning and assessment than ever before.

Ambitious targets to get many more people into further education, training and higher education, and for them to achieve more qualifications, put new pressures on educational institutions and training organizations and on the teachers working in them. There are also looming pressures from the Learning and Skills Council to rationalize education and training provision in local areas and gear it more closely to the needs of local labour markets. At the same time, there are calls for education to achieve goals of social inclusion and citizenship and to motivate people to be lifelong learners. At a DfES conference in 2002, the Minister for Lifelong Learning offered a scenario where educational achievement is supposed to combat everything from poverty and low skills to poor health, low self-esteem and single parenthood! And yet, in addition to these bold claims, institutions and teachers are under other pressures to be efficient and cost-effective in getting more learners through the system more cheaply.

The demands are therefore very great and finding your own goals, values and educational ideals among them all is no easy task. Although policy-makers have a legitimate interest in the quality of post-16 teaching, a teacher training course also has to support you in working out your own motives to teach young people and adults. As the writers of this textbook show so enthusiastically, teaching gives us the chance, at least occasionally, to glimpse what it is like to inspire people, to work together on something new, difficult or just plain interesting. You may meet jaded and cynical teachers but you will also be lucky enough to work with staff who are still passionate about getting this occasional glimpse, even after many years of teaching. And, if you approach this teacher training course with openness and enthusiasm, you are likely to experience it yourself as a student!

The more you can identify your own motives for teaching, your own strengths and weaknesses in studying and learning and the educational values you care about, the more it is possible to understand and deal confidently with the profound pressures arising from political interest and resource constraints. This book, together with the course you are on, are an invaluable support and you should really maximize everything you can gain from it, for your own growth and skill development and for colleagues in your group.

It's also worth knowing that behind the FENTO Standards that underpin the course there have been heated debates and disagreements over the past ten years about how best to train people to be effective, even inspiring, teachers in post-16 education. The university and college team who design and run your course have been at the heart of these discussions. The changes that have been made to the FENTO Standards therefore reflect the views of very experienced post-16 teacher educators. They are now a far cry from the narrow, instrumental competences that were first proposed in 1994.

But however broadly framed a standards-based qualification is, it still offers two options for students and teachers. The first is to treat the Standards instrumentally, to 'get through them' as quickly and painlessly as possible, to accumulate the evidence in order to 'tick off' the Standards and get the qualification. The second is to see them as a vehicle for reflection and self-assessment, as a diagnosis of your strengths and weaknesses at the beginning and a way of developing skills and insights. All the post-16 teacher educators I know will motivate you to take the second option.

It's also interesting to reflect as you contemplate the Standards and what's going to be involved in meeting them, how the students you teach might choose between the two options. If they choose the first, it is unlikely that you or they will glimpse the delight of deep involvement in learning that lies at the heart of good teaching. But if they choose the second, and you helped them do so, you would be making a really important contribution to the goals of lifelong learning as a love of learning, not as an instrumental compliance with assessment targets.

That's why doing a teacher training course is so fascinating, but also why it places such a responsibility on you. How you decide to get involved in your own learning will say something about the expectations you have of your students. The designers and teachers of your course hope that you will maximize the chance to become a better teacher and a better learner. The pressures in post-16 education and training have never been greater but the opportunity to glimpse what it means to be an excellent teacher is too good an opportunity to miss.

Dr Kathryn Ecclestone
Senior Lecturer in Post-Compulsory Education
November 2002

Teaching and supporting learning in post-compulsory education and training

Fred Fawbert

An overview of the National Standards as a basis for the professional development of teachers, trainers and support workers in the Learning and Skills Sector

Key concepts in this chapter

Certificated Stage, Collaboration, Collegiality, Inclusiveness, Intermediate Stage, Introductory Stage, Key Area Specifications, Key Teaching Purposes, Personal Development Journal, Post-Compulsory, Practitioner File, Reflective Practice, Standards

Index to Chapter 1

1.1 INTRODUCTION

Teaching is an art, which many of us practise, but only on very infrequent occasions perfect. This is probably because only rarely do all the elements coincide to become the ideal, interactive relationship between teacher and taught which can lead to the exciting discovery of those concepts and relationships that lead to unexpected insights into both the subject and the self. Most of us have to be content with occasional, but rewarding glimpses of what might be achieved in a situation where there is the time and the opportunity to use this foundation of mutual trust and shared achievement as a base for an exploration of the not-yet-known.

Despite all of the pressures, many teachers do achieve the excitement of this shared bond with their learners, where there is a willingness by both to emerge for a time from behind physical and psychological barriers into a more open, trusting relationship. Because of their position, it is teachers who must initiate such a relationship and this demands a particular understanding of all the characteristics of the specific educational context in which they are working. This includes the more tangible features such as environment, subject content and assessment requirements as well as those equally important but less well-defined elements, such as the dynamics of the learning group at that particular time, the internal and external influences which bear down on their progress and the teacher's current disposition towards them.

Probably the least understood, simple but influential factor is timing. In any relationship there is a time to press forward and a time to hold back. Get it wrong and you may have to retreat and rebuild. This level of insightful relationship cannot be taught, let alone measured. And yet it can mean the difference between success and failure.

This book is essentially about identifying and then nurturing this relationship between learner and teacher through consciously reflective practice. Our focus is the post-compulsory sector of education within the United Kingdom but the ideas and concepts we will discuss should have more general relevance to all teachers of students aged 14 and above whatever their particular situation.

Teaching effectively within any context is often a hugely rewarding task but, as with all complex processes, particularly in the early stages, it is also fraught with difficulties. Sometimes learners are receptive and sometimes, of course, they are not. The reasons for this are many and varied and are usually peculiar to that setting. The same may equally be said about the dissemination of good practice, particularly to teachers. Sometimes the suggested approach seems to be significant and relevant and sometimes it appears inappropriate and trivial. Again the reason for this variation in responses is often situational. Naturally, there are times when teachers are open to new ideas and, conversely, there are just as many instances where the security and familiarity of the known has much more appeal than innovation. This is particularly true when, as many of us are, the practitioner is working under pressure.

It follows then, that there will be times when this book may be seen as a welcome resource and others when it will represent only additional stress. For this reason, my colleagues and I have attempted to present this collection of ideas and approaches as a series of suggested solutions to familiar teaching problems. This is partially because we are only too aware of the connotations attached to concepts such as 'standards' or 'competence' and wish, at the outset, to look beyond the fairly common but limited interpretation that they can only represent prescription or compliance.

The FENTO Standards form the structure of this book. We believe that through the establishment of these national Standards for teachers in post-compulsory education, after the significant and extensive consultation with key players from the sector which marked their production, Graham Peake and his colleagues have provided us with an excellent basis for professional development.

However, our stance is that the Standards are merely a benchmark or a signpost, which should most definitely *not* be seen as a final destination. Of course, we do also realize that the real danger in articulating so clearly such guidelines to performance, is that those who are concerned with accountability rather than development may take a damagingly instrumental approach that focuses on simplistic measurement at the expense of the more important, subtle and holistic indicators of enhanced performance. Our concerns are based on the simple perception that learning is not predictable and teaching is not an exact science. Treating them as though they are is not, in the long term, a valid or reliable way to mark progress.

So, although each of the chapters that follow will be based on the eight Key Areas of the FENTO Standards and will include a detailed specification grid, the text is based on the practice and theory related to that particular stage of the teaching and learning process. We see this book as a guided-study programme, which identifies a range of useful sources for teachers. It is deliberately *not* assessment-led; however, the theoretical deliberations and the related practice-based activities are designed to address the FENTO outcomes. Fortunately, the Standards are not overly prescriptive in that they do not specify 'range statements' or the 'underpinning knowledge' related to each and every criterion.

We are realistic enough to accept that we cannot anticipate the special characteristics of every learning situation. However, although good practice in one situation could well seem an unnecessary indulgence in another, if the insights that it represents can be identified then decisions about teaching and learning will be better informed.

The authors are all experienced teacher educators from the sector and have drawn on their work to provide appropriate examples of teaching methods and the related concepts. This process has provided some insightful case studies that illuminate the core skills defined in the chapters that follow.

1.2 CHAPTER CONTENT

You will find that each chapter is a consecutive step in a familiar teaching/training cycle, but we start in *Chapter 2* with Janet Hobley's discussion about the notion of the teacher as a reflective practitioner. This is an important exploration of the principles discussed above, namely that, if they are to be effective, teachers should become the experts within their own particular situation because only they have had the opportunity to develop the insights into the range of variables which currently influence their practice. Some of the specific features that could be considered are their own values and objectives, the special subject characteristics, the needs of their students, the demands of their department and the culture of the college, etc.

Janet also carries this debate forward in *Chapter 3* by focusing on individual learner differences (aptitude and ability, etc.) and the ways of identifying and responding to learner needs (supported by appropriate theory) including diagnostic testing, student action-plans, basic skills, etc. Building on this knowledge of the learners, Margaret Postance considers in *Chapter 4* some of the ways of developing and planning different teaching and learning programmes and sessions within a safe, supportive learning environment.

Following this practical application, in *Chapter 5* Karen Lowe moves to a more theoretical consideration of teaching through an analysis of the social, cultural and emotional factors, which affect individual and group learning. Tricia Semeraz takes this theme of the effective learning environment (setting targets, structuring learning, developing materials, introducing basic and key skills) further in *Chapter 6* by considering in more detail such management of teaching processes as effective communication, interaction and learner empowerment. Lyn Butcher moves beyond classroom practice in *Chapter 7* to include quality and accountability dimensions such as reviewing learning process, establishing effective working relationships and the necessary quality measures.

In *Chapter 8*, Alison Barton moves us forward by taking a learner-centred approach to pastoral care. Again this entails identifying student needs, their counselling and referral to other care agencies which involves learning contracts, health and safety, student entitlement, access to services, information and resources, review procedure, progression. *Chapter 9* focuses on approaches to assessment using different measures for a range of purposes including student motivation and achievement.

Yvonne Hutton proposes in *Chapter 10* that the systematic evaluation of your own performance is the basis for developing future practice to meet learner and college needs.

Chapter 11 considers the recent history of the post-compulsory sector and the range of policies which have been developed to changing national priorities.

Finally, in *Chapter 12* we summarize some of the important agencies responsible for establishing and maintaining standards within PCET.

1.3 | CHAPTER STRUCTURE

The content of each chapter, as described above, is placed within a consistent structure that relates directly to the FENTO Standards. It is believed that the signposts provided by this framework will facilitate access to any information required by a practitioner involved in a FENTO-based programme. Table 1.1 (opposite) is designed as a summary of the common features found in each chapter.

1.4 | FENTO STANDARDS

Launched in January 1999 by Tessa Blackstone, the Minister of Education and Employment, these professional development standards were developed by the Further Education National Training Organization. Over 18 months the defined outcomes were constructed by Graham Peake and his team and modified through widespread consultation with further education managers, staff developers and teachers. During this time the agreed Standards moved considerably from the initial 'hard' NVQ style of competence statement to a definition of teacher/trainer Standards, which has much in common with the more flexible learning outcomes that have been in use by most university Certificate in Education programmes for a number of years. However, these Standards are designed for a wider audience than the traditional Certificate in Education/PGCE. Because three broad stages have

Table 1.1 Chapter structure

- *Chapter titles*   The FENTO Standards are presented under eight Key Areas and so the relevant core chapters (3 to 10) use these as the basis for their titles.

- *Purpose*   Under each title will be a simple statement clarifying the purpose of that Key Area.

- *Key concepts*   Each chapter starts with a summary of the concepts to be covered.

- *Chapter index*   The beginning of each chapter has a guide to the contents and the 'activities'.

- *Activities*   Within each chapter will be a series of 'activities' designed to identify the sources and then develop appropriate evidence against the Standards. One basic form of this evidence will be the details of teaching practice within the *Practitioner File* (for more information see 1.5 in Chapter 1).
  Another of the main forms of evidence will be reflections within the suggested *Professional Development Journal (PDJ)* see 1.6 in Chapter 1.
  The 'activities' will usually be based on reflection about a completed task.
  Each of these activities will be signalled by a *clipboard graphic* incorporating the exercise reference. These are, of course, optional.

- *Reading*   Each reference to sources within the text will be signposted by a book graphic in the margin.

- *Website*   Throughout the book the website graphic indicates that further material on that topic is also available on our website *tipcet.com*

- Useful sources   Our authors have added a short annotated list of recommended books and websites at the end of each of their chapters.

- Rationale   Each chapter has a simple justification explaining why and how teachers should address the Key Area Standards at the appropriate level (FENTO Stage 1, 2 or 3).

- Key Area Specifications   The FENTO Standard specifications for each of the Key Areas are included in each chapter after the above Rationale, together with a summary of how appropriate evidence may be drawn from chapter activities, the Practitioner File and the Personal Development Journal (PDJ).

- Self-assessment table   This is included at the end of Chapter 1 to allow practitioners to make an initial appraisal of where they stand in relation to their own professional development and the FENTO Standards. This self-identification of needs is a preparation for the study to come.

- Accreditation grid   This overall grid is included on the *tipcet.com* website to allow practitioners to record their progress against the Standards.

- Key Skills Mapping   In Chapter 12 there is a grid which indicates how the process of generating evidence against the FENTO Standards will also provide evidence of some of a teacher's generic Key Skills.

- Ofsted   Chapter 12 discusses the implementation by Ofsted of the Common Inspection Framework and its relevance to the FENTO Standards.

- Composite bibliography   A full bibliography incorporating all sources is included at the end of the book.

- Index   Complete reference to issues, concepts and sources.

been identified (Introductory, Intermediate and Threshold) the Standards are flexible and applicable to the wide variety of roles that teachers, trainers, instructors, demonstrators and support workers have within the post-14 sector. The development of these Standards was informed by the values and purposes summarized below.

1.4.1 Reflective practice and personal development

Teaching in the post-compulsory sector involves working with a wide range of learners, using diverse methods of teaching and learning. Teachers are constantly assessing the needs of learners and planning how to meet these needs. The ability of teachers to reflect on their practice and to employ appropriate methods, therefore, is a crucial one and this programme of guided study is centred around that philosophy. As a focus for reflection, you will be asked to develop two files during the study; the first is the Practitioner File (PF) which is a collection of evidence of practical teaching (see details in 1.5).

The second is your Personal Development Journal (PDJ) which is, in effect, a reflective diary of your professional development during and beyond this programme (see 1.6). Teaching, studies, reflection and personal development will underpin your wider professional role as you manage the learning process, develop the curriculum and guide and support learners in partnership with others in the organization and the local community. The next chapter helps you to begin this process through discussion and a range of activities to promote Reflective Practice.

1.4.2 Collegiality and collaboration

Since the Education Reform Act in 1988, the post-compulsory sector has been involved in a series of radical changes (discussed more fully in Chapter 11) and, consequently, for any standards to be effective they must promote flexibility and adaptability. The role of practitioners in post-compulsory education is, by its very nature, extremely diverse and will inevitably change over time as a reflection of both the developing interests of the teacher and the changing nature of the learner.

Despite their apparent isolation in the classroom, teachers and teaching teams frequently work in partnership with external groups such as employers, parents, other members of the educational community and related agencies. They are automatically involved in different levels of practical and theoretical collaboration in order to ensure the relevance and responsiveness of their learning programmes. The purposeful development of collegial relationships is therefore an extremely important aspect of practice. From time to time during this programme it is suggested that you collaborate with colleagues during various analytical exercises and also to identify practitioners you would like to work-shadow. In addition, it is recommended that you identify a colleague to act as a mentor. All of these activities are designed to develop the notion of collegiality and the dissemination of good practice.

1.4.3 Learning and learner autonomy

Another important concept promoted by FENTO is the belief that teachers and teaching teams should value the autonomy of learners and promote the centrality of learning. By this they mean that teachers should seek to provide learners with the skills and abilities to work effectively on their own and promote an attitude to learning which views it as a lifelong process rather than the short-term acquisition of a set of specific skills. The development of a learner's key skills is an integral part of the promotion of autonomy and each of the following chapters will identify not only appropriate evidence against the FENTO Standards, but also how related evidence may be used to accredit appropriate Key Skills (see also 1.7 below).

1.4.4 Entitlement, equality and inclusiveness

Equality of opportunity is also a basic principle within the Standards as a crucial foundation upon which good teaching, learning and assessment are based. Simply put, this means optimizing the learning experience of all students because all learners should have access to appropriate educational opportunities regardless of ethnic origin, gender, age, sexual orientation or degree of learning disability and/or difficulty. Consequently, the values of entitlement, equality and inclusiveness are seen as being of fundamental importance to teachers and teaching teams.

1.4.5 The context of post-compulsory education

This book is designed for teachers within the post-compulsory sector of education and consequently programme members may be drawn from continuing, further and adult education as well as public service and private training providers. The values listed previously and the characteristics defined below indicate something of the distinctive nature of this particular context:

Main characteristics of post-compulsory education (PCE)

- wide range of learner
- broad diversity of levels
- the emphasis upon guiding and supporting learners and the assessment of their needs
- the application of vocational knowledge and experience
- the degree of liaison with employers and of working in partnership with other agencies
- involvement in work-based assessment and learning
- the wide use of outcomes-based curricula
- the dynamic nature and complexity of the curriculum
- the emphasis on student retention and achievement
- the central role of the teacher in key skills development
- the central role of the teacher in helping people to return to learning

The above characteristics are a clear indication of the tremendously wide variety of teaching and learning which takes place within the post-compulsory sector. The FENTO Workforce Development Plan (April 2001) states that around 2.3 million people are currently learning in further education and more than 500,000 are studying full-time at the 512 FE colleges in Britain. There are 400,00 staff in these colleges and about 70 per cent of these are in a teaching role as lecturers, trainers or support staff. This makes FE the biggest provider of learning opportunities outside of the school system. Further education learners will range from 14 year olds involved in vocational development programmes to Higher National Diploma course members. Continuing education prepares students for progression to higher education through A Levels and vocational subjects and adult education caters largely for non-vocational courses from basic crafts to theory and practice within the Arts. The government views the sector as extremely important and the establishment of the Department for Education and Skills (DfES) after they won the election in May 2001 is a clear indication of their perception of the link between education, employment and the national economy. During recent years there has been a drive to move towards equivalence between the sectors (i.e. Primary, Secondary and Further) and spearheading this is the government's concern to improve professional standards. The principle vehicle for this process is the FENTO Standards.

In many instances, teaching within PCE involves work with students who have progressed from schools and who will progress into higher education. Familiarity with other phases of education is clearly important for PCE staff, as is familiarity with the workplace and the world of work in general. The sector as a whole is discussed in more detail in Chapter 11.

1.4.6   The key purpose of the teacher in post-compulsory education

The following definition of the key purpose of the teacher and those involved in supporting learning has been used to guide the structure and content of the FENTO Standards. The Standards are based on the assumption that those who teach in the sector already possess *specialized subject knowledge, skills and experience*. Therefore, the Standards (and this programme of study) address the generic, professional development of teachers and teaching teams rather than the development of their *subject* expertise. This generic approach to professional development may be summarized in the following key aim of FENTO:

> **The key purpose of the post-compulsory teacher and those directly involved in supporting learning is to provide high quality teaching, to create effective opportunities for learning and to enable all learners to achieve to the best of their ability.**

Naturally, post-compulsory teachers have responsibility for ensuring high standards of teaching and learning, as well as contributing to curriculum development and the development of their subject knowledge. Good teachers will always ensure that the educational opportunities provided meet the needs and aspirations of their learners and those learners achieve to the best of their ability. It is envisaged that teachers and teaching teams will play a key role in guiding and supporting their learners, as well as in assessing learners' achievements. In part this programme is designed to promote a teacher's awareness of how their subject contributes to the overall educational experience of their learners.

In essence then, this is the beginning of a career-long personal and professional development during which teachers will take on a variety of different roles, depending upon their interests, abilities and experience. In addition to their role as teachers, they may become course leaders or subject coordinators or take up responsibility for liaison with employers, pastoral support or curriculum and subject development. Some teachers may move into managerial roles or specialize in other functions related to the work of the organization such as entrepreneurial development, finance, marketing, staff development or personnel management.

1.4.7 Defining the FENTO National Standards

The use of the FENTO Standards as a basis for practitioner development involves the disaggregation of the above key purpose into eight Key Areas of the teaching and training developmental process.

KEY AREAS

A   assessing learners' needs

B   planning and preparing teaching and learning programmes for groups and individuals

C   developing and using a range of teaching and learning techniques

D   managing the Learning Process

E   providing learners with support

F   assessing the outcomes of learning and learners' achievements

G   reflecting on and evaluating one's own performance and planning future practice

H   meeting professional requirements

Several of these eight Key Areas contain more than one Standard and consequently there are a total of **26 sets of Standards** that are common to both the Cert Ed and the PGCE programmes (see overleaf).

1.4.7.1 Standards and levels

FENTO have defined three stages of their teaching/training qualifications:

- Stage 1
  Introductory – basic classroom skills (equivalent to the City & Guilds 7307 Teachers' Certificate Part One)

- Stage 2
  Intermediate – competent teaching (equivalent to the City & Guilds 7307 Teachers' Certificate or the Certificate in Education, Year One)

- Stage 3
  Certificated – full professional (equivalent to the Certificate in Education/PGCE)

However, it is important to point out that the above stages do not necessarily relate to length of service or the amount of teaching hours that are currently being undertaken.

Our understanding of the FENTO Standards is that the level of achievement that it is necessary for a particular practitioner to achieve will relate very much to that teacher/trainer's role. For example, a teacher/trainer may be full-time and have a fairly limited role that could be met by a Stage 2 qualification, while a part-time teacher may have a more substantial role that would require the acquisition of the Stage 3 Standards. To gain a *FENTO endorsed* award, teaching practice must be

Table 1.2 FENTO Standards

No.	Key Area	Standard	
I	A		ASSESSING LEARNERS' NEEDS
1		A1	Identify and plan for the needs of potential learners
2		A2	Make an initial assessment of learners' needs
II	B		PLANNING AND PREPARING TEACHING AND LEARNING PROGRAMMES FOR GROUPS AND INDIVIDUALS
3		B1	Identify the required outcomes of the learning programme
4		B2	Identify appropriate teaching and learning techniques
5		B3	Enhance access to and provision of learning programmes
III	C		DEVELOPING AND USING A RANGE OF TEACHING AND LEARNING TECHNIQUES
6		C1	Promote and encourage individual learning
7		C2	Facilitate learning in groups
8		C3	Facilitate learning through experience
IV	D		MANAGING THE LEARNING PROCESS
9		D1	Establish and maintain an effective learning environment
10		D2	Plan and structure learning activities
11		D3	Communicate effectively with learners
12		D4	Review the learning process with learners
13		D5	Select and develop resources to support learning
14		D6	Establish and maintain effective working relationships
15		D7	Contribute to the organization's quality assurance system
V	E		PROVIDING LEARNERS WITH SUPPORT
16		E1	Induct learners into the organization
17		E2	Provide effective learning support
18		E3	Ensure access and guidance opportunities for learners
19		E4	Provide personal support to learners
VI	F		ASSESSING THE OUTCOMES OF LEARNING AND LEARNERS' ACHIEVEMENTS
20		F1	Use appropriate assessment methods to measure learning and achievement
21		F2	Make use of assessment information
VII	G		REFLECTING ON AND EVALUATING ONE'S OWN PERFORMANCE AND PLANNING FUTURE PRACTICE
22		G1	Evaluate one's own practice
23		G2	Plan for future practice
24		G3	Engage in continuing professional development
VIII	H		MEETING PROFESSIONAL REQUIREMENTS
25		H1	Work within a professional value base
26		H2	Conform to agreed codes of professional practice

within an FE context. Your line manager would be the appropriate person to consult about target levels and practice contexts.

In order for this programme to provide the maximum flexibility, the above FENTO Standards will form the basis of a *'spiral' curriculum* where the same elements will be visited during Stages 1 (Introductory), 2 (Intermediate) and 3 (Certificated), each time with a more demanding level of study. The use of the *same* standards of competence for all three stages of the programme within a spiral approach does require that the performance and knowledge criteria must *differentiate* between the stages. The 26 defined Standards and their related performance criteria can be interpreted at whatever level is required, but the more practical teaching/training activities would, necessarily, be confined to Stages 1 and 2. We are therefore concentrating on a simple hierarchy of skills and understandings, within Stages 1 and 2 related to *basic, fundamental teaching skills*, and Stage 3 more concerned with *evaluation and the development of the teacher as an autonomous practitioner*. All three levels will be concerned with reflective practice, but this will become more analytical as we progress through the stages. Key Area Specification is provided at the end of the relevant chapter (3 to 10) and within these we have given details of each of the 26 Standards and their related *performance criteria*, plus the *specific* and *generic knowledge*.

1.4.7.2 Key Area Rationales

Although the disaggregation of the teacher's role into these various components does enable work-based accreditation, unfortunately it also often tends to foster what has been termed a 'technicist' approach. Each element of assessment becomes divorced from the whole, with the inherent danger that programme members become concerned with a mechanistic, reductive process of evidence gathering that doesn't allow them to gain a holistic view of the teaching and learning process. In addition, the language used within competence frameworks is often couched in difficult jargon. In an attempt to counteract these tendencies, you will find that *before* the Key Area Specifications in each chapter, there is a Rationale for those particular Standards. These Rationales present in a simple FAQ form, justifications for the assessment requirements from a holistic view of the teacher's role and respond to eight fundamental questions. In addition, these responses are directed separately to Stages 1, 2 and 3 skills in order to clarify the differentiation between the level requirements.

Following these Key Area Rationales each of the Standards is listed separately together with its *defined purpose*. The performance criteria are also listed alongside indicative details of specific and generic knowledge requirements. Finally, each specification contains suggestions for the form of evidence that is appropriate to each of the three stages, together with a reference to the Activities suggested in each chapter, which will generate the coverage required.

1.4.7.3 Standards and evidence

The achievement of all of the essential 26 Standards is the aim of this programme. There are no optional standards in this list. However, although each of the Key Area Standards must be addressed, if some criteria within the Standard are not appropriate to a particular teaching situation, the practitioners are recommended to provide a rationale for *not* addressing that particular criterion. Completing the self-assessment grid at the end of this chapter will help to identify those Standards that may be problematic.

The Activities in each chapter, together with the practice-based work and supported by reflections within the Personal Development Journal are the means of generating evidence of these competences, but we have avoided the straitjacket of having a direct one-to-one relationship between the Standards and the chapters. This would have resulted in having Activities that have value only to the Key Area related to that chapter. This is not necessarily the most effective way to organize development but, more importantly, many of the Standards (particularly those at Stage 3) could be achieved and reinforced through several of the Activities. Note that practitioners are not expected to address the Standards within Key Area 'H' separately, but should provide evidence of these two aspects of professional knowledge (i.e. value base and codes of practice) as they address the previous seven Key Areas. There are two key documents, which we suggest you use to develop appropriate evidence against the Standards: the Practitioner File is suggested as a means of collecting together experiential evidence of continuing professional development and the Personal Development Journal is an ongoing reflective commentary on this process.

| 1.5 | PRACTITIONER FILE |

Introduction

The Practitioner File is designed to record not only evidence of your assessment through teaching observations during the programme, but also the development of particular areas of interest and expertise. Whereas, in order to meet the requirements of the teaching assessment you will provide your observer with a Lesson Plan and Rationale for each session you will also, at other times, be generating all sorts of evidence of your developing skills as a practitioner. These may take the form of an analysis of student needs, action plans for meeting those needs, teaching materials, assessment schemes, student evaluations, etc.

The manager of the particular programme of teacher training which you are undertaking will provide you with details of how your observed teaching assessment will be carried out. The information within this Practitioner File will support the process. We suggest that you include the records discussed below. *For your convenience, appropriate blank pro formas for each evidence-generating activity are available on the tipcet.com website.*

1.5.1 Teaching Log

This is intended to be a record of all the teaching you carry out during the programme. FENTO have a requirement that you achieve 60 hours' practice during Stages 1 and 2 and a further 60 hours during Stage 3 (120 hours in total). In general, a simple one-line record of the different teaching commitments will be sufficient. In order to qualify for a FENTO-endorsed award, teaching must be carried out within a further education context (suggested pro forma in the Appendix). You may, if you wish, insert a copy of your contract and refer to it on the Teaching Log pro forma. This will eliminate the need to complete the pro forma in detail. You may need to get these entries confirmed by a signature.

1.5.2 Session Plan

Your programme manager will have provided you with the requirements of each Teaching Observation and inevitably this will involve developing a Session Plan. This process is discussed in detail in Chapter 4 and a blank pro forma is in the Appendix.

1.5.3 Rationale

Often an observer will ask you to justify the approach you are taking when teaching a particular class. This Rationale may contain such considerations as reflections on learner characteristics and needs, the learning environment plus a justification for your selection of defined learning outcomes, teaching methods, principles of learning, use of resources, assessment and evaluation, etc. You may add some reflections on how earlier teaching sessions (perhaps with the same group of students) have affected your chosen approach. It is useful if each observation is developmental (i.e. building on earlier observations) and is used (at least in part) to address related criteria within one or more of the Key Areas defined within the FENTO Standards.

1.5.4 Generic Self-Evaluation Schedule

A retrospective analysis of your teaching session is a valuable form of evidence in relation to FENTO as it allows you to establish your own ability to identify the successful and less-successful aspects of the observed session and any other examples of your teaching. This Schedule should be completed shortly after the teaching session while all of the subtle details are still fresh in your memory. If possible you should discuss your completed self-evaluation with your observer and relate it to your own Rationale for the session and to the observer's written report. Further details and examples are contained in Chapter 10 and in the Appendix.

1.5.5 Specific Self-Evaluation Schedule

As you progress (to Stage 3 for example), instead of using the above pro forma (which provides you with the evaluation criteria) you may wish to define your own criteria so that your analysis may focus more precisely on what you perceive to be the most significant characteristics (strengths and weaknesses) of your teaching performance. This Evaluation pro forma which is also discussed in Chapter 10, allows you to define the ten most appropriate criteria and then to add your response.

1.5.6 Progress Summary

It is suggested that these pro formas should be completed with your observer during the debriefing after each Teaching Observation. It is intended to record your progressive development during teaching practice throughout the programme. The strengths and areas for improvement identified during previous observations should inform the selection, planning and delivery of subsequent observed sessions. For example, if in the first observed session a weakness is identified in the design and use of learning aids, the debriefing should include action planning to address the weakness. Ideally, the next observed session should include an opportunity to demonstrate significant improvement in this respect. Each observed session should consciously have built into it at least one aspect which differs from earlier observations and there should be clear evidence of progression.

Stage 3 observed sessions in particular should demonstrate an awareness of differentiation between students in the group, including techniques for catering for different levels of ability and interest. There should also be evidence of purposeful use of group activities.

Your observer may respond to the evidence you provide against criteria and knowledge goals in a Key Area (as shown on your Lesson Plan and Rationale) and will confirm those which have been met in the appropriate column of the Progress Summary.

1.6 PERSONAL DEVELOPMENT JOURNAL

1.6.1 Introduction – teachers as reflective practitioners

Whereas the *Practitioner File* (the previous document which we suggest you might develop) is clearly designed to record each stage of your *practical* development as a teacher, the purpose of the activities in the *Personal Development Journal* is the improvement of your cognitive development through *reflective* practice.

The purpose of reflection is to learn from experience in order to modify and develop strategies and principles for future action and to increase awareness of the actual learning process itself. Teachers who evaluate and plan in this manner not only improve their own performance but, in doing so, create a responsive and supportive learning environment which, in turn, will help their own students to become independent, aware and able to *learn about their own learning (meta-learning)* and to begin to take responsibility for it. These themes are developed in Chapter 2, 'Reflective Practice in PCE' and in Chapter 10.

1.6.2 Completing the Personal Development Journal

The purpose of the PDJ is the production of a reflective commentary to accompany the various types of evidence that will be presented for the accreditation of the 26 FENTO Standards.

As mentioned earlier, the Standards are structured around eight Key Areas of the teaching and training developmental process and within these areas are defined the 26 broad Standards. For the sake of clarity, these Standards have been further disaggregated within the eight Key Areas (Chapters 3 to 10) into 205 performance criteria against which are identified related specific and generic knowledge.

These criteria and knowledge specifications are used as guidelines to inform the gathering of evidence against each of the 26 broad elements of competence. So, to repeat, the central activity of our accreditation procedure is to address these 26 defined Standards with evidence which meets the *majority* of the criteria and their related specific and generic knowledge requirements. If you find it impossible to address any of the 205 criteria you should provide within your PDJ a written rationale, which explains why that criterion is not appropriate within your teaching situation.

The Specification Sheets, which begin with Key Area 'A' in Chapter 3, have been designed as a way of facilitating the process of identifying the relevant practical and theoretical activities which are the core of teaching and training and which should be the basis of the presented evidence and related reflections. We have prefaced each Key Area Specification Sheet with a simplified Key Area Rationale for undergoing each of the defined teaching and training activities.

Written in plain English, these justifications are presented as straightforward answers to what we expect will be frequently asked questions (FAQs) about the reasons for incorporating the FENTO Standards into your everyday work teaching and developing learning.

The Key Area Rationales are not specific to any subject specialism but are generic to post-compulsory sector teaching and have been written at three levels. Stage 1 represents the achievement of basic skills, Stage 2 is seen as more rounded competence and Stage 3 is the full, professional threshold award as represented by the Certificate in Education. When accredited within a university credit accumulation scheme, these three levels are equivalent to a third of an undergraduate degree programme.

As the Key Area justifications indicate, Stages 1 and 2 will involve the practical implementation of each area of skill and at Stage 3 you will be analysing not only the effect of the implementation, but also the external and internal influences on the chosen teaching/training methodologies and their particular context.

Stages 1 and 2 evidence will, in the main, be drawn from teaching processes, administration, resource and material production, etc. The evidence, which will facilitate accreditation against the appropriate Standard, will be generated in the teaching context (classroom, workshop, laboratory, etc.).

Although Stage 3 evidence will also draw heavily on practice, it will be more conceptual and will be based on more lengthy and detailed analysis of aspects of the teaching and learning process and the PDJ commentary on this process; in addition the observations will provide valuable confirmatory reflections.

Common to both years of the programme and, obviously, the source of a wealth of appropriate evidence, are the teaching observations. Depending on which accreditation centre is used, a number of successful teaching observations have to be carried out in each year of the programme and these, together with the associated documentation (contained in the Practitioner File), will provide evidence for some of the criteria and knowledge requirements in all 26 of the Standards.

1.6.3 The assessment process

It is important that assessment is not viewed as a series of independent tasks but should be considered as a whole and as an integral part of the learning process. One piece of evidence, such as an entry in the PDJ, a completed 'activity' from the Key Area chapters, a teaching observation or an academic assignment, will be relevant to more than one Standard. In fact, most of the forms of assessment are, or can be designed to be, relevant to all of the Standards. When gathering evidence, care should be taken to cross-reference each item of evidence to the Standards to which it refers.

1.6.4   Sources of evidence

Evidence may be derived from

- *Observation of performance.*   For a Stage 3 award you must undertake a minimum of 120 hours' teaching practice and a number of these sessions will be observed. The evidence from these observations may address any of the eight Key Areas.

- *Product evidence.*   This may consist of documentation produced as a natural part of a teacher's normal work and could include schemes of work, learning resources, assessment records, etc. In addition to routine documentation, within the Practitioner File, there are available optional pro formas (described below). By using these, programme members may produce appropriate and useful additional documentation such as Rationales, Progress Summaries, Session Plans, PDJ entries and so on.

- *Evaluation reports.*   It is suggested that programme members carry out a self-evaluation of their observed teaching sessions. You may also draw on evaluations you carry out as part of your organization's quality systems and within the PDJ you should also evaluate other aspects of your work in order to produce the necessary evidence.

- *Witness testimony.*   Evidence from others may be produced as a result of direct observation of performance (for example, teaching observation). In addition, experienced colleagues (such as your mentor) may well provide testimony of performance during collaborative or team teaching exercises.

- *Evidence of knowledge and understanding.*   A wide range of knowledge and understanding is required to achieve the Standards for teaching and learning within post-compulsory education. Confirmation that teachers have such knowledge may be inferred in part from their performance. This however, will not always be sufficient and other assessment will be required – for example, the chapter-based activities and assignments, the entries in the PDJ and questioning during observed teaching.

1.6.5   Using the Key Area Specification Sheets

These follow the Rationale at the end of each chapter. There are a different number of Standards to each Key Area; some have only two, while other Key Areas have seven. However there are 26 in total and they are listed together with the relevant performance criteria, each of which must be addressed.

1.6.6   Criteria

If you find it impossible to address a particular criterion within your teaching situation, you must provide a written rationale within your PDJ explaining why it is not appropriate or relevant within your teaching context. The final Key Area (H) is concerned with professional requirements and is separated into two categories –

working within a professional value base and within an agreed code of practice. Unlike the others, this Key Area should not be treated separately, but the evidence should be generated while addressing the previous seven Key Areas.

1.6.7 Key Area Rationales

Placed before each of the eight Key Areas there is a Rationale for incorporating the Standards into your practice which also suggests the kind of teaching and learning activities you may use to generate evidence appropriate to that stage/level and how you might reflect on the various types of evidence you have produced in order to demonstrate wider reading and underpinning specific and generic knowledge.

1.6.8 Structured tasks

Rather than rely only on personal reflections as the basis of your journal of evidence, you may wish (with your Programme Leader's permission) to use the more prescriptive *structured tasks* encompassed within the 'Activities' contained in all of the Key Area chapters (i.e. Chapters 3 to 10) as a means of generating all or part of your evidence against the Standards.

1.6.9 Reflective commentary

The PDJ (Personal Development Journal) is an individual reflection on teaching and learning experiences, which may take many forms. You may wish to analyse recent events, you may like to articulate a problem-solving process you have recently been involved with, or you could evaluate aspects of practice. The clipboard graphic identifies each of the specific 'Activities' within this and the following chapters. The reflections suggested in these activities should be carried out in your Professional Development Journal (PDJ) so that you build up a developmental log during your teacher education programme.

Remembering that this log is meant to be *personal*, most reflections will take one of two basic forms:

EXPERIENTIAL	Descriptive, setting the teaching/training in context and providing details of the various activities
THEORETICAL	Analysing the process and offering justifications, explanations, evaluations and action plans

Experiential reflections

Initially, it is expected that your Journal entries will, in the main, be descriptions of the practical teaching you are involved with. For example, although you may use the pro forma from the *Practitioner File* to provide your observer with the necessary details about a planned observed session (completed *Lesson Plans* will provide an outline of your intended teaching and the *Rationales* will be used to give a justification for your chosen approach and methodology) you may also wish to add in the PDJ a commentary on your experiences not only in the classroom, but also within the teacher education course. Reflect on the preparations you made, completing the documentation, implementing your chosen teaching method, being observed, completing the Evaluation Sheets, etc. Try to give an insight into what you value about the process and the aspects which are less than helpful, but keep in mind the need to generate evidence against the knowledge requirements and to show wider reading.

Theoretical analysis

As valuable as it is, it is important that you should go beyond a review of practical activities and begin to conceptualize and analyse your work in order to meet the specific and generic knowledge requirements of FENTO. Your commentary should incorporate important principles and concepts and show a familiarity with important theory in order to provide appropriate evidence, *particularly at Stage 3*.

1.7 | PREPARING FOR STUDY

As this chapter closes and in preparation for what follows, we have included below two simple exercises which are designed to lay the foundation for the concepts which will be developed later in this study programme. Firstly (in Activity 1a) we are asking you to consider the characteristics of one of your own groups of learners and then (in 1b) to think about your experience in relation to the Key Areas of the FENTO Standards.

1a   Identification of learner characteristics

During the following chapters you will be asked to carry out various activities in relation to your own work as a teacher. It will be helpful if you begin now to develop an analysis of the characteristics of your learners and build on this during the forthcoming tasks. Identify one particular group who you teach regularly and who could be the focus of similar activities to come. This could be a small or large group who may be easy to work with or may have particular demands that make them interesting. Make this your first entry in your Personal Development Journal. Write about 200 words in which you try to capture the nature of the group. In addition to a basic description (number, age, gender, experience of the subject, etc.) think how they respond to you at different times and how they go about tackling the different types of work you set them.

1b   **Table 1.3 Self-assessment against the FENTO Standards**

How to complete: This exercise follows on from the previous activity in 1a. As you consider the current level of your own professional development, bear in mind the group of learners you have identified and consider, not only the Standards, but your current ability to meet their needs. There are three Stages in teacher/trainer development. Stage 1 is *Introductory* and is equivalent to C&G Stage One (i.e. Basic Skills), Stage 2 is *Intermediate* and is equivalent to C&G Stage 2 or the first year of the Cert Ed. Stage 3 is *Certificated* (equivalent to the full Certificate in Education). There are eight Key Areas of FENTO which are broken down into groups of Standards and these are listed below in the left-hand column. To assess in broad, general terms your current level, make an estimate of which Stage you are at in being able to meet the Standards. Insert a tick under the appropriate Stage in relation to the 26 teaching and learning skills and summarize in the right-hand column your strengths and weaknesses in this area. If you need more detail about the Standards you may need to look these performance criteria up within the Key Area Specifications in Chapters 3 to 10.

	Stage 1	Stage 2	Stage 3	Comments on strengths and weaknesses
A Assessing learner need				
A1 Identify and plan for the needs of potential learners				
A2 Make an initial assessment of learners' needs				
B Planning and preparing teaching and learning programmes for groups and individuals				
B1 Identify the required outcomes of the learning programmes				
B2 Identify appropriate teaching and learning techniques				
B3 Enhance access to and provision of learning programmes				
C Developing and using a range of teaching and learning techniques				
C1 Promote and encourage individual learning				
C2 Facilitate learning in groups				
C3 Facilitate learning through experience				
D Managing the learning process				
D1 Establish and maintain an effective learning environment				
D2 Plan and structure learning activities				

1.8 | SUMMARY OF CHAPTER PROGRESSION

Each of the following chapters have been designed to fit in with the familiar Teaching and Training Cycle and they may be summarized as follows:

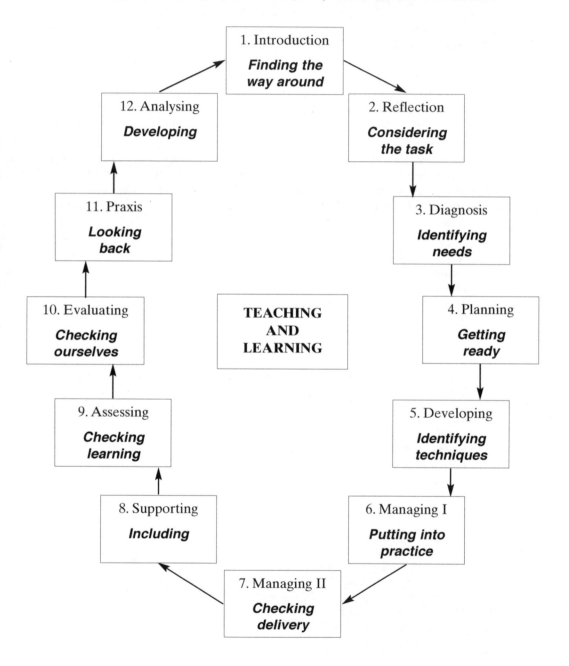

CHAPTER 2

Reflective practice

Janet Hobley

Reflective Teaching and the implications for practice

Key concepts in this chapter

Absolutist, Abstract Conceptualization, Active Experimentation, Concrete Experience, Dualistic View, Hard Highground, Knowing-in-Action, Messy Swamps, Personal Construct, Poiesis, Praxis, Reflection on Action, Reflective Action, Reflective Observation, Relativist, Routine Action, Technical Rationality, Thematized Learning

Index to Chapter 2

Chapters 1 and 2 Activities designed to generate evidence against the Standards

Ref	Activity	Page	Ref	Activity	Page
1a	Identification of learner characteristics	18	2e	Influences on chosen teaching and learning methods	29
1b	Self-assessment against the FENTO Standards	19	2f	Knowing-in-action	29
2a	A significant learning experience	25	2g	Selection of means	30
2b	Planning teaching	26	2h	Principles of teaching and learning	31
2c	Responding to student need	27	2i	Values underpinning approaches to teaching	32
2d	Problem solving	27	2j	Relationship between previous reflections	32

2.1 INTRODUCTION

Although it is often highly rewarding, the role of the teacher (as with other professions) does undoubtedly involve constantly coping with a range of competing demands. Within such a pressurized world there may be a temptation to think of Reflective Practice as the sort of luxury you can enjoy when you have time available, much as you would quiet contemplation. Unfortunately, such an approach not only misunderstands the notion of active reflection, but may also cause a practitioner to overlook a skill that could well light a pathway to success in our very demanding world. Reflectivity is not an indulgence, but a prerequisite for effective teaching and, in fact, the FENTO Standards require evidence that it is taking place.

The reason is relatively simple but, as you would expect, the realization takes time and conscious effort. The explanation for the value of Reflective Practice in today's hectic environment is premised on the fact that teachers, trainers and support workers quite often become the 'experts' within a particular learning context. Over time your close involvement provides you with the opportunity to become better informed about the characteristics of your learners, the environment you are working in and more aware of what may be achieved than anyone else. As you become conscious of this developing expertise you become more confident, relaxed, flexible and responsive, and as your students learn to trust you they will often respond with an openness that makes the whole process easier to manage and more rewarding. Refining this highly valuable 'responsive expertise' is the purpose of Reflective Practice. It is the ability to identify *and prioritize* all the subtle indicators within your learning environment.

2.2 CONCEPTS OF REFLECTION

The concept of Reflective Practice dates back to Socrates, Plato and Aristotle, but perhaps the most influential exponent was John Dewey. In 1938 at a time of very traditional, formal approaches such as learning by rote, Dewey was emphasizing experience, experiment, purposeful learning, freedom and progressive education. He anticipated the writings of Paulo Freire when he claimed that:

> The traditional scheme is, in essence, one of imposition from above and from outside
> . . . .. Learning here means acquisition of what is incorporated in books and in the heads
> of the elders.

Earlier in 1933, Dewey had contrasted *routine action* with *reflective action*. According to Dewey, routine action is the day-to-day working life, guided by factors such as tradition, habit and authority and by institutional definitions and expectations. By implication, it is relatively static and is thus unresponsive to changing priorities and circumstances. Reflective action, on the other hand, involves a willingness to engage in constant self-appraisal and development. Among other things, it implies flexibility, rigorous analysis and social awareness. For Dewey, reflective activity involves the perception of relationships and the connections between the parts of an experience. This experience may be the raw material, but it has to be processed through reflection before it can emerge as learning. It is not sufficient simply to have an experience in order to learn, because without reflection it may be forgotten and its learning potential lost.

Gibbs (1988) makes the important link between theorizing and action:

> it is from the feelings and thoughts emerging from this reflection that generalisations or concepts may be created. It is generalisations, which enable new situations to be tackled effectively. Similarly, if it is intended that behaviour should be changed by learning, it is not sufficient simply to learn new concepts and develop new generalisations. This learning must be tested out in new situations. The learner must make the link between theory and action by planning for that action, carrying it out and then reflecting upon it, relating what happens back to the theory.

Gibbs is interpreting the experiential learning cycle developed by David Kolb (1984) from the work of Lewin (1951) (see also 5.7 in Chapter 5). This cycle moves from *concrete experience* through *reflective observation, abstract conceptualization, active experimentation* and back again to concrete experience. Kolb believes that learners may enter the cycle at any point depending upon their individual learning style, but it is important that they work around the cycle. For example, those who prefer concrete experience (doing) should be persuaded to try out their ideas in order that future hypotheses will be better informed through experience. Kolb's view is that it is not sufficient to do or to think in order to learn from experience; learners should also be aware of their own development through the testing out of their concepts and explanations.

To illustrate this process in action in the classroom, a teacher may begin (though not necessarily) with a *concrete experience* such as trying out a new teaching method or a different assessment technique. *Reflective observation* would then involve a consideration of the process and how it might be done differently and then *abstract conceptualization* would be promoted by gathering more information (reading, talking to colleagues, etc.) and forming a hypothesis as to how to be more effective.

Active experimentation would then involve trying out new ways, which may well be a synthesis of the original approach combined with new ideas gained subsequently. Summarized simply, the process consists of *doing, thinking, planning, experimenting* and then *doing* once more. In this manner, reflective learning becomes 'whole person' learning as it involves intellectual, emotional and psychological development.

2.3 REFLECTION IN THE PERSONAL DEVELOPMENT JOURNAL

Taking the lead from Kolb, you will be encouraged throughout this book to build on your ideas and insights. At different times during this programme, you will be asked to add to the two reflections within your PDJ which you hopefully completed at the end of Chapter 1 in response to Activities 1a and 1b. These Activities will build up to form a personal analytical theme which you can then develop further in relation to your own practice. However, as William Perry (1970) observes, many learners (particularly at first) find the process of meaningful reflection very difficult indeed and they often need guidance to move from what he calls the *absolutist* mode, where they are prepared to accept implicitly the content of a course as they believe that all important knowledge is 'exterior' to themselves (i.e. it lies with the lecturer or teacher).

Perry believes that with encouragement learners' conceptualization will develop, bringing about a cognitive shift. First of all, they may move to what he calls a *relativist* position, where they begin to perceive that the course content is manipulated by tutors, and consequently they may consider that all presented theory is ephemeral and transient and that teachers are laying assessment traps for them. Often, at this stage, the students adopt an instrumental approach using 'shallow' learning to overcome these assessment hurdles.

The final stage in this development, as outlined by Perry, is when students gain an *independent commitment* to an area of study. As they develop their enjoyment and involvement in the subject they become aware of their own development and begin to reflect on the process they are involved in. In relation to the subject they are studying, they often come to realize that there is not just one singular, authoritative point of view. Through study they realize that the perspectives of teachers and authors often differ in some minor way and, in some cases, there may be a major difference of opinion. As students think about thinking (meta-cognition) they become more ready to accept a range of different perspectives and, as a consequence, begin to place more value on their own views.

Usher (1985) shares a similar view to Perry, in that he believes that students must be persuaded to move from what he calls a *dualistic view* (which considers that knowledge is either true or untrue) to a perspective-dependent attitude that accepts the relative merits of knowledge and is prepared to evaluate according to the context of the learning. Usher's term for this particular context is *thematized* learning, which has much in common with Kelly's (1955) view that each person has an individual and unique perception of events, which Kelly calls a *personal construct*.

Although this difficult concept is compatible with student-centred learning, it often clashes with the notion that the teacher should be seen as a 'paragon' at the centre of the learning process. However, Usher (reflecting Dewey's earlier view) believes that students who experience only teacher-centred learning so undervalue their own experience that they have great difficulty in drawing upon it. Instead they resort to anecdotal evidence without articulating the underlying principles and generalizations from their experiences. This interpretive experience is often so disappointing to them that the students (unable to see the value of the exercise) insist upon returning to the secure ground of the didactic presentation and push their teachers back into a leadership role. Usher believes that the way forward is to encourage students to make a conceptual shift to a 'thematized' (perspective-dependent) view that will help them to realize that their own experiences (modified via interaction with the learning situation) are of paramount importance.

As Bain *et al.* (1999) have pointed out, in recent years student journals have been used extensively in education as a means of facilitating reflection, deepening personal understanding and stimulating critical thinking. This is particularly so in the field of teacher education where, as pointed out by Zeichner (1992) and Calderhead and Gates (1993), reflection has come to be widely recognized as a crucial element in the professional growth of teachers. Calderhead (1988) argued that the need for reflective teacher education has been justified on the grounds that it facilitates the linking of theory and practice, subjects the expertise of teachers to

critical evaluation and enables them to take a more active role in their own professional accountability. Given the importance attached to the development of
reflective skills and propensities, it is not surprising that a range of teaching tools
for this purpose has emerged in the literature. Reflective journal writing is one such
technique that has been advocated by educators in many fields as a means of
stimulating reflective learning. There are examples from counselling (Eldridge
1983); psychology (Hettich 1990); nursing (Landeen *et al.* 1992); management
(Leary 1981); leadership (Walker 1985); sociology (Wagenaar 1984) and teaching
(Yinger and Clark 1981).

Ballantyne and Packer (1995) defined a learning journal as an

> exercise in which students express in writing their understandings of, reflections on,
> response to or analysis of an event, experience or concept.

Below you will find the first of this chapter's Activities (2a) to add to your two
earlier reflections in your PDJ. Please take time to do these exercises and be as
thoughtful and honest in your reflections as possible. However, don't agonize too
much over your response; there isn't a right or wrong answer and only you will be
able to judge the value of your deliberations in relation to developing you own
meta-cognition (thinking about thinking) and *meta-learning* (learning about your
own learning).

2a *A significant learning experience*

Building on your previous reflections about your learning group and your
current level of professional development, this is the third entry into your PDJ.

Try to identify a 'significant learning experience' related to your own per-
sonal/professional development. This could be recent or several years ago, it
may have been a positive/rewarding experience or a less enjoyable/negative
event. However, it should be something you recall as being, for one reason or
another, an important learning process (either formal or informal). Now,
please analyse and critically reflect on that experience. You might start simply
by describing the experience, but you should then go on to reflect on the event
and your part in it and, finally, say what value the experience was to your own
personal/professional development (about 200 words).

2.4 THINKING AS AN EDUCATIONAL EXPERIENCE

After this short bout of 'thinking' you may wish to consider Dewey's views on the
importance of developing this skill which, of course, is now heavily represented
within the national Key Skills. In an early book, *Democracy and Education* (1916),
Dewey not only anticipated lifelong learning, but also stressed the need for
'thinking' in education. Although he used the somewhat formal, stilted language of
the time, the conceptual process he identifies has equal relevance today:

> the important thing is that thinking is the method of an educative experience. The
> essentials of method are therefore identical with the essentials of reflection. They are
> first that the pupil has a genuine situation of experience – that there be a continuous

activity in which he is interested for its own sake; secondly, that a genuine problem develop within this situation as a stimulus to thought; third, that he process the information and make the observations needed to deal with it; fourth, that suggested solutions occur to him which he shall be responsible for developing in an orderly way; fifth, that he has opportunity and occasion to test his ideas by application, to make their meaning clear and to discover for himself their validity. (p. 163)

Although it is a long and at times difficult quote, Dewey is making several important points about the process of student thinking and reflection, namely that they should involve:

- a real situation/experience as the focus
- an interesting and continuing activity
- problem/s
- the student developing appropriate solutions in a systematic manner
- the student testing the solutions which have been developed in order to be aware of their value

Consider how Dewey's principles are represented in the following activity:

2b Planning teaching

A teacher is attempting to introduce students to the concept of nutrients for the first time. The teacher first asks the students to list the food they have eaten during the week on a day-to-day basis. Next the students are introduced to the five main nutrients needed for health and the teacher asks them to see how much of each nutrient is included in their diet. The students are given food tables and begin to calculate their own values of the major nutrients from their lists. The tutor then goes on to introduce the concept of digestion, and the way that enzymes work in order to break down the food. The sessions are then followed up with experiments planned by the students to test some of the theory provided by the tutor.

Can you try to analyse the teacher's approach to the sequence and activities? What steps were taken to make it interesting to the students? In what way were Dewey's ideas being used in these sessions?

The first step was to involve the student's own experiences; this provides interest and the students would have fun comparing different food intakes. Then a problem was set and developed in a way which presented the students with the need to process appropriate knowledge. Finally, the students were allowed to experiment in order to test the knowledge and to view it in different ways. Using this strategy the students were engaged in 'thinking' about the problem through reflection. It would, perhaps, have been easier for the teacher to lecture them, but such a didactic approach would make it more difficult to engage the students in problem-solving *activity*.

A further consideration of related theory about reflective practice may help us to understand this. Building on Dewey's work in the first part of the last century, Boud, Keogh and Walker (1985) consider that:

reflection in the context of learning is a generic term for those intellectual and affective activities in which individuals engage to explore their experiences in order to lead to new understanding and appreciations.

They note three stages during the process of reflection:

- returning to the experience
- attending to feelings during the experience
- re-evaluation of the experience

We all have times when planned teaching and learning activities are not as successful as anticipated – to put it mildly! Although it is often painful, the earlier you are able to reflect on the problems which arose during the session, the sooner you will identify the problem and dispel those lingering anxieties. Try the following activity as a starting point.

2c Responding to student need

Consider this teaching scenario and compare it to the previous one in Activity 2b.

A tutor asks a class to work through a set of instructions and to produce a desk-top-published page. One student is 'trigger happy' with the mouse and makes a few 'clicks' that take her way past the point of no return. She is then forced to ask the tutor for help. The tutor grabs the mouse, proceeds to click and move the screen about while the student looks on. The tutor then says, 'You're OK now, carry on.' How do you think the student would feel? Would she know how the tutor solved the problem? Would she be any closer to solving the problem herself? Make notes about your views on this in your PDJ.

Your PDJ should be starting to develop now after five entries. It may be time to start adding to these initial reflections by drawing on your own interests. You may, for instance, wish to collect interesting newspaper cuttings and add comments about the relevance to your own teaching. Jennifer Moon (1999) discusses how to achieve learning through the reflexive use of journals:

Journal writing provides a means by which learning can be upgraded – where unconnected areas of meaning cohere and a deeper meaning emerges.

She goes on to note that journals can be used to record experience, enhance other learning, develop 'critical thinking' and a whole range of extended thinking skills such as problem-solving and creativity. She believes (like Dewey) that reflective activity is very powerful in allowing a novice practitioner to develop, enquire and refine practice in the light of experience. Moon uses the term 'metacogitition' and the power of journal writing to develop this process of 'overviewing one's own mental functioning'. Try thinking about your own thinking as you tackle the next activity:

2d Problem solving

Try to remember how you first went about grasping a difficult concept in a complex subject. Did you need to 'see' it from different angles? Did you try to solve it in different ways? How did you get the insight that allowed you to solve the problem? After being baffled at first, did you feel a rising sense of achievement at having found a solution? Make notes about your own particular experience.

2.5 SCHON'S SWAMP

Of course, each of us will have our own approaches to the solving of complex problems. In some situations our methods may be similar, and yet in others we will differ greatly. This will naturally be affected by the urgency of the situation; however, our preferred learning styles, personal contructs and individual needs will also have a significant bearing. These issues will be tackled in the next two chapters but, for now, let us consider the sheer inherent complexity of each educational situation. Donald Schon (1987) manages to capture the essence of this dilemma when he metaphorically declares that:

In the varied topography of professional practice, there is a high, hard ground overlooking a swamp. On the high ground, manageable problems lend themselves to solution through the application of research-based theory and technique. In the swampy lowland, messy, confusing problems defy technical solution. The irony of this situation is that the problems of the high ground tend to be relatively unimportant to individuals or society at large, however great their technical interest may be; while in the swamp lie the problems of greatest concern. The practitioner must choose. Shall he remain on the high ground where he can solve relatively unimportant problems according to prevailing standards of rigor, or shall he descend to the swamp of important problems and non-rigorous inquiry?

As you will have realized, we are all working in the 'messy swamp' of complex classroom practice, but many of our managers and evaluators measure what we are doing from the relative safety of the high ground.

In developing this argument Schon contrasts two differing approaches to practice. On the one hand practitioners may act as instrumental problem solvers who select the technical means best suited to practical purposes. He uses the term *technical rationality* to describe a process of relying on formal knowledge about a profession in the manner of textbook information. In the case of teaching this would involve knowledge about lesson plans, schemes of work, learning outcomes, etc.

Schon, however, goes on to argue that professionals also use what he calls *professional artistry* and *knowledge in use* as well as propositional knowledge. He uses the example of a skill that practitioners can display in unique, uncertain and conflicting situations. According to Schon, a skilled professional can call upon a range of strategies and can think creatively in different situations. In doing so, he is using a process of reflection to produce effective action. Schon uses the phrase 'knowing-in-action' to describe this process of reflective thinking and uses this expression to refer to publicly observable, physical actions and private, contemplative actions. In both cases, according to Schon, the 'knowing' is in the action. To him, knowing in action is dynamic whereas rules, procedures and theories are static. So as teachers we operate within such static 'rules' as the syllabus and the timetable but knowing in action is the way that individual teachers and trainers achieve learning.

As you consider the activity below, think in terms of these twin influences on what we do.

2e Influences on chosen teaching and learning methods

Consider the teaching and the learning strategies that you currently employ. Think in terms of their usefulness and select one approach which springs to mind as being the most effective. Describe the approach and how you arrived at it and then go on to summarize what learning principles you feel underpin the method (for example, 'Always let the students know exactly what is expected of them' or perhaps, 'Before moving to practical applications the students must have a thorough grounding in relevant theory'). However, remember that you should draw out the underlying principles *after* you have intuitively identified the successful teaching and learning methods.

Schon believes strongly in moving away from mere *technical rationality* in classroom practice. Teachers should primarily respond to the needs of their learners and the context in which they are working. A basic principle of this approach would be to consistently encourage different forms of feedback from students so that the teacher can be clear that they are understanding and keeping up with the development of the session. Even though you are working to a lesson plan it is pointless ploughing on towards the intended outcomes if there are clear signs that earlier concepts are not yet understood. It would be more appropriate to return to the concept that is obviously causing some of the students problems and go through a process of recapitulation, perhaps encouraging those who have grasped the idea to articulate their understanding in their own words for the benefit of those who are still struggling. Schon would term this *knowing-in-action*.

2f Knowing-in-action

A tutor is currently teaching a class the simple basics of ICT. He informs the class that in the future all information will be placed onto floppy disks. He holds up a floppy disk and shows it to the class and then quickly moves on. However, one brave student asks in a quiet voice, 'What's one of those?' What do you think the tutor should do now?

Of course, the tutor would explain what it is, how it works and what it does. Now try to analyse what the tutor may have *learnt* from this example?

The tutor could have ignored the question and carried on with the next topic on the lesson plan. However, if the tutor merely engaged in always delivering the same pre-planned teaching without taking into account changing variables and factors, many learning opportunities, particularly in the case of one member of his class, will be lost. Competence based only on technical knowledge would be fine if every class and every session was the same. However, as practising teachers we know they are not and one fundamental principle of teaching is that it is important not to assume knowledge just because we have it. Knowing-in-action is one way of compensating for such oversights and, in this case, ensured that an unfortunate knowledge gap was addressed. At the same time, the teacher will have demonstrated to the class as a whole that, not only will they not be ignored or ridiculed for admitting to ignorance but that it is a very acceptable and responsible way for a member of the class to respond. As Schon points out 'We may reflect-on-action, thinking back on what we have done in order to discover how our knowing-in-action may have contributed to an unexpected outcome.'

2g   Selection of means

Consider the example of two sessions involving the same subject, one given to a group of adults on a Thursday evening, and the other given to 16–19 year olds on Monday morning. Try to identify what the differences in approach, attitude of the students, classroom management and delivery style would be. Think also in terms of pace, questioning techniques and checking of learning.

Schon's answer would be that when practitioners recognize a situation as unique, they cannot handle it solely by applying theories or techniques derived from their store of professional knowledge. In addition, in situations of value conflict, there are no clear and self-consistent ends to guide the technical selection of means. In other words, in spite of technical expertise gained through training, the teacher needs to look beyond this in order to 'see' the situation differently. 'Reframing' is necessary to question previous constructions of practice in order to perceive things afresh with different eyes. This leads to a process that Schon describes as 'a sequence of "moments" in a process of reflection-in-action'. He believes that students cannot be 'taught' the knowledge, but should be coached towards it. 'Nobody else can see for him, and he can't see just by being *told*. However, the right kind of telling may guide his seeing and thus help him see what he wants to see.'

2.6   PRINCIPLES AND VALUES

During this chapter we have discussed a number of important and sometimes difficult concepts. You may not have agreed with them all because there, in the background influencing all teaching, are the implicit values and purposes of the teacher. Concepts inevitably build into principles of operation and those that are held dear are those which form the core of, not only the chosen methodology, but also the underpinning ideology or fundamental beliefs.

As an example here is a principle identified by Ferenc Marton from the University of Göteborg that may, at first, seem a simplistic statement of the obvious (principles often are), but which can provide a real insight into effective pedagogy:

> Whenever you fail to make someone understand something, it is because you have taken something for granted which you shouldn't have taken for granted.

The next exercise is about the principles of learning that are formed from the range of concepts which the practitioner feels are important within a particular context. Of course, if this programme you're reading is at all effective, these principles will inevitably change and develop during the course of it. You may find the activity to be difficult at first, but please give as much time to it as you can spare.

2h Principles of teaching and learning

This reflective activity builds on those you have completed previously. Consider those aspects of teaching and learning which you feel are most important. Now list (if possible in priority order) eight general principles, which you feel would apply to any teaching/learning situation (not just your own). Once again, be aware that there are no right or wrong answers to this and your views will probably change over time.

A simple example of a basic principle could be *At the start of a session make it clear to your students what you are going to cover with them.* Not exactly rocket science, we know, but a very important principle that is sometimes forgotten. *Varied and interactive teaching methods* may have occurred to you as well as the need to *Check learning at regular intervals.* These are some of the key principles of teaching and learning and obviously others will emerge during the chapters that follow.

However, in general, principles will usually relate to the stance you take as a teacher. For example, one dimension to consider could be the question, *Should education stress the importance of Self or Society?* If you feel that the teacher's only responsibility is to dispense the essential knowledge and skills related to the subject, you will have a different set of principles to the practitioner who feels that a teacher's role is to facilitate the student's developing knowledge of him or herself and promote informed scepticism. These extremes may well be seen as somewhat exaggerated examples. Often a practitioner's values will move between ideological positions according to the situation they are working in.

The concept of Reflective Practice may be viewed as a process of moving from a subject base (and relative safety) to a more considered position of thinking about the learning process and educational issues that impact on classroom practice. It involves the tutor moving from the mechanics of imparting knowledge, through a series of personal learning experiences, to becoming a facilitator who guides students in their exploration of the subject being studied in order to develop and value their own insights.

Parker (1997) notes that:

> The literature paints a picture of the reflective practitioner as one who turns her attention to the wider issues of education – its aims, its social and personal consequences, its ethics, the rationale of its methods and its curricula – and to the intimate relationship between these and the immediate reality of her classroom practice.

To support this, Parker also notes that the reflective practitioner is one 'who attempts to bring about improvement in her practice by applying critical thinking to her situation; an approach which is modulated by her appreciation of that situation's uniqueness and its resistance to ready-made descriptions and interpretations'.

2i Values underpinning approaches to teaching

You have probably realized that your identification of learning principles during the previous reflections will inevitably have also given some indication of those aspects of teaching and learning which you most value. Please try to be more precise about your own educational values by expressing (again if possible in priority order) what, for you, are six important *purposes* of education. Remember, there are no right or wrong answers.

We all have certain values that we bring to the education arena which are personal and which differ from individual to individual. These values are based on our own experiences and it is these that influence what goes on in the classroom. For example, one person might think that education should involve freedom of speech and so allow all their students to discuss issues in order to develop critical thinking. Another tutor might believe that education should be about preparing for a useful role in society, which may involve a degree of conformity. The effect on students of these two differing value-bases may well be noticeable in their overt behaviour.

2.7 | CONCLUSION

It is possible that your own views on educational purposes may well develop and change during this programme. On the other hand they may be established on such a firm value-foundation that you cannot envisage any room for manoeuvre. But how do your values equate to the teaching that you are currently doing? This is a difficult issue and one which may well be highly political within the setting in which you work. Remember again that there are no right or wrong answers, particularly in this instance. Be as honest as possible, but also be aware of the political sensitivities within your working environment. The final reflection is designed to be a summative evaluation of your own views as expressed within all your reflective activities to this point and a consideration of how compatible these perceptions are with aspects of your current teaching:

2j Relationship between previous reflections

Please look back through your previous reflections once more and notice how your early identification of a *significant learning experience* (2a) and your preferred approaches to *problem solving* (2d) and *teaching and learning* (2e) relate to your later articulation of *principles and values* (2h and 2i). Consider the nature of your 'significant learning experience' and your preferred 'teaching and learning styles'. Do they contain or represent any of the principles and values you identified later? In what way do your expressed values and principles relate to your present work as a teacher?

Please write between 50 and 100 words analysing each of these two aspects (summarized below):

- relationship between own teaching and learning *approaches* and educational values and principles
- compatibility of current teaching *responsibilities* with educational values and principles

If there are no tensions then that is excellent! However, you may have found that some of the values you believe in are compromised to some extent by the constraints within the present education system. In Chapter 10, Yvonne Hutton suggests how reflection may be used as a means of active self-evaluation. Chapter 12 will address many of these issues which affect the validity of education, but the plain fact is that colleges are currently under great pressure and have to make some sacrifices to survive within the present climate.

To counteract this rather pessimistic note, it is worthwhile ending the chapter with a consideration of why, despite the need for technical rationality within management, teachers should continue to explore theoretical issues as well as cope with the more instrumental influences on practice. Wilfred Carr (1995) introduces the concept of 'poiesis' and contrasts this with the opposing concept of 'praxis'. Carr's theoretical examination of practice has led to his identification of two approaches. The first he characterizes as 'rule-following action' (poiesis) and contrasts this with practice that is 'morally informed and morally committed action' (praxis).

Praxis according to Carr is reflexive action that can 'transform the *theory* that guides it'. Poiesis, on the other hand, is seen as a non-reflexive 'know-how' that does not affect its guiding 'techne'. To Carr *techne* is a term for technical expertise and knowledge.

Stephen Kemmis (1985), a contemporary of Carr, draws heavily upon the idea of 'critical thinking' in teaching and the need for reflective practice. He too notes the need for 'praxis'.

> reflection is action-orientated, social and political. Its product is 'praxis' (informed, committed action), the most eloquent and socially significant form of human action.

In other words, teachers have the opportunity to continually reconstruct theory in response to their own praxis (active reflection). In this way they are involved with the ongoing development of knowledge related to their own practice and are not restricted to Dewey's 'routine action', Schon's 'technical rationality' or Carr's 'poiesis'.

Knowledge is developed through practice but is only visible when it is illuminated by theory. Teachers who, in addition to recording events that are happening in their classroom, are also willing (through praxis) to consider *why* they are happening, are taking the first steps towards knowledge creation in contrast to routine knowledge replication. But they need the light of theory to guide them. The FENTO Standards state that:

> Reflective practice and scholarship should ... underpin the wider and professional role of the teacher in managing the learning process, developing the curriculum and guiding and supporting the learner in partnership with others in the organization and the local community.

Perhaps the final word on praxis (active reflection) should go to the great Brazilian educationalist Paulo Freire (2000).

Liberation is a praxis: the action and reflection of people upon their world in order to transform it.

2.8 | USEFUL SOURCES

Schon, D. (1987) *Educating the Reflective Practitioner*. Jossey-Bass
This readable book is one of the 'authorities' on Reflective Practice. Schon uses real examples of practice to show how people move from everyday know-how through to a process of reflection and thinking about what they do. The concepts noted in this text such as Knowing-in-Action and Technical Rationality are made clear through appropriate examples.

Dewey, J. (1916) *Democracy and Education*. New York: Free Press
An old book that has set the foundations for educational discourse. Dewey's work inflenced government policy changes between 1940 and 1960. Recent critics of the current accountability drive draw upon Dewey for support. A return to his problem-solving approach seems to be underpinning recent political debates.

Dewey, J. (1938) *Experience and Education*. Collier Macmillan Publishers
Similar to the above work in a philosophical sense, but in this text Dewey draws upon student experience as a powerful learning tool and one that any educational practice should employ. Dated in some respects, but again critics of the current economic utility model of education would do well to seek it out.

Carr, W. (1995) *For Education towards Critical Educational Inquiry*. Milton Keynes: Open University Press
This text is a more recent philosophical debate regarding the nature of education. Carr questions what educational practice is and raises issues such as how theory and practice are related in terms of broader educational debates. Very relevant to the ideas behind reflective practice, Carr is able to develop aspects of critical enquiry that are designed to promote a further consideration of educational values.

Elliott, G. (1996) *Crisis and Change in Vocational Education and Training*. Jessica Kingsley
An excellent text that draws upon actual research undertaken within the further education sector. Elliott uses actual practitioner comment to reflect what he sees as an escalating crisis brought about by recent government reforms in education. He questions the businesslike approach to education and training and illustrates the impact of the policies on practice.

Parker, S. (1997) *Reflective teaching in the Postmodern world. A manifesto for education in postmodernity*. Milton Keynes: Open University Press
A strong text on the use of reflective teaching and its place within an economic environment of education. Parker provides some useful definitions of Reflective Practice that places it firmly within a broader concept than that of classroom practice. His work provokes thought and challenges some concepts that have previously been taken for granted.

Moon, J. (1999a) *Reflection in Learning and Professional Development Theory and Practice.* London: Kogan Page
A practical book which draws upon a range of theory to relate Reflective Practice to actual examples. Moon is down to earth in her approach to using Reflective Practice as a tool for real learning, but at the same time presents a very useful overview of the major writings on Reflective Practice. A very helpful text on the use of journals as a powerful learning tool.

Moon, J. (1999b) *Learning journals: A handbook for academics, students and professional development.* London: Kogan Page
This book draws on the previous title, but pays particular attention to the aspect of journal writing. Moon provides a powerful argument for the use of journals as a reflective vehicle to promote learning at a deeper level. She explains how journals can create meta-cognition through a process of reflection about one's knowledge and understanding.

Kemmis, S. (1985) 'Action research and the politics of reflection', in Boud, D., Keogh, R. and Walker, D. (eds) *Reflection: Turning experience into practice.* London: Kogan Page
Kemmis is well known for his opinions on education as a form of social change. This work draws upon action research for teachers as a powerful tool for liberation and social change through education. He uses examples drawn from practice that illustrate how action research can change and develop education, teaching and learning towards better practice through a cycle of reflection, analysis and evaluation.

You will also find a range of materials which promote active reflection on the *tipcet.com* website.

Assessing learners' needs

Janet Hobley

Key Area 'A' Identifying and responding to the characteristics and needs of student groups

Key concepts in this chapter

Abstract Random, Abstract Sequential, Accreditation, Action Plans, APEL, APL, Cloze Technique, Concrete Random, Concrete Sequential, Deductive, Diagnostic Tests, FOG index, Holistic, Inductive, Intellectual Skills, Interpersonal Skills, Intrapersonal Skills, Learner Dependence, Learner Independence, Learner Needs, Learner Skills, Learning Cycle, Learning Strategies, Learning Styles, Mediation Channels, Practical Skills, Serialistic, Student Autonomy, Student Profiles, Teaching Styles

Before you begin this chapter you may wish to check the FAQs on pp. 62–4

Index to Chapter 3 (Key Area A)

Chapter 3 Activities designed to generate evidence against the Standards

3.1 INTRODUCTION

Preparing for a new group of students is probably one of the most interesting aspects of teaching. Many experienced teachers will tell you that, despite having gone through the process many times before, an incoming group of learners inevitably causes the familiar tingle of an adrenalin rush. The fresh challenges that this initial process brings are exciting partially because they are, to some extent, as yet unknown. Even though you may have background information about each of the students as individuals, you cannot predict accurately how the dynamics of the newly formed group will operate. Your anxieties may be about the learners' mental, physical and social responses to your preparations. In other words you may worry about what they will think about your chosen approach, how they cope with any physical demands required of them and their reactions to each other, to you and to their new environment. Try the following activity as a starting point for this process of needs assessment:

A3a Preparing for your first meeting with new students

Imagine that you are about to have your first meeting with a new group of learners. Make a list of any advanced information you could be given which would help you to prepare more effectively for your initial meeting. Remember, first impressions do count.

It is likely that you will be provided with a class list, but this information is only of limited value. You will then know the number of learners in the group, their gender and perhaps their age. At this stage additional advanced information that would help you to plan your first session can be summarized as follows:

Venue: The time of day and the room you are meeting in can have an effect on the outcome of the session. Facilities you may take for granted such as sufficient seating, a working overhead projector, a surface to project on, a white or blackboard, chalk or marker pen, adequate ventilation have been known to be absent. If your session is the students' second or third meeting during an induction day, it will probably affect how you approach your introductions to the topic.

Age: This information is helpful, for example, in ensuring that learners meet the requirements of a professional body and indicating whether they are school leavers or more mature students.

Experience: These details will let you know, for example, if they moving to you from another education environment, are mature students with no post-school experience, have taken other programmes since leaving school, or are entering your college after or while continuing in employment.

Qualifications: You need to know if their qualifications meet the course prerequisites. Also these details will give you an indication of their areas of interest/expertise and whether they are inclined towards academic or vocational study.

Special Needs: You may need to make arrangements if your incoming group contains students who require particular provision because of physical or learning difficulties.

Given some or all of the above information, you can plan the first session with much more confidence. However, as is true of each of us, you may still be caught out on the day by the unexpected, but at least you have attempted to cover the obvious eventualities.

3.2 | LEARNER NEEDS

Chapter 4 which follows is concerned with teaching and learning techniques; our concern now is to build upon the information gained in Activity A3a (above) in order to be aware of the range of needs which may exist within a particular group. You have already got together the basic data needed for you to start establishing an effective working relationship with the group. Even so, though a teacher or trainer may be very experienced within their own particular subject, they will still be faced with the need to present it in a way that will catch and hold the interest of the incoming students.

In this regard, subject expertise is valuable but it does not necessarily guarantee that the teacher will be able to convince the learners of its intrinsic worth. Any particular student group will inevitably contain a range of differing learner characteristics and knowing these qualities may help you to promote a positive teacher/student relationship. Conversely, ignoring them could well reduce the effectiveness of teacher–student and student–student interaction. Obviously, the needs of any individual will be related to the particular qualities they bring to a situation. Try the next exercise as a further step forward in your learner needs' analysis:

A3b   Learner skills

Consider a student or trainee group (perhaps your focus learning group identified in Chapter 1) with whom you are so familiar that you already have most of the information discussed in Activity A3a. Now try to identify the range of skills that individual learners bring to your sessions.

Stoker (1994) has identified the following skills which learners will possess in varying degrees:

a)   practical skills – ability to use equipment and carry out actions

b)   intellectual skills – related to knowledge and how the learner applies this, and concerned with activities such as planning, identifying priorities, problem-solving and decision-making

c)   interpersonal skills – the ability to communicate, form relationships and generally 'get on' with other people

d)   intrapersonal skills – concerned with the learner's self-confidence, self-control and awareness of her own abilities and the effect they have on others

Although it is clear that the level of the above skills possessed by the student/ trainee will certainly affect their overall performance, information about each student's ability in each of the above areas will not necessarily be readily available. In any case, all of these skills may well vary dependent upon the context in which the student is operating. For example, if for some reason a particular environment affects their self-confidence, then (c) and (d) may well be undermined.

3.3   DIAGNOSTIC TESTS

Obviously, as you work with the learners over the first few weeks of the programme, you will collect more data about their skills which, in turn, will enhance your individual profiles. However, you may wish to be more systematic about your data gathering. Turning once again to Stoker's list (above) try the following new activity:

A3c   Diagnostic tests

Suggest some of the ways you might go about identifying the levels of ability of your learners in each of Stoker's four areas – practical, intellectual, interpersonal and intrapersonal.

It is relatively easy to identify previous learning of 16 year olds with GCSE results and details from the secondary school about their abilities within the four areas. Not so easy for adult returners who have not attended an educational institution for several years and it is harder still to identify the range of needs that individuals with communication difficulties might have.

However, we must remember that FENTO does apply to *all* aspects of post-compulsory education and training. Tutors must consciously develop strategies to build up a profile or picture of their own students in order to decide what teaching methods will be most appropriate for the different student needs.

●   *Practical skills* – on the face of it, this is probably the most straightforward of the areas in which to diagnose ability. A tutor could ask students to carry out a task which contains important skills. However, in these situations it is very easy to misinterpret hesitancy on the part of the student as a lack of competence. In fact, all manner of features within the testing situation may be quite different to those that the learner is used to and their performance may not yet reflect their true ability

- *Intellectual skills* – most problem-solving or decision-making situations where knowledge may be applied can be used to give an indication of cognitive ability. However, it is as important to know what the student *can* do, as well as what they are unable to achieve. So the diagnosis should also provide the opportunity for the learner to demonstrate at what level *in relation to a particular task* they are able to perform within the cognitive hierarchy of behaviours (see further details in Chapter 4)

- *Interpersonal skills* – obviously, an aware teacher will be able to observe evidence of these abilities as well as collect data from student work. However, once again it is important not to jump to conclusions because, although some people take longer to develop confidence in group situations, they may well be responding to and supporting their colleagues, but in a less obvious manner

- *Intrapersonal skills* – again a difficult area in which to gain accurate information about true ability. Students are often influenced by factors not immediately obvious within the social setting where diagnosis is taking place. Self-esteem and self-control may differ radically dependent upon the other personalities present (see more in Chapter 4)

There are, of course, several diagnostic techniques, which can be undertaken *prior* to enrolment. Students may be interviewed and given guidance about course options and care can be taken to ensure that learners are sure about their own and their tutors' initial course decisions. This involves a process of induction and pre-course guidance that allows for arrangements to be put in place for early course changes as necessary. With this initial assessment of needs comes the use of early pre-course testing to gauge student levels and existing abilities. Examples include reading tests, mathematical tests, aptitude tests and other subject-specific tests that can give the tutor an insight into student ability and knowledge. These are all useful techniques that can aid course design. After all, if each of your students can already do, for example, differential equations, there is no need to spend hours teaching this. A short diagnostic test will help to determine the learner's abilities in a subject. From the results, a tutor could plan the sequence of lessons and indeed the level.

3.4 READING AND WRITING SKILLS

It is easy to assume that by the time they enter further education, all students will have developed their reading skills to the required basic level, but often this isn't the case. The reading age of students who have learning difficulties will often not match their chronological age and, in a minority of cases, the problem may be more serious. By using questions that involve short answer tests, tutors may also obtain a valuable indication of the reading and writing skills of the students in order to see if extra support in these areas needs to be given. Further diagnosis may involve testing the learners' reading age using measures such as the APU vocabulary tests.

Simple steps which lecturers themselves can usefully take in relation to reading would be to check that the materials they are using are pitched at an appropriate reading age for their own students. Two such methods, the FOG index and the Cloze Technique are used as the basis of the next two activities (A3d and A3e):

A3d FOG index

Take a typical example of text which you have used or will use with your own students and select a passage of 100 words which you can use to test the reading age of the material following the guidelines below.

3.4.1 FOG index

This is a useful indicator of the reading age of written materials and is based on the notion of the number of difficult words within a passage of writing, or the 'Frequency Of Gobbledegook'. For your test use extracts from appropriate textbooks or handouts. The steps are as follows:

Step 1   Select a passage of 100 words
We have selected the following extract from the beginning of *Using Video in Training*.

> The recorded image whether on film or videotape has become such a familiar part of our lives that we now treat it as we would a member of our family. In general, we enjoy its company uncritically and only when it fails us do we see it in a new light. For a brief moment we become aware of its limitations. We cannot rely too much on these accidental revelations, instructive though they may be. We must attempt to develop our awareness of these characteristics in order to be more precise when using the moving image to achieve training goals.

Step 2   Count the number of complete sentences
In our case, the above passage has five complete sentences.

Step 3   Count the words in each of the complete sentences
Our answer is 30, 21, 10, 14 and 25.

Step 4   Find the average sentence length (L)
In other words, 100 words divided by 5 = 20 words on average per sentence.

Step 5   Count the number of words of three or more syllables (polysyllabic) in the 100-word sample (we will call this N)
In our case this is 10 – recorded, videotape, familiar, company, uncritically, limitations, accidental, revelations, instructive and characteristics.

Step 6   To arrive at the reading age, add L and N, multiply by 0.4 and then add 5. Written as a formula this is 0.4 (L + N) + 5 This is the reading age
In our case the calculations are as follows:
20 (Step 4) + 10 (Step 5) = 30
30 × 0.4 = 12
12 + 5 = 17 years

Obviously, if your students have a reading age of 14 years, the above passage (which has a reading age of 17 years) is not going to be suitable. The problem is the number of words with three syllables or more and it is a simple task to replace these polysyllabic words by rewriting the piece.

Step 7   Although the re-drafting has increased the number of words to 110, it has taken out the polysyllabic words and consequently the reading age has been reduced to less than 14 years:

> As we develop new methods, it becomes easier to record an image onto film or tape. These days, film and video have helped moving pictures to become so common that we tend to take them for granted. It is only when we have reason to check them with more care that we see some good and bad things about them. If we are to learn to use moving pictures well, we must also know the key rules about choosing an image. If we want to say something clearly using moving pictures, we also need to know about the effect of images and how they can help or hinder our work.

The calculations this time are as follows:

22 (Step 4) + 0 (Step 5) = 22

22 × 0.4 = 8.8

8.8 + 5 = 13.8 years.

A3e   Cloze technique

This test is more concerned with your students' understanding and their ability to express themselves in writing. Find another example of text that would be appropriate for your learners and use the following test with them and then record the results.

3.4.2   The cloze technique

Although relatively crude, this type of test can provide some useful information about a student's level of comprehension and writing ability. If you have designed a test, or some guided study materials for example, you may wish to have an indication of how the learners will cope with it. The cloze process is based on the gestalt psychology notion of 'closure', which occurs when a person perceiving an incomplete form automatically adds the missing elements, sometimes correctly and sometimes, when their understanding is poor, incorrectly.

The procedure is relatively simple. Take the material or (if it is lengthy) part of the material you wish to test and after omitting every *ninth* word give it to your students to write what they think the missing words are in the blank spaces. Allow them sufficient time to consider the alternative words carefully but not so long that they become bored waiting for all the slowest members to complete. When it comes to marking, interpretations differ as do the recommended intervals between the omitted words. However, a simple guide is that, if a student gets less than 65 per cent of the replacement words correct, then the materials are too demanding. A 65 to 80 per cent score indicates that they will need some guidance with terms and concepts, and any score of 80 per cent and over shows that the target group should find the materials manageable. Obviously, if you already know what the reading age is for the passage that you have used for the Cloze Test, you will also have an indication of the students' reading ability as well as their level of comprehension and vocabulary.

3.5 | DEVELOPING STUDENT PROFILES

During this opening part of the chapter we have been developing an awareness of the many and varied needs which learners will bring to your sessions. You will agree that the majority of learners attending colleges of further education have far more than just academic needs. Of course, the subject being studied is very important, but it is also crucial to understand how the student is responding to both the subject and the learning environment in which they have been placed.

The learners' life experiences will inevitably colour their perceptions of what they find when they commence their chosen learning programme. If tutors are able to develop an insight into these personal constructs, then the management of the students may well be less problematic. All that they encounter during their induction period, and often events occurring even before they attend their new place of learning, will influence the attitudes of new students. These attitudes change very rapidly and it is important that tutors are aware of the range of subtle influences that can affect the learners' attitudes, confidence and their openness to new experiences.

The essential ingredient in any positive and productive relationship is trust and, despite the fact that most of the parties involved (teachers and students) are willing to give the others the benefit of the doubt, this trusting relationship is often very difficult to achieve. It does take time and you will usually find that by the end of the term/semester the students will have moved a long way towards trusting you. However, progress in this direction does very much depend on whether or not you have intentionally or accidentally given them any reason to doubt that you have their best interest at heart. An essential feature in developing a trusting relationship is consistency. This doesn't just mean treating all members of the group equally, although that is important. It involves the difficult skill of responding in what may be called a professional manner to all eventualities. For example, although you may find that some students have naturally developed more attractive characteristics than others, you are able to avoid any inclination towards an overt demonstration of favouritism.

Another important aspect of consistency its that the learners should begin to anticipate accurately how you will respond to their performance or behaviour. In other words, they learn to understand the values that you feel strongly about and expect you to react in a particular way if these values are not respected. If your reaction to minor infringements is over the top and, on other occasions, you ignore major transgressions, the learners will inevitably be uncertain about where they stand. Students will usually respond well if they are secure in the knowledge that their teacher has established a productive learning environment where a consistent relationship thrives that is based on values they understand.

Try the following activity:

A3f Student trust

Think of the characteristics of a particular group of students whom you teach. Make a list of indicators (for example, changes in behaviour) that you might become aware of at the end of term, which show how the students' trust has developed since the term commenced.

Naturally, these indicators will reflect the characteristics of a particular group and so it is difficult to generalize. However, you could expect the following indications:

- small positive signs, such as smiles, openness, shared news, etc., which show that the students are actually pleased to be there and which outweigh any negative reluctance or resentment
- a general readiness to begin the session (and even some signs of anticipation)
- a willingness to follow a tutor-led change of direction during the ongoing discussion without signs of apprehension such as needing to know where it is leading
- student willingness to put forward their own views, even on unfamiliar topics
- a concern among the learners that the teacher doesn't misunderstand them
- a willingness to persuade reticent fellow students to contribute
- student acceptance of assessment results and a willingness to improve

We have stressed that teachers need as much information as possible about their new charges. However, perhaps as an initial 'them and us' reaction, it is fairly common for a novice tutor to perceive the student group as an amorphous whole. Try the following activity as a first step in considering student/trainee learning preferences:

A3g   A starting point for study

Imagine that you are teaching for the first time a familiar topic from your own subject area to a particular group of learners. How would you structure the session?

3.5.1   Deductive and inductive learning approaches

When delivering learning programmes within post-compulsory education, there is a natural tendency for trainers, teachers, learning support workers, etc. to turn to approaches that they have experienced to good effect themselves. This often involves presenting the students with the *theory* first. This theory may be in the form of rules, principles, guidelines, formulae, recipes, instructions and so on. Whatever way this essentially theoretical content is presented it will inevitably be *abstract* in nature and the learners will be involved with trying to *deduce* a conclusion from the information they have received.

A familiar example presented by Conan Doyle in the Sherlock Holmes stories is that the great detective relied on *deductive reasoning* where he ensured that the conclusions he inferred when investigating a situation were based only on the evidence that was available. Holmes established a premise (a theoretical proposition or hypothesis) and then set about collecting evidence to prove or disprove it.

When deductive approaches in teaching are used, the learners will first be given rules (the theory) and then will usually have the experience of investigating these through laboratory work, field work, the real situation, etc. A simple way to represent the process is to say that deductive learning is RULE/EX, i.e. the rules followed by the experience/example.

As you would expect, a simple way to represent the alternative *inductive* approach to reasoning or teaching is EX/RULE. Although, inductive teaching is more obvious within the primary or secondary sectors, many would suggest that it should be used more extensively in further education (see Chapter 5). It involves providing the learners with the experience *first* and then drawing the rules and principles out of the experience. Sand and water play are good examples from early years' education, where children develop a range of abstract concepts from concrete experiences. These would include addition, subtraction, conservation and spatial and volume relationships. Some teachers continue this approach in a more structured manner during Year 3. For example, a walk in the countryside with the children may involve the teacher encouraging the children to identify the characteristics of different flowers or trees and then, back in the classroom, they will perhaps develop through discussion the 'rules' of what characteristics a particular plant, flower or tree must have in order to belong to a specific category. So, in this way the theory is drawn out of the experience and often, because the development of the theory is based on rich, concrete experiences involving many of the senses, the learners' grasp of these rules and principles is firm, long-lasting and easily recalled.

Of course, teachers in post-compulsory education will be aware that, although the inductive approach may well be successful, it is also very demanding of resources, particularly time. However, given the premise that, in any given learning situation, students/trainees will have a preference for a particular learning style (even though they may not express it) it is clear that some of these learners will have real difficulty with the theory first, deductive approach. An alternative definition of inductive/experiential approaches could be *building on learners' previous experience* rather than basing the learning entirely on new experiences. Again this will help learners because you are starting from a basis they are familiar with and are using previous cognitive structures to develop new knowledge. Now try the following activity:

A3h   Different group reactions

Consider the following two examples:
1. A tutor delivers a session on *King Lear* to a GCSE group of 16-year old males and females at 10 a.m. on a Monday morning. The session involves tutor-led readings and explanations of the key ideas of two Acts, followed by a 15-minute video of a recent Stratford production. The session finishes promptly at the point that the tutor required.
2. The same tutor then attempts to deliver a similar session to a mature GCSE adult evening class consisting of 15 female students. Five minutes into the tutor's explanation of why King Lear disinherits his youngest daughter, the class begins to argue and debate the tutor's input. At the end of the session, the tutor has only covered a quarter of the material.

Try to identify the factors that have caused the change in student response.

Obviously, the time was different; but so were the students' age, sex, experience and motivation. Also, many 16-year olds find it difficult to contribute on a Monday morning, their experience of Shakespeare may well be limited and their reasons for studying GCSE will be totally different to that of the adult returners. The experience and possibly the gender of the second group would inevitably help to promote a healthy debate about the relationship between King Lear and his youngest daughter.

It is worth remembering that within classes and between classes there will inevitably be myriad student 'types'. It is possible that a particular student group could consist of adults who come from many different walks of life in order to study subjects that they may have missed at school, together with restless 16 year olds who 'need' a particular GCSE in order to gain access to a particular course and experienced people who have held down responsible jobs in industry or commerce and who are studying for pleasure and relaxation. On top of all this, the teacher may well be faced with personality clashes. For example, the extrovert who will not shut up and the introvert who remains silent throughout all discussions. In adult groups the students may range from 18 to 90 and may come from all occupations and all social classes. There are issues of gender and race as well as age, ability and self-esteem. This notion of dealing with multifaceted learners may initially be very threatening to a novice teacher even though they are very experienced in their subject area. Although you have a good awareness of how you learnt your subject it very soon becomes evident that not all students learn in the same way.

It is because we are faced with this complex range of learner differences that we turn to diagnostic assessment as a vital aid to our understanding of student needs. The information gained through diagnosis can relate to several areas. Simple examples could be that it may be important if you teach a physical subject to find out the health of your students and if cookery is your subject, you may need to identify if they have any allergies to foods. We mentioned earlier student writing and reading skills and you may also need to know if they are able to add up and subtract simple numbers. The precise nature of the diagnostic tests you use will usually be directly related to the subject you teach. A useful starting point then would be to reflect on the skills, attributes or attitudes that are needed to do well in your subject. Try the following:

A3i   Subject-specific skills

What made you want to pursue your own subject/area of interest? Identify the skills and knowledge that would be needed to succeed in this topic. Now, identify a few questions or tasks that will identify whether or not students have these abilities and understandings. Don't forget that attitudes play a part as well. After all, hairdressing isn't just about skilfully cutting hair; a student also needs to be able to communicate effectively with customers.

3.6   ACTION PLANS

When you have developed the most effective way of obtaining basic information about your students' skills and knowledge, you need to process it in some way. This could involve producing individual action plans for each student. For example, you may have identified that one student has some difficulty in spelling and needs extra support. In this case it might be useful to suggest some form of study support to develop this aspect of performance. An individual action plan is just that, an individual prescription for a specific student. No two action plans should be the same. Take the following examples:

Action Plan 1	
Student: Judith Smith	*Course:* NVQ Level One Hairdressing
Skills:	Previously worked for 12 months in a children's nursery. Can already shampoo hair as a result of working for eighteen months in a salon, positive comments from supervisor. Is computer literate but has no qualification in IT.
Knowledge:	Knows the theory of shampooing, but not any other techniques in hairdressing. Has Key Skill Level One Communication and Working with Others.
Diagnostic results:	Some spelling problems identified, but your essays are becoming more structured due to the implementation of essay plans.
Action:	Study support needed to improve spelling To be entered for Clait to gain an IT qualification.

Action Plan 2	
Student: Albert Ainsworth	*Course:* 'A' Level Spanish
Skills:	Can speak three languages already
Knowledge:	Has GCSE Spanish, but taken 10 years ago. Has a Diploma in Management Studies.
Diagnostic results:	Other languages can get in the way of speaking Spanish. Written Spanish very poor.
Action:	Subject-specific study support weekly to improve written work. To sit in on a current GCSE Spanish class alongside 'A' Level students.

Collecting this sort of information is the first step in ensuring that, where it is needed, the right support is provided at the optimum time. Try the following action planning activity:

A3j   Action planning

Using a simple format (along the lines of the above examples), construct action plans based around the known profiles of three or four of your students/trainees. Try to make your 'action' as realistic and appropriate as possible, bearing in mind the needs of the learners and the current range of provision that is available to them.

For example, in some cases the information might show that the course was not the right one for the student at that particular time. A structured induction period will identify problems early while it is still possible for students to change courses and to be placed on one that is more suitable. *For instance, an AS Level Spanish may be more suitable for Albert Ainsworth in Action Plan 2.*

What you write must be understood by all parties concerned and, like feedback, should be constructive and helpful. Try to use positive statements, clarifying what the learner has achieved. See Judith Smith Action Plan for examples. When completing the action plan, make sure tasks are clear with definite target dates. There may be room for students to complete their own comments – and they should be encouraged to do so in order to develop their reflective skills. Timely diagnostic assessment and individual action plans can often prevent many students experiencing early failure or withdrawal.

3.7 ACCREDITATION OF PRIOR LEARNING AND EXPERIENTIAL LEARNING (APL AND APEL)

A part of identifying student needs involves a consideration of their *prior learning and experience*. Although the Accreditation of Prior Learning (APL) and the Accreditation of Prior Experiential Learning (APEL) are relatively new processes in education, they are becoming increasingly important as a means of ensuring that a student's previous endeavours are not only acknowledged but, where appropriate, are also translated into some form of credit within their current programme of study.

Unfortunately, the process is necessarily complicated. This is because it essentially hinges on an interpretation of equivalence and this may often be controversial. Even when accrediting a *certificated* qualification, there is sometimes disagreement about its value to the target programme and consequently what credit it should earn. Those involved talk about the APEL currency (i.e. how long ago was the certificate or experience undertaken) or relevance (i.e. what it has in common with aspects of the target programme).

However, it is important to remember that a student may enter your institution with a range of different experiences or qualifications which may not only positively influence their ability to benefit from a course (i.e. their prior learning gives them advanced standing), but in some cases make part of the course redundant because it will only be repeating what has been previously learned.

Using Albert Ainsworth from our example of an action plan, it might be useful to consider whether he would have any previous learning that might have influenced the way he was able to perform on his current programme of study:

A3k   *Prior learning and experience*

Refer back to Judith Smith and Albert Ainsworth (Action Plans 1 and 2 above) and decide if they have any knowledge or experience that could have affected their learning within their chosen programme of study.

You may have identified the value of Albert already speaking three languages. This goes some way towards indicating that this person has a natural flair for language and that he could do well on an academic study route.

With Judith Smith you may feel that she deserves some credit for her shampooing skills. It may be possible in this sort of case to give a student credit in *advance* of the course for this aspect of learning. However, as stated before, some aspects are difficult to measure. Try the following activity to investigate this further:

A3l   Accreditation

Given the case of Judith Smith, what information would you need to know that would convince you that this candidate really did have the skills of shampooing? If you were convinced that she had these skills, ask yourself how it would be possible to accredit them.

You would certainly need to see them in action and would probably need a witness statement of support from her employer. A tutor's role in using APL is to collect as much data as possible about the previous learning and to assess it in the light of the new learning being undertaken. It may be that the previous learning was many years ago and did not involve current technology or techniques and is therefore redundant knowledge because it doesn't have currency. In that case, the tutor would reject the claim for the accreditation of previous learning. It may be that the previous learning is substantial both in terms of duration and level of difficulty and is equivalent to a whole unit within the current programme. Whatever the scenario, each case needs to be considered on its own merit and it is the subject tutor's role to define what is needed for a particular course and what can be accredited through previous experiences, both formal and informal. Most programmes and courses have a regulation that states what percentage of the award may be accredited on the basis of prior experience or certification.

Some courses allow *credit exemption*, which occurs when there is some APL/APEL, which may allow the student to be exempted from parts of the programme of study. In the case of Albert Ainsworth (Action Plan 2), if he were to take a programme which includes a Management Unit, he may well be exempted from all or part of it because he holds a DMS.

Some courses also allow *credit transfer*. This is because the APL/APEL is directly relevant to the target programme. In Judith Smith's case, if she were entering a programme such as Childhood Studies, she may receive some credits because of her nursery nursing experience. If this were the case, the credit would be transferred directly onto the student's profile and this will reduce the amount of credits needing to be attained. Tutors may also consider the value of APL/APEL from another useful perspective. If, when planning a programme of learning, the lecturer takes into account any prior knowledge and experience which the learners *as a group* may have previously developed, it often helps to counteract any potential there may be for student disinterest or demotivation. For example, reference during teaching to any ideas, people, places or theories which are already familiar to the group will help to reduce any anxieties they may have and provide valuable shared interest and communication points which may quickly be built upon. These mutual frameworks for the structuring of concepts and principles provide wonderful signposts or reference points which may be used over and over again during the forthcoming teaching. In simple terms, there needs to be a system integrated into the planned programme which not only credits the prior learning that has already taken place, but also values learners as a group by designing a programme which builds on their experience and meets their needs. If they are to fully achieve their potential, the tutor needs to ensure that the learner can transfer existing skills and knowledge to either a new setting or a new learning programme. Learners need to know what is to be learned so that they can make an informed choice as to planning their own personal needs. It is true that some learners do want to run before they can walk and this may be linked to the fact that the learners have identified some gaps in their own learning and are eager to address these omissions. In other cases, and possibly because of their previous learning experiences, some learners lack motivation. If the tutor is to help such learners to progress the underpinning causes of demotivation need to be identified and addressed in both a confidential and empathetic manner.

One method some tutors use to obtain details about each of the individuals in a group is to use a questionnaire, which asks for specific details about each individual. This approach needs sensitivity on the part of the teacher, particularly in the wording of the questions and also in making it clear when introducing the questionnaire that it is optional. From the experience of those who use such a data collection method, the process *cannot* occur prior to the commencement of the programme, as it is human nature not to disclose personal information to an 'unknown entity' (i.e. a tutor they have yet to develop any trust in). Practice has shown that if a carefully worded document is issued some two to three sessions into the programme and is complemented by a verbal explanation relating to the usefulness of such *optional* information, most students will agree to complete the questionnaire. Also, of course, students would have to be reassured that this information is for short-term use and will not be kept on a database. Some of the most useful areas on which to collect data are given below, together with a rationale for obtaining this information:

- *number and nature of dependants* – to ascertain the demands on the student's time outside of the learning context
- *medical conditions or learning difficulties* – that might affect learning (this may including illnesses such as asthma, diabetes, epilepsy, as well as barriers to learning such as dyslexia and colour blindness)
- *previous related learning* – allowing the tutor to attempt to ascertain the prior experience and knowledge an individual might have, as well as academic ability with regard to the curriculum content
- *individual expectations of the programme* – potential insight into additional reasons why the leaarner has chosen to come onto the programme, e.g. raising confidence, building self-esteem, proving to themselves that they can achieve, etc.)
- *fears of the programme* – as with previous topic, responses in this area often highlight the major concerns of the potential learner. Those who come into post-compulsory education for a 'second chance' often have a strong fear of failure. It is crucial that the tutor is aware of the strength of these concerns

A3m   Individual needs

Return to your focus learning group and, without naming them, reflect on how the above sort of information would enable you to more effectively meet their needs, improve their learning experience and enhance their potential for achievement.

Provided that tutors use the data collected through the suggested questionnaire in a sensitive and confidential manner, it will often give an excellent insight into the basic needs of their learners and provide the vital knowledge necessary for an effective planning process.

3.8   TEACHING STYLES

In theory therefore, by following the above guidelines, you should be able to ensure that your students have access to the most suitable course and that they will then go on to enjoy it and achieve success. However, the reality is that some students will still struggle with certain topics and in particular with certain teaching styles and methods. Try the following activity as an introduction to teaching and learning styles:

A3n   Solving problems

Focusing on one of your classes, reflect on why some students need time to work out problems, while others constantly ask you to explain everything several times.

If you have been able to identify several student behavioural traits by reflecting on their learning styles, then you will have some understanding that not all people learn in the same way.

A3o   Starting a task

Ask yourself whether you would read instructions first before assembling something, or whether you would prefer to get on with it and learn by trial and error.

We all know that in obvious ways people are different to each other. We are often different in size and have different hair colours and it is accepted that these differences are genetically based. What is less easily seen is that we also differ in our approaches to learning. There are many theories related to our preferred styles of learning and this has been a growing area for research from both an educational and a psychological perspective.

Although the theorists may not entirely agree on the effects, in order to be aware of the extent of student needs it is important that tutors do have some awareness of the possible effects which these differences may have in the classroom. This insight is often the key to effective lesson planning. As a starting point, try the following activity:

A3p Approaches to learning

Consider a group of learners with differing learning styles who, in a practical 'Cooking for Pleasure' lesson are involved in planning and preparing a meal. Obviously, some learners will prefer a step-by-step approach where they first see the tutor demonstrate the task and then attempt to copy these skills. Reflect on two other ways in which the students/trainees might prefer to approach the learning task.

Possibly, for some learners the starting point would be a meal, which is familiar to them, and they would then already have some knowledge of and possibly practice in the required task. Some may be more creative and would, for example, enjoy an exercise where they are asked to make the best use of a prescribed set of ingredients. Others may like to see a finished meal and then work out how best to achieve that result.

Building on the earlier theories of Lewin and Kolb (see previous chapter), two researchers have identified four basic learning styles – pragmatist, activist, reflector and theorist. To Honey and Mumford (1982) a pragmatist would take a planning approach, activists like doing things, reflectors enjoy thinking about issues and experiences and the theorists enjoy analysis as a means of explaining things. Although these styles seem widely different, it is possible for a teacher to plan a session which does accommodate to varying extents each of the above styles. Try the following exercise:

A3q Using different styles

Focusing on your own teaching subject, reflect on how you might plan one of your sessions to include learning activities which appeal to each of Honey and Mumford's styles.

A simple approach would be for the tutor to present a problem (theorist), follow this with a practical (activist), then ask the students to identify another situation where the process which they are discussing would be relevant (reflector) and finally plan how the process might best be implemented in that situation (pragmatist). Of course, this teaching process can very easily be carried out in a different order. Now attempt to apply the above approach to your own teaching situation by carrying out the following activity:

A3r Accommodating learning styles within your own teaching

Take the above simple explanation of Honey and Munford's approach and apply it to one of your lessons. Use the strategy suggested above in any order which is appropriate and then give details of how each activity in turn addresses a particular learning style.

One example of the above during an English Literature class would be to first show a video extract from *King Lear*, followed by a series of questions related to the scenes shown and then a group discussion on various aspects of the scenes and their relation to the main plot. So far, the tutor has addressed the styles of reflectors and theorists (thinking and analysing). The next part of the session may involve planning a role-play exercise related to the play that will involve all the class and then carrying it out. The pragmatists will relate well to the planning and organization of this activity and the actual role-play is very appropriate for activists. However, although these sessions will probably be well received by the learners, it is timely to add a word of caution at this point. If a tutor allows the reflector to continue reflecting and the pragmatist to continue to plan, etc., the students may still not learn a great deal despite the appropriateness of the activities. We will introduce the teaching and learning cycle here as a way of explaining this apparent contradiction. You will notice its similarities to our book plan at the end of Chapter 1.

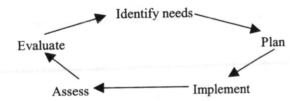

Teaching and learning cycle

This is a simple but useful model in which, first of all, the teacher identifies the needs of the learners. This is basically what this chapter has been about and, as you know, we have already looked at the use of diagnostic assessment and the use of the resultant individual action plans. We have also considered ways of identifying our students' learning styles using such techniques as learning style questionnaires. Hopefully then, we are now in a position to plan a structured lesson based on these identified needs.

Following the above model, we next deliver the planned session, check student learning using appropriate assessment techniques, evaluate how the process went and then, armed with this knowledge, start the process off again. This time, our experience of delivering the planned session and our evaluation of the result, will usually have changed our perception of the *actual* needs of the learners.

As teachers and trainers, we too have particular preferred learning styles and we may well be very effective in some aspects of the above teaching and learning process, but not as good in other areas. This may be illustrated by adding Honey and Mumford's categories to our teaching and learning model:

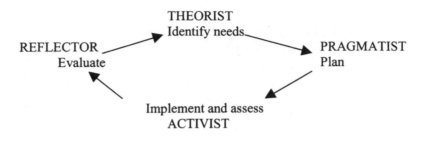

Teaching and learning model with learning styles added

Obviously, in order to optimize your development as a teacher or trainer, it will be necessary for you to improve in those areas which might not necessarily come naturally to you. If you are good at planning but not as effective in delivering, then you will know you must improve in that active area. Alternatively you may be totally comfortable with the actual teaching process, but are reluctant to reflect on the process. Kolb (1984), Honey and Mumford (1982), Gibbs (1988) etc., would all say that in order to maximize development you must be willing to push yourself round the cycle. *This is also true of your learners.*

Teaching and learning involves moving the learner from their 'comfortable/ familiar' point on the cycle round and through the complete cycle. Only then can the learners reflect on their own experiences and actions. In this way, we develop Schon's (1987) 'knowing-in-action' as discussed in the previous chapter.

Therefore, although as an essentially practical person, the *activist* may be more inclined to move immediately onto the next task, he or she needs to *reflect* about the implications of what has taken place before the subtle signs and meanings are forgotten. Similarly, even though he or she may be unwilling, the *reflector* needs to be persuaded to *develop a theory*, which will enable the fruits of his or her con-templation to be applied.

This is one of the more difficult aspects of teaching and this is where the skills of planning a session become most significant. The tutor needs to consider activities and exercises that will move each learner throughout the cycle so that each one can become aware of and further develop the important skills which lie in areas their natural inclinations may have led them to neglect. So the *theorist* should be encouraged to *apply* their ideas to practice and the *pragmatist* should move on from merely planning to becoming *actively involved* in the task. Consider ways of moving your own learners on by trying the following activity:

A3s *Moving round the cycle*

Take the above simple explanation of Honey and Munford's approach and apply it to one of your lessons. Use the strategy suggested above (in any order that is appropriate) and then give details of how each activity would, in turn, address a particular learning style.

As we said earlier in this chapter, a well-used starting point for FE and HE teaching is to begin with the exposition of a theory (the deductive approach). You then need to consider how you could introduce some activities based on the theory in order to develop an understanding of the key concepts. You could encourage your students to become engaged in a planning process such as applying the theory in a particular situation (e.g. surveying students using theodolites to measure a road junction). You might choose to start with a practical exercise (the inductive approach) such as applying the concepts to be learned within a given context (e.g. students learning a foreign language asking for directions to a particular destination). You may then decide to follow this up by involving the learners in some sort of experimentation (e.g. using a key concept in another way as when catering students move from making bread to baking pastry). Problem solving could be used as a means of reintroducing the theory (e.g. asking accountancy students to analyse an annual financial report in order to identify the main features of the particular company's performance). The final stage may involve some sort of evaluation where you could ask the students to report on their perception of the learning process and say how it could be changed or improved.

3.9 STUDENT LEARNING STRATEGIES

Gordon Pask (1976) built on these notions of learners adopting a preferred approach to understanding. He identified *two* strategies that students adopt when learning. The first of these he called the Holist Strategy and he identified particular attributes as common to those students/trainees who predominantly used that approach to learning. Such learners preferred a *broad, global approach to learning* and were by nature idiosyncratic and intuitive. In addition, they were impatient of rules, structures and details. During their learning, they liked to jump in anywhere and to work from a big picture back to detail. This type of learner may well demonstrate the following familiar characteristics:

Flexible and creative	Good visual memory
Good at improvisation	Inspired
Good at problem solving	Risk taker
Lateral thinker	Good in discussions
Ability to have a good overview	Ability to make unusual connections

Pask's second type of learning approach is the Serialist Strategy and he noted that this type of learner likes a *step by step approach with a narrow focus.* In contrast to a holistic slant, this type of trainee/student enjoys rules and structures. They build their learning around steps or stages and can deal with these either in order or separately in isolation and will work towards the bigger picture through a series of small steps. Pask also noted that they were logical rather than intuitive and factual rather than using their own experience. Characteristics which this group demonstrate include:

A good sequential memory	Good reading and writing skills
Clear concept of boundaries	Good logical thinking
Achievement of steady measurable progress	Ordered and organized

Now try the following activity:

A3t Holistic or serialist traits

Write about some examples of your students demonstrating the two learning strategies identified by Gordon Pask.

Perhaps you have someone who likes to have an overview of a topic in relation to previous learning. Maybe there are students who can only deal with small amounts of learning at a time, while others want to know it all at once.

Although this identification of preferred strategies will give you some insight into Pask's theories, take care not to place your learners into overly rigid categories. Remember that students do respond to the situation they are in and their learning can be affected by many different factors. Learning theories are there to give you an insight into student needs and should not be treated simply as a set of rules. Use the following exercise to summarize your reaction to the styles considered so far:

A3u Responding to learning style theory

Reflect on the learning styles covered so far and decide how, why and if these theories are important to teaching and learning. If they are, what are the implications for practice? If you accept the notion of learners being individual and often idiosyncratic, how should a teacher respond in the reality of the practice setting?

One practical thing you can do when you commence a programme is to provide the learners with an overview. This will make clear to the learner what will be taking place over the coming weeks.

For example:

> This programme will consist of a series of taught sessions that consist of a one-hour input by subject specialists. Following this hour, students could be put into groups to discuss the issue under study. Following the group sessions, students will be expected to present their findings to their peers and to accept questions. Topics covered will include the following...

Given this information, a holistic learner would probably search out information on the unfamiliar subjects, while a seralist would be comfortable in the knowledge that programme members are expected to research topics at regular intervals. In addition, the tutor can provide a more detailed week-by-week breakdown of activities and topics that will be covered over the course. This allows a more seralistic learner to plan and order their readings, research, etc. in a structured way. Using a framework such as this allows the student to either break down the pro-gramme into manageable slices, or to research the entire course at once. Their learning style will influence what they do, but it is their choice; you provide the framework that they as individuals can use according to their needs.

3.9.1   Mediation channels in learning

 Gregoric (1984) developed a further model of learning which has some similarities to Pask's, but is founded on the concept that there are *two* channels through which the mind receives and interprets information. He calls these 'mediation channels' and considers that they are primarily involved with the *perception* and *ordering* of information.

Considering first the process of perception, Gregoric claims that some people like to deal with thoughts, concepts and feelings in a reflective and theoretical manner and defines this as *abstract thought*. He claims that other people prefer to deal with a 'real' world that they can sense and experience. This type has a *concrete* or more solid sense of perception.

Within the 'ordering' mediation channel, Gregoric has noted other differences between individuals. He believes that some individuals like to think sequentially and in a linear manner, whilst others prefer to think in a random and non-logical fashion. He identifies the following characteristics:

Concrete sequential:	very practical and ordered, preferring to work with facts and reality
Concrete random:	more experimental than ordered, but still fairly practical
Abstract sequential:	logical and rational preferring concepts and patterns
Abstract random:	more concerned with feeling and emotions, good at 'insight' into problems

In order to build on this model, try the following exercise:

A3v   Addressing feelings and rationality

Assume that you are teaching your own subject to a group of learners and you wish them all to undertake a task which will give them an insight into a particular process. Then consider how best you could present the task to a student/trainee who, being primarily concerned with feelings, falls into Gregoric's *abstract random* category. Next, think how you might come at the same task from a different angle in order to encourage another learner, who is very practical and who prefers to operate with facts in an orderly manner (*concrete sequential*), to tackle the exercise.

As a simple, hypothetical approach to the above fairly complex analysis we will take as an example the familiar process of changing a wheel on a car. Although essentially practical, this task does require some understanding of simple theory, for example in relation to gaining effective leverage, safely securing and supporting the vehicle while the wheel is taken off, or ensuring the even distribution of pressure when tightening up the wheel nuts.

As the process of changing a wheel is essentially sequential and practical, learners who prefer an *abstract random* approach will probably present a particular challenge to a tutor attempting, in their own interests, to persuade them to conform to a particular safety regime. However, in setting the context of the task, the teacher can deliberately introduce a number of elements which can be tackled in an imaginative or creative way, before the learner gets down to the prescribed procedure (in this case changing the wheel) which must be done carefully in a particular order.

For example, the time of day, weather or situation (e.g. motorway hard shoulder) may add unexpected problems which must be addressed to ensure the safety of the passengers and the person changing the wheel.

The *concrete sequential* learners will be comfortable with following the structure of an established routine and with the practical processes involved. However, it may be good to challenge them by suggesting an unusual context.

Coping with an unusual situation will be a welcome challenge to the *concrete random* student but their inclination to experiment would be challenged by the need to follow a precise order.

Finally, the *abstract sequential* learner would enjoy exploring how the various concepts involved in the process (i.e. leverage, pressure, distribution) build into rules and procedures to be followed. They may be surprised to be confronted with practical difficulties such as a tight wheel nut or the need to chock the wheels.

3.9.2 Student autonomy

Of course, the ultimate need of any learner is that, in relation to the subject they are studying, they will eventually be able to function effectively and independently, without the support of their teachers.

Although, when contrasted with the beginning of this chapter where we discussed how learners might be encouraged to trust their tutors, this intended outcome may now seem a little perverse, it is in fact consistent with the notion of teachers always having the best interests of their charges at heart. When faced with the fact that the students/trainees will inevitably move on, it would be grossly irresponsible of a tutor, either deliberately or accidentally, to encourage learner dependence.

> ### A3w   Emancipation or dependence?
>
> List some of the ways in which teachers may, either deliberately or unconsciously, encourage learner dependence.

As you will know, at the present time teachers have to operate within a climate of strict accountability and are only too aware that they (and their department or institution) will be judged by their students' performance. Under these circumstances, it is only natural for teachers to monitor student progress systematically and to apply remedial teaching as soon as there is a hint of failure. Although it may be argued that this is the responsible thing to do, too much supervision does often encourage learner dependence and the adoption by students of surface-learning strategies in order to meet the assessment requirements. We will discuss these relationships in more detail in the following chapters, but it is worth noting here that cognitive learning is often enhanced when students are allowed to make and then correct their own mistakes. For now we will raise the issue by introducing the continuum below as an indication of the various ways in which a teacher's good intentions may well be counter-productive:

Encouraging learner dependence	*Encouraging learner independence*
Encourage instrumental learning which addresses only the defined assessment requirements	Get students into the habit of consolidating learning, correcting mistakes and developing new skills and a deeper interest in the subject
Set tasks which are too easy or too difficult	Set tasks which build appropriately on previous experience
Explain task in great detail in order to eliminate student questions	Don't always break things down in order to make learning easy; students encouraged to do this themselves
Repeat things many times	Don't always give the complete, definitive answer to students, merely hint at a way to arrive at a solution and let them know that they have to work it out
Carry out difficult part of the exercise for the students	Get students to discuss how they intend to go about learning something
Belittle student attempts and compare them unfavourably with others	Make students aware that they have a contribution to make and take notice of their views
Supervise students to ensure they don't make mistakes	Students allowed to work things out for themselves
Merely mark assessed work right or wrong	Get students to check their own work and to assess the standard attained
Give unrealistic feedback that contains undue praise or criticism	Give accurate feedback, which doesn't merely confirm what they have achieved but identifies how learners may progress

3.10 CONCLUSION

Our consideration of the different models of learning theories has demonstrated that it is the tutors' responsibility to determine the learning styles and character-istics of their learners and to accommodate them all within their sessions. Key Area

A1 and A2 of FENTO (around which this chapter is based) require a tutor to have some knowledge of the different ways that people learn so that diagnostic assessment can be developed and planned to identify the range of different styles present in the learning group. However, a word of caution: in reality we often adapt our approach to learning to the context in which we are operating and in this way are, in fact, amalgamating several styles. It would be crude and inaccurate to label students and to box them into a category. Tutors need to know and recognize traits in their students that they can build on and then help these learners to develop a range of abilities that will be required for successful lifelong learning.

So armed with this knowledge we can now progress to Key Area B, that of Planning and Preparing teaching programmes for groups and individuals. However, because our deliberations in this chapter clearly touch on assessment as well as structured learning, it might be useful at this point to consider how interrelated the whole teaching and learning process is and how significant the choices which teachers make about approaches, methods and styles are in relation to ultimate success.

A3x   Which comes first?

Consider once again your own particular subject and a particular group of learners. The success of your teaching could be said to depend upon *a) your intended aims and objectives, b) the selected content, c) your chosen delivery, d) the assessment methods* and *e) how effectively you evaluate your success.*

Select a starting point from the above five aspects of practice and give a reason for your choice.

The teaching and learning process is cyclical and each time you complete a cycle and prepare for the next, you should consider the evaluative data and then identify possible areas for improvement. It seems obvious then that, if evaluation comes last, the above *order* must be correct. However, we stressed earlier that teaching and learning should be treated as an essentially holistic process, so we should consider the effect which each of the parts have on each other and on the whole (i.e. the total student experience). For example, although the learning outcomes identified and tested during the *assessment* stage should reflect the aims and objectives of the curriculum, sometimes assessment is defined first and may heavily influence the whole process. In other cases, some of the implicit intentions of the teaching are difficult to observe and measure. It is because of these and other significant variables that we need to hold onto a view of the whole, rather than concentrating exclusively on the disaggregated parts.

3.11 | USEFUL SOURCES

Thomas, E. (2001) *Widening Participation in Post-Compulsory Education.* London: Continuum
Thomas examines in detail a range of barriers to education including class, race

and disability and suggests realistic strategies for increasing participation. This informative debate is supported by well-considered studies.

Honey, P. and Mumford, A. (1982) *The Manual of Learning Styles*. Maidenhead: Peter Honey

This is a very popular reader for educational teacher training teams. Honey and Mumford are pioneers of the concept of learning styles and this book provides a detailed account of the main learning styles that are attributed to Honey and Mumford. These are activists, pragmatists, reflectors and theorists. Each type is described in detail and a questionnaire provided which allows the reader to determine his or her own style. Aimed at teacher trainers it allows teachers to determine their own student profile and the book indicates how this information can inform and develop teaching strategies in order to maximize learning

Pask, G. (1976) 'Styles and strategies of learning', *British Journal of Educational Psychology*, 128–48.

This article provides a different concept of learning styles and these relate to the idea that individuals think either in terms of a whole, or in small pieces and in a seralist fashion. Pask gives an academic account that is based in psychological theory and describes the underlying reasons for these types of thinking patterns. He provides an educational rationale for the development of these styles of thought and this has been an influential book on educational practice.

http://www.edwdebono.com (Edward de Bono's site)
http://www.brains.org (good site for learning styles)
http://www.csrnet.org/csrnet/articles/student-learning-styles.html (applying what we know: student learning styles)
http://www.tipcet.com (our site with additional material related to learner needs)

3.12 RATIONALE FOR KEY AREA A ASSESSING LEARNERS' NEEDS

FAQs	At Stage 1	At Stage 2	At Stage 3
Why do it?	The essential starting point for effective teaching is to know your students. To help anyone to learn you need to find out about their current knowledge, ability and aptitudes.	To make your assessment of the needs of learners more accurate you need to develop appropriate techniques. You should aim to accommodate individual learning styles, needs and preferences and be aware of the ways in which the physical and social environment will influence learning.	In order to effectively reflect on your ability to assess the needs of learners you need to be sure that you have really understood the individual characteristics of your learners and the manner in which they are influenced by the total learning context.
Where are we going?	You are attempting to optimize the provision for your particular learners. This will involve recognizing and valuing and helping them to recognize and value their previous learning.	You are moving towards an understanding of each group of learners and how their individual characteristics influence the interactions and responses of the whole group.	You are evaluating your own performance in order to become more precise in the way you identify the very subtle variations in each situation which affect the quality of student experience.
How do we get there?	Begin to move beyond intuitive decisions (as valuable as they may be on occasions) towards deliberately collecting and analysing appropriate data about your learners without infringing data collection guidelines. Use any information provided by the institution about their previous performance, their expectations or their preferred learning styles.	Collate information on previous educational background. Test for literacy/numeracy and other key skills. Test for subject-specific skills/ knowledge. Use induction exercises, 'ice-breakers', progress reviews, student attitude surveys, counselling sessions, tutorials, etc. in order to gain more useful and varied knowledge. Support the learners as they settle in and respond to their new environment.	All of your judgements and actions related to optimizing student learning should be evaluated in terms of their appropriateness, flexibility, timing, accuracy, breadth, depth etc., in order to continually improve your provision.

Is this the best way?	You need to remain aware of all indicators of your learners' needs, rather than accepting all provided data at face value. Talk to the students, consider their progress and their evaluations of the work they have been doing.	College or departmental procedures may well be adequate, but you may need to improve your own access to general information, or to set up your own diagnostic or monitoring systems. Confirm that you have a flexible system for recording students' prior learning and achievement and for diagnosing student needs. You will need to monitor student progress effectively and identify potential problems.	Confirm that all of the information is available and accessible. Check if there are problems balancing accessibility and confidentiality. Find out if students are given opportunities to talk about their needs. Consider whether your record system is too paper bound and if IT could help with record keeping. Ensure that you take the initiative in identifying student need. Evaluate how sensitive your systems of identifying and recording needs are.
When is the right time?	Check if you have appropriate information before you meet the students. Confirm what (if anything) has been done during induction.	Check if reviews are used at fixed points during a programme. Confirm how progress is monitored and how you should deal effectively with diagnosed problems. Make sure you know at which point a student is considered to have failed and the ways in which they can recover from this and try again.	Consider the stage at which you achieved all of the valuable information which helped you to diagnose student needs. Inevitably some would have been more valuable if it had been received earlier – how do you rectify that next time round? Confirm that the order of gathering data was the most appropriate. For example, would it be more motivating to the learners if possible APL/APEL had been identified earlier?
Who needs to know?	Initially, you and the students.	Confirm how information about students is shared and whether this information is passed on adequately to the students themselves, and to teaching and support colleagues, educational managers, parents, employers, etc.	Each of those teaching and supporting the students will require different sorts of information to help them to become more effective. You are the key to this process of developing more accurate information.

How do we know when we've got there?	When you feel that you know enough about your students to make reasonably well-informed decisions about what is appropriate teaching, learning and assessment.	Check student satisfaction, student retention, pass rates, grades, progression, survey results, employment statistics.	Evaluate how effective the dissemination of information about student needs is. For example, does vital information reach support staff early enough?
Has everyone had a fair chance?	Consider the information you have gathered on which you have based your decisions. Does the data adequately represent their experience, needs, ambitions and constraints?	Confirm that you are asking the right questions, that your procedures are adequate to identify differences in need arising from age, sex, class, ethnicity or disability.	Reflect on the 'value added' achieved and think not only of the outcomes gained but the distance travelled. Consider equally the less obvious learning achievements such as social abilities, improved confidence, trust, openness, etc.

3.13 KEY AREA A SPECIFICATIONS – ASSESSING LEARNERS' NEEDS

Purpose: Teachers and teaching teams need to be effective in identifying the needs of potential learners and in making an initial assessment of learners. This involves matching learners' experiences and attainments to the requirements of programmes within one's own area of expertise. For an analysis of this process at FENTO Stages 1, 2 and 3 see the rationale above.

Please note: The FENTO Standards listed below are relevant to the following three levels of award: Stage 1 (Introduction), Stage 2 (Intermediate) and Stage 3 (Full Certification). All of the standards are required at Stage 3, only those in italic or bold are required at Stage 2 and only those in italic are required at Stage 1.

Unit A1. Identify and plan for the needs of potential learners *In order to do this teachers should*

Demonstrate that they are able to:	*and have specific knowledge and critical understanding of:*	*plus generic knowledge of:*	*Summary of appropriate evidence in this Key Area:*		*Relevant Chapter Activities*
a	*Criteria:* *acknowledge the previous learning experiences and achievements of the learners*	• Organizational record keeping and information processing systems	• The broad range of learning needs, including the needs of those with learning difficulties and/or disabilities	a	Group and individual profiles and records of attainment	A3b, A3i
		• An understanding of resource constraints and how to present relevant and coherent arguments for strengthening resources	• Sources of information about learners' previous experiences and attainments		APL/APEL accreditation	A3k, A3l
b	enable learners to review their past experiences in a way which reveals their strengths and needs		• The requirements of individual learning programmes	b	Diagnostic testing and individual 'interviews' with students	A3c, A3d, A3e
c	recognize when additional specialist assessment is required and take appropriate action		• Ways of evaluating different information about learners against the requirements of specific learning programmes, including the	c	Various specialist assessment	A3m, A3n, A3o, A3p, A3q, A3r, A3s, A3t, A3u
d	support learners while they deal with unfamiliar circumstances	How to match resources to the needs of individual	accreditation of prior learning and experience	d	Individual student action plans	A3j, A3m

65

e	assist learners to explore and articulate their personal aspirations	The accreditation of prior experience and learning, why it is important and what are the processes and procedures for carrying it out	• Appropriate forms of initial assessment and how to conduct them • Individual differences in aptitude and ability • Training needs analysis, methods and techniques	e	As above (integrated within established organizational procedures)	A3f, A3g, A3h, A3i, A3j, A3u, A3v
f	identify and confirm any exemptions to which learners are entitled	Record of liaison with line managers.		f	Identification of particular exemptions	A3k, A3l
g	provide information to, and negotiate with, colleagues to ensure that the learning needs of individuals can be met in a realistic way			g	Specific teaching strategies	A3c, A3j; A3m

Plus commentary in PDJ on the purposes and value of the above together with records in PF of teaching observations, lesson plans, rationales, self-evaluations and progress summary.

Key to above standards required at each FENTO Stage:

Introduction Stage – italic
Intermediate Stage + bold
Certification Stage – all

Unit A2. Make an initial assessment of learners' needs *In order to do this teachers should*

	Demonstrate that they are able to:	and have specific knowledge and critical understanding of:	plus generic knowledge of:		Summary of appropriate evidence in this Key Area:	Relevant Chapter Activities
a	**Criteria:** *consider and apply a range of assessment techniques*	• Learning programmes and their requirements • Appropriate assessment procedures for evaluating learners' potential to achieve the required learning outcomes • Appropriate selection criteria • The intellectual and related demands of the learning programme	• The broad range of learning needs, including the needs of those with learning difficulties and/or disabilities • Sources of information about learners' previous experiences and attainments • The requirements of individual learning programmes • Ways of evaluating different information about learners against the requirements of specific learning programmes, including the accreditation of prior learning and experience • Appropriate forms of initial assessment and how to conduct them • Individual differences in aptitude and ability • Training needs analysis, methods and techniques	a	Group profiles and records of individual attainment	A3b, A3c, A3d, A3e, A3i, A3j, A3k, A3l, A3m, A3n, A3o, A3q
b	use a variety of methods for assessing the previous learning experiences and achievements of learners including their basic skills and key skills			b	Diagnostic testing and individual 'interviews' with students individual student action plans as above (integrated within established organisational procedures) identification of particular exemptions record of liaison with line managers	As above
c	consider a range of selection criteria appropriate to learning programmes			c	Admissions decisions and specific provision	A3c, A3j; A3m
d	identify the implications of a disability or learning difficulty for an individual's learning	• Sources of additional specialist assessment and how to assess them		d	Specialist assessment and specific provision	As above

	Activity	Knowledge	Document	See
e	establish with learners the requirements and limitations of the programme	• The organization's recording and documentation procedures	programme specifications and learning outcomes	Chapter 4
f	assess the experience, capabilities and learning styles of individual learners in relation to the identified learning programme	• Ways of eliciting and evaluating learners' previous experiences • Techniques and procedures for basic skills screening	Diagnostic Tests	A3c, A3j, A3m
g	prepare for and carry out the initial assessment	• Procedures for conducting relevant assessments and interpreting the results	Diagnostic Tests	As above
h	*provide feedback to the learner on the outcome of the assessment and its consequences*	• Ways of presenting and explaining the initial assessment • Ways of weighting, verifying and corroborating previous experience and attainment	Diagnostic Tests and Action Plans	A3c, A3j, A3m
i	direct the individual learner to the most appropriate programme	• How to assess levels of commitment and personal characteristics relevant to a programme of study	Action Plans	As above
j	liaise with colleagues and other interested parties throughout the initial assessment process, as necessary	• The differences of individuals, methods of learning	Diagnostic Tests and Action Plans	As above

Plus commentary in PDJ on the purposes and value of the above together with records in PF of Teaching Observations, Lesson Plans, Rationales, Self-Evaluations and Progress Summary

Key to above standards required at each FENTO Stage:

Introduction Stage – *italic*
Intermediate Stage + **bold**
Certification Stage – all

CHAPTER 4

Planning and preparing teaching and learning programmes for groups and individuals

Margaret Postance

<table>
<tr><td colspan="3">Key Area 'B' The organization of schemes of work and individual sessions</td></tr>
<tr><td colspan="3">Key concepts in this chapter</td></tr>
<tr><td colspan="3">Additionality, Affective, Awarding Bodies, Behavioural, Cognitive, Curriculum, Diversity, Holistic View, Key Dates, Layout, Non-behavioural, Objectives, Objectives Model, Planning, Preparation, Prerequisites. Prioritizing, Process Model, Programme, Programme Aims, Psycho-Motor, Scheme of Work, Syllabus, Topic Order, Topics</td></tr>
<tr><td colspan="3">Before you begin this chapter you may wish to check the FAQs on pp. 98–100</td></tr>
<tr><td colspan="3">Index to Chapter 4 (Key Area B)</td></tr>
<tr><td>Section</td><td>Subject</td><td>Page</td></tr>
<tr><td>4.1</td><td>Introduction</td><td>70</td></tr>
<tr><td>4.2</td><td>Approaches to planning</td><td>71</td></tr>
<tr><td>4.3</td><td>Defining the curriculum</td><td>71</td></tr>
<tr><td>4.4</td><td>Particular needs</td><td>72</td></tr>
<tr><td>4.5</td><td>Schemes of work</td><td>74</td></tr>
<tr><td>4.6</td><td>Writing aims, objectives and learning outcomes</td><td>81</td></tr>
<tr><td>4.7</td><td>Session plans</td><td>90</td></tr>
<tr><td>4.8</td><td>Conclusion</td><td>96</td></tr>
<tr><td>4.9</td><td>Useful sources</td><td>97</td></tr>
<tr><td>4.10</td><td>Rationale for Key Area B planning and preparing teaching and learning programmes for groups and individuals</td><td>98</td></tr>
<tr><td>4.11</td><td>Key Area B specification – planning and preparing teaching and learning programmes for groups and individuals</td><td>101</td></tr>
</table>

Chapter 4 Activities designed to generate evidence against the Standards

Ref	Activity	Page	Ref	Activity	Page
B4a	Syllabus or curriculum?	72	B4l	Scheme of work layout	79
B4b	Moving towards a curriculum	72	B4m	Aims and objectives	82
			B4n	Defining programme aims	82
B4c	Identifying needs	73	B4o	Identifying session aims	83
B4d	Awarding body requirements	73	B4p	Differentiating between objectives	84
B4e	Learners' needs	74	B4q	Objective characteristics	86
B4f	Institutional needs	74	B4r	Writing objectives	87
B4g	Topic identification	75	B4s	Ensuring achievement	87
B4h	Sequencing	76	B4t	Defining levels	91
B4i	Confirming the order	77	B4u	Moving beyond knowledge	92
B4j	Prioritizing	77			
B4k	Flexible content	77	B4v	Developing more rounded learners	94

4.1 | INTRODUCTION

In Chapter 1 we discussed the drive to improve standards within all sectors of education. The focus for this accountability process is, as you would expect, the quality of the learners' experience, be it during classroom teaching, fieldwork, laboratory experiments, workshop sessions, gymnasium exercises, etc. *However, always underpinning these various delivery processes will be the effectiveness of the planning and preparation carried out by the teacher or trainer.*

We have also stressed the individual nature of each teaching and learning situation and the importance of taking a holistic view of these complex relationships. We will further develop these themes during this chapter by stressing the need for the practitioner not only to understand the particular characteristics of these contexts, but also to respond effectively to them during the planning process.

In addition to the familiar subject specialisms, teachers must be aware of their responsibility for the incorporation into any scheme of work of a range of generic requirements such as:

- key skill implementation
- basic skills initiatives
- ICT and ILT strategies
- work-based learning
- inclusive learning
- widening participation
- lifelong learning

4.2 | APPROACHES TO PLANNING

Although the above more general requirements have been introduced at this early stage because it is important to bear them in mind during the planning, the predominant influencing factor will always be the syllabus or programme. This may be provided by the awarding body in the form of study units, competence statements or learning outcomes. Naturally, practitioners will respond in varying ways to these central prerequisites as they will be aware of the needs of their particular groups of learners (see Chapter 3), their own skills and, inevitably, the demands of the host institution.

It has often been said that 'if you fail to plan, then you plan to fail'. Never has this old adage been more true than it currently is within all sectors of education. Systematic planning is crucial if the delivered curriculum is to meet both the needs of the learners, the other issues previously mentioned and the various accountability processes.

However, students within post-compulsory education share a significant, distinguishing characteristic. In no other sector is the range of learners so diverse. It is possible for a learning group to contain members from the age of 16 to 90. Recent developments (see Chapter 11) have now lowered this entry age, so some provision will be directed towards learners as young as 14. Also, because very often in post-compulsory education a programme will have broad entry requirements, there may be graduates alongside those who have no prior academic achievements. In addition, a group may contain people who are extremely motivated, as well as those who feel they have to some extent been coerced to attend.

Another familiar characteristic encountered among students in FE are those learners who, for any number of reasons, are taking a 'second chance' to return to study and whose first experience of education was sufficiently unsupportive to leave them anxious about the whole process. It is also very possible that there will be individuals who, because of their learning difficulties, have previously been working in discrete groups separate from the mainstream.

At this point, you may well be asking whether it possible for a teacher to plan effectively to meet the extremely varied needs of such groups of learners while, at the same time, grappling with the ever increasing curricular demands and quality targets. Castling (1996) points the way forward:

> Planning is the bridge between your identification of learners' needs and the learning activities they undertake. It is a vital stage in the teaching/training cycle and deserves your full attention whether you are planning whole programmes, courses or single sessions. Planning is the process of making decisions about the directions that learners will take and the activities they will engage in to help them meet their long and short-term goals. It may involve negotiation with learners and other staff, and will need to be followed up by thorough planning.

4.3 | DEFINING THE CURRICULUM

One of the first tasks which a practitioner must carry out is the thorough review of the curriculum that is being offered. Initially, the tutor will commence this task by completing a comprehensive interpretation of either the syllabus or the criteria indicated by the awarding body. Daines and Graham (1997) suggest that:

> You may be working to an external syllabus and feel that you are compelled to teach all the content it specifies. If you find out what your students already know, and what they feel they need, you should be able to select what material is essential, what is peripheral, and what they already know sufficiently well for you to be able to move on. Syllabuses rarely indicate the structure and emphases to be placed on particular topics, nor do they usually specify the approach that should be taken. You are quite at liberty to decide, in consultation with your group, how the topic is to be tackled. There is probably much greater freedom to select and prioritise the content defined by a syllabus than would first appear. Syllabuses are as much guides as directives.

B4a   Syllabus or curriculum?

We may seem at times to be using the terms syllabus and curriculum as though they are interchangeable. Discuss briefly how, in your experience, the two differ.

The *syllabus* is really a list or an indicative content that is usually provided by the awarding body. This may come in alternative or additional forms such as competence statements, programmes of study, directives, learning outcomes, bibliographies, etc. It is essentially static and is brought alive by the teacher's interpretation, whereupon it begins to become a *curriculum*. The curriculum is dynamic, and incorporates the whole of the learners' experience, both formal and informal. As a starting point for your planning, try activity B4b below:

B4b   Moving towards a curriculum

Obtain a copy of your own awarding body's specifications that will be in the form of a syllabus, competence statements, directives, etc. Familiarize yourself with the content before you carry out the activities which follow.

Having studied the awarding body's guidelines, how comfortable do you feel about interpreting the content and translating it into learning experiences for your students? Is there a clear, coherent, developmental sequence identifiable in the way it is presented? Are there ambiguities, which may be difficult to resolve? Most of all, is the syllabus deliverable within the time-frame specified by your institution?

4.4   PARTICULAR NEEDS

One of the shared goals held by the majority of learners is the need to learn and achieve. As we highlighted in the previous chapter, learners attending further education establishments also possess their own learning agendas, as well as their own preferred learning styles. Clearly, if the learning is to be considered 'effective', the planning process carried out by the tutor has to take into account, not only all of the above, but also the personal perceptions of the tutor in respect of their role, and their own personal style of delivery. Armitage *et al.* (1999) support this complex task by stating:

> No teaching takes place in a vacuum. Even though we may see teaching as a partly planned and partly spontaneous act, our approach to it, our interpretation of our role, our attitude to our students and our view of what we should be teaching are shaped by a variety of factors. These include our personal belief system, our own experience of being taught, our personality and our theoretical understanding of the teaching and learning process.

B4c   Identifying needs

Bearing in mind your awarding body's specifications, make a list of the range of needs which must be taken into account when planning a programme of study. The list should include institutional as well as the personal needs of the learners and the teachers. Give a brief justification for the needs that you feel should be considered and an indication of the ways in which you might address them.

First of all, we must take into account the expected standards articulated by the awarding body in their document. These include subject coverage and the expected achievement by the learners. These are often, but not always, expressed as learning outcomes, which we will discuss in more detail below. As a lead in to this, first try activity B4d below:

B4d   Awarding body requirements

Summarize the range of awarding body requirements that you are aware of and indicate how you would expect to meet these.

The learners' needs will usually include new skills and knowledge, but they will also seek reassurance in relation to other areas because most learners within post-compulsory education have far more than academic needs. For many who attend our establishments, life experiences colour their perception of what they find when commencing their chosen learning programme. Tutors need to consider these characteristics and how they may respond to them. Above all, learners need to feel valued if they are to fully achieve their goals. The tutor should ensure that the learner can transfer existing skills and knowledge to either a new setting or a new learning programme. Learners need to know what is to be learned so that they can make an informed choice when planning their own personal approach. Many learners will wish to run before they can walk because, often for the first time in their lives, they have had assistance in systematically identifying gaps in their own learning and now urgently wish to fill them.

Other learners may lack motivation, possibly because previous learning experiences have not been successful. If the tutor is to help such learners to progress, the underpinning causes of their anxiety need to be elicited and addressed in both a confidential and empathetic manner.

B4e   Learners' needs

As we develop our scheme of work, the next few activities will focus on your learners. To establish consistency and for the process to be developmental, during these tasks you should use the same familiar learning group. Identify which of your student cohorts you will use and then summarise the particular needs of these learners. Think in terms of both their personal and practical requirements.

Finally, there will be a number of institutional needs, which should be taken into account. The obvious ones are timetabling, key dates and use of resources:

- Most teaching establishments are obliged to operate fairly complex systems to ensure that teaching sessions occur at the required time and in the designated venue. Nothing upsets new students more than being unable to find their class at the published time because it isn't being held in the room advertised. Often there are good reasons for this, but it still makes the student feel inadequate or frustrated and if the experience is repeated it will have a serious effect on retention.

- The planning of a programme must also take into account the important dates that have been previously decided by the institution or the awarding body. These dates may be rigidly set in order to accommodate examinations, internal/external verification, submission of results, award ceremonies, etc.

- Many courses require access to institutional resources that are in great demand and so there must be an effective allocation system. One obvious example is the library, but there are many others including ILT, directed study materials, sports facilities, laboratories, workshops, etc.

B4f   Institutional needs

Consider the above bullet points as you summarize the institutional needs, but also remember such requirements as enrolment, retention, inclusive learning, widening participation, etc.

4.5   SCHEMES OF WORK

Now, having developed an understanding of the needs within your own learning context, you can begin to move your 'plan' towards fruition in the form of a scheme of work. This is essentially a strategy for turning the static nature of a prescribed syllabus into an active, living curriculum composed of relevant and beneficial, formal and informal student experiences.

We should consider the following important 'component parts' when beginning our design of a scheme of work:

- the course/programme aims
- the learning outcomes/objectives

- the content (subject matter)
- the teaching and learning strategies (methods)
- ways of monitoring and reviewing learning
- methods of assessing achievement
- approaches to course/programme evaluation

It is worth remembering at this stage that schemes of work (which may well have been perceived by many in the past as merely a 'paper exercise'), while remaining a significant tool in the process of successful and effective planning, have also moved to a key position within the quality framework.

The scheme of work should identify the *topics* to be covered within the programme under study. Simply put, a topic is an aspect of the subject being taught which can be presented as a separate learning focus. In practical terms, you may decide to use a particular topic for each session, or a topic may span a number of sessions. Try the following activity:

B4g Topic identification

Identify the topics into which a syllabus you are familiar with may be usefully broken down for the benefit of a particular group of learners (preferably the learning group you identified earlier).

Of course, you would expect each teacher to disaggregate a study programme into topics in a different way to their colleagues. This is because you will be looking for learning entities, i.e. topics that can stand alone as a basis for teaching, which are appropriate to your particular learners. This is always, in a sense, an artificial process because understanding much of what is contained in a syllabus is dependent upon having a grasp of other parts of the learning process, or developing a holistic view. However, because learning is delivered in digestible 'chunks' the separation into topics is an unavoidable process. Some teachers will feel that the syllabus naturally falls into themes, each of which contains selected topics. Others will perceive it as a series of developing concepts or a linear progression. Topic identification will often reflect a preferred teaching style, but it is important to remember that the resulting curriculum should also respond to the students' preferred learning styles (see Chapter 3). Once identified, the topics will be presented in a particular order and it is important to consider the learners as you grapple with this structure. There may be times when you deliberately use a more 'inductive' teaching approach by introducing your learners to something new without prior warning in order to develop their skills and confidence in tackling the unknown. However, generally it is important that the learning process moves the student from the 'known to the unknown' so that learning is perceived by them to be logical and sequential. This systematic process of development will often help to nurture successfully the skills of retention, recall and application. Now try the following activity:

B4h   Sequencing

Using your previously developed list of topics, develop a notional *order* for your programme of study. Remember to also consider how the order you select will fit in with such institutional imperatives as key assessment deadlines, venue availability, vacations, etc.

Obviously, the manner in which you sequence a programme is extremely important. However, there are so many variables involved in each of these difficult curricular decisions that, during its implementation, some parts will, inevitably, be more successful than others. Even so, the next time you deliver the programme, other areas that have previously gone well may cause you problems. This can be extremely frustrating, but unfortunately the cumulative effect of such factors as student group dynamics, your own performance, institutional pressures, etc., cannot be predicted with absolute certainty.

The following suggestions may be helpful, but please avoid treating them as definitive rules. As you would expect, the most useful guidance will come from your learners themselves in the form of formal and informal evaluative feedback (see Chapter 10):

- *start with the easiest topics first* – this will help to reduce any threat which the learners may perceive and will give them the opportunity of being motivated by some achievement before progressing to more difficult and challenging topics

- *logical sequence* – in many subjects there will be a clear order for the topics through which learners need to progress and understand before moving on to more complex learning, i.e. 'known to the unknown'

- *timing* – clearly the length of time a particular topic will take to deliver may influence its position within your scheme. It is unwise to commence a topic if it cannot be completed before a vacation. Timing can also apply to those curricular areas where there might be seasonal considerations, e.g. catering, floristry and horticulture. Here, the availability of materials or the production of specific items may be related to or governed by the time of the year

- *commence with topics which you will enjoy teaching* – remember, moving from the known to the unknown applies to tutors as well as learners! Teachers are far more intrinsically motivated when delivering a learning session they know well and have had success with in previous programmes. Conveniently, this approach will also give you more time to consider the less-familiar topics and prepare an approach which most effectively meets the needs of the learning group

- *meet the assessment schedules* – many of the current awarding bodies have pre-set dates within their programmes by which time the learners need to complete various forms of assessments (see also Chapter 9). If this is the case, it is particularly important that the order of scheme topics is compatible with the specified assessment dates

B4i   Confirming the order

Revisit the session order you devised for activity B4h and see if your notional plan a) plays to your strengths, b) allows for awarding body requirements and c) still has a logical order if the above bullet points were implemented.

In addition to sequencing, the planning of learning must also take into account the *quantity* of topics to be covered. Realistically speaking, it is generally true that most syllabuses have more information contained within them than there is time to deliver effectively. Consequently, another difficult task for the tutor is the development of a system of prioritization, which will ensure that the most important content is delivered.

B4j   Prioritizing

Look again at the topic order you have developed. Have you already excluded some areas of the curriculum which you feel you haven't time to deliver? Have you a clear idea of what you would omit if any internal or external college influences brought further pressure to bear on the teaching time available? Try to indicate those areas which are, regrettably, the most expendable.

There will obviously be particular institutional requirements which impinge on teaching time and cannot be identified here. However, the following guidelines may help you to develop a policy for prioritizing curriculum topics and activities:

Include topics which the learners:

- *MUST know* – if these areas are omitted it will cause serious damage to the overall learning experience and may possibly lead to non-achievement of learning outcomes and even the target award
- *SHOULD know* – these are the areas which really need to be included in the programme in order for the learners to have as full an understanding of the content as possible
- *COULD know* – these are the topics which might offer 'additionality' to the programme. These areas are clearly related to the subject, but should they be omitted they would not be detrimental to the students' successful completion of the programme. This then is the 'flexible' section of the scheme which will include topics that may be cut should one or more of the above 'must' and 'should' areas take longer than originally planned

B4k   Flexible content

Looking back at your evolving curriculum, identify those topics which you may have omitted because you felt they were less essential, and also those you may have included but which you felt were marginal to the students' ultimate goal. Use these topics to structure potential additionality should, for some reason or other, the currently available time/resources be increased.

The scheme of work is the first, very important step to the effective management of teaching and learning. If you are a member of a team which is teaching the same or similar subjects, then obviously it would be very beneficial for this group of tutors to work collaboratively to ensure that the final content represents, as well as is possible, each of the member's preferences.

In a lot of post-compulsory establishments, the schemes of work are required to be passed to a line or quality manager, in order to ensure that the document meets the standards set by both the LSC and the employing institution. Writing a scheme of work can be tedious but, providing that you use a thorough, holistic approach that considers all of the aspects suggested above, it will pay dividends throughout the delivery of the programme. Clearly, it is important to remember that a scheme of work is a flexible document, which should not be perceived as being set in 'tablets of stone'. Throughout the delivery of the programme it is important that you should monitor the progress of the students to ensure that their learning experiences are beneficial and that the curriculum is progressing at a suitable pace and pitch (see Chapter 10 for further information about evaluation). As we discussed in Chapter 2, an effective teacher is a consciously reflective practitioner who develops the habit of continuously questioning themselves about the purpose of their actions. With regard to planning and preparation, David Minton (1991) suggests that we should ask ourselves the following useful questions:

WHO?
Who am I going to teach?
What age are they? What is their background?
Why are they in this class?
What do they want, or what do they need to learn?
Why do they need to learn it?
What do they know? Or what can they do already?
What are they expecting of me?

WHAT?
What are they going to learn?
What do they have to do in order to learn that?
What do they need in order to do that?
What are they going to learn with?
What do I have to do in order to provide that?
What do I have to do to help them learn?

WHERE?
Where are they going to learn? Or where am I going to teach?
What kind of help and support will they find there?
What kind of difficulties are they likely to find there?
What equipment can they and I use?
How do I get hold of it, set it up, find out how to use it?
What reorganization and preparation must I do?

WHEN?
How much time have I and they got for each class? And for the programme?
What time of day will it happen?
How often will they meet?
What might be the effects of time of day or frequency?

HOW?

Where are they starting from? Where should I start?

How are they going to learn?

How am I going to teach? What pace of learning?

How will we agree a learning goal?

How will I get them working and committed?

Can I assume that they will want to learn what I teach?

How do I engage them in the learning?

What kind of problems are they likely to have in learning?

What can I do to make it easier to do?

How can I anticipate these problems and make it easier?

How shall I know whether they are learning – and what?

How shall I get feedback, and how shall I use it?

How should I adapt what I do to what they need?

How flexible should my learning/teaching programme be?

Having used Minton's checklist to confirm that your intended scheme of work is complete, you now need to find an appropriate presentation format. You will probably be required, by your institution or by the awarding body, to incorporate considerable administrative information in addition to the topics to be covered. Some information that may be required could include:

- the venue
- the academic year
- the group to be 'taught'
- the proposed number of learners
- the person/s responsible for the scheme design
- application of Key Skill areas
- general aims of the programme
- assessment strategies for the programme
- resource-based learning/ICT (information communication technology)/ILT (information learning technology)

B4l Scheme of work layout

You should now be in a position to gather together the information you have developed and present it as a scheme of work. Most establishments will have an in-house pro forma, which they use for this. A completed first page of an imaginary scheme of work is included as an example overleaf. If you wish to use this layout, you will find a blank pro forma on the *tipcet.com* website.

SCHEME OF WORK EXAMPLE

Title of Learning Programme: Introduction to Humour	No of weeks in Scheme: Thirteen – (13)	Venue: Lecture Room 3
Academic Year 2003/2004	Start Date: W/c 15.9.03	Name(s) of Scheme Designer: Ivor Funnybone
Semester/Term One	Finish Date: W/c 20.12.03	Date Scheme Written: July 2003 (Scheme must be updated at least every two years)

Aims of the Programme	Specific Learning Outcomes of the Unit/Module	Individual Learning Needs will be met by
• to promote an understanding of the role and value of humour • to develop awareness of the historical origins of humour • to identify different forms of humour within present-day society • to evaluate the role of humour in communication • to identify explicit and implicit barriers to using humour • to understand cultural differences in comedic expression	On completion of this module, students will be able to • identify examples of humour within at least five contemporary forms of communication media • describe three traditional forms of humour still evident in society today • analyse the purposes of humour evident in four examples of popular media • describe the cultural differences between two major examples of popular comedy	• the provision of a full spectrum of delivery strategies • regular positive and constructive feedback at all levels of programme assessment • provision of self-study materials • support being offered on an individual basis via a supportive tutorial system

Week number	Date	General Objectives (or objective reference number where applicable)	Teaching and Learning Activities (in outline including resources to be used)	Assessment Strategies
1	15.9.03	• participate in an icebreaker exercise • complete the college induction procedure • view a 15-minute video extract from a popular comedy programme • work in groups to identify how script, direction, acting, set and music contribute to the overall humour within the video example	• welcome to the college/module – verbal/Q & A • introduce module and portfolio assessment • present video extract • working with groups to produce flip-chart summaries of sources of humour in video extract • provide photocopies of cartoons • discuss and ask class	• group flip-chart summaries • Q & A • discussion

		• discuss in groups photocopies of cartoons • collect other examples of cartoons before next session	to collect examples for next week	
2	22.9.03	• consider examples of cartoons collected by class • view exemplar cartoons (British, American, European) from last 100 years • discuss humour, politics and culture • group work on humour and political purposes • consider three topical verbal jokes • collect other jokes on identified themes for next week	• introduce examples of cartoons collected by class • show exemplar cartoons (British, American, European) from last 100 years • initiate discussion on humour in politics and cultural influences • work with groups on use of humour • provide three topical jokes and ask group to collect jokes for next week	• Q & A • discussion • developing portfolio on examples of humour
3	29.9.03	• consider descriptions and illustrations of clowns from the Greek theatre and contemporary circus • relate connected to the role of the medieval clown • consider humour, incongruity and narrative • working in groups to identify morality tales • collect gender-based humour examples for next week	• introduce examples of cartoons collected by class • show exemplar cartoons (British, American, European) from last 100 years • initiate discussion on humour in politics and cultural influences • work with groups on use of humour	• Q & A • discussion • developing portfolio on examples of humour

4.6 WRITING AIMS, OBJECTIVES AND LEARNING OUTCOMES

You will be aware that, in writing this chapter, we have assumed that either the awarding body or your establishment will be providing you with the syllabus and the defined outcomes of the learning. As you become more experienced, it is quite likely that you will be given the responsibility of designing the curriculum, which involves important decisions about content and outcomes. This is further referred to in Chapter 12.

However, even though at this stage it is likely that the programmes you are involved with may be carefully prescribed, you will still be required to write out-comes for each of the topics or segments into which you have disaggregated the provided syllabus. These will form the core of each of your session plans, which will be a more fully developed presentation of the teaching and learning activities summarized for each of the separate weeks in the scheme of work above.

For obvious reasons, it is important that you consider the aims and objectives of any learning session. As discussed earlier in this chapter, the planning of the cur-riculum will encompass the requirements of the syllabus in terms of the distribution of the underpinning content, the appropriateness of the selected level and the needs of the target learners. Depending upon their particular conventions, the educa-tional establishment involved may require the tutor to write aims and objectives for both the scheme of work and the constituent sessions. However, it is more often the case that *only* the scheme of work will include aims and objectives. The more detailed session plans will concentrate on specific behavioural objectives or defined learning outcomes. As a lead-in to this process, try the following activity within your PDJ:

B4m   Aims and objectives

If you have completed the earlier exercises you should by now have attempted to draw up a scheme of work for at least part of your syllabus and this scheme should include the aims of the programme and the general objectives. Look back at your plan and try to explain how your defined aims differ from your objectives.

4.6.1   Aims

An aim is a general statement of the overall direction of the course. It indicates what the teacher intends to achieve. It does *not* indicate how it is to be achieved – this is what the tutor decides during the planning process. Aims will usually be specified first for the whole course or programme, and then for the individual parts of it (sessions for example). The scheme aims tend to be *long-term, broad state-ments* which need to be translated into more immediate intentions. Here are two examples:

- to prepare learners for a role in the travel and tourism industry
- to enable learners to familiarize themselves with the structure, functions and applications of a range of information technology

B4n   Defining programme aims

Revisit your scheme of work and ensure that your aims are long-term. If you have only written one, try to add a second aim to develop the breadth of the programme.

As you will be aware, the *programme aims* that you have defined are, in effect, only 'signposts' and lack a detailed description of your destination. To achieve this, you now need to break down this general concept into definitions of the more precise *intentions* of the course or programme. As within our previously discussed scheme of work, these intended outcomes will be represented within each of the session plans. Although not quite as overarching, individual *session aims* are still quite broad and are based on what the teacher intends to do. Some examples are:

- to revise mathematical conversions relating to binary and decimal systems
- to highlight the causes of food poisoning and indicate the methods of prevention
- to demonstrate and give practice in techniques of subjective examination for patients with musculoskeletal disorders

B4o   Identifying session aims

Consider now the session aims you have defined for your scheme of work. Do they adequately represent the curriculum indicated by the programme aims, or do they need adding to? Remember, you are still working at a general level and are not yet considering the *detailed* objectives or learning outcomes, which are typical of a session plan.

An aim, then, is a generalized statement of intent, often encompassing broad areas of the planned curriculum. An aim is not measurable, but highlights what it is that the syllabus (and tutor) wishes to cover. As an example, if we apply this concept of a broad umbrella statement to a teacher education programme, one example of an appropriate aim could be

> to promote an understanding of the learning theories underpinning effective teaching and learning

or,

> to encourage learners to develop an awareness of the diversity of students' needs

Both of these statements would be difficult for anyone to 'measure', but are acceptable as broad terms used to explain the primary purposes of a teacher education programme.

Discussing aims, Petty (1998) stresses their importance as signposts:

> Aims are like compass directions, indicating the general direction in which the teacher wishes to travel. As such they are vital; but they are not specific enough to help the teacher pick learning activities, or assess whether learning has taken place. There is no general agreement about how to decide aims and objectives, or precisely how they should be written. But there is an agreement that aims are vitally important.

The aims then provide a general understanding of the conceptual area from which the more specific objectives will be drawn.

4.6.2   Behavioural objectives

It is their more precise nature that makes objectives a sub-group of the original devised aim. We are moving now from the broad intentions of the programme to the specific requirements actually placed on learners during the teaching/training session itself. Each facet of their expected performance is stated as an objective, for example, 'The students will be able to list the qualities of a good leader.'

Verbs such as *list, explain, justify, evaluate*, etc., are used to define *behavioural objectives*. In other words, the students are able to demonstrate their learning by doing something (in one of the above cases, *listing*) that can be observed and measured.

It is obvious that, in encouraging the learners to develop the skills of listing, selecting, rejecting, etc., the tutor will be also helping them to practise *non-behavioural objectives* such as *thinking, appreciating* and *understanding*. Although they remain a central part of learning and development, non-behavioural objectives are much less specific and cannot be observed or precisely measured in the way that behavioural outcomes can.

B4p Differentiating between objectives

Look back at the aims and objectives you defined within the scheme of work that you developed earlier. It should be easy to identify the behavioural objectives from the above description. However, also see if you can identify *non-behavioural outcomes* (i.e. those that will be difficult to express as an observable behaviour), which are either within the aims of the programme or are implicit within the defined objectives.

Within our current educational climate where there is such an emphasis on standards and accountability, it is to be expected that teachers and trainers delivering learning sessions will focus on the actual, measurable progress being made by individual learners. This is most effectively achieved by checking them against specific behavioural objectives or defined learning outcomes.

Educational Objectives were developed by Bloom and his colleagues (1956) when they developed their taxonomies for the Cognitive (thinking), Affective (feeling) and Psycho-Motor (doing) areas of learning. They are essentially hierarchies of behaviours, which the authors referred to as 'Domains' and which attempt to articulate an ascending, progressive development. So, for example, within the cognitive domain, Bloom defined behaviours which became more complex and demanding as they moved from Knowledge through Comprehension, Application, Analysis and Synthesis to Evaluation (see also Chapter 9).

However, although behavioural objectives are undoubtedly useful as a means of making educational purposes more transparent, the complex processes involved within the higher levels of learning are sometimes impossible to capture sufficiently accurately when using only behavioural objectives, and often the overall aim of a programme will be expressed in non-behavioural terms. Cohen and Manion (1989) rightly point out that although the present currency is certainly behavioural, there is a useful place for both methods of expressing the intentions of a curriculum:

> Behavioural objectives might well be most effective when the subject matter and intended learning is skill-based and can be demonstrated easily, or where overt writing or speaking can demonstrate appropriate levels of learning, or where learners need small, behavioural stages brought into the subject matter to provide clear, attainable targets. Non-behavioural objectives might be best used when the intended learning is more complex or less specific, is developmental and almost impossible to view in terms of behaviour without reducing the learning to an absurd level.

4.6.3 Curriculum theories

Two major curriculum paradigms have dominated education during the last 50 years. Perhaps the most familiar one was introduced by Ralph Tyler (1949) as the *objectives model*:

This simple design, which is clearly influenced by behaviourist approaches, is the forerunner of our present teaching and learning cycle. Tyler proposed that our starting point in curriculum design must always be the aims and objectives which, of course, are based on the values and purposes of the educational provider. Next, when stated precisely, the aims and objectives will indicate what teaching and learning methods will be the most effective in achieving these outcomes. Finally, student assessment and course evaluation will indicate how effective the implementation of the design has been. Using this information, it may be necessary to adjust parts of the framework to improve future provision.

Developed partially as a reaction to the behaviourist, deductive approach promoted by Tyler, Lawrence Stenhouse (1975) proposed the *process model* in order to focus less on prescribed outcomes and more on inductive development.

The essence of Stenhouse's approach is that teachers are able to design for learners significant, beneficial experiences without being constrained by defined outcomes. It is the teachers' expertise which allows them to identify holistic learning processes, which aspects to give priority to, and the most effective means of consolidating this procedure.

4.6.4 Designing objectives

The Common Inspection Framework, which is now the basis of the accountability processes implemented by Ofsted and ALI (Adult Learning Inspectorate) (see more details in Chapter 12), together with the management of the sector through the Learning and Skills Council has, as you might expect, been based on the Tyler approach rather than that of Stenhouse. However, the central concern is still the *quality of the learning experience* enjoyed by each individual within post-compulsory education sessions. As the effective planning of these learning experiences depends very much on the range and value of the objectives devised by teachers, it is clear that it is important for tutors to develop the skill of articulating intended outcomes.

The first step when defining behavioural outcomes is to write an opening statement, which makes clear just what you wish to achieve. For example:

- At the end of this session (or unit/module) the students/learners will be able to

Remember, your intention is to *achieve* the objectives which follow the statement, so you do not need to qualify these intended outcomes by using 'should' in preference to 'will.'

Also, the objectives provide an indication of how much each individual has progressed against the expressed measure during each learning session.

We can take it therefore, that:

- If the objectives commence with a verb, then this usually ensures that the resulting evidence is 'measurable'

In an educational context, objectives are precise descriptions of how you wish the learner to behave as a result of the successful learning. So it follows from our opening statement, that objectives should always be expressed from the *point of view of the learner*:

- State clearly what the learner will be able to do

The following are examples of this approach:

Describe the binary system
Convert binary numbers to decimal
Explain the need for such conversions in practice
Put the client at their ease before questioning
Question in a logical sequence
Record the client's responses during questioning

B4q   Objective characteristics

Analyse briefly the major common characteristics which the above six objectives share

It is clear that each of the objectives:

- begins with a verb
- is specific
- refers to activity which can be seen/heard and measured
- uses simple sentence structure and plain language (the exception could be specialist terms, the understanding of which are, of course, part of the learner's curriculum)
- links into the key areas for assessment – informal or formal
- sets targets for learners to achieve
- provides the teacher with evidence of learning
- helps the teacher to evaluate the effectiveness of their teaching – i.e. has the lesson helped the learners to achieve their targets?

It is evident from these examples that objectives are easy to specify for all kinds of subject areas and provide a good guide to the content of the sessions, to the tutor's choice of teaching/learning strategies and to the assessment vehicle. Now try the following activity:

B4r   Writing objectives

Bearing in mind our discussion above, write two objectives to match each of the short-term session aims you considered in activity B4o previously.

Referring back to our (fictional) specific learning objectives in the example of a scheme of work (activity B4l above), it will help us to illustrate a point here. The aims were to:

- identify examples of humour within at least five contemporary forms of communication media
- describe three traditional forms of humour still evident in society today
- analyse the purposes of humour evident in four examples of popular media
- describe the cultural differences between two major examples of popular comedy

As you will have realized, the *evidence* from each of the above assessment activities meets the important characteristics we defined above (i.e. can be observed by the tutor). In order to clarify this still further, some *incorrect* objectives for that same 'humour' context might be to:

- *know* examples of humour within communication
- *appreciate* forms evident in society today
- *value* the purposes of humour evident in the media
- *understand* the differences between major examples of comedy

Use the above examples as a basis for activity B4s:

B4s   Ensuring achievement

Would the learner have a clear idea of how much evidence is required and the type of information needed? Would the tutor have any evidence to be absolutely sure that the objectives had been achieved by the learners?

Unfortunately, despite the fact that the above objectives are worthy, they are non-behavioural and so would not generate the evidence required by most of our assessment processes. Also we have taken out the descriptors, which clarify how much work is expected of the student (i.e. 'four examples of media')

The problems associate with such omissions are indentified by Petty (1998) when he states that: 'specific objectives should:

- specify precisely and in concrete terms what the student should be able to do
- be written in such a way that it is possible to determine whether or not the objective has been achieved

Table 4.1 Session planning considerations

Topic to be covered: You may decide to have some variety in the way you distribute the different topics to be covered, or you may wish to develop a topic over a number of weeks.	**Learning environment:** It may be that certain facilities are needed for a particular topic and these are only available on certain dates. Or the arranged venue may have particular characteristics which must be considered.	**Nature and composition of the student cohort:** The learning characteristics of the group will influence your planning, for example, group dynamics, learning styles, level of ability.
Number of learners in the group: Naturally, small group teaching can be quite different to the approaches you need to take with a larger group.	**Age of the learners:** If there is a wide age mix, you will need to provide appropriate compensation and stimulation in order to hold the interest of all the learners. If they are roughly the same age, you will need to try to differentiate.	**Maturity of the learners – both social and emotional:** Naturally, you will respond to the levels of responsibility that your students are able to accept.
Length of the session: Approaches will be quite different for one-hour sessions where some steps are more urgent when compared, for example, to half-day or full-day programmes.	**Time of day of the session:** Sessions immediately after lunch (on a Friday in particular) will need to be approached in a way which takes account of the learners' disposition and uses appropriate strategies to counteract any lethargy.	**Desired outcome/s of the session:** The objectives to be achieved will, of course, be a central consideration when deciding on the teaching and learning methods to employ.
Previous session/topic covered: Obviously, the success of the previous session in achieving the desired outcomes will have a significant bearing on at least the opening of the following session.	**Next session/topic to be covered:** It is often useful to prime the learners about what will be discussed at the next session and where possible to encourage them to prepare for it in some way.	**General knowledge of the learners:** In placing a subject in the context of the students' level of experience, it is valuable to know to which areas of general knowledge you can rely on them being able to respond.
Special knowledge of the learners: If the learners have a similar understanding of the subject, it is easier to design the learning than if the students have widely differing levels of ability.	**Significant learning needs:** If your learning group contains students with particular physical or emotional needs, you will obviously have to plan your methods of sustaining inclusion carefully. This could include gaining the cooperation of the other learners in advance of the session	**Constraints and difficulties anticipated:** Planning sessions usually involves negotiating some problem or other. This could relate to the venue, to the timing, to activities taking place near to your sessions, etc. General awareness of establishment-wide developments and commitments is needed.

Main teaching and learning methods envisaged:	Resources and teaching/learning aids required/available:	How the session will be evaluated:
It is clear that the methods which you intend to implement during the session need to be carefully considered in advance in order to ensure that you are familiar with the content and, most importantly, how you will deliver the key content in a successful manner.	You need to know, for example, not just that there is an overhead projector in the venue, but that it is working and that the projection surface is acceptable. Designing particular aids to learning can make the difference between a moderately successful session and a memorable one.	Even though the evaluation processes you employ may be just an informal Q & A exchange, you should have a clear idea, *before the session*, of the areas on which you need information in order to improve your practice and how best to get it. A clumsily managed evaluation can easily do more harm than good. You should also know if you need formative or summative information.

- usually be short-term
- be drawn up by the teacher to suit the resources, the teacher and the students
- optionally, define the circumstances under which the objective is to be demonstrated and/or what constitutes an achievement

4.7 | SESSION PLANS

Having designed the scheme of work, the next task is for the tutor to plan the delivery of learning in the form of the individual sessions. Each of the particular sessions will be free standing but must build on earlier sessions and prepare the way for what follows. It is, of course, necessary for the objectives set out in the scheme of work to be covered in the session plans and for there to be a particular progression in terms of content and conceptual understanding. The following are some of the many aspects that must be considered:

4.7.1 Depth and breadth in learning

So far in this chapter, we have mainly discussed the accuracy of the defined outcomes we use in order to plan our programmes. Despite the importance of these considerations, if we didn't look a little beyond them, we could end up with precisely written outcomes which meet the observable and measurable requirements, but which also, unfortunately, are so undemanding as to be virtually useless. Learning is directed towards many different situations and purposes and some are simple, while others are much more complex and have to be achieved over time.

Gronlund (1985) discussed the fact that quite often it is necessary to achieve lower level objectives before moving on to more demanding development:

> Learning outcomes that are considered *minimum essentials* are typically low-level outcomes that can be rather easily achieved by students and that serve as *prerequisites* to further learning in the area. Those outcomes at the *developmental level* represent goals toward which students may show different degrees of progress but which they never fully achieve. The ability to *understand*, to *apply*, to *interpret*, and to *think critically*, for example, typically depend on an extended period of development. Their *complete* attainment is not expected in any given course.

Gronlund is making the point that many curriculum designers and teachers tend to treat all objectives as minimum essentials, which must be achieved. If this approach is taken, the outcomes tend to be written to cater for the lowest common denominator and the quality of the total student experience is diminished. On the other hand, if the more demanding objectives are the only focus, the students may not be sufficiently versed in the knowledge and skills which are prerequisites for such higher-level learning.

Bloom (1956) made the ascending developmental stages that all learners must go through very clear in his description of the Cognitive Domain and Gronlund (ibid.) provides a very useful summary of this hierarchy:

Major categories in the cognitive domain	
1. Knowledge	Knowledge is defined as remembering of previously learnt material. This may involve the recall of a wide range of material, from specific facts to complete theories, but all that is required is the bringing to mind of the appropriate information. Knowledge represents the lowest level of learning outcomes in the cognitive domain.
2. Comprehension	Comprehension is defined as the ability to grasp the meaning of material. This may be shown by translating material from one form to another (words to numbers), by interpreting material (explaining or summarizing) and by estimating future trends (predicting consequences or effects). These learning outcomes go one step beyond the simple remembering of material, and represent the lowest level of understanding.
3. Application	Application refers to the ability to use learnt material in new and concrete situations. This may include the application of such things as rules, methods, concepts, principles, laws and theories. Learning outcomes in this area require a higher level of understanding than those under comprehension.
4. Analysis	Analysis refers to the ability to break down material into its component parts so that its organizational structure may be understood. This may include the identification of the parts, analysis of the relationships between parts and recognition of the organizational principles involved. Learning outcomes here represent a higher intellectual level then comprehension and application because they require an understanding of both the content and the structural form of the material.
5. Synthesis	Synthesis refers to the ability to put parts together to form a new whole. This may involve the production of a unique communication (theme or speech), a plan of operations (research proposal), or a set of abstract relations (scheme for classifying information). Learning outcomes in this area stress creative behaviours, with major emphasis on the formulation of *new* patterns or structures.
6. Evaluation	Evaluation is concerned with the ability to judge the value of material (statement, novel, poem, research report) for a given purpose. The judgements are to be based on definite criteria. These may be internal criteria (organization) or external criteria (relevance to the purpose) and the student may determine the criteria or be given them. Learning outcomes in this area are the highest in the cognitive hierarchy because they contain elements of all of the other categories, plus conscious value judgements based on clearly defined criteria.

B4t Defining levels

Consider your developing session plan and look again at the *levels* of the outcomes you have written, referring to Bloom's Cognitive Domain above. Are many of your objectives concerned only with knowledge and comprehension, or are you moving the students up towards application and analysis?

It is possible that you may think that your learners are not yet at a stage to develop beyond application, yet many apparently simple tasks also involve analysis, synthesis and evaluation. If we examine a very fundamental process such a shopping, you will see from Table 4.2 that the learners very quickly move beyond the mere comprehension and application levels.

Table 4.2 Possible cognitive levels demonstrated during shopping through the learner being able to:	
Knowledge	*List* items intending to purchase. *Name* the stores that may hold the required commodities. *Justify* the amount of money which is available for the intended goods.
Comprehension	*Explain* the characteristics of the items to be purchased. Give *examples* of categories of goods. *Defend* the range of products identified as necessary purchases.
Application	*Relate* the choice of goods in one store with those available elsewhere. *Change* the order of priority within the shopping list. *Discover* previously unconsidered possibilities.
Analysis	*Relate* available goods to original shopping list. *Identify* good value. *Differentiate* between two competing choices. *Separate* imperative buys from possible purchases.
Synthesis	*Recognize* how intended purchases will relate to goods already owned. *Plan* to delay the purchase of some of the items in favour of more desirable goods. *Revise* shopping list.
Evaluation	*Appraise* the final list of possible choices. *Discriminate* between two similar items. *Justify* a final short list. *Conclude* the process with appropriate purchases.

Of course, our debate above is focused only on the Cognitive Domain but, as we stressed earlier, we feel that it is very important to promote holistic learning which involves more than just thinking. There are basic physical skills to be developed (the Psycho-Motor Domain) and most learning is also about the development of values or feelings (the Affective Domain).

B4u   Moving beyond knowledge

Revisit your defined session objectives once again and consider what psycho-motor and affective skills will also be learned by your students as they grapple with the cognitive element of their programme.

The following summaries of the Affective Domain, taken from Krathwohl (1964) and the Psycho-Motor Domain, taken from Simpson (1972) provide a useful hierarchy of behaviours and related learner actions which indicate how objectives at each level may be expressed (see Table 4.3).

Remember when planning a curriculum or a range of assessment tasks that there are other important outcomes in addition to cognitive objectives. You need to achieve a balance of *Cognitive, Affective* and *Psycho-Motor* outcomes set at appropriately *demanding levels*.

Table 4.3 Affective and Psycho-Motor Behaviours and appropriate objectives			
AFFECTIVE *(Krathwohl 1964)*		**PSYCHO-MOTOR** *(Simpson 1972)*	
Receiving stimuli	Listens attentively. Shows awareness. Accepts differences. Attends closely.	Perception of sensory stimulation	Relates the taste of food to the need for seasoning. Detects differences in temperature. Differentiates between stimuli.
Responding	Shows interest. Accepts school rules. Participates in discussion. Completes homework. Enjoys helping others.	Mental, physical and emotional set	Knows sequence of steps in a particular process. Demonstrates correct stance for a physical activity. Responds with interest to a particular opportunity.
Valuing	Appreciates good literature/art/music. Shows concern for the welfare of others. Demonstrates belief in the democratic process.	Guided response	Imitates actions demonstrated by an instructor. Uses trial and error to develop a technique. Determines best sequence for optimum effect.
Organizing	Accepts responsibility for own behaviour. Understands and accepts own strengths and limitations. Recognizes the need for balance between freedom and responsibility.	Mechanism of performance	Writes smoothly and legibly. Is able to touch-type when operating keyboard.
		Complex overt response	Automatically takes up correct position during ball games. Plays from music.
Characterizing by a value	Begins to develop own value system. Demonstrates self-reliance. Behaves in a consistent and predictable manner.	Adaptation	Adjusts play to counteract opponent. Modifies use of machine to allow for unusual conditions
		Origination	Creates an original dance step. Develops a new style of painting. Uses established procedure for a new purpose.

> ### B4v   Developing more rounded learners
>
> Continue to think holistically about your students' development. Consider not just the knowledge, skills and values you wish them to acquire, but also their stance in relation to study, work and relationships. Are you encouraging gradual independence, or is your over-supportive approach prolonging their dependence?

Our previous discussion has been concentrating on the development of depth (*i.e. concern for levels*) and breadth (*i.e. holistic concerns*) when writing objectives, by consciously incorporating variable outcomes related to feeling and doing in addition to thinking. It is clear that, even more important than precision in the writing of outcomes, is our ability to ensure that we stimulate the learners' interest and enthusiasm for the subject by stretching them in terms of the range and complexity of the abilities they develop. As Alan Rogers (1994) stresses when talking about the education of adults:

> If we have a narrow objective, aiming at some specific competency or externally moderated achievement, we will tend to lay greater stress on the part played by the teacher than on the learners' activities. If, on the other hand, we set our sights more on the growth of the individual, then the emphasis of our programme will rely more on the activities engaged in by the participants, less on the work of the teacher.

Rogers is pointing up one of the serious problems of systems that are heavily dependent on closely prescribed outcomes. Such a process inevitably leads to 'teaching to the test' which limits both the teaching and the learning to the inevitably limited objectives (because language cannot encompass all the nuances of learning) and students become concerned more with knowledge replication, rather than knowledge creation. Rogers also indicates a further implication of such an approach: the teacher assumes a dominant role as the holder of the knowledge and the assessor of the defined outcomes, which leads to the learners accepting a passive role as the receivers of the prescribed knowledge and the subjects of the assessment demands. It is difficult for the potentially rewarding learning partnership between teacher and student to flourish during such a relationship because the implication to the learners is that the really valuable knowledge is external to themselves.

It may seem incongruous that we have introduced these imprecise notions of breadth of study and shared responsibility towards the end of a chapter which has been so concerned with systematic planning. However, as we pointed out at the start of this book, although the need for accountability is accepted, we believe teaching to be more of an art than a science. We accept that some accountability is necessary in order to ensure consistency of standards, but believe that there must be room for student flair and teacher judgement. We will continue this debate in Chapter 12.

4.7.2   Session plan layout

Below is an example of a possible way of laying out a Session Plan. It is based on the *second* session of the imaginary scheme of work that we used in activity B4l.
You will note that:

- the teacher has a notional timing for the session (although this is open to adjustment depending on how the students respond to each of the intended activities)
- the four defined learning outcomes are identified clearly at the top of the session plan
- the defined learning outcomes are related in column 2 to each of the teacher activities. This establishes clearly that the identified learning outcomes are covered during the session
- although this may be a non-vocational programme, the student achievement is assessed in various ways throughout the module. The tutor makes clear the assessment approaches

SESSION PLAN						
Date	22nd September 2003		Time of session:	19.00 to 21.00 hours		
Venue:	Lecture Room 3					
Programme:	Adult non-voc Leisure Class		Unit:	Introduction to Humour		
Group:	Part-time evening		Topic:	Purposes of humour in cultural contexts		
Session aims	Promote an understanding of humour					
Learning outcomes:	a) Extract humorous and subject themes from collected cartoons		c) Identify how humour is used for cultural and political purposes			
	b) Identify the historical origins of present-day humour		d) Analyse topical verbal jokes to identify themes			

Time	Outcomes	Teacher activity:	Learner activity:	Resources:	Assessment method:	Comments:
19.00	a)	Discuss cartoons collected by class	Bring in collected cartoons	Collected cartoons	Informal	Formative Assessment used to accredit student contribution
19.15	b)	Present examples of historical cartoons	Viewing presentation	PowerPoint proj & Lap-top	None	
1935	b)	Establish groups to discuss cultural and political humorous themes from cartoons	Form groups to discuss humour and politics	Group experiences	Q & A	

19.45	a) & b)	Describe discussion task during break	Receiving directions	None	None	
19.50	None	Break	Break	None	None	
20.00	a) & b)	Instigate continuation of discussion	Discussion	Group experiences	Observation	
20.15	a) & b)	Coord feedback from discussion groups	Feeding back	Group experiences	Observation	More formal summative assessment to be used at the end of the module.
20.25	c)	Encourage groups to identify topical verbal jokes	Discussing current jokes and selecting three.	Group experiences	Observation and Q & A	
20.40	c) & d)	Org pres of three jokes by each group	Helping with presentaion	Group preparation	Observation and Q & A	
20.50	c) & d)	Themes and purposes identified	Analysing jokes for themes	Previous presentation	Observation and Q & A	
20.55	a), b), c) & d)	Summary and encourage-ment of groups to collect verbal jokes on identified themes for next week	Noting requirements for following week	Earlier cartoons. Summary of historical pres. & topical jokes.	None	

4.8 | CONCLUSION

On the face of it, the planning of teaching sessions may seem to be a straightfor-ward, uncomplicated process. However, as this chapter has indicated, in reality the teacher must achieve the difficult balance between, on the one hand, being overly prescriptive and, on the other, allowing disorganized classroom chaos which demotivates all the learners. The planning must, of course, produce a clear fra-mework, which articulates exactly what the teacher wishes to achieve. Even so, it is imperative that the teacher's planning should allow for the unexpected in the various possible ways the learners may respond to the teaching.

Because of all the reasons we have so far discussed, teaching and learning are not predictable. The practitioner who pushes ahead with a planned session, despite all the indications that the learners are not receiving the message, is doing nobody a service. Sticking to the planned session and continuing to fire didactic missiles when it is clear they are not reaching their target is clearly not effective teaching. Keeping to a notional timing in such a situation is, in fact, wasting everybody's time.

Even so, becoming reflective and responsive does not mean that planning becomes redundant. Reflecting on practice and developing strategies that have the appropriate teacher response ready to hand demand considerable prior thought and organization.

However, the key to the whole process is *resonance* rather than prescription. In these stressful days it is undoubtedly difficult to retain the ability *and the willingness* to respond positively to our students. To do this successfully, we need to spend time getting to know the learners well, to attune ourselves to their wavelength, so that we are able to understand most of the subtle signals that are transmitted between the students and the teacher and between student and student.

Once we have the ability and the motivation to read accurately how the majority of our learners are receiving both the taught material *and the manner in which it is being presented*, our planning and preparation will inevitably begin to have much greater accuracy and meaning.

Rather than preparing ourselves to fail because we fail to prepare, we must plan to prevail by becoming more aware of even our smallest weaknesses. Mapping our failures is often very difficult and uncomfortable, but it is the most reliable way of illuminating the path to learning success.

4.9 | USEFUL SOURCES

Armitage, A. (ed.) (1999) *Teaching and Training in Post-Compulsory Education*. Milton Keynes: Open University Press.
This book looks at what it is like to teach in the Further Education sector. Chapters include Teaching and learning, Resources, Assessment, Course design and Developments in the post-compulsory sector. This is a good all round introduction for the new FE teacher.

Daines, D., Daines, C. and Graham, B. (1993) *Adult Learning, Adult Teaching*. Nottingham: Continuing Education Press.
A useful handbook for teachers who are new to teaching adults. It begins by identifying the characteristics of adult learners and explores planning for learning, teaching methods and reviewing learning.

Reece, I. and Walker, S. (2000) *Teaching, Training and Learning*. (4th edn.) Business Education Publishers.
Nine chapters full of detail about teaching and learning. A good first chapter about the role of the teacher. A good attempt has been made to relate methods and theory to the FENTO Standards although, as these tend to be threaded throughout the book, the relationship is not always entirely clear.

 Further materials and blank pro-formas are available on the *tipcet.com* website.

4.10 RATIONALE FOR KEY AREA B PLANNING AND PREPARING TEACHING AND LEARNING PROGRAMMES FOR GROUPS AND INDIVIDUALS

FAQs	At Stage 1	At Stage 2	At Stage 3
Why do it?	You are involved in delivering learning which will help your students/ trainees achieve specified outcomes and the less you leave to chance, the more likely you are to meet your targets within the resource limitations which every programme must acknowledge	To facilitate effective learning many factors need to be considered in addition to the immediate problem of delivering an identified content to particular learners. If important factors (current level of ability, needs, attitudes, learning styles, etc.) are ignored all your efforts may be in vain.	You need to evaluate your curriculum planning in order to identify to what extent it is affecting the quality of student experience and achievement. Your future planning will become better informed as you learn to take account of the range of variables.
Where are we going?	You need to be clear about what you wish to achieve within a particular lesson/unit/ course. Your destination will be clearly indicated by the aims and objectives of the programme you are involved in and often more precisely spelt out within the defined learning outcomes that your trainees/students must achieve. You should also have begun to plan appropriate diagnostic tests.	You could express the intended outcomes as objectives or competences or as a process you wish to take the learners through, but you *must* know the purpose of the educational experience you are planning. Don't forget to include goals from the affective (feeling) and psycho-motor (doing) category, as well as the obvious cognitive (thinking) domain. Also be aware of the development of key skills.	You are developing the ability to reflect actively on curriculum processes in order to identify the range of intentional and unintentional influences which are affecting the learning outcomes. You are moving towards a planning approach which is supported, but not constrained, by an appropriate structure while remaining able to respond effectively to the needs of learners.
How do we get there?	Consider carefully any information you have been given such as a *scheme of work, syllabus* or *curriculum*. Identify the key content of which the learners *must* gain an understanding and plan a *realistic* progression to these learning outcomes. Identify your assessment strategy and don't forget to take into account the times when important assessment must take place.	An obvious beginning is the content of syllabus. Use your experience and intuition to prioritize the major themes/points you wish to include and also an appropriate introduction which will enable your students to build on earlier ideas and draw out from the experiences you provide the key concepts and principles they will need later.	Start by reflecting on the more obvious aspects of teaching and learning such as achievement of defined outcomes, student interest and motivation, management of time, etc. Consider later the more subtle influences of planning such as teaching and learning styles, physical environment, timetable position in relation to other subjects, etc.

Is this the best way?	Look again at what you intend to do and try to separate content that is essential from that which would be your ideal. Allow extra time in the early stages for learners to get used to your delivery and aspects of the learning environment. Keep an ongoing record of effectiveness and use this formative evaluation to consider if any modification is needed in later session.	Examine what you have planned objectively. Ensure you have selected the optimal order and allow time for remedial work whenever necessary. Check that you haven't included too much, and that what you have selected is relevant to your defined outcomes and the agreed assessment strategy. Beware of self-indulgence when planning the syllabus.	Confirm that the lesson plan/scheme of work has a linking coherence and development. Ensure variety of presentational methods and planned student experiences. Confirm that learners are able to see the value of your intended provision. Check underpinning values and purposes as well as planning, delivery and assessment.
When is the right time?	You have to accept that you will only rarely have enough time, but obviously the earlier you start planning and preparing the better. Remember to plan some form of induction into the programme for the learners and think of appropriate ice-breaker exercises to promote group cohesion.	Be aware of the timing of significant events/ experiences and inputs so that you allow the students time to absorb these important ideas before being expected to develop and build on them. Watch out for key events such as visits/ fieldtrips, availability of resources/guest speakers and assessment deadlines.	Evaluate and modify your approach during the teaching (i.e. formative) in order to correct any problems encountered in the delivery of teaching or the development of learning. It may be too late to correct student misunderstandings or teaching ambiguities at the end of the process.
Who needs to know?	Obviously, the students need to know about the intended schedule. Check that the library and the learning resource centre have been told about the needs of your programme. Confirm that your teaching room is adequate for the intended session, that you have ordered any specific audio/visual/IT hardware/software. Ensure that what you have organized will not disrupt other classes held during, before or after your session.	Do you need a translator, or an interpreter? Perhaps you need to arrange access or learning support for students with specific learning difficulties. The detail of your planning will obviously be influenced by the success of your earlier teaching, particularly with the target group. If you can, build on their earlier learning and use familiar terms and references to help them develop a mental 'set' in relation to the learning to come.	The analysis of the effectiveness of planning will affect present and future students, but it will also inevitably affect colleagues involved directly in that provision or indirectly in terms of support, use of resources and changes in department culture, etc. Managers will also need to know if there are resource implications or if a particular problem such as retention is being addressed.
How do we know when we've got there?	Your planning has been effective when the majority of your students/ trainees have enjoyed the	All the key aspects of the curriculum have been incorporated and the delivery is varied and	Analyse how effective the planning has been in terms of the allocation of resources and time to the

	programme and have achieved the learning outcomes. Obviously, it is important to consider the retention data. However, the reasons for drop-out are often complex, so do not immediately think that you are automatically at fault if some students stop attending.	interesting. The planned sessions are manageable and although the content is challenging, the teaching is not over-demanding on the students and you and your colleagues. Where necessary, there is time for remedial work with the students before the assessment processes take place.	key stages. Ensure that preferred student learning styles have been accommodated and that you and your colleagues are comfortable with the designed teaching and learning strategies and are confident that they will achieve the desired learning outcomes.
Has everyone had a fair chance?	As noted in the previous chapter, meeting the particular needs of every student is extremely difficult. Start by considering whether such broad aims as the provision of an appropriate, orderly environment, where the views of individuals are respected and where learning is a common goal, are met.	Ensure that your intended strategy doesn't discriminate in some way against some members of the group. Think about how the less able will cope. Check that the high-fliers will be able to demonstrate their range of skills adequately and will be fully occupied during the class.	Reflect on your response to perceived student need and confirm that you have made optimum use of available resources. Consider if your teaching strategies could be detrimentally affecting students' perception of their own abilities and autonomy as learners.

4.11 KEY AREA B SPECIFICATIONS – PLANNING AND PREPARING TEACHING AND LEARNING PROGRAMMES FOR GROUPS AND INDIVIDUALS

Purpose: Teachers and teaching teams need to be effective in interpreting curriculum requirements in order to devise learning outcomes, programmes of study and assessment strategies as well as adopting appropriate teaching and learning strategies. This involves devising programmes of study which meet the demands of the curriculum and set clear targets for individual learners within a supportive and flexible environment for learning. It also involves encouraging the take-up of post-compulsory provision and the widening of participation. For an analysis of this process at FENTO Stages 1, 2 and 3 see the rationale above.

Please note: The FENTO Standards listed below are relevant to the following three levels of award: Stage 1 (Introduction), Stage 2 (Intermediate) and Stage 3 (Full Certification). All of the standards are required at Stage 3, only those in italic or bold are required at Stage 2 and only those in italic are required at Stage 1.

UNIT B1. IDENTIFY THE REQUIRED OUTCOMES OF THE LEARNING PROGRAMME *In order to do this teachers should:*

Demonstrate that they are able to:	and have specific knowledge and critical understanding of:	plus generic knowledge of:	Summary of appropriate evidence in this Key Area:		Relevant Chapter Activities
a Criteria: *interpret curriculum requirements in terms of syllabus, objectives and schemes of work for learning programmes*	How to select appropriate learning programmes	• The broad range of learning needs including the needs of those with learning difficulties and/or disabilities • Sources of information about learners' previous experiences and attainments • The requirements of individual learning programmes	a	Schemes of work, Devised outcomes, Topic sequencing, Prioritizing order, etc	B4a, B4b, B4c, B4d, B4e, B4f, B4g, B4h, B4i, B4j, B4k, B4l
b **produce learning outcomes for programmes of study**	Ways of establishing learning outcomes for programmes of study		b	Learning outcome development	B4m, B4n, B4o.F9j, F9k
c establish precise learning objectives and content	The content required to achieve particular learning outcomes		c	Schemes of work, Session plans	B4p, B4q.F9h, F9n

101

	Standard	Essential knowledge	Evidence		Reference
d	*define the subject/technical knowledge and skills required*	• Ways of evaluating different information about learners against the requirements of specific learning programmes, including the accreditation of prior learning and experience • Appropriate forms of initial assessment and how to conduct them • Individual differences in aptitude and ability • Training needs analysis, methods & techniques	Scheme of work, syllabus, session plans	d	B4o, B4q, B4r
e	**fulfil validating and awarding body requirements, where relevant**	Programme validation criteria and procedures	Validation documentation	e	B4d
f	ensure the basic skills and Key Skills are integral to provision, as required.	• Ways of ensuring that basic skills and Key Skills are integral to learning outcomes • How to derive individual learning programmes from required learning outcomes • Possible progression routes and their implications for the learner • How to analyse and evaluate skills, knowledge and values within a curriculum area • The importance of inclusive learning and ways of ensuring that teachers meet the needs of all students		f	B4a to B4v See also Chapter 12
			Plus commentary in the PDJ on the purposes and value of the above, together with records in the PF of Teaching Observations, Session Plans, Rationales. Self-Evaluations and Progress Summary		

Key to above standards required at each FENTO Stage:

Introduction Stage – italic
Intermediate Stage + bold
Certification Stage – all

UNIT B2.   IDENTIFY APPROPRIATE TEACHING AND LEARNING TECHNIQUES In order to do this teachers should:

Demonstrate that they are able to:	and have specific knowledge and critical understanding of:	plus generic knowledge of:		Summary of appropriate evidence in this Key Area:	Relevant Chapter Activities
Criteria: a *encourage learners to adopt styles of learning which are appropriate to the required outcomes and most likely to enable learners to achieve to the best of their abilities*	• How to structure learning to achieve the required outcomes	• The broad range of learning needs including the needs of those with learning difficulties and/or disabilities • Sources of information about learners' previous experiences and attainments	a	Scheme/s of work which incorporate student review of success of their individual action plans	B4a to B4l
b **select appropriate teaching techniques to accommodate different styles of learning**	• Appropriate teaching techniques • The information and learning technology resources available to learners	• The requirements of individual learning programmes • Ways of evaluating different information about learners against the requirements of specific learning	b	Session plans, Schemes of work	C5a to C5v
c **use individual, small group and whole group teaching techniques as appropriate**	• The advantages and disadvantages of individual and group teaching/learning and when to use these approaches	programmes, including the accreditation of prior learning and experience • Appropriate forms of initial assessment and how to conduct them	c	Session plans, Schemes of Work	C5a to C5v
d **set precise targets with individual learners that match their capacities, make the most of their potential for achievement and meet the required learning outcomes**		• Individual differences in aptitude and ability • Training needs analysis methods and techniques	d	Schemes of Work, Session plans,	A3j and A3m
e *create a safe learning environment based on trust and support*			e	Learning Support audit, Schemes of Work, Session Plans	A3j and A3m. E8g and E8k

			A3c, A3j and A3m
f	encourage learners to see the relevance of what they are learning to other aspects of the curriculum and to apply their learning in different contexts		Action Plans, Session Plans Schemes of Work,
		f	Plus commentary in the PDJ on the purposes and value of the above, together with records in the PF of Teaching Observations, Session Plans, Rationales. Self-Evaluations and Progress Summary

Key to above standards required at each FENTO Stage:

Introduction Stage – italic
Intermediate Stage + **bold**
Certification Stage – all

UNIT B3. ENHANCE ACCESS TO AND PROVISION IN LEARNING PROGRAMMES				
Demonstrate that they are able to:	and have specific knowledge and critical understanding of:	plus generic knowledge of:	Summary of appropriate evidence in this Key Area:	Relevant Chapter Activities
a maintain contact with those who coordinate the links between other institutions and the organization and across different curriculum areas	• Local and national networks to which the organization belongs	• The broad range of learning needs including the needs of those with learning difficulties and/or disabilities • Sources of information about learners' previous experiences and attainments	a Links to learning support, ITC, Library and Learning Resources	B4d, B4f E8g, E8i, E8o
b maintain effective links with appropriate agencies to enhance curriculum delivery		• The requirements of individual learning programmes • Ways of evaluating different information about learners against the requirements of specific learning programmes, including the accreditation of prior learning and experience	b Learning Support, External Agencies	B4d, B4f and E8m
c contribute to the activities which improve access to the organization's learning facilities			c Cross Organization Committees, External Support	D6m, D6o E8m, E8o
d support a culture of open access and widening participation	• How to make learning programmes more accessible and why this is important • Flexible processes and procedures for delivery and assessment • The role of information learning technology in creating new modes of learning that are attractive to potential learners	• Appropriate forms of initial assessment and how to conduct them • Individual differences in aptitude and ability • Training needs analysis methods and techniques	d Learning Support	D7e, E8j, E8m.
e offer a range of flexible opportunities for learning including learning facilitated through information technology			e ITC materials, Library and Learning Resource Links	D6n, D6o
f identify and overcome potential barriers to participation in learning programmes			f Action Plans, Learning Review	D7e, D7l, E8k

g	ensure, where possible within resource constraints, the potential learners are able to experience aspects of the programme before committing themselves to it	Open Days, Taster Sessions	A3r, D6h, D7g,
h	recognize the organizational and resource constraints influencing participation and make the most of opportunities to achieve wider participation in learning programmes;	Learning Support	E8j; E8k
Key to above standards required at each FENTO Stage: *Introduction Stage – italic* **Intermediate Stage + bold** Certification Stage – all		Plus commentary in the PDJ on the purposes and value of the above, together with records in the PF of Teaching Observations, Session Plans, Rationales. Self-Evaluations and Progress Summary	

CHAPTER 5

Developing and using a range of teaching and learning techniques

Karen Lowe

Key Area C Promoting individual, group and experiential learning

Key concepts in this chapter:

Accretion, Advanced Organizer, Andragogy, Behaviourist, Comrades in Adversity, Conceptual Structure, Conditions of Learning, Controversy, Cooperative and Competitive Learning, Disinhibition, Dynamics and Roles, Eclectic Approaches, Experiential Learning, Exposition, Group Learning, Higher-Level Thinking, Iconic and Symbolic Learning, Individual Accountability, Inhibition, Instrumental Conceptualism, Internal and External Knowledge, Mental Set, Positive Interdependence

Before you begin this chapter you may wish to check the FAQs on pp. 139–40.

Index to Chapter 5 (Key Area C)

5.1 INTRODUCTION

As teaching practitioners we have a widely varied range of delivery and assessment methods available to us and, even though it is possible for us to identify our own personal preferences, various accountability and pedagogical pressures make it increasingly difficult to stick intransigently to these.

Different learners, courses of study, environmental and organizational demands and the requirements of awarding bodies, all necessitate flexibility, if not from individual tutors, then from the teams who have responsibility for the delivery of learning.

Also, as we observed earlier, education within the learning and skills sector is concerned with such a variety of learners within so many diverse educational contexts that, inevitably, each teacher will draw on many different theories in order to develop an appropriate method of organizing and delivering learning.

In this chapter we will introduce a range of educational theories and relate these to individual, group and experiential learning. As a starting point it may be useful to consider some of the key questions that arise when we consider the value of *learning theory* and how this relates to the development of teaching and learning techniques.

C5a Why consider theory?

Reflect on the value of learning theory to a busy practitioner who is coping well in the present situation by using familiar methods and adopting departmental practices

You may well have raised some of the following questions:

- How will my learners benefit?
- How will I benefit?

- If it isn't broken – why fix it? My students already have a reasonable learning experience.
- Why change? I am comfortable with the range of methods I already use.

Despite their obvious competence in the classroom (or perhaps because of it) many teachers are hesitant about entering into theoretical discussions about pedagogy. This reluctance may be related to a perception that the pressurized realities of the chalkface are a million miles from the vague, abstract world of academia.

However, it is worth remembering that the actual *source* of most, if not all, knowledge is some form of *practical* endeavour and not the reflections of erudite academics. The value of their scholarly activity is that, through analysis and synthesis, they identify the validity and wider implications of the new knowledge. Eventually, through the integraton of these interpretations within evolving theories, the generalizability of these practices to other settings is achieved. Over time, as the theories are refined during testing within actual practice, they gain acceptance, thus allowing new knowledge to emerge and the cyclical process to continue.

If we bear this process in mind as we return to our rightly sceptical questions, perhaps the following simple responses have some value:

a) *Finding the problem.* Compare teaching to something familiar, such as owning and driving a car. In the early days, the methods used are often a copy of other styles which have been taught or observed and may well be successful for a time. However, should that practice become, for one reason or another, less successful, it is often useful if your analysis of the problem is informed by theory. For example, if this problem is in teaching, it could be related to the effect of group dynamics. In the car analogy, the problem could be problems in starting the engine on a winter's morning. It is very possible that both difficulties will be solved more quickly if our analysis is informed by theory.

b) *Justifying the methods.* Within current inspection frameworks, we may well be asked to justify our chosen approach and, obviously, arguments based on established theories will provide useful support for any rationale.

c) *Repeating our success.* After we have moved beyond the understandable enjoyment generated by achieving a certain amount of success, we will usually wish to know what we did that was so right, so that we will be able to repeat whatever aspect of our performance was so effective. If we are to evaluate the success of our methods usefully, the analysis should rely as much on theory as intuition.

The central fact is that there are extremely valuable basic principles which have been developed by the theorists and assimilated by us the practitioners over the years. In this chapter we will explore these theories and relate them to the accepted and conventional teaching strategies, with which we are all fairly familiar. You are not expected to become an expert in the range of methods discussed, only to develop your awareness of them and thus make informed choices about their application, validity or usefulness.

The following discussion falls naturally into two parts – Learners and Teachers and their particular characteristics and relationships. It is hoped to identify and extract from each area some theoretical ideas which may have general application and from these principles to arrive at guidelines for the organization of successful learning within post-compulsory education.

5.2 | LEARNERS

Of all the characteristics that affect a learner's achievements within post-compulsory education, it is perhaps their level of *self-esteem* which is the most influential. Learning and performance is significantly affected by the students' views of their own self-worth and this predisposition towards achievement or failure will already have been established long before they arrive in your classroom. Interaction with parents, friends, peers and previous teachers, each of whom have offered differing levels of interest, acceptance and love, will have helped to shape how positively or negatively they regard themselves.

C5b   Self-concept summaries

Identify some examples of which you are aware, where learners have been positively and negatively affected by parents, friends, peers, employers, previous teachers, etc.

This group of 'significant others' is a valued reference group who have helped to shape the student's view of him or herself. Cooley (1912) introduced the theory of the 'looking-glass self' suggesting that one's self-concept is significantly influenced by what the individual believes others think of him. Tomatsu Shibutani (1971) considers that deliberately, intuitively or unconsciously, each of us performs for some kind of audience, not actual but conceptual. Although this influential audience may not be actually present, our conduct is oriented towards certain people whose judgement we see as important.
Bruner (1966) agrees:

> Human beings fall into a pattern that is required by the goals and activities of the social group in which they find themselves.

Mead (1934) reinforces the fact that when we adopt the behaviours that we feel our 'significant others' would accept, we are recognizing and sharing the meanings which this audience has attributed to us. This performance helps us to define ourselves as a specific role-player in a given relationship.

C5c   Significant teachers

Of all the 'significant others' we have mentioned who influence a student's self-esteem, teachers are perhaps the most influential of them all. Think in terms of your own educational experience and situation, then comment on whether you think this is so and why it should be.

It is important to note that of the three predominant groups of 'significant others' (parents, peers and teachers), only the teacher is in a *formal, systematic, institutionalized, evaluative role* during which they produce *recorded assessments* of the learner. Outside of the educational situation we can avoid assessments or rationalize them away, but once inside a formal establishment, they become official.

Where, previously, should the learner prefer not to risk any damage to her or his self-esteem by becoming involved in an exposed situation where public evaluation can take place, then there would usually be available appropriate strategies to minimize involvement.

William James (1890), a founder of research into self-concept formation, wisely pointed out:

> with no attempt there can be no failure, with no failure no humiliation. So our feeling in this world depends entirely on what we back ourselves to be and do.

Consequently lecturers in post-compulsory education are in an extremely responsible position (as are all of us teachers) where they may promote or destroy the self-esteem of each of their students according to the way they either involve or neglect them during the learning process.

We will discuss further these attribution aspects of lecturers' responses in the next section. For now we will continue to concentrate on the novice learners whose previously established attitudes will considerably influence how they perceive their teachers, colleagues and the demands of the learning within their new college.

C5d   Coping learners

Consider some of the ways in which learners, who have a relatively secure self-esteem, cope with the various college demands and requirements.

Learners with high levels of self-esteem will usually have the advantage of being able to see these important aspects of their educational situation in a positive manner and to cope with them adequately, despite the fact that they themselves may not be competent in *all* of the areas they are studying. After an initial period of evaluation they will begin to respond to their new teachers in a context-specific way, which they feel is appropriate. With formal teachers they may demonstrate the required 'academic' norms; with less formal teachers they will often establish a productive relationship and take advantage of the more flexible situation.

C5e   Low self-worth responses

Now compare the coping strategies of those who have less confidence in their self-worth.

The students with a relatively low self-esteem are less likely to be as effective in the early decisions they make about the qualities of different teachers and will often treat them uniformly as a group of 'significant others' who each have the power to affect their levels of self-worth. Because they find it difficult to differentiate between them, their response to each teacher is not necessarily always appropriate. Also, as some students grow to accept this more passive role as 'receivers' of whatever their tutors wish to present to them, they are more likely to see worthwhile and desirable knowledge as *external* to themselves. They often perceive the learning they value as being possessed and dispensed verbally by 'respected academics'. Burns (1982) again observed that:

> In traditional classrooms verbal intelligence has generally been recognised as the major, if not the sole basis for determining who is capable and likely to succeed. Teachers in these classrooms have generally failed to teach children to recognise, use and value their other skills and abilities. Consequently, many children who are not in the top quarter in verbal intelligence feel that they are incapable and are virtually doomed to failure.

Although Burns is referring to the compulsory sector of education, his comments apply equally to post-compulsory, where many less academic students are marginalized, despite their high levels of commitment and range of vocational skills, because of their limited verbal communication.

Related to this is the use by confident students of the *surface* approach to learning. Whereas the less confident learners may be committed to learning the knowledge 'prescribed' by their teachers because they see that as the authoritative version that they must master, the securely confident students adopt an instrumental, surface learning approach dedicated to a replication of 'prescribed' knowledge, because they see this as the simplest route to exam success.

C5f Surface approaches

Try to identify among your students those learners who stand out as being able to use 'surface' approaches to learning. Reflect on the ways in which they differ from other learners who do not use surface approaches.

A key point here is that the students with high self-esteem are able to select the most effective route to success, while those with less confidence are not aware of the alternatives. All students should be encouraged to develop their cognitive skills to reflect on particular processes and concepts and, to do this, they need to be able to take a more objective stance and to question fundamental, widely held beliefs and practices. This requires considerable confidence and independence that, very often, learners with low self-concepts have not been encouraged to develop. It seems that, in order to encourage a conceptual shift from the passive, absolute acceptance of 'external' knowledge to a more questioning, reflective, evaluative mode of operation, learners must be persuaded to believe more in themselves and less in those established processes of education which create physical and psychological barriers to their personal development.

C5g Developing self-esteem

Summarize some ideas of how students with less confidence in their abilities may be persuaded to value their contribution more.

Usher (1985) believes that we need to encourage the less confident students to move to a view that it is their *experience* of education which is of paramount importance, rather than the 'often sterile academic input'. It is our task to persuade them that reflection and the *awareness of the process of learning* have equal importance to the product and we must show that we value their prior formal and experiential learning.

The views of George Kelly and Carl Rogers have much in common with the above concerns for the learners' self-esteem and the importance of individual interpretation. Rogers (1983) is concerned with student-centred, experiential development based upon 'whole person' learning, that is intellectual, emotional and psychological. This is dependent upon the creation of an appropriate ethos characterized by friendliness and informality and a spirit of mutuality between teachers and students as participants in learning. The teacher here acts more as a facilitator providing regular and supportive feedback sessions in order to promote a conscious evaluation of the processes and serving to indicate that the learners' experiences are valued. Rogers' aim is to reduce any threat to the learner's self, so that the student is able to develop the skill to judge the value of the learning experience that has been provided. Only when learners can perceive experience in this differentiated fashion and relate it to their own needs will effective learning be achieved.

Kelly's (1955) constructivist view of learning often anticipates the humanistic perspective of Rogers as both share a focus on the individual and believe in active interaction with the environment as a means of structuring knowledge as a response to experience. Kelly also shares a holistic view of learning and considers that the development of knowledge is not so much a process of 'accretion' (i.e. merely adding to previous knowledge) but, more importantly, is process of *restructuring* previous knowledge as a consequence of learning received during a new experience. Rogers and Kelly also believe that existing concepts should be challenged by planned experiences so that new and more appropriate ideas may be developed.

C5h Challenging experiences

Consider one of your areas of teaching and think about the stereotypical notions which many students bring to their studies. Take one such perspective and consider what sort of educational experience you could plan which would challenge their preconceptions and make them reconsider their present ideas.

The ideas of 'self-directed learners' that were developed by Malcolm Knowles (1984) clearly relate to the work of Kelly and Rogers. Knowles compared andragogy (adult learning) with the more familiar pedagogy which, in his view, places too much of the responsibility for learning with the teacher or the institution, i.e. setting goals, determining the curriculum and using more authoritarian and didactic teaching methods. Knowles preferred to promote andragogical methods where responsibility is shared and the role of the teacher is more facilitative and, as a consequence, the learners are more responsive and participative. Knowles had a considerable influence on adult education and the current development and use of 'learner contracts' owes a great deal to his push towards increasing learner autonomy.

Our examination so far of the relationship between the individual person and learning does have obvious limitations as it is biased towards a humanist/constructivist standpoint and seriously neglects a *behaviourist* perspective. However, we may usefully draw from the above brief discussion the following *five principles*, to which we will add during this chapter, so that we may arrive at a composite review of the implications for post-compulsory education of relevant learning theory.

Practitioners should ensure that:

1. each learner's prior learning and experience is valued
2. where possible, any threat to the learners' self-esteem is removed
3. the purpose of the provided learning is understood by the learners
4. students are encouraged to become aware of their own learning processes
5. the development of learners' independent thinking is encouraged

5.3 | TEACHERS

Very often lecturers have a predilection for teaching in a style similar to the way they themselves were taught and their chosen approach will usually have a bias towards either student- or teacher-centredness.

Carl Rogers (ibid.) points out that often the self-esteem held by a teacher will influence how he or she will teach and those with a self-perception of relatively low worth will find security in an authoritarian style. Those with more confidence will allow the learners increasing participation in the organization and evaluation of learning experiences.

Rogers, along with Kelly, emphasizes repeatedly the importance of providing learning experiences that allow the students to develop their own concepts through the construction of their own interpretations, which will be related to their own needs. Bruner and Gagne would also stress a real consideration of the learner's conceptual development, but Gagne's theories would be more at home within a didactic approach than an experiential mode.

Robert Gagne (1985) groups together all factors influencing learning through his discussion on the 'conditions of learning' where he states that the changes brought about by learning are related to the situations in which they occur. He divides these conditions into two types. Firstly, there are the conditions *internal* to the learner and he suggests that we find evidence of these from studying his or her existing capabilities. Second are the *external* conditions, which he considers to be any exterior factors that may influence or initiate learning.

Gagne provides a taxonomy of learning in the form of a hierarchy moving from attitudes through motor skills, verbal information and cognitive strategies to intellectual skills including discriminations, formal concepts and developing rules. He analyses each learning category in detail and suggests appropriate learning methods. However, he does not say that a given learning task can be related to one of his categories. He believes that the task itself must be analysed into steps to reveal its procedural characteristics, which are a series of sub-tasks that must be performed in a particular order. This process produces a number of instructional objectives, which represent the whole task.

C5i Procedural analysis

Take one reasonably small learning task which you use in your teaching and analyse it into sub-tasks as suggested by Gagne. Place these in order of completion and identify the instructional objectives which you must achieve to ensure the student is able to understand the whole task.

Morris Bigge (1982) summarizing Gagne's approach to teaching states that:

> instruction means arranging the proper conditions of learning that are external to the learner. These proper external conditions include the teacher communicating verbally with the student to inform him of what he is to achieve, reminding him of what he already knows, directing his attention and actions and guiding his thinking along certain lines.

A further three principles may be drawn from Gagne's work. Practitioners should ensure that:

6. learners are stimulated to recall previously learned capabilities
7. the desired mental sets of the learner are activated
8. the learner receives appropriate feedback from the teacher

Bigge (ibid.) believes that Gagne is not sympathetic to experiential learning as he proposes *providing* student problems rather than allowing their negotiation and development and Bigge notes that:

> the discussion class is not primarily concerned with learning at all, but with transfer (generalising) of what has already been learned .... To get learning to happen is still the basic problem. The conditions that bring learning about are not those of the discussion class.

Although Gagne has much in common with Bruner with regard to the importance of developing the appropriate mental 'sets', they differ considerably with regard to the experimental dimension.

Jerome Bruner (1966) sees learning as involving three almost simultaneous processes. First, there is the acquisition of new information, which could either be the refinement of existing knowledge, or perhaps it may run totally counter to current beliefs. The second characteristic Bruner proposes is the transformation of knowledge, which takes place when learners manipulate what is known in order to address new problems. In this way the student goes beyond what is known in a creative manner making assumptions about untried situations by extrapolating from accepted knowledge. The final stage takes place when the learner checks the 'pertinence and adequacy' of gained information through an evaluation of its usefulness in relation to the current problem or task. This cognitive growth Bruner labels 'instrumental conceptualism' and is based on two tenets:

a) a person's knowledge of the world is based on his constructed models of reality
b) such models are first adopted from one's culture, then they are adapted to one's individual use

During the perceptual process, a learner will form a hypothesis as to what the incoming stimulus is. This process is based on previous experience and involves making an inferential leap. Bruner believes that the process of learning involves *enactive, iconic* and *symbolic* modes of representation. A learner's representations collectively constitute his model of reality. The *enactive mode* occurs when a learner does not require imagery or words to represent learning, but achieves it through motor responses. For example, a child *enactively* knows how to ride a bike or tie a knot. *Iconic* representation takes place when a learner uses internal imagery to represent categories of events, and Bruner believes that this mode of representation is usually at its height when a child is between the ages of five and seven and is extremely dependent upon personal sensory images.

The final mode of representation, the *symbolic*, is the most relevant to post-compulsory education. Approaching and during adolescence, language becomes increasingly important and gradually the learner moves from a preference for sensory imagery to an increasing use of *symbolic representation*. Language, the most used of these abstract forms, enables a person to manipulate real or imagined concepts, to solve problems and to evaluate. This is the basis for reflective thought mentioned earlier in this essay during the discussion on self-concept.

Bruner too places great importance on the negative effect of weakened self-images in students:

> the one most pervasive thing that prevents man from reaching his full potential is a lack of confidence not only in his own capacities but also in the ability to develop them further.

Bruner believes that, in order to improve their confidence, students should be encouraged to see the value of their own perceptual ability. Bruner also sees great value in developing students' *problem-solving skills* through their ability to transform acquired knowledge to new situations. He feels that being confronted with materials and problems should motivate students. Through their own manipulation of these phenomena the students become more independent learners and develop their own value-system through understanding when they are right and when they are wrong. This independence and self-appraisal demands intellectual honesty. Bruner believes that this development may be promoted through experiential learning:

> discovery, whether by a schoolboy going through it on his own or by a scientist cultivating the growing edge of his field, is in its essence a matter of rearranging or transforming evidence in such a way that one is enabled to go beyond the evidence ... to new additional insights.

From Bruner's writings the following further four principles may be extracted. Practitioners should ensure that:

9. they share the process of learning with learners in order to reduce the effects of culturally based resistance

10. learning is organized in order to build on previous learning (e.g. the spiral curriculum)

11. learning is clearly structured to show relationships and continuity

12. problem-solving techniques are used to challenge previous perceptions

David Ausubel (1965) shares with Bruner the view that it is important that teachers promote conceptual structures, but he does not agree with any over-emphasis on discovery learning. Ausubel argues that much instruction, particularly at higher levels of education, is (and always has been) successfully performed by the process of exposition leading to meaningful reception learning. He is concerned with the value of didactic methods arguing that it is not possible for a learner to have the time to rediscover the whole of the intended curriculum and that, in any case, experiential learning does involve reception learning, it is merely the style of presentation which differs.

Ausubel believes that proponents of discovery learning often confuse reception learning with rote learning and discovery learning with meaningful learning. The popular misconception, he believes, is that discovery learning is automatically meaningful and that reception learning automatically involves rote methods. Ausubel agrees that rote learning is *not* a route to understanding and because of the discrete, compartmentalized nature often results in a lack of retention. He believes that long-term learning is often achieved through presentational style methods, which are appropriate to meaningful reception learning. This involves relating new material to previous conceptual structures and Ausubel feels that only up to the age of eleven or twelve is experiential learning necessary in order to build up these schemata.

Ausubel has much in common with Bruner in his views that subsequently learners begin to move to a more symbolic means of representation where they are increasingly able to manipulate abstract concepts. Ausubel stresses the importance of using 'advanced organisers' to facilitate the reception of related concepts and principles. These organizers are substantive structures or schemata, which are stable and discernible from related conceptual systems.

> These organisers are introduced in advance of the learning material itself, are for-
> mulated in terms that are already familiar to the learner, and are also presented at a
> higher level of abstractness, generality and inclusiveness.

C5j   Advanced organizer

Identify a discrete area of learning which you present to your students and plan a structure which would help them to see the relationship between the component parts, for example, a 'tree' of ideas or steps in a process.

Ausubel explains in detail how a well-designed organizer acts as a 'subsumer' in that it is able to subsume a great number of related concepts or principles. It is this 'tree' of understanding on which many concepts are hung which enables the learner to successfully manipulate abstract hypotheses on the way to solving related problems. As problems are solved, new concepts emerge, related rules of operation are developed and that particular 'tree' is enlarged.

Ausubel is highly critical of curriculum designers and authors who, despite this psychological evidence, structure content in discrete categories which do not draw out their relationship to the gestalt of the overarching conceptual system. From Ausubel's discussion three additional principles may be added to our list.

Practitioners should ensure that:

13. meaningful reception learning is used in order to develop existing conceptual systems

14. teaching is organized around concepts and principles which potentially have the widest explanatory power, inclusiveness, generalizability and reliability to the chosen content

15. a sequence of presentation is selected which best illustrates the characteristics of the chosen cognitive structure in terms of clarity, stability and integratedness

Although Ausubel is primarily concerned with cognitive processes he does often use behaviourist explanations for the process of learning. The behaviourists, on the other hand, consider the structure of internal thinking and learning processes as irrelevant to the process of instruction. Their concern, as exemplified by B.F. Skinner (1938), is for the structuring of the environment in such a way as to maximize the probability of the desired new behaviour being learnt. These desired behaviours are taught by a series of successive approximations, which begin with an already established behaviour and work towards the learning objective.

The process is based on the principle of reinforcement expounded by Skinner which was a more precise restatement of Thorndike's (1931) law of effect. This law of effect states the observed phenomenon that behaviour, which produces desirable or pleasant effects, tends to be repeated. Skinner helped to develop this classical conditioning theory relating to voluntary behaviour and recognized two different kinds of learning:

> *Respondent behaviour* is elicited by specific stimuli and given that stimulus the required response occurs automatically. This follows the pattern of classical conditioning where a new stimulus is paired with the one that already elicits the response and after a number of such pairings the new stimulus comes to elicit the response.

A simple example of an existing stimulus would be an animal salivating at the sight or smell of food. If this is deliberately paired with the sound of a bell, eventually the animal will salivate on hearing the sound. However, Skinner maintained that most behaviour is of a different sort, which he refers to as:

> *Operant behaviour.* The characteristics which differentiate operant behaviour from respondent behaviour is that it operates on the environment to secure particular consequences. There is no specific stimulus that can be identified which will consistently elicit an operant response.

Skinner speaks of operant behaviour as being emitted by the person or organism rather than elicited by stimuli. Most behaviour is of this sort – walking, talking, working and playing are all made up of operant responses. Skinner does not mean to say that operant behaviour is not influenced by stimuli (and much of his analysis of behaviour is brought under the control of stimuli) and that such control is only partial and conditional. For example, the operant response of reaching for food is not simply elicited by the sight of food; it also depends on hunger, social circumstances and a variety of other stimulus conditions. In these respects it is in contrast to the jerking back of one's hand from a hot stove in a respondent manner which would, of course, be elicited almost without regard to other conditions.

Because of this distinction, Skinner does not consider it useful to think of operant behaviour as made up of specific stimulus-response connections in the sense that respondent behaviour is. He concentrates instead on the fact that if an operant response (sometimes referred to just as an operant) occurs and is followed by reinforcement, its probability of occurring again increases. So even though the actual stimulus or stimuli for an operant is uncertain, if it is followed by a reward it is likely that the response will occur again.

Operant behaviour and the resulting patterns of learning are Skinner's chief concern. Series of operants become organized into a chain, for example, a person rising from an armchair to switch on the television set. Each of the steps in the process may be seen as individual operants, but the whole may be considered to be a single operant because it is the chain of responses which will be reinforced by the reward of sitting back and enjoying a television programme. This would be considered to be positive reinforcement. If, however, the television programme should have some kind of irritating content (perhaps a poor presenter), then the viewer will often switch off the set. This removal of the irritant (a negative reinforcer) could be considered to be a reward.

Thus a response can be reinforced either by presenting a *positive reinforcer* (the enjoyment of television viewing) or by removing a negative one (the irritating content). Both types of reinforcers may be conditioned. If a stimulus occurs repeatedly with a positive reinforcer that reinforcer tends itself to acquire the capacity to reinforce behaviour; this is called a conditioned positive reinforcer. For example, the title of a previously enjoyed television programme in a newspaper schedule of the evening's entertainment would be associated with pleasure and would lend to an anticipation of switching on the television in readiness for the broadcast. Conversely, the description of a disliked programme would lead to avoidance and is acting as a *conditioned negative reinforcer*.

C5k   *Positive and negative reinforcers*

Identify a student behaviour you wish to encourage and then suggest both a positive and a negative reinforcer that it would be appropriate to use to stimulate this behavioural response. Add your own comments on the relative value of these suggested reinforcers.

Skinner believes that a learner will rarely perform the target behaviour without having to be trained towards it. The teacher must gradually mould the students' behaviour to the desired learning outcome. This is done by the teacher's employing *shaping*, through reinforcing that behaviour which successively approximates toward the desired outcome. Behaviour that is not reinforced gradually stops. This is known as *extinction*. From these behaviourist concepts a further five principles may be drawn:

Practitioners should ensure that:

16. learning is regularly rewarded during the early stages that should consist of short steps. In later stages variable reinforcement is preferable in order to avoid extinction

17. reward quickly follows the appropriate response. Motivation is increased by immediate feedback

18. desirable behaviour is reinforced and unwanted behaviour is, as far as possible, ignored (since attention can often be a strong reinforcer). Emphasis should be on praising and encouraging desirable behaviour and not on punishing undesirable behaviour. Undesirable behaviour should, as far as possible, be extinguished

19. negative reinforcement is used with care even though it is preferable to punishment. Punishment should not be used since it often has emotional side-effects (anxiety inhibits learning) and will produce avoidance behaviour (learners start missing lessons)

20. lessons are carefully planned in order to encourage desired behaviours by eliciting necessary responses through appropriate reinforcers

Obviously, behaviourist approaches have proved to be extremely valuable to education and training over the past fifty years and are still very much in evidence within the many national Standards we have today. However, some critics would point out that, when we attempt to disaggregate more sophisticated skills into behavioural outcomes, it often proves impossible to articulate clearly the nuances of the range of complex outcomes that are involved. Also, when several psycho-motor responses are occurring simultaneously (such as learning to drive a car) it is difficult (and even dangerous) to attempt to shape them using Skinnerian procedures.

As Bigge points out:

> Reinforcing the learner for each successive approximation to the final correct use of each of the controls would not only be maddeningly slow, it would also give little assurance that the learner would survive the training course, considering how a person would be likely to drive who had achieved only a first approximation to mastery of the steering wheel and brake!

The fact that a learner can observe and imitate an experienced practitioner who is also providing verbal instructions and interpretations greatly increases the speed of learning. Bandura and Walter (1963) expanded this concept of modelling (which is, in fact, a sophisticated form of imitation) and discussed the process of 'identification,' where the learner is trying as well as possible to be the other person. Bandura and Walter talk about two other forms of imitation, *inhibition* or *disinhibition* of already learnt responses and the eliciting of an already learnt response.

In the case of inhibition, a learner sees from observing others that a learnt response is not appropriate in that context and conversely disinhibition involves a situation where a learner, who has understood from previous experience that certain behaviour is not acceptable, now sees others exhibiting that previously unacceptable behaviour and realizes that constraints have been removed. Teachers hope that inhibition by observation will take place when they reprimand a student for being disruptive and then other students will also learn what the desired behaviour is. Disinhibition occurs where the disruptive students persuade others to abandon their previous inhibitions and become disruptive.

C5l *Inhibitive action*

Discuss a situation where you have tried to inhibit undesirable behaviour by reprimanding an individual student. Comment on the success or otherwise of your strategy and suggest how you might develop this process.

The third manner in which imitation can operate is through the eliciting of an already learnt response. This occurs in a situation where the observation of a model of behaviour (such as painting) creates a positive desire in others to join in the activity. Depending on how the teacher responds to the displaying of particular behaviour, vicarious reinforcement will take place. The giving of rewards (i.e. displaying the resultant work of art) will increase the likelihood of the observer imitating the behaviour and the handing out of punishment will make it more likely that the observer will refrain from imitation.

A great deal of social behaviour is learned through modelling or reciprocal interaction with the teacher and his or her students operating as personal, behavioural and environmental determinants of one another's behaviours. Bandura has lent a cognitive focus to behaviourist principles through the notion of vicarious reinforcement and has included humanist concerns by stressing the importance of a learner's self-efficacy. Bandura's work provides another three principles.

Practitioners should ensure that:

21. behaviours and tasks which the students are expected to learn are modelled, preferably by them. For example, being punctual, showing enthusiasm or taking a critically reflective stance

22. students are aware that desirable behaviour is being reinforced

23. students are also used as models. For example, during group work, pair the confident, successful students with those who are less successful and try to build a mutually supportive relationship

5.4 | GROUP LEARNING

During the previous discussions in this chapter the presumption has been that, although we are debating learning strategies for cohorts of students, we have been considering *individual* responses. Although many of the theories we have discussed have real relevance to both individual and group performance, we have not, so far, considered collective responses, nor the effect that the dynamics of a group may have on individual members. This may be due to the fact that during a time when so much emphasis has been placed on 'individual striving', concern for the processes within all manner of social and economic 'collectives' has diminished. Nevertheless, groups do exist and provide an experience for members, which is subtly different to an isolated perspective. As Asch (1956) pointed out:

> We need a way of understanding group processes that retains the prime reality of the individual and group, the two permanent poles of all social processes.

Large and small student groups are an inevitable feature in the majority of educational situations. We have all been either members of short-term learning groups (at a conference for example) or have belonged to a cohort of students who have been together for a semester or even for all three years of an undergraduate programme. Our experiences within such contrasting learning collectives are likely to be very different because, for example, the purpose, the quality of the relationships and the commitment of the members will vary so widely. However, in retrospect, it will be the particular nature of these relationships that will remain in the memory long after the subject being studied has been forgotten.

It is safe to say that the majority of people will appreciate that learning within a group is usually a much richer experience than learning in isolation. Not necessarily more rewarding but, coloured as it will be by the many interactions at all the differing levels, it will be an experience that is dense in detail and contains many surprising and often subtle insights.

C5m   Rich learning experiences

Try to identify a rewarding group learning experience and summarize all the details you can recall about the situation and the nature of the learning. Say why you think this incident has remained so clearly in your memory.

5.5 | GROUP DYNAMICS

Usually a group of people gathered together for a particular purpose will very quickly develop characteristics of its own as, through the initial interactions, the members begin to evolve a role with which they feel comfortable. Our discussions earlier in this chapter about the 'significant other' and levels of self-esteem have important parts to play in this process. The dynamics of this process are themselves fascinating and a great deal of research has analysed these interactions and the range of roles which members assume or have ascribed to them.

Belbin (1981) suggested *eight* different roles with which individuals can identify and, given the opportunity, would choose for themselves. Although Belbin was referring to an employment context, his conceptualization of group processes has much relevance to education and his role descriptions give an insight into the complexity *and the potential for learning* of the dynamics existing within most groups.

Each group role within Belbin's categories has a different function to perform which is compatible with the individual's abilities and their current disposition towards the task in hand and the other members. Belbin characterized these roles as follows and argued that a successful team must contain many, if not all, of these contributors:

- *Company worker.* This team member is practical, organized and reliable and has the capacity to turn ideas into actions and see them carried out.
  Characteristics: practical, methodical, organized, not easily discouraged, but may flounder in times of change.

- *Team worker.* This person is sensitive, sociable and supporting and brings to a group the capacity to foster team spirit by supporting other members.
  Characteristics: helps communication, builds on ideas, counters friction, likeable and popular, dislikes personal confrontation, but may seem 'soft' to some members.

- *Chairperson.* This person is seen as calm, self-controlled and self-confident. They strive to get the team working together to produce results.
  Characteristics: clarifies, coordinates, is disciplined, probes, listens, brings out the best in people, but is not particularly creative or innovative.

- *Plant.* This person may be unorthodox, serious and individualistic as they suggest new ideas and strategies to solve problems.

Characteristics: innovative, imaginative, creative thinker, pays special attention to major issues, may be radical at times but can make careless mistakes on detail and may respond poorly to criticism.

- *Completer/Finisher.* This member is conscientious, detail-conscious and delivers on time. Will take care that details are not overlooked and that pace is maintained.
  Characteristics: checks detail, meets deadlines, relentlessly follows through, dislikes a vague approach, but can get 'bogged down'.

- *Monitor/Evaluator.* This team member is highly analytical and objective. Uses judgement to evaluate team ideas, analyse problems arising and critique contributions.
  Characteristics: analytical, 'feet on the ground', good judgement, assimilates and assesses data, but can lack tact and fail to accept new ideas.

- *Resource investigator.* This member is enthusiastic and curious. Often an extrovert who is externally orientated which allows him/her to create and develop outside contracts to help the team progress.
  Characteristics: energetic and positive, has masses of contacts, follows interests, goes outside of the team for information and ideas, but may be poor on follow-through and can be elusive.

- *Shaper.* This person is outgoing and dynamic and seeks to direct the team and get the desired results.
  Characteristics: dominant and extrovert, they challenge and respond to challenge. They give shape to a discussion, but can be seen as arrogant and abrasive, impulsive or impatient.

C5n   Group roles

Think of a fairly well established group that you teach and try to identify where members have taken on one of the roles described by Belbin. Are there other roles that members have assumed in addition to Belbin's categories?

It is often useful to look at the composition of the groups with which you work and also to consider the type of person you are yourself in relation to the groups within which you function. As a member of a course team, do you have preferred functions or particular characteristics, which either suggest you for a role or let you slip into one? As you will have noted above, in addition to showing how various roles may contribute to successful outcomes for the group, Belbin was also able to identify how potential characteristics have significant disadvantages that may inhibit the progress of the group.

C5o   Counterproductive characteristics

At the end of most of his role descriptions above, Belbin has added a qualification which identifies potential weaknesses or problems with that particular role characteristic. Give some examples of such problems which you have encountered and how you have dealt with them.

Of course, this aspect of group dynamics is both the strength and the potential weakness of collective operation. Even though they may be reluctant to admit to it, as well as their positive qualities, members will usually also have areas where their performance could be stronger. For example, the person in the role Belbin describes as 'Plant' is good at innovative thinking, but careless when dealing with detail. These characteristics may well create internal dispute when the group is working under stress.

Part of your responsibility will be to encourage your learner group members to 'play to their strengths' and, in so doing, compensate for those less proficient in this particular role. In this way, the collective has more resources than the individual.

5.6 GROUP PRODUCTIVITY

Given that a group has more potential for achievement than an individual learner, it is important that the achievement of this anticipated, enhanced performance is monitored. Douglas (1992) examined groups from a *performance* point of view and suggested a number of activities which he feels groups perform more successfully than individuals:

- tasks requiring a division of labour
- producing a *range* of solutions to a problem
- using resources efficiently
- social motivation
- increased productivity
- arriving at superior judgements during tasks involving random error
- sustaining tenacity of purpose
- providing involvement, participation and a high level of commitment

However, the group's *social* processes may well inhibit the group's *potential* productivity, creating what Steiner (1972) termed *group deficit*. This occurs because groups are very seldom able to utilize their resources to the full because there are often losses due to processes within the group, which impede the group's maximum attainment.

> ### C5p   Facilitating group productivity
> Again consider your own group of students, which you identified in activity C5n above, and identify the social interactions and processes that may affect the total performance of the group.

It can be argued that groups exist on two levels: *the task for which the group comes together* and *the hidden tasks and activities* or the social relationships which are an integral part of everyday group interaction. The quality of verbal and non-verbal interactions will help to determine the effectiveness of the group, but members will need to spend as much time listening as they spend talking. As you can imagine, for some this is a serious challenge! Being sensitive to the feelings of others is also crucial during the development of a collaborative climate and will be one of the determinants when establishing the norms of acceptable behaviour.

Another key dimension is 'crowd behaviour'. Individuals should not become so overwhelmed by more dominant members that they are unable to express themselves and so relinquish the power to make decisions to others, consequently forgoing their own individual rights and responsibilities. Obviously, if a person's role is diminished in this way it will create ongoing resentment, which may fester for a while before erupting in angry confrontation.

C5q Managing conflict

Similar conflicts to the above can arise from the personal differences of individuals and from different role expectation. Identify ways that your groups manage this sort of conflict themselves and the situations where you need to use your skills to manage it on their behalf.

Addressing such problems, Hackman and Morris (1978) and other theorists concerned with group processes, believe that group 'deficit' (i.e. not achieving their potential) occurs when groups are left to work 'spontaneously' through a task. In other words, insufficient attempts have been made to improve the *facilitatory* processes such as effective communication, decision-making and action planning. Obviously, facilitating the optimum performance from a group of learners is the responsibility of the teacher, trainer or support worker. Commonly conflict may be dealt with through:

- *avoidance* – redirecting the focus of the situation to more positive aspects, i.e. what *has* been achieved
- *defusion* – reducing the cause of the problem, i.e. indicating misunderstandings or taking responsibility for part of the confusion
- *confrontation* – challenging consistently inappropriate behaviour or malicious practice, i.e. as a last resort when all other forms of persuasion have been of no avail

For a group to function effectively its members must agree on mutual roles and norms of behaviour. Each member needs to make a contribution and, although individual members will subordinate their own needs to those of the group, this should not result in these needs being totally submerged. Other factors, which affect interpersonal interaction in groups, are:

- *distractions* – both internal and external, psychological and physical
- *irrelevant topics* – learners can easily wander, or be drawn into topics which are irrelevant or out of context
- *domination* – group members who are over-dominating can affect the behaviour and performance of others within the group
- *reluctance* – a reluctant learner can bring with them a set of issues which cause disruption and need to be addressed

Belbin's concepts and those of Hackman and Morris add two more principles to add to our list.

Practitioners should ensure that:

24. when forming learning groups they are aware of the personal characteristics of members and their influence on the dynamics of the group

25. effective group operation is facilitated by developing or providing skills and resources

5.7 | EXPERIENTIAL LEARNING

Because by its very nature group learning is *experiential*, our previous discussion has led us into our penultimate teaching and learning technique of this chapter. Traditionally within post-compulsory education the balance between theory and practice has been heavily influenced by the predominant educational context. Within workshops, laboratories, etc., learning has been essentially 'on-the-job', practical and experiential in nature, while in the classroom learning would often be related to theory taught in a didactic manner.

These two approaches are not, of course, mutually exclusive and represent either end of the spectrum of learning processes. The teacher/facilitator would settle at a point along this continuum that adequately satisfied both personal preferences and the demands of the learning situation. Usually, the introduction of theory would be followed by appropriate opportunities for application and practical experience would be accompanied by reference to underlying concepts and principles.

However, the present concern to promote more active learning across all subjects does not depend, as it once did, upon the nature of the task in hand or the actual *content* of the curriculum. Previously, in most cases, academic theory would automatically be presented through lectures, seminars and tutorials, and practical skills through demonstration, drill and practice. Both of these delivery methods would be directed towards an audience who, although receptive, would also usually be quite passive.

C5r Attitudes to learning

Summarize how students' attitudes to learning may be affected by sessions delivered in the conventional, didactic manner described above.

As we discussed earlier (see 2.3 in Chapter 2) learners receiving a conventional, didactic presentation will respond in what William Perry (1970) describes as either the 'absolutist' or the 'relativist' mode, that is, either believing implicitly in the content, or considering *all* theory to be ephemeral and transient and therefore not worth the trouble of learning.

These attitudes would usually lead to either rote or surface learning designed only to meet the needs of assessment. Very few students would progress to what Perry describes as 'commitment', where learners develop their own values which allows them to make judgements about the relative worth of the expert view compared to their own active participation.

On the other hand, students involved in the development of practical skills would often not be encouraged to reflect on their learning or to consider how processes could be developed and their skills transferred to other areas.

C5s   Experiential implementation

Describe how you could move from the traditional instructional approach you analysed in activity C5r to a more experiential approach.

The purpose of experiential learning is to transcend the limitations discussed above. It is equally concerned with theoretical and practical subjects and can successfully address learner development within each of the hierarchies defined by Bloom and his colleagues – the cognitive, affective and psycho-motor.

This approach has been derived from the work of Kurt Lewin (1952) who had a considerable influence on post-war group psychology. 'Experience' is stressed in the name given to his perspective of learning, partially to highlight its link to the work of Dewey and Piaget but also, as David Kolb (1984) explained:

> to emphasise the central role that experience plays in the learning process. This differentiates experiential learning theory from rationalist and other cognitive theories of learning that tend to give primary emphasis to acquisition, manipulation and recall of abstract symbols, and from behavioural learning theories that deny any role for consciousness and subjective experience in the learning process.

Kolb stresses that experiential learning is a holistic, integrated perspective. It is essentially student-centred, involving as it does the intellectual, emotional and psychological development of the learner. Central to these ideas is the process of *meta-learning* or learning about learning. This need not only to learn about the learning process, but also for learners to take on the responsibility for their own learning, is graphically captured in Lewin's (1952) experiential model, which has since been further developed by Honey and Mumford (1982) and Kolb (1984):

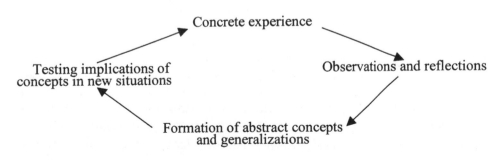

An important feature of the Lewinian model is that there is an emphasis on current, *concrete experiences* as a basis for the assimilation of later more abstract concepts. This immediately places value on the internal, personal experience of the learner and reduces the traditional classroom focus on the knowledge of the 'expert' (teacher or textbook) which, because it is external to the learner, may affect their perception of their role, moving it from an active involvement in the development of knowledge to a passive acceptance of the knowledge provided.

In addition, the cycle of operation provides the opportunity for *feedback* on the concrete experience, firstly from observations, which are reflected on in order to develop theories. These are then tested so as to identify new approaches and experiences. Simply put, the learner, having done something, reviews its effectiveness, develops ideas on how to do it better, and then tries out the modified approach.

The important point made by Lewin and Kolb is that many people have experiences and do not learn from them. It is the reflective processes that enable the memorizing and the learning that are so important. From these meta-cognitive deliberations emerge concepts and generalizations which allow the ideas to be developed and transferred to other contexts. Similarly, it would not be sufficient merely to learn concepts and generalize them in the abstract. These theories must be tested out in the actual situation to enable the learner to establish the links between theory and practice by working through the cycle of theory, experiment, experience and reflection.

C5t   The importance of experience

Given the above explanations of the importance of the experiential cycle, relate the cycle of theory/experiment/experience/reflection to your own subject and your own learners. Make notes about how you can use this process to help the students to respond in an active manner, owning the learning rather than responding passively to tutor input.

Of course, introducing experiential approaches can be problematic within an educational culture which is primarily concerned with the achievement of accountability outcomes; it may be difficult to create the opportunity for students to understand the value of learning about their own learning and through this meta-cognition being able to recognize that the *quality* of learning is heavily dependent upon the context in which it takes place. For example, surface learning (which can be successfully employed to achieve good assessment results) may not lead to the deeper levels of personal and academic insights which are so satisfying and long-lasting.

Obviously, not all experiences will be conducive or relevant to learning and consequently, as teachers, we are responsible for the selection and organization of appropriate learner activities. Ideally the learner should have some involvement in this planning process but, because they will not always have the prior learning necessary to make informed decisions, it will often be a shared activity between facilitator and learner. Knowles (1975) makes the point that:

> The function of planning consists of translating diagnosed needs into specific educational objectives (or dimensions of growth), designing and conducting learning experiences to achieve these objectives, and evaluating the extent to which these objectives have been accomplished. In andragogy, responsibility for performing this function is a mutual one between the learners and the teacher.

Learning from experience may be gained through learner interaction in the context of group processes organized around such activities as buzz groups, fish bowl exercises, shout-outs, syndicates, encounter groups, etc. Even more elaborate interaction-based learning exercises using designed materials and equipment could involve role-play, simulations and games.

C5u Learning for life

Although the above activities do create group interaction, how effective do you feel that they can be in encouraging students to develop the ability to transfer their learning to other situations, perhaps even beyond the classroom?

The type of activities we have suggested above may be seen as 'active' learning which is an improvement on passive, receptive learning. Even so Reg Revans (1980), the inventor of 'action learning', would have concerns that although simulations do allow learners to run through various important interactions, they lack the crucial dimension of *responsibility* that is inevitably present in real experiences. Revans promoted the concept of 'comrades in adversity', which occurs when colleagues, faced with difficulty within a work situation, solve the problem *collaboratively*, and stressed that taking responsibility in this way developed crucial context-based learning which is not present when the issue is solved either by an authoritarian management decision or the employment of an external consultant.

The theories of Lewin, Kolb and Revans add three more to our principle categories.

Practitioners should ensure that:

26. the learners' previous experiences are valued

27. no matter at which point they commence, students should move through each step of the learning cycle

28. students should be encouraged to take responsibility for their own learning

Experiential education then, is not merely about learning by doing, but is essentially about the learner both identifying the need to develop and then taking on responsibility for their own learning to meet a particular objective. This brings us to this chapter's final example of theory in practice, 'collaborative learning', which is another aspect of the same experiential debate.

5.8 GROUP COLLABORATION

David Johnson and Roger Johnson (1990), who have carried out extensive and detailed research into the relationship between learning and cognition in *co-operative* and *competitive* educational situations, have shown absolutely categorically that collaborative learning is by far the superior method. Their findings raise serious questions about our preference for competitive arrangements within both education and the workplace. To Johnson and Johnson *cooperative learning* involves small groups of students working together to maximize their own and each other's learning. Within such groups, students are given *two* responsibilities –

to learn the required material and to make sure that *all* other members of the group do likewise. The success of individual students is measured by their *own* achievement and the achievements of *all* other group members.

The researchers believe that simply placing students in groups and instructing them to work together does not, in itself, promote higher achievement or higher level reasoning because there are many different ways in which the learning can fail. In order to be productive, cooperative learning groups must be structured to include the essential elements of *positive interdependence,* i.e. each member can succeed only if all members succeed. The positive interdependence is facilitated by *face-to-face interaction* during which learners assist and support each other's efforts to achieve *individual accountability*, which ensures that all members do their fair share of the work.

In addition, Johnson and Johnson facilitate the development of the *interpersonal and small group skills* which are required to work cooperatively with others and the *group processing awareness* which helps members to reflect on how well they are working together and how their effectiveness as a group may be improved.

It is useful to compare these collaborative learning processes with what Johnson and Johnson term *individualistic* learning. In a *competitive* learning situation individual students work against each other to achieve grades that only a few students can attain and consequently, within such a situation, students seek an outcome which is *personally* beneficial and ignore as irrelevant the efforts and achievements of other students. Crucially, according to the theories of Johnson and Johnson, the *interpersonal interactions* that promote cognition and metacognition (thinking about thinking) *do not take place*.

In many hundreds of studies which have taken place in the USA and elsewhere during the last 20 years, cooperative learning experiences have promoted *higher achievement* than competitive and individualistic learning. Achievements which indicated this success are the quality of reasoning strategies, the generation of new ideas and solutions, and the transfer of what is learned to other situations. Apparently, the more conceptual the task, the more problem-solving that is required, the more creative the answers need to be, the more long-term retention is desired, the greater the superiority of cooperation over competitive and indivi-dualistic learning.

Within performance situations where considerable advantage is given to learners who

a) engage in critical, higher-level thinking
b) know what thinking strategies they are using
c) modify their strategies to perform better in different situations

the following reasons are given by Johnson and Johnson for the success of co-operative learning strategies:

1. The expectations among learners that they will have to summarize, explain and teach what they are learning has a direct effect on the learning processes they use. The manner in which students conceptualize material and organize it cognitively is different when they are learning material to teach to others compared to when they are only learning for their own benefit.

2. Discussion within cooperative learning situations promotes on the part of the learners more frequent oral summarizing, explaining and elaborating of what one knows. This oral rehearsal promotes long-term retention.

3. Cooperative learning groups thrive on the heterogeneity of group members. As they accommodate themselves to each other's perspectives, strategies and approaches to completing their assignments, divergent and creative thinking are stimulated. This is especially so the more divergent the group members are.

4. In most cooperative learning situations, students with incomplete information interact with others who have different perspectives and facts. In order to understand all the relevant information gained by everyone involved, students must actively attempt to understand the content being presented and the cognitive and affective perspectives of the person presenting it. They must also at the same time evaluate the relationship of these ideas to their own and other's beliefs. It is their ability to understand other perspectives which enables the use of the wide range of information available.

5. Cooperative learning group members must externalize their ideas and reasoning for critical examination by their peers. As a result, there is often significant monitoring and regulation of learners' thinking and reasoning. This contrasts with individuals working in isolation who often get involved in a lengthy and aimless wild goose chase.

6. Within cooperative learning groups members give each other continuous feedback regarding the quality and relevance of their contributions and how performance may be improved.

7. Participation in co-operative learning groups inevitably produces conflicts among the ideas, opinions, conclusions, theories and information of members, i.e. *controversy*. Johnson and Johnson (1979) consider that the promotion of controversy is one of the most important routes to learning. In summary, because controversies are resolved by engaging in the discussion of the advantages and disadvantages of proposed actions aimed at synthesizing novel solutions, there is an advocacy and challenging of each participant's position which is based on the synthesis of both perspectives. When managed constructively, controversy promotes uncertainty about the correctness of one's views, an active search for new information, a reconceptualization of one's knowledge and conclusions and, as a consequence, increased motivation to achieve and retain deeper understanding.

C5v   Collaborative learning

Try to design a learning activity for your students based on Johnson and Johnson's seven concepts. Remember, each group has a responsibility to ensure that each member not only achieves the assigned task, but is also able to explain and defend their point of view in relation to the learned content.

Johnson and Johnson's theories help us to add two final principles to complete our list.

Practitioners should ensure that:

29. they encourage collaboration by making learning a collective responsibility

30. once cooperative learning has been established, they deliberately stimulate intellectual conflict by structuring academic controversies

5.9 | BECOMING ECLECTIC

So as a basis for our eclectic approach we have now selected thirty principles from the fields of humanist, cognitive and behaviourist theory. Of course, this is not a definitive list; we have selected these principles for their generic nature and relevance to post-compulsory education. Many related principles from each of these fields, which have more currency within the compulsory sector, have been ignored. Nor have we presented any critical discussion on the relative merits of each of the psychological theories. Instead they have been left to stand alongside each other and a review of the list now does not seem to present any discordant contradictions. True there are different areas of focus, but none of the principles selected creates problems of congruence in relation to others in the list. There are many areas of overlap, more notably between the humanist and the cognitive fields, which can be tightened up in our final set of guidelines to successful lessons in post-compulsory education.

First, in order to help us arrive at a notional order, we have summarized in the following table each of the principles discussed previously and related them to the sort of action a teacher may take in order to implement them. Of course, this is only a convenient device to illustrate how principles underpin many of our routine processes. We realize that our simplistic interpretation of these complex principles will not be universally accepted in the abridged form that is presented here and in the Session Guide that follows. However, although many of the principles also underpin other teaching processes that have not been included, we feel that, on the whole, the exercise does illustrate good practice.

In the table opposite (5.1) each of the 30 principles which have been discussed above is summarized and, by way of illustration, an example is given of how it may be implemented in practice. As pointed out previously, this table presents a limited number of implementations of a particular theory; there will be many others within each different context.

5.10 | A SUGGESTED FRAMEWORK FOR SUCCESSFUL SESSIONS

The eclectic set of principles which we have collected together in the table opposite (5.1) and presented as a summary guide to successful sessions in Table 5.2 (pp. 136f.), could just as easily have been obtained, almost intuitively, from many experienced teachers without resorting to the survey of psychological theory contained in this chapter. However, the exercise has helped to identify the research behind many empirically tested and now accepted methods of delivering learning and it does indicate that a study of one particular field of psychology does not necessarily undermine principles drawn from another. As a consequence of the many variables within a teaching and learning relationship, each area of study does of necessity focus upon a particular facet. The resulting guidelines for the teaching

Table 5.1   Summary of theoretical principles translated into teacher actions

	Practitioners ensure that:	Theoretical sources	Relevant teacher action
1	each student's prior learning and experience is valued	Bruner, J. (1966) Kelly, G. (1955) Rogers, C. (1983) Ausubel, D. (1965)	be aware of student entry behaviour; use experiential methods where appropriate
2	where possible, any threat to the learners' self-esteem is removed	Cooley, C.H. (1912) James, W. (1890) Mead, G.H. (1934) Rogers, C. (1983) Shibutani, T. (1971)	create a supportive learning environment
3	the purpose of provided learning is understood by the learners	Burns, R (1982) Kelly, G. (1989) Rogers, C. (1983) Skinner, B.F. (1938)	set clear, achievable objectives
4	students are encouraged to become aware of their own learning processes	Perry, W (1970) Usher, R.S. (1985) Ausubel, D. (1965)	adjust pace according to elicited student responses
5	the development of learners' independence is encouraged	Knowles, M. (1984) Kelly, G. (1989) Rogers, C. (1983)	avoid prescription, encourage learner independent thinking
6	learners are stimulated to recall previously learned capabilities	Gagne, R.M. (1985) Perry, W (1970) Usher, R.S. (1985)	consider student responses in order to evaluate understanding
7	the desired mental sets of the learner are activated	Gagne, R.M. (1985) Bruner, J (1966) Ausubel, D. (1965) Rogers, C. (1983)	use probing, high order questioning; promote consolidation/ transfer
8	the learner receives appropriate feedback from the teacher	Gagne, R.M. (1985) Perry, W. (1970) Usher, R.S. (1985) Skinner, B.F. (1938)	provide appropriate feedback to support students
9	they share the process of learning with learners in order to reduce the effects of culturally based resistance	Bruner, J. (1966)	encourage and consider carefully student feedback with a view to improving future teaching and learning
10	learning is organized in order to build on previous learning (e.g. the spiral curriculum)	Ausubel, D. (1965) Bruner, J. (1966)	relate new knowledge to previous learning
11	learning is clearly structured to show relationships and continuity	Ausubel, D. (1965) Bruner, J. (1966)	plan the session – the individual parts should be clearly related to each other and previous learning in an appropriate way; break the skills or knowledge down into a logical sequence; form a link to the next session

12	problem-solving techniques are used to challenge previous perceptions	Ausubel, D. (1965) Bruner, J. (1966)	challenge learners to solve problems
13	meaningful reception learning is used in order to develop existing conceptual systems	Ausubel, D. (1965) Bruner, J. (1966)	identification of definite stages and relationships to the whole; use aids to competently stress key words and essential stages
14	teaching is organized around concepts and principles which potentially have the widest explanatory power, inclusiveness, reliability and generalizability to the chosen content	Ausubel, D. (1965) Bruner, J. (1966)	provide successful closure – major purposes, principles and constructs are summarized to form a cognitive link between past knowledge and current achievement
15	a sequence of presentation is selected which best illustrates the characteristics of the chosen cognitive structure in terms of clarity, stability and integratedness	Ausubel, D. (1965) Skinner, B.F. (1938)	provide a statement of objectives, explanation, purpose, relevance of topic, process to be followed, etc.; use presentational approaches where appropriate
16	learning is regularly rewarded during the early stages that should consist of short steps. In later stages variable reinforcement is preferable in order to avoid extinction	Ausubel, D. (1965) Skinner, B.F. (1938) Thorndike, E.L. (1931)	break skills or knowledge down into a logical sequence, reinforce behaviours
17	reward quickly follows the appropriate response. Motivation is increased by immediate feedback	Skinner, B.F. (1938) Thorndike, E.L. (1931)	use appropriate motivators and incentives; provide appropriate feedback to support student development
18	desirable behaviour is reinforced and unwanted behaviour is, as far as possible, ignored (since attention can often be a strong reinforcer). Emphasis should be on praising and encouraging desirable behaviour and not on punishing undesirable behaviour. Undesirable behaviour should, as far as possible, be extinguished	Skinner, B.F. (1938) Thorndike, E.L. (1931) Bandura, A. and Walter, R.H. (1963)	use positive reinforcement to reward desired student behaviour

19	negative reinforcement is used with care even though it is preferable to punishment. Punishment should not be used since it often has emotional side-effects (anxiety inhibits learning) and will produce avoidance behaviour (learners start missing lessons)	Skinner, B.F. (1938) Thorndike, E.L. (1931)	use voice, manner, language and personal characteristics to reassure learners and facilitate learning
20	lessons are carefully planned in order to encourage desired behaviours by eliciting necessary responses through appropriate reinforcers	Skinner, B.F. (1938) Bandura, A. and Walter, R.H. (1963)	stimulate interest/attention using a variety of verbal and non-verbal techniques
21	behaviours and tasks which the students are expected to learn are modelled, preferably by the tutors. For example, being punctual, showing enthusiasm or taking a critically reflective stance	Skinner, B.F. (1938) Bandura, A. and Walter, R.H. (1963)	communicate clearly, maintain eye contact; model behaviours
22	students are aware that desirable behaviour is being reinforced	Bandura, A. and Walter, R.H. (1963)	demonstrate subject expertise and enthusiasm and encourage students to respond
23	students are also used as models. For example, during group work, pair the confident, successful students with those who are less successful and try to build a mutually supportive relationship	Bandura, A. and Walter, R.H. (1963)	encourage student rapport and interaction
24	when forming learning groups tutors are aware of the personal characteristics of members and their influence on the dynamics of the group	Belbin, R.M. (1981) Hackman, J.R. and Morris, C.G. (1978)	form viable learning groups
25	effective group operation is facilitated by developing or providing skills and resources	Belbin, R.M. (1981) Hackman, J.R. and Morris, C.G. (1978)	facilitate effective group operation
26	the learners' previous experiences are valued	Kolb, D.A. (1984) Lewin, K. (1952) Revans, R. (1980) Kelly, G. (1989) Rogers, C. (1983)	move learners through cycle but allow to start at different points according to their preferred learning styles
27	no matter at which point they commence, students should move through each step of the learning cycle	Kolb, D. A. (1984) Lewin, K. (1952) Revans, R. (1980) Knowles, M. (1984)	promote learner independence and self-direction

28	students should be encouraged to take responsibility for their own learning	Knowles, M. (1984) Johnson, D. and Johnson, R. (1989)	develop student awareness of group dynamics and processes
29	they encourage collaboration by making learning a collective responsibility	Johnson, D. and Johnson, R. (1989)	establish collaborative learning groups
30	once cooperative learning has been established, they deliberately stimulate intellectual conflict by structuring academic controversies	Johnson, D. and Johnson, R. (1989)	structure learning activities which encourage students to explain, defend and challenge ideas

of sessions are by no means definitive, but they do contain a set of useful, generic and heuristic principles for practitioners, which represent a reasonably balanced approach to teaching. Certainly, most teaching will be improved through their inclusion.

Table 5.2 contains a summary of one approach to teaching or training which draws on established principles that have been incorporated into a generic session framework in a particular order. Of course, the purpose of the various methods can be achieved in many other ways, in a different order or in a range of contexts. This is merely an illustration and should be used as an example rather than a rigid prescription. Our emphasis, as always, is on responsive teaching which has been informed through practice and theory.

Table 5.2 A suggested framework for successful sessions (Theorist and Principle Number from Table 5.1 included in brackets)	
1. Preparation	
1.1	Be aware of student entry behaviour and build on learner's previous experience (1 Rogers, 12 Ausubel, 26 Knowles, Kelly, Rogers)
1.2	Set clear achievable objectives (14 Ausubel, 19 Skinner) Plan lesson – the individual parts should be clearly related to each other and previous learning in an appropriate way (9 Bruner)
1.3	Create a supportive learning environment (4 Rogers)
1.4	Form viable learning groups (24 Belbin, Hackman and Morris)
1.5	Structure learning activities which encourage students to explain, defend and challenge ideas (30 Johnson and Johnson)
1.6	Develop student awareness of group dynamics and processes (29 Johnson and Johnson)
2. Introduction (short opening period)	
2.1	Stimulate interest/attention using a variety of verbal and non-verbal techniques (20 Bandura and Walter)
2.2	Use voice, manner, language and personal characteristics to reassure learners and facilitate learning (4 Rogers)

2.3	Provide a statement of objectives, explanation, purpose, relevance of topic, process to be followed, etc. (2, 3 Rogers, 6 Gagne, 8, 10 Bruner, 13 Ausubel)
2.4	Relate new knowledge to previous learning (1 Rogers, 5 Gagne, 9 Bruner, 12 Ausubel)
2.5	Communicate clearly, maintain eye contact (20 Bandura and Walter)

3. Development (major period)

3.1	Demonstrate subject expertise, enthusiasm (20 Bandura)
3.2	Break skills or knowledge down into logical sequence (10 Bruner, 14 Ausubel)
3.3	Identification of definite stages and relationship to whole (13, 14 Ausubel)
3.4	Competent use of appropriate learning aids (19 Skinner)
3.5	Use suitable, probing, high order questions (3 Rogers, 5 Gagne, 11 Bruner, 14 Ausubel)
3.6	Consider student responses in order to evaluate understanding (6 Gagne, 12 Ausubel)
3.7	Adjust pace according to elicited responses (12 Ausubel)
3.8	Use appropriate motivators and incentives (15 Skinner)
3.9	Use presentational approaches where appropriate (12 Ausubel)
3.10	User experiential methods where appropriate to move learners through theory, experiment, experience and reflection cycle (3 Rogers, 11 Bruner, 26, 27 Lewin, Kolb, Revans)
3.11	Use positive reinforcement to reward desired student behaviour (15, 16, 17 Skinner, 21 Bandura and Walter)
3.12	Facilitate effective group operation.(25 Hackman and Morris)
3.13	Promote learner independence (28 Lewin, Kolb and Revans)

Closure (short, closing period)

4.1	Provide successful closure – major purposes, principles and constructs are summarized to form a cognitive link between past knowledge and current achievements (13 Ausubel, 10 Bruner)
4.2	Stress key words and essential stages (15 Skinner, 14 Ausubel)
4.3	Promote consolidation/transfer (6 Gagne, 10 Bruner, 14 Ausubel)
4.4	Make any assessment relevant to objectives (11 Bruner)
4.5	Form a link to next session (14 Ausubel, 10 Bruner)
4.6	Promote and consider student feedback with a view to improving future teaching and learning (1 Rogers, 9 Bruner, 14 Ausubel)

5.11 | CONCLUSION

As is so often the case, when considering National Standards the overlap between professional areas of practice becomes apparent. Taking into the account the needs of learners, supporting, planning and assessing them, all have their part to play in informing our selection from the range of appropriate teaching and learning methods available for particular student groups.

What seems clear is that, even when teachers have established a preferred approach, they must also be willing to consider new methods from the increasing variety which are available, in order to ensure that they are taking the necessary steps to promote the growth of *all* their learners. Although the teacher's 'tool kit' that we have presented may seem overly complex, many of its devices will be appropriate only in particular contexts and for specific purposes. However, although we all grow to rely on our favourite methods, the better we are informed the more quickly we will be able to select the optimum approach when faced with new or difficult situations.

5.12 | USEFUL SOURCES

Bigge, M. (1982) *Learning Theories for Teachers*. New York: Harper & Row.
Quite a 'weighty' book which does explain in detail the main learning theories and identifies how theorists such as Bandura, Gagne, Bruner, Bloom and Skinner impact on the classroom. There is a tendency by the author to assume an existing knowledge of basic psychological schools of thought.

Buzan, T. (1993) *The Mind Map Book; Radical Thinking*. London: BBC Books.
One of a series of books by Tony Buzan. They are all very easy to read and tend to prompt the reader into thought and reflection rather than presenting theory in a formal way. Hints and suggestions about ways to improve the thinking process and memory. A good read to supplement some of the more academic publications available.

Berryman, J. (1991) *Psychology and You*. London: British Psychological Society.
A good introduction to psychology and theories about the human personality. Highly readable with two particularly useful chapters on memory and learning, and thinking. Small and portable and a good book to 'dip into'.

Dryden, G. and Vos, J. (1994) *The Learning Revolution*. Accelerated Learning Systems.
This book looks at ways to use your mind to enable you to learn as much as possible as quickly as possible. It is very much a 'fun' text which should be read with an open, but critical mind. Very much an international book which makes references to New Zealand, Australia and USA. Lots of quotes from other researchers in the field of learning and education.

Shaffer, D. (1999) *Developmental Psychology* (5th edn). Brooks/Cole.
A detailed psychological text which looks at childhood and adolescence. It contains useful chapters on learning and thinking, information processing and intelligence.

The section on the development of 'self' is also relevant when considering motivating factors in education. All major theorists are discussed and most learning theories are examined. A higher level psychological text.

 Other material related to Learning Theory is available on the *tipcet.com* website.

5.13 RATIONALE FOR DEVELOPING AND USING A RANGE OF TEACHING AND LEARNING TECHNIQUES – KEY AREA C

FAQs	At Stage 1	At Stage 2	At Stage 3
Why do it?	In order to provide good learning experiences for your students which help them to develop towards their full potential and to prepare them for an active and useful role in society. If the strategies you implement are not optimally effective, you are not maximizing the benefits the students may gain or attracting other students to your programme/department/ college.	As you develop as a practitioner and become more aware of a range of different approaches to teaching, you will want to find out about the basic theories of teaching and learning. An understanding of theory will help you to see the principles and concepts underpinning various methods and help you to modify and transfer methods to new situations.	As a reflective practitioner you will be concerned to understand the changing and developing abilities of your students so that you are able to modify your approaches continuously in order to provide new challenges and experiences. You need to balance the use of didactic with experiential methods, inductive with deductive approaches and individual student endeavour with collaborative work.
Where are we going?	You are developing an understanding of the needs and characteristics of your learners and also your own preferred approaches to teaching. This involves developing the skills of analysis both of your own performance and that of your learners. Naturally, this is all taking place within a particular context which you also need to understand because it will have an influence on the success of your planned sessions.	Your aim is to achieve the learning outcomes which you have identified for your programme in as professional a manner as is possible within the constraints which teachers/lecturers inevitably face. You also have a responsibility to make the programme as enjoyable and beneficial as possible for the students. Your ultimate aim is to facilitate their development as independent, effective learners.	As you develop the process of collecting and organizing data about your own teaching you will gradually become an active researcher into your own practice and will develop and test a range of theories within the context of your own teaching. Although this action research will be context-specific you will, nevertheless, be able to make more informed judgements about teaching and learning as you become an expert within your particular context.

How do we get there?	Essentially by becoming more reflective, so that you are aware of the range of variables which are affecting your practice. You will be improving through practice the teaching and learning approaches you are familiar with and becoming aware of other approaches used by colleagues and suggested in the texts you may be reading. The learning experience of your students is the most important measure of your success and so this should be a guide as you adopt new methods.	You need to facilitate learning through the didactic, experiential, group and individual strategies which you have devised based on the needs of the learners, the subject you are teaching and the environment in which you are working. You also need to develop your students' study and social/collaborative skills. Working with and supporting colleagues and liaising with a range of support staff are also important developmental processes.	To be effective, this level of reflection cannot remain merely at an intuitive level but should become organized and systematic. Your analysis will become 'grounded' within your working context as you develop and test a range of hypotheses about how learning is enhanced or impoverished. An effective, reflective practitioner must remain open-minded, committed and responsive.
Is this the best way?	At the end of the day, you are to become the 'expert' in your particular educational context. You should know the characteristics of your learners, the effect of other influences and your own strengths and weaknesses in order to improve your practice.	As a reflective practitioner you will become aware of the effects of different teaching and learning approaches and you will develop a repertoire of appropriate methods. Just as important, you will begin to test and record the effectiveness of this range of approaches.	In order to develop an eclectic approach to teaching and learning you need to analyse the effectiveness of different methods and develop a synthesis which draws on a range of methods to arrive at a model which is the most appropriate for your particular context.
When is the right time?	Very often, the time of day, the place the session occupies in the learning schedule, or its position in relation to term-time, will influence the effectiveness of selected teaching/learning methods. Approaches which go well first session in a morning may not be nearly as effective after lunch. Also, immediately prior to your session, the students may have experienced other methods used by a colleague, which can also affect how they respond to you.	You are probably finding that, as you become more responsive to your learners and the context in which you operate, you are able to modify your approach very quickly to the prevailing conditions. This could be a change in the student group dynamics or a subject-based difficulty which requires an adjustment to the time allocated to different topics. Responsiveness is a better indicator of mature teaching, than rigid adherence to session plan timing.	Analyse the relevance of timing in relation to the practice of different teaching and learning methods. Check on within-session timing in relation to changing approaches, sustaining interest, developing knowledge transfer, consolidation of theories, etc. Consider within–programme timing in terms of key events such as visits, expert speakers, assessment, etc. Reflect on cross-programme timing in terms of integrated projects, common induction sessions, external speakers, etc.

5.14 KEY AREA C – DEVELOPING AND USING A RANGE OF TEACHING AND LEARNING TECHNIQUES (SEE C1, C2 AND C3)

Purpose: Teachers and teaching teams need to be effective in selecting and using a range of appropriate methods of teaching and learning including individual and group learning. This involves developing an awareness of the effect of different styles of teaching on the learning process in order to plan and deliver suitable programmes. There is also a need for teachers to evaluate the effectiveness of the learning programme based in part on feedback from learners. Unit C3 focuses on the skills and knowledge required to facilitate learning through experience. This is a particular aspect of both group and individual learning but it is identified separately. For an analysis of this process at FENTO Stages 1, 2 and 3 see the rationale above.

Please note: The FENTO Standards listed below are relevant to the following three levels of award: Stage 1 (Introduction), Stage 2 (Intermediate) and Stage 3 (Full Certification). All of the standards are required at Stage 3, only those in italic or bold are required at Stage 2 and only those in italic are required at Stage 1.

UNIT C1.   PROMOTE AND ENCOURAGE INDIVIDUAL LEARNING *In order to do this teachers should:*

	Demonstrate that they are able to:	and have specific knowledge and critical understanding of:	plus generic knowledge of:		Summary of appropriate evidence in this Key Area:	Relevant Chapter Activities
a	**Criteria:** establish and agree individual learning needs, aspirations and preferred learning style	Ways of assisting individual learning	● Learning theories and how they affect teaching and learning ● How to select appropriate teaching methods on the basis of learning theory ● The use of differentiated learning materials ● The range of information and learning technology available to support learners and how to make the best use of available resources	a	Group learning profiles and records of individual attainment	A3a to A3x, B4c to B4v, C5a to C55n, C5s to C5v
b	agree learning goals and targets which support individual needs and aspirations within available resources			b	Development of Individual Learning Plans	A3j; A3m
c	produce learning plans which encourage individual learning	How to structure individual learning programmes		c	Individual Student Action Plans	A3j; A3m

	Standards	Knowledge and understanding		Evidence	Codes
d	*identify and produce appropriate teaching and learning materials which engage learners' interest and reinforce their learning*	Different learning materials and how to produce them Specialist equipment and its uses in supporting learning	d	Materials for individual learning	D6h, D6l
e	recognize and build on the experiences which learners bring to the programme	How individual learning is affected by social, cultural and emotional factors	e	a and b above	C5s to C5v
f	agree a learning contract with the learner	The difference between learning plans and learning contracts and how to use both effectively	f	b or c above	D6i, D7d
g	*evaluate the effectiveness of learning*	• Evaluation strategies and methods • How to analyse information on teaching and learning and extract what is relevant to modify future learning stategies • How to evaluate learning programmes in terms of efficiency, effectiveness and equity	g	Data from evaluations	G10d to G10g
h	**acknowledge the effect of resource constraints and make best use of available opportunities**	The availability of resources and how this affects learning	h	Session Plans	D7o

Key to above standards required at each FENTO Stage:

Introduction Stage – italic
Intermediate Stage + bold
Certification Stage – all

Plus commentary in PDJ on the purposes and value of the above together with records in your PF of Teaching Observations, Lesson Plans, Rationales, Self-Evaluations and Progress Summary.

UNIT C2. FACILITATE LEARNING IN GROUPS *In order to do this teachers should:*

Demonstrate that they are able to:	and have specific knowledge and critical understanding of:	plus generic knowledge of:	Summary of appropriate evidence in this Key Area:		Relevant Chapter Activities
a Criteria: plan and select learning opportunities which involve group activity	Group methods and when to use them	• Learning theories and how they affect teaching and learning • How to select appropriate teaching methods on the basis of learning theory	a	Session Plans	C5l to C5r D6l, D6m
b *produce Learning Plans which encourage learning in groups*		• The use of differentiated learning materials	b	Session Plans	C5l to C5r D6l, D6m
c encourage learning through sound group management including appropriate interventions in group activities	Group dynamics and the effective management of groups	• The range of information and learning technology available to support learners and how to make the best use of available resources • Evaluation strategies and methods	c	Group Learning Plans	C5l to C5r D6l, D6m
d facilitate learning through the use of collaborative exercises and encourage learners to support each other	The importance of collaborative working practices and peer group support and how to encourage these	• How to analyse information on teaching and learning and extract what is relevant to modify future learning	d	Collaborative learning strategies	C5l to C5r D6l, D6m
e *ensure that all members of the group are involved in learning activities*		• How to evaluate learning programmes in terms of efficiency, effectiveness and equity	e	Session Plans	C5l to C5r D6l, D6m
f *produce appropriate learning support materials using information learning technology where appropriate*	Different learning support materials, when to use them and how to prepare them		f	Appropriate materials	D6n, D6o

g	evaluate the effectiveness of learning and modify teaching plans where necessary	Evaluation feedback	D7i and G10d to G10g
h	acknowledge the effect of resource constraints and make the best use of available opportunities	Session Plans, Schemes of Work	D6o, D6p

Plus commentary in PDJ on the purposes and value of the above together with records in your PF of Teaching Observations, Lesson Plans, Rationales, Self-Evaluations and Progress Summary.

Key to above standards required at each FENTO Stage:

Introduction Stage – italic
Intermediate Stage + bold
Certification Stage – all

UNIT C3. FACILITATE LEARNING THROUGH EXPERIENCE *In order to do this teachers should:*

	Demonstrate that they are able to:	and have specific knowledge and critical understanding of:	plus generic knowledge of:	Summary of appropriate evidence in this Key Area:	Relevant Chapter Activities
a	**Criteria:** identify learning objectives amenable to learning through experience	The appropriateness, advantages and disadvantages of learning through experience	• Learning theories and how they affect teaching and learning • How to select appropriate teaching methods on the basis of learning theory • The use of differentiated learning materials • The range of information and learning technology available to support learners and how to make the best use of available resources • Evaluation strategies and methods • How to analyse information on teaching and learning and extract what is relevant to modify future learning strategies • How to evaluate learning programmes in terms of efficiency, effectiveness and equity	*Schemes of Work, Session Plans*	*B4n to B4r, C5s to C5v, F9i to F9k*
b	produce Learning Plans which encourage learning through experience	The importance of ensuring that all learners have opportunities to learn through experience		*Appropriate Session Plans*	*C5s to C5v*
c	plan and structure opportunities for groups and individuals to learn through experience, including opportunities to demonstrate and practise skills	• Appropriate opportunities for learning through experience • The importance of the learner's experience in practising skills		*Appropriate Session Plans*	*C5s to C5v*
d	encourage and support individuals in identifying personal experiences which enhance their learning			*Action Plans, Learning Review*	*C5s to C5v*
e	ensure that learning is appropriately structured, safe and adequately resourced	Health, safety and environmental controls during learning through experience		*Learning Support, Learning Agreement*	*B4m to B4s, C5s to C5v*
f	support learners as they learn			*Learning Support Audit*	*E8b to E8g, C5s to C5v*

145

g	provide appropriately constructive feedback to learners and reinforce the learning gained through experience	Ways of conducting debriefing and providing constructive feedback to learners	*Assessment Feedback, Learning Review, Action Plans*	*C5s to C5v, F9a, F9b*
h	evaluate the effectiveness of the learning process and modify Teaching Plans where necessary		*Session Plan, Schemes of Work, Evaluations*	*C5s to C5v, G10d to G10g*
i	acknowledge the effect of resource constraints and make best use of available opportunities for experiential learning		*Session Plans, Evaluations*	*C5s to C5v, D6l, D6m*
Key to above standards required at each FENTO Stage: *Introduction Stage – italic* **Intermediate Stage + bold** Certification Stage – all		*Plus commentary in PDJ on the purposes and value of the above together with records in your PF of Teaching Observations, Lesson Plans, Rationales, Self-Evaluations and Progress Summary*	

Managing the learning process (Part 1)

Tricia Semeraz

Key Area D (Part 1) Maintaining an effective learning environment, planning learning activities

Key concepts in this chapter

Assignments, Buzz Groups, Demonstrations, Effective Environment, Entry Characteristics, Formal Teaching, Games, Hierarchy of Needs, Ice-Breaking, Keeping Track, Learner's Agreement, Learners as a resource. Learning Contracts, Learning Resources, Lecturer-centred, Lectures, Motivation, Projects, Resonate, Role-play, Search, Self-concept, Seminars, Sensory Experience, Session Management, Simulation, Small-group tutorials, Student-centred, Syndicates, Team-teaching, Values and Attitudes

Before you begin this chapter you may wish to check the FAQs on pp. 199–202

Index to Chapter 6

Chapter 6 Activities designed to generate evidence against the Standards

6.1 INTRODUCTION

It is clear that each of us has particular views about the interacting relationships which make up the learning process, but our analysis will be greatly enhanced if we can develop the skill of not only seeing the individual parts, but also that particular situation *as a whole*. For it is the *totality* of the learners' experience which is our primary concern and the effect of the various components on this intricate amalgamation of interacting parts is often difficult to predict. However, as teachers this is our task and it is, after all, what makes education and training so difficult, fascinating and, ultimately (when we finally get it right), so richly rewarding.

There is, of course, some value in separately addressing each of the parts which make up the whole. This disaggregated view invariably helps in our analysis because the whole is often so intimidatingly complex that it defies examination. Even so, it is only after we have taken an informed *holistic* overview that we will become aware of the role and importance of some of the less obvious components and it is then that we will be able to judge how accurate our analysis has been. In a sense, in writing this chapter, we are faced with a similar dilemma. We are concerned to develop an effective discussion about *Managing the Learning Process* that FENTO have broken down into five separate Standards. Obviously each of these discrete areas is related, but there is also considerable overlap.

Therefore, in order to present this debate as digestible pieces we will, in this chapter, consider *the learning environment, learning activities* and *learning resources*. In the following Chapter 7, we will discuss *reviewing learning, working relationships* and *effective communication with learners*. It is our intention, as you consider how each of these six facets is related to your own practice, to try to sustain a sense of the totality of management practices and the importance of the inter-connectedness of each of the component parts which form Chapters 6 and 7.

6.2 THE LEARNING ENVIRONMENT

As you know, effective teaching is not a haphazard process whereby the eagerly awaiting students automatically consume any knowledge or skill that might be presented to them. Previous chapters have discussed how we increase the likelihood of effectiveness by purposefully planning our teaching, taking into account the learner and subject characteristics. However, this interaction takes place within a particular environment or setting which may well have its own characteristics that can significantly affect the quality of the ensuing interactions.

D6a First impressions

Imagine that a new group of learners has entered for the first time the learning environment that you manage. Consider what the students may be feeling as they arrive for the first time, the nature of their apprehensions and the range of attitudes they may adopt. What practical steps can you take to encourage them to react positively?

Naturally, the learners will be looking for any explicit or implicit indications that the experience in which they are about to take part will be positive, enhancing, non-threatening, enjoyable, rewarding, challenging, organized, entertaining, cool, surprising, etc. These hopes and aspirations will, of course, differ from student to student and you will *not* be able to predict or change the attitudes they bring to the session. However, there are many things that you can do to reassure them, whatever their needs are, that you and the environment you have created will be positively responsive. Try simple things, such as:

- ensure that the setting looks cared for, decorate with colourful pictures, play music
- minimize authoritarian notices or instructions, use humorous, interesting displays
- smile, reassure, explain, use their names as soon as possible
- encourage questioning and respond sincerely as a facilitator
- inform the students, provide choice, trigger positive emotions
- emphasize success, use upbeat language, avoid stressful references
- trigger positive emotions, suggest targets they can achieve, introduce hope
- find something about each of them to like

D6b Building on good beginnings

As the students settle in, their questions will become more specific and personal to them. Reflect on the sort of anxieties they may have and the questions these attitudes will generate.

Naturally, students need to feel that their contribution to the learning is valued. These needs challenge the teacher to manage the learning process in a way that may provide answers to the following notional questions. Will the teacher –

1. provide opportunities for me to be involved and motivated?
2. know who I am?
3. know what I'm doing?
4. explain to me what I should be doing?
5. provide varied, appropriate and interesting sessions?
6. facilitate my success on this learning programme?

These six fundamental questions may be used to evaluate the success of your chosen approach for whatever learning group you may be working with. The answers will provide a good guide as to how conducive to learning your learners themselves *perceive* the environment to be. We will use these questions as a basis for our investigation of an effective learning environment.

6.3 MOTIVATION

The above questions indicate an essentially humanistic approach, which we discussed briefly in the previous chapter. During the development of these ideas more than 50 years ago, Carl Rogers (1983) and Abraham Maslow (1970) were concerned with the individuals' willingness to accept and participate actively in their environment. This aptitude is very much dependent upon their own self-concept and related levels of motivation or 'self-actualization'. This in turn affects their perception of their learning environment as something that they can *affect and manipulate* or something they must *accept as unchangeable*. Maslow believed that self-actualization was a human need, which he placed at the top of his notional hierarchy, as he believed that other needs must be met *before* this ultimate level of fulfilment could be achieved:

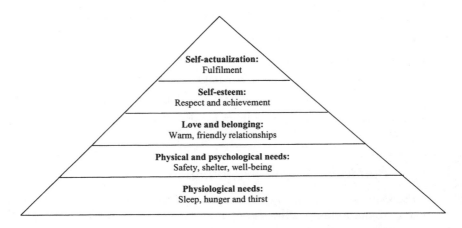

Maslow's hierarchy of needs

The ascending order of needs identified by Maslow begins at the bottom with basic physiological demands (*hunger, thirst, etc*) that require satisfying before moving up to comfort requirements such as *safety and shelter*. *Love and belonging* helps to establish *self-esteem* needs (pride), which provide a platform for the cognitive and conceptual needs of *self-actualization*. Thus physical survival needs must be satisfied in order for people to concentrate on higher needs. Maslow believed that the final self-actualization level may only be achieved by some people and then perhaps only for a short time. However, this higher level of fulfilment, which is mainly experienced on a conceptual level, may take many different forms and is open to all of us.

D6c Hierarchy of needs

Consider Maslow's theory that the lower need must be satisfied before moving on to a higher need and then relate it to your particular learners. Is it true, for example, that the motivation related to the establishment of self-esteem cannot be achieved without gaining love and belonging first?

It is true that if students are made to feel comfortable and involved in their learning they will be much more likely to succeed. Even so, sources of motivation take many forms within a whole range of different human activities and often lead to surprising levels of learning and achievement, which enhance the individual self-esteem of people who do not appear to be endowed with a well-developed sense of belonging. Their motivation is often a powerful but intrinsic force.

D6d A motivational structure

In your PDJ, develop a list of practical ways in which you could improve the motivation of your particular group of students. Give a brief explanation of why you feel that each particular method would work with your learners.

Of course, as we have stressed several times, each learner group will be motivated by *different* things and many of the motivational forces will be *specific* to your own particular context (e.g. competing with another group, bettering previous performances, helping other learners). However, the following are some more generic approaches, which are often successful (notice the importance of assessment, feedback and evaluation):

a) set clear objectives at the beginning of the session so that you and the learners have expectations of what they should be able to achieve by the end of the session. *This helps to encourage the learners to establish a positive mental 'set'*

b) try to develop differentiated objectives. *These cater for the range of abilities within the group. In this way, the outcomes are more appropriate and learners will feel either less patronized (by easily achieved objectives) or less stressed (by being presented with overly difficult targets)*

c) ensure that, although there will inevitably be a spread of marks, everyone should be able achieve a reasonable result. *This may seem patronizing, but if*

151

you develop the skill of devising an appropriate assessment that the learners know is a challenge, but during which they also anticipate that, if they do the work, they will be able to do reasonably well, they will find it reassuring, motivating and rewarding

d) during all classroom activities your students should be encouraged to feel that, should there be anything that they are unsure of, it is *expected* they will seek clarification. *Try to **avoid** putting the onus for any lack of understanding on them. Try asking 'Have I explained everything clearly?' rather than 'Is there anything you don't understand?' which will often result in silence as they do not wish to appear to be the only one with a problem*

e) all contributions should be acknowledged and, where appropriate, praised. *Resist the temptation to make jokes at the learners' expense*

f) try to use a range of techniques to make the session interesting, involving and stimulating. *Think in terms of **varying compatible methods**, rather than an all singing and dancing extravaganza*

g) where possible, provide an opportunity for *formative* assessment so that students know that they are on the right track. *The earlier they are aware of any misunderstandings, the more time they have to correct them*

h) try to make feedback constructive with clear points for development. *The learners need to know how to recover if they have made serious errors. Sometimes it isn't very helpful to receive only **confirmatory** feedback (i.e. 'you have listed all the components correctly') Because your students need to know about any potential way forward, always try to ensure that the feedback is also **developmental***

i) take steps to demonstrate to the students the *relevance* of the session to the syllabus *as a whole. They need to see the total problem to appreciate the function and value of the parts. This provision of a gestalt or whole view helps to develop a level of understanding that often cannot be achieved through a study of the parts*

j) ensure that your final assessment of the learners' work incorporates *summative* comments, which look back at what has been covered, together with *constructive* comments, which help to prepare the student for the next piece of assessment. *It is often possible to incorporate into assessment feedback acknowledgement or praise together with suggestions of how particular elements can be developed further within the next piece of coursework*

k) don't forget that the intention is to develop *independent* learners, so try to suggest ways forward which are not overly prescriptive. *Let the student make choices and decisions by suggesting a **number** of ways, rather than stipulating what you consider to be the 'proper' or 'ideal' method*

6.4 SELF-CONCEPT

We included a lengthy discussion about the theories of group dynamics and the effect on learning in the previous chapter. The implications were that *only a very limited number of people* within a typical learning environment *wish to remain anonymous*. Most want their fellow learners to be aware of their interests, experiences and needs and, usually, they also wish to know about their peers. Very often, even individual learning is promoted by the security of a group of fellow students who are sharing the same experiences and difficulties. An important part of this security is the knowledge that their teacher or trainer not only knows them, but also is concerned for their well-being. Try to think of a means of informally getting to know more about your learners by completing the following activity:

D6e Getting to know the learners

Think again about a particular group of learners you know well and suggest an enjoyable, less formal activity which will not only encourage the class members to get to know more about each other, but also will let them know that you (the teacher/trainer) are also getting to know them and allowing them to know more about you.

There are many interesting 'ice-breaking' exercises and we suggest two of these below. As you would expect, it is essential when undertaking such exchanges that the learners are not embarrassed by interactions they cannot handle or stressed by exercises they have difficulty completing.

a) *Presenting*: one simple way is to allow groups of two or three students to talk to each other for about ten minutes in order to discover as much as possible about each other and what their reason for joining the particular class was. In turn, they will then introduce their 'interviewee' to the rest of the class, providing as much detail as they have managed to glean

b) *Signatures*: a second method would be to organize an 'autograph hunt' by finding as many different questions (or signatures) as there are people in the group, including yourself. Get the class to help you find out who:

1. speaks more than one language
2. has bathed a baby this week
3. has a younger brother or sister
4. has a relative who lives abroad
5. is new to this area, etc

D6f Interactive activity

When you have tried one of these interactive 'getting to know you' exercises with your learners, reflect on the process. Consider if and how they helped you to get to know the group and the group get to know each other and you. Reflect on the usefulness of this type of interactive activity. For example, would it have been just as effective if you had just told everyone the name of each group member? Would it work for all learners, at any time, in any setting? What influences this?

6.5 | KEEPING TRACK

You will probably realize that, even though you have spent time building up the trust of your students through various interactive activities, you can easily damage this very precious relationship. Your careful nurturing of them towards independence can be undermined should they suddenly realize that *you* don't really appreciate all of the different ways in which they are developing. Students can be extremely disappointed to find that a tutor, whom they believed to be attuned to their interests and achievements, is not in fact aware of the strides they have recently made. Nevertheless, teachers are extremely busy and cannot be expected to be aware of every development which is taking place in learning environments other than their own.

D6g   *Significant student development*

How can you possibly keep abreast of student development? Summarize the ways in which you remain aware of significant development being achieved by each learner.

6.5.1   Learning contracts, agreements and journals

One obvious device which would allow you to keep abreast of your learners' developing areas of interest and exploration would be to encourage them to keep a reflect log or learning diary/journal (see guidance in Chapter 2). An occasional review of this record together with the student will allow them to explain their interests and how they wish to develop further.

A more formal approach, which effectively places some of the responsibility on the learners themselves, is the use of *learning contracts* or a *learning agreement*. This device may seem to be merely 'passing the buck' but, if implemented with integrity, the process can be a vehicle for the genuine sharing of the learning process between tutor and student, where progressively the formal *teacher and taught* relationship is replaced with the notion of a learning partnership or community. This process clearly embraces philosophies of learner-centred learning by encouraging individuals to articulate and then realize their own goals. Along the way they are helped to identify more clearly the abilities, potential and progress which they have already achieved and those that they will achieve as they proceed through their chosen programme of study.

A simple definition of any contract is 'a written or spoken agreement'. It is important that this agreement should make explicit what the expectations of both the learners and the tutors are within the particular establishment context.

D6h   *Developing a learning contract*

Again take your own learners within your own establishment as your focus. Summarize the things that you feel it would be important to include in any learning contract. Think of the separate and the shared responsibilities of the parties involved. Remember that this is essentially a *mutual* agreement

> between *equals*, rather than a formal, legally binding contract characterized by *authority and compliance.*

The contract should focus on the *process* of learning, rather than solely on the product of the learning process. You will probably be concerned to ensure that not only should the achievement at the end of the programme be important, but also the quality of each individual learner's journey to the selected goal. The 'value added' will not only be quantitative (i.e. the award achieved) but also qualitative (the range of subtle experiences along the way).

Dart and Clarke (1991) believe that a learning contract will help learners to develop habits related to lifelong learning. The current educational processes for many of today's learners encourage, and indeed expect, them to be autonomous individuals in charge of their own learning, and the use of contracts fosters that autonomy. The ownership of learning becomes a reality and individual learning is the result.

6.5.2 Learning agreements

On the next page we have gathered typical statements from a Learning Agreement which you may consider including in your learning contract/agreement. You will note that the responsibilities of both the learner and the educational institution are made clear to both parties.

D6i Learning agreement details

Compare the contract/agreement you have designed with the example overleaf and make any adjustments you may consider appropriate.

McAllister (1996) made the point that this focus on what is to be achieved is an essential part of education today:

> teachers should not deny their teaching and learning expertise and so should continue to advise, guide and encourage students to meet their learning objectives. If such an approach is not integral within the planning process, it may well be difficult, if not impossible to attempt to 'change' once a programme is being delivered.

The teacher's task is inevitably demanding. Not only is it important to plan a purposeful lesson, but also it is equally important to be able to manage the lesson to meet the varying needs of the students so that they are motivated to learn. The four important steps in structuring this process may be remembered through the acronym *REAL:*

Resonate   This simply means that before you can initiate any learning, you need to get on the same 'wavelength' as your students. You must develop strategies that ensure that your input is being received and understood.

Educate   Having established two-way transactional communication, you can now introduce your key concepts to the group.

155

Learning Agreement

between *(full name of programme member)* and *(full name of institution/establishment)*

Institutional/establishment commitment:

On the.................................programme, the *(name of establishment)* undertakes to provide:

a)   teaching by suitably qualified and experienced staff

b)   adequate accommodation to meet the demands of the course

c)   an opportunity to negotiate a learning programme

d)   a system for the accreditation of prior learning

e)   a programme tutor and a personal tutorial system

f)   a validated system of assessments and accreditation

g)   access to appropriate equipment and facilities

h)   access to college-based library resources

i)   access to appropriate services, e.g. student services, counselling, health support

j)   a formative review system

k)   an understanding that it may be necessary for a member to leave the programme if continued attendance would not appear to he in her/his best interests or the interests of other members

l)   an appeals procedure

Programme member's commitment

Following enrolment onto the...........programme and after initial assessment and guidance, I undertake to:

a)   follow an agreed programme of learning, which can only be amended after negotiation with personal tutor/course tutor

b)   attend all sessions/activities as required in the agreed programme and provide written explanations in the case of absences

c)   make appropriate contact with the programme during any 15 working-day (3-week) period

d)   cooperate in all administrative matters covering enrolments, attendance, assessment and programme evaluation

e)   provide a Learning Agreement for any programme being undertaken at another institution

f)   where I have indicated that a sponsor will pay my fees, if for any reason the sponsor does not pay, I will be liable for the debt

g)   in signing this form I agree to comply with the College Learner Agreement and Code of Conduct, details of which can be found in the Student Handbook

I accept the commitments stated above:

Student Name:................................. Signature:.................................. Date:......................

I accept the commitments stated above on behalf of: *(institution/establishment name)*.................

....

Programme leader name:................. Signature:.................................. Date.......................

By signing this form, you are agreeing that the college is entitled to use the information provided both on this form and for your student membership card, for purposes connected with the college as an educational institution, including publicity and marketing. The information collected will be stored on the college computerized student record system. Some or all of the data may be supplied to other organizations, as described in our registration under the Act. The information you provide on this form will be passed to the Learning and Skills Council, which is registered under the Data Protection Act 1998. The registration is primarily for the collection and analysis of statistical data, but it also allows the council to share information with other organizations for the purpose of detecting fraud. Further information about data confidentiality is available by written request to the Central Administration Unit.

Activate   Don't leave the learners sitting there merely receiving information for too long. Get them more involved through relevant activities.

Liberate   Think about how, through your teaching, you are going to start to move your students gradually towards *independent operation*. You should begin these small steps towards autonomy as soon as possible because the longer they remain dependent upon you to provide all of the answers, the more difficult they will find it to stand on their own two feet.

D6j   Getting REAL

Observe an experienced teacher and analyse how they operate these important concepts of classroom management. Compare this to your own methods and reflect on how you might improve the students' engagement with the learning process and redress poor motivation.

A device which might help during this developmental/analytical process is the checklist below which suggest some ways of developing our REAL concepts. You may use this as a planning sheet, as a way of recording for yourself key incidents during an observed session, or as a framework for giving feedback to a practitioner after an observed session.

(This pro forma is available on the ***tipcet.com*** website.)

SESSION PLANNING OR OBSERVATION SHEET	
Steps	**Comments**
1. Resonate • ice-breaking or introductory phase – getting to know them again • show the learners respect, know their names, interests, etc. • brief overview of the session using familiar terminology • link to previous learning • identifying intended learning outcomes • earn their trust by trying to understand and meet their needs • stimulate interest through glimpses of what each of them can achieve • challenge by passing to them some responsibility • differentiate by setting individual targets	
2. Educate • provide information using a range of appropriate methods • communicate clearly • use open, directed questioning • deliberately develop their understanding and skills • avoid spoon feeding or unnecessary repetition	

3. Activate • vary the pace, introduce activities • get the learners to summarize what they have learned • facilitate learning wherever possible, instead of lecturing • use collaborative learning exercises • help learners to appreciate and share your enthusiasms • don't let them lapse into a passive/receptive mode	
4. Liberate • let the students summarize what has been learned • share understandings • discuss how they arrived at their conceptualization of key points • identify areas of concern and let others suggest ways forward • revisit targets and stress their achievability • suggest how their learning will be developed further in subsequent sessions • let them bring ideas to the next session	

6.6 ESTABLISHING AN EFFECTIVE LEARNING ENVIRONMENT

Perhaps the most essential feature of an effective learning relationship is that students always know exactly what they should be doing. Admittedly, it is difficult to achieve this ideal state consistently. However, the establishment of an ethos where learners are consistently encouraged to become informed, independent and motivated will often depend on setting certain ground rules for both staff and students. Obviously many of these guidelines will be specific to the actual educational context and are difficult to generalize about, but some possible examples of these prerequisites might be:

• all tutors should support the underpinning values of the programme

• learning should be active and student-centred

• high expectations of learner performance should be demonstrated by setting challenging but achievable targets

D6k Underpinning programme values and attitudes

Consider what you would expect of colleagues who are teaching on a programme you manage. What would be their core values and how would they be expressed in their interactions with your learners?

Good tutors show that they care about students. They engage with them and take responsibility for dealing with problems. They have high expectations: ensure good attendance, homework completion and achievement. They follow up students when they fall behind required standards and they inspire students and communicate their own enthusiasm about their subject to them.

The above is a summary of some fairly basic principles, which also set good examples for students. These first steps begin the gradual process of developing student independence (which eventually will encourage them to take on more responsibility) and may be further broken down into the following activities:

- try to get to know learners as quickly as possible so that you can address them by name
- remember what it is like to be a beginner learning a new skill
- where possible, make use of the students' knowledge and experience
- spend time finding out about their background, culture and reasons for doing the course
- set high standards at the start of the course, for example 100 per cent pass rates
- generate enthusiasm and thus a positive work ethic by allowing students to see your own genuine delight in their achievements
- praise students' success and encourage them when they encounter difficulties
- communicate non-verbally as well as verbally
- use metaphors and real examples to provide insight into difficult problems
- remember that teaching and learning is a two-way process; you can learn new skills and ideas from your students
- occasionally provide something special, such as a trip or a guest speaker

6.6.1 Session management

It is fairly obvious that very little positive learning will take place during our teaching sessions if we do not achieve an effective management of the proceedings. That is not to say that we must impose strict controls over each of the learning processes; that would be far too heavy handed, particularly for more mature or sensitive students.

However, as teachers, the activities and interactions *are* our responsibility and, as we stressed earlier, planning for success is essential even if we find the need to modify our approach in the light of the learners' initial response. Ironically, this is even more true of a laissez-faire, experiential session where the outcomes are deliberately kept vague or unknown. In such a situation, a whole range of variables will need to be anticipated and planned for if we are to avoid unproductive chaos.

Most learners will enter our taught sessions wishing to achieve a positive outcome and we have a responsibility to establish an environment where they may use the strategies with which they feel comfortable to achieve that success. Students must be encouraged to respect fellow learners and this includes trying to ensure that their behaviour is not intrusive to others.

As tutors, we will find if difficult to manage learning effectively if students are not attentive or able to concentrate on the session. We have the responsibility of establishing an environment which is conducive to the learning of those present and to do this we need to establish clear ground rules for the behaviour of all members:

1. be punctual and expect your students to be punctual, start session on time
2. develop respect between the student and the teacher

3. discourage disruptive behaviour which distracts others such as chatting while you are teaching

4. use positive reinforcement, good humour and a pleasant disposition as your key session management strategies

5. support college rules and procedures

6. adhere to breaks in long sessions

7. begin with and maintain a friendly, approachable authority in your dealings with students

8. take immediate action to challenge abusive, sexist or racist language and comments

9. always check up on absences

10. ask students to turn off mobile phones

11. make sure that students have work to be going on with

12. ensure that productive work is being done when tasks are set in groups or pairs

D6l Managing group work

Imagine that you have a large group of students with varying abilities and personalities. You find that a group of more capable students prefer to sit together and object to being separated and placed in pre-selected groups on the grounds that, while they may well each be able to contribute a great deal to the overall group performance, they will individually gain very little because they will not find the experience sufficiently challenging. How would you manage this situation?

Compromise will be the keynote here. The high flyers do work well together and always remain focused on the task. The rest of the class seem to prefer to have the composition of the group changed with each new activity as they enjoy exchanging learning with as many others as possible. Obviously, the class should not be exposed to any sense of elitism in their midst since our aim is to make all students feel equally valued. However, at the same time we should give equal recognition to the needs of all students, taking account of their widely differing abilities, aptitudes and learning styles.

A solution could be for the tutor to continue to organize the groups, but to discreetly arrange different patterns of membership according to the task at hand. For example, where the activity is to investigate what has been learnt, the problem group will stay together and will, in this way, benefit from peer pressure at their own level of learning. When they feedback during a plenary, the rest of the class will benefit from their ideas. When the group activity involves practical implementation of earlier learning or revision exercises, then the more capable students will join other groups so that eventually all learners have the opportunity to work with each other.

6.7 | TEACHING AND LEARNING METHODS

Earlier chapters have discussed the planning of sessions and the theories of learning which should underpin these plans. Using broader terms, a teacher has a limited number of choices to make when deciding what are appropriate methods to use. True, when planning a session, it is important to be aware of the range of student learning styles or particular needs which will be present in the class.

However, a major choice, which will affect other decisions, is between *lecturer-centred delivery* and *student-centred processes*. Even though the specific learning activities will inevitably vary, most sessions will be a combination of these two strategies. At some stages the lecturer's input will be have a more crucial bearing on the learners' development and during others it will be more important that the learners' active involvement predominates.

D6m Selecting a teaching approach

Take one of your planned sessions and look at the balance between teacher-centred and learner-centred activities. Adjust the strategies if you wish and then provide a brief justification for the balance you have achieved.

As you would expect there are a range of different approaches, which may be considered in three simple categories. The first and most commonly used methods involve various forms of *presentation* and as you would expect these are essentially teacher-centred. *Search* approaches are more focused around the learners' exploration of sources and the third strategy, *interaction*, is again learner-centred and experiential but will often involve much more student collaboration. As a basic reference, in the tables overleaf (6.5.1 to 6.5.3) we have listed these different models of learning, together with a list of advantages and disadvantages.

6.8 | LEARNING RESOURCES

Johann Amos Comenius, a seventeenth-century philosopher and one of the founders of modern educational theory, stressed that

> to exercise the senses well about the right perceiving of the differences of things will be to lay the grounds for all wisdom and wise discourse.

More than three hundred years ago he was providing an insight into teaching and learning which, despite all the resources of modern technology, we still often ignore within our classrooms today. We cannot claim to be 'exercising our senses well' if our preferred methods (i.e. formal teaching) continue to be predominantly dependent upon communication through *hearing*, a sense which provides us with less than 20 per cent of the information we gain through sight as we try to understand the world around us.

As you know, the models of learning presented in the tables referred to above (6.5.1 to 6.5.3) are designed to promote different aspects of learner development according to the aims of the particular session. However, choosing the most

Table 6.5.1 Presentation (teacher-centred models)

Method	Purpose	Characteristics	Qualities	Limitations
Lectures	For use with large groups of learners, where participation is limited because of time or student numbers	Didactic delivery, usually with a minimum of audience interaction	The transfer of large amounts of information in a limited time which lends itself to Ausubel's theories of meaningful reception learning (see Chapter 5)	Passive learning due to lack of learner participation
Formal teaching	Again, the transfer of large amounts of information during a limited period of time	Again an essentially deductive approach but may use a range of techniques and allow questions and debate	Charismatic presentations remain memorable and lend themselves to the use of 'advanced organizers' to enable the formation of cognitive structures	One-way communication, so the teacher has little idea how the various concepts are being received
Demonstrations	The transfer of skills but this often requires follow-up practice	The unpacking of a particular skill or process and the provision of an insight into specific expertise	The more difficult aspects of a process may be highlighted through the disaggregation of the whole into constituent parts. However, learner errors or bad habits must be addressed early in the process before they become learnt.	Without the aid of CCTV this process will usually be directed at relatively small groups and the lack of 'hands-on' experience may limit the extent of the learning
Individual/small group tutorials	A more personal exchange of opinion and feedback, often on a one-to-one basis	Useful for reviewing progress and discussing specific assignments and projects; an opportunity to provide individual guidance and counselling	Insufficient time may be available for tutorials	The development of competence-based education and training with its highly individualized approach requires tutors to spend more time coaching individual learners, helping with study problems, negotiating and re-negotiating targets and generally providing guidance and support on an individual basis

Table 6.5.2 Search (learner-centred models)

Method	Purpose	Characteristics	Qualities	Limitations
Projects and assignments	Important aspects of coursework, which are often integrated activities – involving more than one subject (i.e. cross-curricular)	Promotes student-initiated investigations of subjects either identified by them or selected from a range of possibilities suggested by the tutor	The breadth of the study and the extended range of sources often motivates students to produce excellent, original work which has involved the development of many new skills and understandings	Demands a high level of organization and preparation because of the cross-institutional contacts. Can be difficult to monitor standards, plagiarism, etc.
Case studies	A history of an event or set of circumstances, where the learners examine the relevant details. These fall into two broad types: those in which the learners diagnose the causes of a particular problem; those in which the learners set out to solve a particular problem.	Particularly suitable where a cool look at a problem or set of circumstances, free from the pressures of the actual event, is beneficial; a useful opportunity to exchange ideas about solutions to common work problems	Learners may not realize that decisions taken in the training situation are different from those which have to be made 'on the spot' in a live situation	Courses focusing on human behaviour; training in decision-making (management); diagnostic work in any subject area
Search or discovery	Learners are placed in situations requiring self-directed learning under the tutor's general guidance. Exercises, tasks or games are used – enabling learners to make their own discoveries.	Allows learners to demonstrate and develop a wide range of skills and personal qualities. These include the ability to show initiative, to take responsibility and plan, to solve problems, make decisions and communicate effectively. Is a highly active and participative form of learning. Opportunity for involvement may encourage poorly motivated learners	Promotes collaborative learning and the learners' ability to take responsibility for their chosen methods and to develop the ability to present and defend their findings. It may also encourage them to support the learning of other group members.	Poorly motivated learners may regard the freedom of learner-centred strategies as an opportunity to do very little

163

Table 6.5.2 continued

Method	Purpose	Characteristics	Qualities	Limitations
Seminars	To disseminate ideas and good practice by allowing individuals or small groups to investigate a topic, report back to the main seminar group and lead a discussion around the topic	Student/s collect information, about a chosen or designated topic sufficiently well to be able to prepare a presentation around the subject and then lead the discussion afterwards	Often stimulating and challenging to students. Helps to develop the learners' ability to craft and present a case. Learning something sufficiently well as to be able to inform others is, in itself, a very rewarding learning experience.	Some students need considerable support and guidance, as leading a seminar can be a very intimidating experience

Table 6.5.3   Interaction (learner-centred models continued)

Method	Purpose	Characteristics	Qualities	Limitations
Buzz group/ Word shower/ Callouts	The generation of solutions to a problem through a concentrated period of free responses from this collective process *(The term 'brain-storming is less used now because of the unfortunate connotations with epilepsy)*	A small group is given a topic or question and for five or ten minutes members say anything that occurs to them in connection with it. A recorder writes up anything that is said (no matter how irrelevant, silly or perverse) on a board or flip-chart. Members then evaluate the ideas and develop selected ones.	The process is a good way of introducing a topic and helps to make everyone feel involved and valued as a contributor. It promotes creative thinking, which often provides new or unexpected perspectives on the topic. It is useful to establish simple ground rules such: as the ideas should be called out in any order without giving or seeking explanations, justifications or comment.	Requires good management because a few members can dominate the session and others will often hold back on good ideas because they feel that they may be too radical
Small groups or syndicates	Groups of learners are split into smaller sub-groups to work (sometimes in competition with the other groups) on related problems/ issues	Provides an opportunity for learners to show initiative; can be highly motivating	Management training; in-service training; often used in conjunction with simulation exercises where groups work concurrently on the same (or different) lifelike problems	Provision of sufficient basic information is essential; groupwork activity must be well planned and prepared, and seen to be relevant
Simulation	Learners may be asked to undertake a particular task, such as solving a problem, using the same procedures as those which operate in a real-life situation. Simulation often involves a practice session or a test of knowledge acquired prior to the exercise.	A highly active form of learning; particularly suitable for any situation where learners need to practice making choices and following through the implications of their choices; frequently used instead of formal tests to find out how much learners have assimilated and how well they can apply new skills	Teaching practice: personal selection; courses for armed forces and 'emergency' services – police, first aid, fire; in-service training in industry and commercial/public sector organizations	Must be realistic and the expected result reasonably attainable by all learners; may be expensive and time-consuming to prepare

Table 6.5.3 continued

Method	Purpose	Characteristics	Qualities	Limitations
Games or Ice-breakers	Games take all kinds of forms, but often involve competition (and cooperation), teams, point-scoring, etc. They are often used to simulate real-life situations and allow learners to experience roles where they are required to make decisions and present a case. Ice-breakers can be used when a group first meets, to establish a good rapport quickly, enable learners to get to know each other and help diffuse possible tensions. Or they may be used at the beginning of regular sessions, to establish an appropriate group atmosphere.	Similar to those of role-plays allow participation by learners of varying ability add variety, assist in problem-solving and in understanding inter-personal relationships. Can be used to introduce competition (or promote cooperation) and provide motivation	Can be used to good effect in most subject areas – but must be used tactfully and skilfully in appropriate situations	If badly handled they can 'fall flat', embarrassing or even alienating and antagonizing learners
Discussion	Knowledge, ideas and opinions on particular subjects are freely exchanged among the tutor and learners.	Particularly suitable where: the content involves matters of opinion; tutors aim to change attitudes. Useful for obtaining feedback about the learners' level of understanding and ability to apply knowledge.	To follow up a visit or a talk by a visiting speaker or the showing of a film or video. Of course, many of the best discussions are spontaneous and unplanned.	Learners may stray from the subject-matter or fail to discuss it usefully Whole session may be unfocused and woolly learners may become entrenched in their attitudes rather than be prepared to change them Group leader may talk too much, intervene too readily to fill silences

Table 6.5.3 continued

Method	Purpose	Characteristics	Qualities	Limitations
Role play	Learners practise being in particular roles by acting out a face-to-face situation that represents real life – a work situation for instance. Each participant should have sufficient background information to allow a proper understanding of the part to be played.	Learners can practise and receive advice and criticism in the safety of a learning situation; practice in role play provides guidelines for future behaviour; learners gain insight into the motives and attitudes of others; a highly active learning experience that enables learners to draw their own conclusions and formulate their own ideas	The training of social workers, managers and others involved in personal relationships; the training of tutors, through microteaching	Learners may: be embarrassed; suffer loss of confidence; not take the role play seriously
Open learning	Open learning is the term used to describe any form of learning in which the provider enables individual choice in one or more aspects of learning. It frequently involves the use of materials developed specially to allow independent learning. The tutor's role is usually a combination of 'resource-manager', guide and advisor.	Particularly useful where access to conventional courses is restricted (e.g. for domestic, work or geographical reasons). Learners can work through open learning materials at their own pace – often at home or during quiet times at work – although the materials may also be used in a college-based workshop. An individual approach is being embodied in the move towards competence-based education and training and the introduction of National Vocational Qualifications. This is likely to lead to increasing use of open learning in educational mainstream classes.	Where learners are well-motivated and willing to work independently for significant periods of time, open learning can be a valuable method.	Open learning requires investment in high-quality materials and in training tutorial and administrative staff to adopt a more flexible, learner-centred role. Where such investment is lacking learners can rapidly become demotivated – especially where there are repeated problems.

appropriate teaching strategy is only the first step. The selected method may, in turn, be communicated and supported using a range of resources to provide a learning experience which is sufficiently rich to be compatible with the learners' needs. If well designed, this approach should be reasonably appropriate to most learner characteristics. The range of learning resources currently available to teachers are so many and varied that ignoring them and relying entirely on the spoken word is perverse and inexcusable. However, because the choice is so wide, it isn't always easy to decide what is appropriate. As an introduction and in order to develop some basic principles, we have gathered various educational media together in the diagram below:

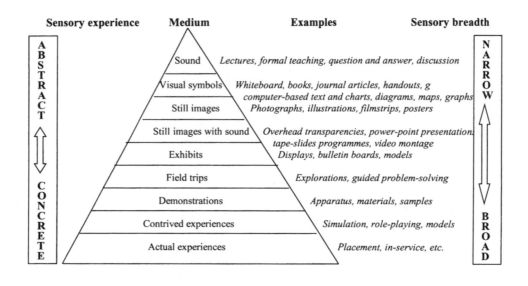

Sensory experience	Medium	Examples	Sensory breadth
ABSTRACT ↕ CONCRETE	Sound	Lectures, formal teaching, question and answer, discussion	NARROW ↕ BROAD
	Visual symbols	Whiteboard, books, journal articles, handouts, g computer-based text and charts, diagrams, maps, graphs	
	Still images	Photographs, illustrations, filmstrips, posters	
	Still images with sound	Overhead transparencies, power-point presentations, tape-slides programmes, video montage	
	Exhibits	Displays, bulletin boards, models	
	Field trips	Explorations, guided problem-solving	
	Demonstrations	Apparatus, materials, samples	
	Contrived experiences	Simulation, role-playing, models	
	Actual experiences	Placement, in-service, etc.	

D6n   Learning aid principles

Again take a particular session you have planned for a specific group of learners and (using the above diagram) suggest how you might enhance the process by including particular learning resources. Remember to consider any information about the group's learning styles, which you may have collected earlier.

Of course, the first principle is that the addition of a learning resource should *enhance* the previously unaided presentation. If it adds nothing to the session, then it isn't worth including. Secondly, as you will see, our diagram above contains two important dimensions. From the narrow top of the diagram to the broader bottom line there is a gradual increase in the *number* of the learners' senses which the particular medium engages. This indicates another basic principle which is that, when more of our senses are used, the communication and the related learning will generally be richer and more effective.

Next we should consider the *nature* of the sensory experience and point out (at the apex of the diagram) that the use of auditory language and visual symbols (i.e. words and letters) involves presenting material in an *abstract* form. We considered earlier in Chapter 3 the ways in which particular, individual learning styles either promote or inhibit learning. Learners who respond better to concrete experiences will find the rich sensory media towards the bottom of the diagram much more rewarding.

For some learners who are adept at abstract conceptualization, the use of sound (i.e. formal teaching) will be effective even though communication is primarily through hearing, which is a less informative sensory path than sight. With these learners, good progress can be made with a minimum of resources.

However, even gifted learners often find that broader, experiential learning is more productive because they simultaneously receive information through more of their senses and this allows them to use this range of memories (i.e. touch, smell, taste, in addition to hearing and sight) to recall more accurately the knowledge and skills they have gained. It becomes richer, kinaesthetic learning. We can also clearly see from the above diagram that the teacher's toolkit contains more than a pen, paper and extensive subject knowledge, and it is good practice to have a bank of resources available to you. These aids could include flip-chart paper and marker pens, dry-wipe pens (remember not to confuse the two!) for use with the whiteboard, sticky tack, craft materials, postcards, post notes, coloured pens and paper. You may also need to know how to access TV/video players, cassette recorders or video camera, computers and digital projectors, or an interactive whiteboard. Most importantly, if you are not technically proficient with the equipment you must remember who and where the technical support can be found, should you need it. Don't forget batteries and bulbs, film for cameras and a cassette for the VCR.

D6o *Selecting learning resources*

Following on from our earlier activity (D6n), and having considered some basic principles, try to identify the selection criteria which you might use when you are considering developing learning resources for your students. Think in terms of the steps in the process.

Remember that learning resources may be used to promote any of the stages within the learning processes outlined in this and earlier chapters. For example, if we use again our REAL acronym, resources may be used to facilitate *resonance* between tutor and learners, i.e. establish communication through humour, common experiences, shared aims, etc. All forms of *education* may be facilitated and supported through resources and *active* rather than passive learning may be stimulated by using search and interactive exercises based around simple resources such as library use. Finally, *learner autonomy* can be promoted through resource-based simulations, field trips and role-playing.

Following our familiar learning cycle, your learning resource selection criteria would need to address the following questions:

- **Target audience:** *Who are the resources for?* As in our earlier session-planning exercises, the more you know about your learners, the more appropriate will be your choice of supporting resources. For example, the images, references and language which you might use will be different for a group of 16 year old modern apprentices compared to a class of non-vocational adult learners.

- **Content:** *What is the subject or topic?* Consider the subject or topic to get an indication of the cognitive, affective and psycho-motor aspects of the syllabus that would benefit from the additional support of resources.

- **Learning outcomes:** *What should the resources achieve?* Resources can be used to address any aspect of the learning cycle. They may for example, be used to motivate, as metaphors to introduce difficult concepts or to break down the steps in a complex process. Resources can also provide an excellent means of differentiating learning to address diverse and individual needs.

- **Delivery:** *How will these resources be provided to the learner?* You need to decide how best the programme learning experiences and materials can be brought to the learner at the optimum period in the programme. For example, you may wish to have reference material constantly available or, at the other extreme, you may feel that providing an impact at a crucial point in the learners' development will be more important.

- **Media:** *What learning media are available to you?* You need to know exactly what learning resources you can utilize and which of them are appropriate for the defined objectives, content and delivery methods.

- **Constraints:** *What restrictions and pressures will you have to cope with?* You will have to consider such things as current budget, deadlines, preferred learning styles, expectations, health and safety requirements, etc.

6.8.1   Learners as a resource

Remember that your various learning groups are themselves a most valuable resource. As discussed in the previous chapter, the members of any large group of people will have within their ranks significant intellectual, practical, organizational and creative skills. Not only that, most of these learners will enjoy being allowed to share their particular skills with their colleagues.

> ### D6p   Resourceful learners
>
> Discuss how the learners within one of your groups or classes have provided or could provide a valuable resource for the other group members. Consider how you may develop this and in what ways you need to lend your support.

As we know, each teaching situation has its own particular demands, but with a little will and organization it is very possible to draw systematically on the strengths of a group of learners. Even more rewarding, as the class start to realize that they have particular qualities, a group identity will often begin to emerge. Many teachers talk with pride about groups of their learners who continue to meet regularly years after their programmes have been completed.

Naturally, the establishment of such unified, collaborative learners will not happen if there are within their classes constraints that restrict the essential opportunities for group interaction. The promotion of such processes isn't always easy, because often the more dominant members do not realize how they are inhibiting the contributions of less confident members. Such situations require careful and sensitive management.

6.9 | CONCLUSION

In this chapter we have explored some of the significant aspects of managing the learning process, and during this discussion it has become clear that when we break such complex relationships down into constituent parts for the sake of analysis we often create difficulties for ourselves. In actual fact, student experience within any educational setting is an amalgam of aspects of the environment, learning activities and the supporting resources.

When you add to these the three topics covered in the following Chapter 7 (reviewing learning, working relationships and effective communication) you begin to appreciate the rich range of experiences provided by most educational establishments. It also becomes clear that one of our key responsibilities as managers of learning is to sustain this seamless web of educational opportunity where students are implicitly encouraged to accept the notion of lifelong learning.

It is important that we allow the disaggregated parts to merge back into one another in order to provide an environment that is consistently conducive to learning, but as managers we have to remain aware of how the various parts may influence the whole.

6.10 | USEFUL SOURCES

Kyriacou, C. (1998) *Essential Teaching Skills* (2nd edn). Gloucester: Stanley Thornes.
This is a very reader-friendly book about teaching which could apply to all sectors. It has lots of practical advice and incorporates cartoons and blackboard summaries of each chapter. The second edition has been updated to include current teaching and learning styles and aspects of mentoring and portfolio assessment.

Walkin, L. (1990) *Teaching and Learning in Further and Adult Education*. Gloucester: Stanley Thornes.
A very good all-round book on the principles of learning. The characteristics of different kinds of learners are identified. Equally the author goes to great lengths to identify the many roles of the teacher. Curriculum development, assessment and reviewing are dealt with in detail.

Siddons, S. (1997) *Delivering Training*. London: IPD.
A slim volume useful for the trainer who needs to know the essentials of planning a course and being aware of the needs of the learners and what to do if things go wrong.

Elliot, G. (1996) *Crisis and Change in Vocational Education and Training*. London: Jessica Kingsley.
A good chapter on being a reflective practitioner and wider implications for managers and college organizations.

Jarvis, P., Holford, J. and Griffin, C. (1999) *The Theory and Practice of Learning*. London: Kogan Page.
An excellent first chapter on lifelong learning, a very readable general book about how people learn.

Coulthard, M. (1992) *Advances in Spoken Discourse Analysis*. London: Routledge.
An interesting read which highlights how much the teacher talks in the classroom compared to the students. It makes one realize the importance of planning the learning for students so that they are engaged in the learning and not passive listeners.

Fairclough, N. (1989) *Language and Power*. London: Longman.
This is worth dipping into to realize the importance of using the appropriate language in the classroom.

Halliday, M.K. (1978) *Language as a Social Semiotic, the Social Interpretation of Meaning*. London: Arnold.
This book again is a good source of material on the importance of understanding not only the language but also the culture of your learners. Teachers can upset their students without even realizing that what they have said is being misunderstood.

Note: The FAQs Rationale at FENTO Stages 1, 2 and 3 is at the end of Chapter 7, Managing the Learning Process (Part 2).

6.12 | KEY AREA D – MANAGING THE LEARNING PROCESS

Purpose: Teachers and teaching teams need to be effective in establishing a productive learning environment and in working with learners and colleagues to structure and monitor the learning process. Central to these activities is the teacher's capacity to communicate effectively with learners and colleagues. Teachers must consider what encourages learners to learn as well as dealing with the practical organization of the environment, including the legal requirements relating to health, safety and security. They must also consider how to resource the varied approaches to teaching and learning and recognize, by forming effective working relationships with others, that successful management of teaching and learning requires collaboration. Finally, teachers should evaluate teaching and learning and play their part in contributing to the organization's quality assurance system. For an analysis of this process at FENTO Stages 1, 2 and 3, see the rationale on pages 199–201 in Chapter 7.

Please note: The FENTO Standards listed below are relevant to the following three levels of award: Stage 1 (Introduction), Stage 2 (Intermediate) and Stage 3 (Full Certification). All of the standards are required at Stage 3, only those in italic or bold are required at Stage 2 and only those in italic are required at Stage 1.

UNIT D1.   Establish and maintain an effective learning environment *In order to do this teachers should:*

Demonstrate that they are able to:	and have specific knowledge and critical understanding of:	plus generic knowledge of:		Summary of appropriate evidence in this Key Area:	*Relevant Chapter Activities*
Criteria:					
a act as an advocate for learners attempting to secure appropriate resources	• The characteristics and purpose of an effective learning environment • The value of effective	• Theories concerning motivation and ways of motivating learners • Ways of structuring and presenting information and	a	Session Plans, Learning Agreements, Learning Resources audit	D6e to D6n
b *ensure an interactive, safe and productive learning environment that fosters learners' security and confidence*	interaction between those involved in teaching and learning • Group dynamics and how to manage groups of learners	ideas • Appropriate media and language forms for presenting information • Different teaching techniques	b	Rationales, Learning Agreements, Learner Support	D6c to D6i and E8a to E8m
c *maintain learners' interest in and engagement with, the learning process*	• The health and safety requirements applicable to the learning environment	• Different ways of learning	c	Chosen learning approaches, Session Plans	D6d, D6i, D6o

173

d	identify and redress poor motivation and challenge inappropriate behaviour	
	• What motivates learners and what constitutes acceptable levels of motivation and behaviour	
	• Their personal responsibilities for health and safety • The organization's learning programmes and available resources • Good practice in catering for the needs of all students including learners who require additional support • The role of information and learning technology in supporting learning and teaching • The importance of pacing teaching and learning appropriately	
d	Learning Agreements, Learning Review, Teaching Plan	D6a to D6k and E8j
	Plus commentary in PDJ on the purposes and value of the above together with records in your Practice File of Teaching Observations, Lesson Plans, Rationales, Self-Evaluations and Progress Summary	

Key to above standards required at each FENTO Stage:

Introduction Stage – italic
Intermediate Stage + bold
Certification Stage – all

UNIT D2. Plan and structure learning activities *In order to do this teachers should:*

	Demonstrate that they are able to:	and will have specific knowledge and critical understanding of:	plus generic knowledge of:		Summary of appropriate evidence in this Key Area:	Relevant Chapter Activities
a	Criteria: use local, national, comparative, organizational and other appropriate data to set clear targets for learning and individual learners' achievements	• The required outcomes of learning programmes and related assessment requirements and opportunities • Ways of incorporating all aspects of the learning cycle in the learning process • Ways of consolidating and reinforcing learning	• Theories concerning motivation and ways of motivating learners • Ways of structuring and presenting information and ideas • Appropriate media and language forms for presenting information	a	Action Plans, Learning Review, Session Plans	A3g to A3j; D6a to D6h, E8a to E8h
b	*set tasks for learners which will foster their curiosity, creativity and ability to work on their own*		• Different teaching techniques • Different ways of learning • Their personal responsibilities for health and safety	b	Session Plans, Rationales, Learning Reviews.	C5b to C5g D6a to D6h, E8j
c	*structure the learning in a way likely to foster and maintain learners' enthusiasm and motivation*		• The organization's learning programmes and available resources	c	Session Plans, Rationales, Evaluations	B4c, B4e, B4g, C5n,D6d, E8m
d	match the format and level of learning support materials to the abilities of learners and the desired learning outcomes		• Good practice in catering for the needs of all students including learners who require additional support • The role of information and learning technology in supporting learning and teaching	d	Learning Support, Rationales, Session Plans	A3b to A3j; B4s, C5m,D6d, D6i
e	select and develop materials of an appropriate design and format to meet the needs of a wide range of students, including those with hearing and visual impairment		• The importance of pacing teaching and learning appropriately	e	Session Plans, Schemes of Work, Learning Review	A3c, A3f, A3g, B4m,B4s, C5p, C5s D6g, D6m

175

	Standard	Knowledge	Records/Evidence	Codes
f	*use a variety of teaching methods to meet the needs of groups and individuals and to provide an environment in which all learners have the opportunity to experience success*	What constitutes acceptable levels of work to enable learners to meet defined learning outcomes	Learning Review, Needs Analysis, Session Plans, Schemes of Work	C4r, C5u, C5v, D6l, D6n, D7f, D7h
g	**provide opportunities for learners to reinforce their knowledge and understanding.**	Appropriate sources of information and learning support for learners and how to access them	Action Plans, Learning Review, Session Plans	C5g, C5m, C5p, C5s, C5t, D6d, D6m, D6n, D7i, D7m
h	*identify and exploit opportunities to improve learners' basic skills and Key Skills*	The basic skills and Key Skills which learners need to meet the demands of their programmes of study	Learning Review, Action Plan Also see Chapter 12	A3j, A3qm A3rm A3u, B4g, B4n, B4s,C5m, D6m
i	*help learners to develop study skills including time management and work organization skills*	Study skills and how to foster these	Learning Review, Action Plans	E8b, E8d, E8g,E8m
j	*encourage learners to take more responsibility for organizing their learning successfully*	How to encourage learners to work effectively on their own	Session Plans, Rationales	C5u, C5v, D6h, D6l

Plus commentary in PDJ on the purposes and value of experiential learning together with records in PF of Teaching Observations, Lesson Plans, Rationales, Self-Evaluations and Progress Summary

Key to above standards required at each FENTO Stage:

Introduction Stage – italic
Intermediate Stage + bold
Certification Stage – all

UNIT D5. Select and develop resources to support learning *In order to do this teachers should:*

	Demonstrate that they will be able to:	*and will have specific knowledge and critical understanding of:*	*plus generic knowledge of:*		*Summary of appropriate evidence in this Key Area:*	*Relevant Chapter Activities*
	Criteria:					
a	identify the resources required to deliver the programme of learning and support learners	• Ways of quantifying the resources needed to deliver programmes	• Theories concerning motivation and ways of motivating learners • Ways of structuring and presenting information and ideas	a	Session Plans, Rationales	D6m, D6n, D6o
b	ensure they are familiar with the range and availability of resources	• The resources available for learning and how to access them	• Appropriate media and language forms for presenting information	b	Session Plans, Rationales, Action Plans, Learning Review	D6m, D6n, D6o
c	*obtain the resources necessary by following the organization's procedures*		• Different teaching techniques • Different ways of learning • Their personal responsibilities for health and safety	c	ICT and audio-visual procedures	D6n, D6o
d	produce an appropriate range of teaching and learning materials which meets the needs of learners, including those with learning difficulties and disabilities	• The teaching and learning materials appropriate for different programmes • How to develop teaching and learning materials	• The organization's learning programmes and available resources • Good practice in catering for the needs of all students including learners who require additional support	d	Exemplar Materials and Session Plans	D6m and D6n
e	**use information and learning technology, as appropriate**	• The learning support needs of learners when using technology-based or distance-learning approaches	• The role of information and learning technology in supporting learning and teaching	e	ICT-based examples	D6m and D6n
f	*evaluate and ensure the appropriateness and effectiveness of teaching and learning materials and resources for all learners*	• Sources of information about resources designed to support students working on their own and how to access them	• The importance of pacing teaching and learning appropriately	f	Evaluation feedback	D6m, D6n, D7i, G10e

g	help learners to identify appropriate ways of working on their own and provide them with advice and support on using resources effectively	• Ways of enabling students to work effectively on their own and the place of these in teaching and learning • Mentoring and coaching within learning support	Learning Review and Action Plans	C5r, D6e, E8b, E8j
h	monitor how learners are responding to teaching and learning materials during the programme and make modifications as necessary		Evaluation, Rationales, Session Plans, Action Plans	D7f, D7i, B4j; and B4l
i	evaluate the effectiveness of the materials and resources used for learning support and update materials and equipment as necessary	• The criteria by which to evaluate the effectiveness of learning support materials	Evaluation Feedback data	D7i, E8m, G10e
j	keep up to date with the development of resources that enable learners to work effectively on their own		Current resource usage	D7i, D7r

Key to above standards required at each FENTO Stage:

Introduction Stage – italic

Intermediate Stage + bold

Certification Stage – all

Plus commentary in PDJ on the purposes and value of experiential learning together with records in PF of Teaching Observations, Lesson Plans, Rationales, Self-Evaluations and Progress Summary

Managing the learning process (Part 2)

Lyn Butcher

Key Area D Communicating effectively with learners, reviewing learning and maintaining effective working relationships

Key concepts in this chapter

Accountability, Communication, Continuous Improvement, Contractual Obligations, Differentiation, Diversity of the Teacher's Role, Evaluation, Giving and Receiving Feedback, Inclusive Learning, Internal/External Customers, Negotiation Skills, Networking, Professional Relationships, Quality Assurance, Quality Culture, Rapport with Learners, Referral of Learners, Reflection, Reviewing Learning

Before you begin this chapter you may wish to check the FAQs on pp. 199–202

Index to Chapter 7

Chapter 7 Activities designed to generate evidence against the Standards

7.1 INTRODUCTION

This chapter focuses on FENTO Key Area D, units 3, 4, 6 and 7. In other words, we are moving away from the management of classroom teaching into the management of the learner's individual progress and into other areas of the teacher's role, including liaison with other professionals and the maintenance of quality. Broadly, these four units cover effective communication, reviewing learning, working relationships and quality assurance.

With the ever-increasing diversity of the teacher's role, there is greater necessity to be aware of the link between you as the classroom teacher and the learners' whole experience within the organization. You need to be aware of how the organization works and your role within it, and how various systems feed into each other in order to create the learners' experience. This in turn will help to enlighten you about the need for the sometimes laborious paperwork which now comes with the job. As a novice teacher, your main concern will undoubtedly be with lesson preparation, delivery and marking, but from the start you will be involved in the tracking of progress, stating of outcomes and evaluation of provision – so be prepared! But rest assured – we have all been there – and in the current climate of continuous change, it is a constant learning curve for us all.

7.2 REVIEWING LEARNERS

As you would expect, effective teaching inevitably means that you must consistently review your learners' progress. How and when you do this may differ from course to course, and between different organizations. However, the main principles are the same. You and your learners need to be aware of the progress being made and your organization will require you to record the outcomes of reviews as part of the quality assurance process.

You may review students as either their subject/course tutor, or as a personal tutor. As the former, you will be aware of a student's strengths and weaknesses through your teaching and assessment methods. As the latter, you will probably have to rely on information from colleagues to help gain an idea of the student's progress in a variety of subject areas. You may be the student's only tutor contact at college, or one of many. The skill comes from using (together with the student) the information gained to draw conclusions and to action plan.

D7a Reviewing learning

Try to identify some of the reasons why you might review the progress of your own learners. What would you hope to gain?

The reasons for ongoing review are many, but often it is carried out to:

- evaluate the progress a student is making
- check if the student is on course to succeed with their studies
- identify and diagnose particular difficulties
- give the student a platform to speak individually about their own learning
- negotiate individual targets
- discuss future aspirations
- motivate learners
- make learners feel valued
- document progress against targets
- monitor attendance, etc.

An informal review can take place at any time to meet particular student needs. However, there are usually more formal scheduled tutorial times, either at frequent intervals or at certain times of the year. It is usual to carry out initial reviews quite early in a course, perhaps immediately following induction. This enables you to check that the learner is on the right programme and to identify any specific needs which may require specialist attention. Depending on the intensity of the programme, further reviews can occur once per term or more often. Other good times are following or during a period of industrial placement, or after assessment has taken place.

D7b   Types of review

Investigate the review process in your own organization, noting the calendar of *formal* reviews. Collect samples of any pro formas used to 'capture' the information discussed and the action agreed. Is the process similar across the whole organization, or do different programmes/courses have different systems? For example, compare the 16–18 programme with that of adults.

Having got to know more about your establishment's approach to review, you now need to think about the process of carrying reviews out with your learners. It is possible to carry out group tutorials, but to evaluate an individual's progress you really need to talk to students on a one-to-one basis. This is easier said than done when confronted with a full class. One way to tackle the problem is to give the group a task to complete while seeing each individual. If there is another room available (and you can trust the group to work) it is obviously better to withdraw learners one at a time so that you can both concentrate. Another possibility is to book individual tutorials away from group sessions. This is often used with adult learners who appreciate being able to negotiate meetings at times convenient to them.

D7c   Interview settings

Given that you have arranged to interview learners at particular times to carry out their reviews, consider how you would ensure that the setting is conducive to an effective discussion.

You would prepare for an interview very much as you would prepare for a teaching session because, during an earning review, it is equally important to create the right atmosphere in an appropriate setting. The relationship between tutor and tutee is extremely important at this time and certain values are central, especially openness, trust and confidentiality. Learners should feel safe to express their views and feelings. You need to be able to deal with potential problems in a calm and logical manner.

Just as you would carefully plan a normal lesson, so you must plan for the review. You may find it useful to draw up an 'agenda' of items to discuss, leaving room for those raised by the learner. The course leader or organization may dictate certain items.

D7d   Review issues

Consider the sort of things you may discuss with your particular learners during a learning review.

Issues that may be discussed in a review include curriculum performance, work experience, attendance, attitude, discipline and rules, application for jobs or Higher Education, compiling profiles, personal problems, etc. You may have a list of criteria against which you need to review the student, but the trusting relationship between you makes it important that your learners are aware of these.

Give the student advance warning of any preparatory work needed on their part, i.e. what they need to bring with them. You may wish them to carry out a self-assessment prior to the meeting (see Chapter 9), to give you a base from which to start. For initial reviews, it may also be useful to use your organization's Learner Agreement especially when talking about commitment and targets. If it is a second or subsequent review, you should have available a copy of actions agreed at the last review – and this is a good place to start. Above all, it is essential to set the scene at the beginning – just as you would in a taught lesson.

Reviewing what the learner has achieved and agreeing sensible targets helps to aid motivation. As you progress through a formal tutorial you will need to record the information discussed. Both of you should sign and take a copy of what you agree. Targets set should be 'SMART':

- *s*pecific
- *m*easurable (for reference in the next tutorial)
- *a*ttainable
- *r*ealistic
- *t*ime-specific (state a date when the target is to be reached)

They should also be negotiated, as this puts more responsibility onto the learner and they are therefore more likely to be met. Targets may be curriculum-related, or more general, in connection with, for example, attitude or attendance. Targets need to be in chunks of a suitable size for each individual learner – remember learners are all different and the principles of inclusive learning (Chapter 8) and differentiation (Chapter 3) should be applied here. You and the learner must monitor these targets if they are to be effective.

An example of a record of a learning review is included below and blank pro formas are available on the associated website *tipcet.com*

LEARNING REVIEW AND ACTION PLAN	
Candidate:	Barbara Gardner
Assessor/Personal Tutor:	Arthur Robinson
Date and Time:	4th December 2002, 16.30 hours
Programme:	NVQ Care Award
Reasons for review:	End of term learning review

Achievements since last review (date): Held on Monday 4th November 2002
Assignment Four: Analysis of clinical setting. Assignment referred because, although well written it is mostly descriptive and lacks any analysis of procedures and patient care.
Case study: Production of a client care plan well carried out according to hospital guidelines and with good insight into specific patient needs.
Unit CU7: Evidence of critical thinking about actions and applied new knowledge well to practice.
Candidate Log: Little disappointing, still a tendency to focus on evidence with very little reflection about the procedures or the patients' reactions.

Action Agreed:
Assignment Four to be resubmitted. To add more careful analysis of procedures, particularly the monitoring of patient care.
Candidate Log to be developed in a more reflective way and to include more detailed reflection on own professional development as a result of experience on the ward.

Agreed Completion Date 15th January 2003

| Signature of Candidate: | BE Gardner |
| Signature of Assessor/ Personal Tutor: | A Robinson |

Top copy to student, middle copy to personal tutor and bottom copy to programme coordinator

As well as target setting, other issues may arise from the review process. You need to be prepared for learners to disclose possible problems, either academic or personal. You may not feel able to deal with these yourself and may need help from other sources. The key here is not to try to deal with issues in which you have little experience, but refer the student to specialized support.

D7e Referral agencies

Assemble a list of the range of internal and external agencies which you are currently able to use to support your learners through a formal referral system.

Some examples are Careers Adviser, Accommodation Officer, Student Union, Study Skills, Student Counsellor, Job Centre, Youth Worker, Social Services, Citizens Advice Bureau. Students should be involved in the referral process themselves and confidentiality is all important in order to maintain the trust built up between you. It is important here to make the distinction between learning support and pastoral care. Pastoral care is what you will be involved in within a Personal Tutor role. This includes caring for the academic progress as well as general well-being of your learners. Learning support is where you may refer learners with specific needs, or those who are struggling in a particular area of their studies – this is discussed in more detail in Chapter 8.

Whatever structure your reviews take, you must summarize the issues covered at the end – again, just like a lesson! This reinforces the key points, and allows learners to clarify anything misunderstood. Get learners to reflect the issues back to you in order to check their understanding.

D7f Practical reviews

Carry out a selection of review tutorials with different learners. Provide examples of completed tutorial log/record sheets and action plans. Include in your sample learners with differing needs and, if possible, evidence of referral to more specialized support.

From the points already raised, you can see that the tutorial role is as complex as the classroom teacher role. It can often prove to be more demanding, especially if you are conducting a series of one-to-one reviews consecutively. You will probably find the first few tutorial sessions thoroughly exhausting as it takes considerably more effort to concentrate on each individual in turn than it does to teach a full class. In between teaching we are able to give a group a task to do while we gather ourselves for the next input. With individual tutorials rest is impossible, as you must give each learner your full attention. When you get tired, you find your mind wandering onto more mundane matters and then realize that you have not been listening to your tutee. It is highly embarrassing to have to ask someone to repeat what they have said, especially if it has taken them courage to tell you something in the first place. Thankfully, it does get easier as your review skills improve and you get faster and more efficient. However, while developing this welcome expertise, ensure that you do not succumb to the temptation to short-change your learners.

D7g Identifying skills

After looking back on the reviews you have carried out, try to identify the skills you are developing and summarize them in priority order.

Creating the appropriate atmosphere is obviously the first most important competence. You may find it helpful to start the review by indulging in idle chat, asking the student how they are, what they have been doing, etc. This puts them at ease.

It is useful to refer here to the theories of Carl Rogers with regard to his 'facilitative conditions' of the 'empathy, congruence and positive reward' required within a counselling situation, but also most important in a review. Rogers (1983) states that some of the goals of being a humanistically oriented teacher are aiming 'toward a climate of trust in the classroom', 'toward a participatory mode of decision-making in all aspects of learning', and 'toward helping students to prize themselves, to build their confidence and self-esteem'. All of these need to be inherent in the tutorial review.

Many other counselling skills come into play in the review situation. These include active listening (watching for verbal and non-verbal messages), attending (being there, concentrating, as described earlier), and probing (trying to gain more information). The skills of effective questioning allow us to probe students for their true feelings. Open questions give them a platform for expressing concerns. Clarifying questions check our own understanding of the facts and student feelings. Empathy helps us to convey our understanding of students' needs back to them. Congruence allows us to negotiate plans of action with which both sides will agree. Respect and trust dictate that we treat learners individually, without bias and in confidence.

Some examples of the types of questions you may use are:

- *Open*: 'How do you feel you are doing on your work placement?'
  'What do you intend to do when you leave college?'

- *Probing*: 'Tell me more about the incident with the customer.'
  'How did you reach the conclusion in your assignment?'
  'Give me an example of a situation in which you feel vulnerable.'

- *Clarifying*: 'So am I right in thinking...?'
  'I think you are saying ... to me, is that correct?'

Building a student's confidence and self-esteem can be facilitated through effective feedback of a learner's performance. Giving appropriate feedback is a skill that you will certainly need to develop. In these situations you will need to cope with giving negative feedback as well as positive, although all feedback should be constructive. You may find that giving feedback is the most demanding area of reviewing learning. As mentioned earlier, you could be reviewing learners from your own course or subject, in which case the results of performance assessment will be familiar to you and you will know your learners quite well. However, you may be a Personal Tutor with many tutees from differing subject areas and information on their progress may come from a variety of sources. Giving feedback which is constructive and supportive, while at the same time being accurate, is a fine balancing act.

D7h   Good feedback

Thinking about your own learners, summarize what you feel would be the essential qualities of good feedback to them. It will be useful to refer to this list when you undertake the next activity (D7i).

Commonly accepted characteristics of giving good feedback are:

- *Timing* – provide it as soon as practical and only when the student is being receptive.
- *A positive orientation* – most students respond favourably to being told that something has gone well. This will usually relax the student and they are more likely to pay attention to any negative feedback that follows.
- *Detail-specific* – deal with particular incidents and avoid being too general.
- *Clear* – explain both the negative and positive comments. Clarify why something worked or did not work, instead of just saying it went well/did not go well. Give reasons.
- *Constructive* – by offering advice to help the student to move forward with their learning. Suggest what could have been done to improve the situation.
- *Tutee choice* – negotiate what you feel is an appropriate response from the student. Insistence or demand on your part may alienate the learner.
- *Tutee understanding* – get the student to reflect back your advice and suggest their own.
- *Supportive* – do not let the recipient flounder aimlessly. They will need some structure around which to make headway.

The most difficult part of giving feedback has to be that of tackling poor performance. One effective way of doing this is to put the ball in the student's court first, by asking them how they feel they are progressing. More often than not they will identify problem areas themselves. If they do not, continue with directed questions related to more specific elements of progress. If you have criteria against which to measure, ask the learner how they feel that they have met the criteria. Obviously, this is general guidance. You may need to develop particular styles to meet different learner needs.

D7i   Review evaluation

Try to evaluate accurately your own performance in tutorials against the criteria you produced for activity (D7h) above. In what areas do you need to improve? Considering the process used in your programme area or organization, how could the system be improved?

In summary, a review is a good medium to use for re-motivating learning and in turn helping to aid retention and achievement. To be effective, a review must be well planned and thorough. Certain skills of counselling need to be employed with care taken to look beyond the obvious. Feedback should be constructive and sensitive, with students fully involved. Targets should be negotiated and agreed by both parties, with regular monitoring. Records should be made of review outcomes and this feeds back into the organization's quality assurance system. Summarize discussions at the end, leaving the learner feeling positive. Remember, it takes time to build up the skills required to be an effective reviewer – you will not necessarily get it right first time!

7.3 COLLABORATION AND NETWORKING

Earlier in this chapter and within previous chapters we have emphasized that teaching should be seen as a *collaborative* activity which, naturally, involves liaison with other people in order to support learners through referral to more specialized help. This section extends on this, looking at how you will need to work collaboratively with both colleagues and external contacts in order to coordinate all aspects of the curriculum.

Although you can often work in isolation, especially as a part-time tutor at an outreach centre, you will undoubtedly be a member of at least one team. How often you actually meet with this team will depend on the management of your organization. You may very well be a member of many teams, certainly if you work in more than one curriculum area. These teams may have conflicting demands on your time – each team wanting to make the best use of you.

In addition, the teams to which you belong may not all have been created for similar purposes. You may belong to a course team where you are all working towards delivery of an effective learning experience for students on one course. You may have the vocational area in common, but not necessarily share subject expertise. Many of the team may have worked in industry and you will all have different experiences. You may all teach the same group of students and meet to discuss planning issues, i.e. when to set assessments so that they do not clash, or to discuss how each part of the curriculum fits together. You may, on the other hand, belong to a subject team such as Mathematics or Information Technology. You will all have the subject in common, but may teach different students and different courses. Cross-college teams will also exist, for example, groups of personal tutors will meet to discuss the personal tutor curriculum. Due to the dynamic nature of post-compulsory education, more specialized project teams will be created to follow up contemporary initiatives. In addition to these teams, each organization will have management teams at a variety of levels. You will certainly be able to identify examples of these types of teams and more within your own organization.

D7j Team membership

List the teams to which you belong both formally and informally. Summarize your role within each of these teams. Say to which teams you feel you make the most contribution and why.

As a consequence of belonging to more than one team, you may find yourself having to take on a variety of roles, some of which will be unfamiliar to you. It may now be appropriate to discuss some theory connected to the creation, structure and life of teams.

In his discussion about teamwork, Morrison (1998) gives a definition of a team as

> a group of people with a common objective, whose members possess different areas of expertise, skills, personalities and abilities that complement one another, and who are committed to working together co-operatively on a common, shared task and a common purpose.

However, you may not choose to be in a particular team, and teams in education are not necessarily hand picked for the purpose. This means that the collection of individuals may not work well together, leading to an ineffective situation. In Chapter 5 (activity C5n) we considered Belbin's theories about the characteristics of group members and the roles they adopt.

Although you may have a tendency towards one of Belbin's characters, you will probably be comfortable in more than one of these roles. Indeed, you may take on different roles within different teams, as mentioned earlier. In theory a team will not work if it comprises of too many people seeking the same role, but it does not necessarily need one of each to work – a good mix will suffice.

Other well-known related theory comes from Tuckman (1965) regarding the development of teams. This theory relates to a variety of occupations but can easily apply to education. Tuckman recognizes four stages in team development:

- *forming* – a collection of disparate individuals gathered to achieve a particular task
- *storming* – reaction to the task ahead and to other group members
- *norming* – development of group cohesiveness
- *performing* – working effectively to achieve the identified task

Tuckman points out that it is the first three stages that will test the group's willingness and ability to direct itself collaboratively towards the agreed task. They may show their enthusiasm for the job in hand, but can become distracted as they test each other out and become orientated with other individuals as well as with the task. Once formed, there may be many arguments, especially if progress with the task is slow. The team begins to lay down its own rules and provides a structure for completion of the task, and roles are decided. The team is mature at the *performing* stage and is able to carry out the assigned tasks. However, many teams do not arrive at this stage, or do not necessarily arrive in the order stated.

Within education this is especially true as stated by Bush and Middlewood (1997):

> with many teams consisting of a fluid mixture of full-time, part-time and temporary staff, experienced and inexperienced teachers, and professional, para-professional and lay members, it is reasonable to assume that team development is a fragmented, non-linear process and considerably more complex than many normative models imply.

Even with a fully mature team, there will still be ups and downs. Perhaps you can relate this theory to a team to which you belong. Within a continuous improvement culture, teams are often 'renewed' or 'reformed' as individual skills and knowledge are transferred to new projects. This process could be seen as adding a fifth stage to Tuckman's model – i.e. '*transforming*'.

As mentioned earlier, teams in education are not always able to be hand-picked which may lead to problems of conflict. It should, in theory, be advantageous to have a team working on a problem, but teaching has not always been seen as a teamwork activity. Teachers have historically had a good amount of autonomy and may not be open to the sharing what is required to make an effective team.

Bush and Middlewood describes the *incompatibility* between classroom teaching and teamwork by referring to an example from Clement and Sullivan (1970) which compares the difference between a team of football players and a team of teachers. The footballers' central aim revolves around a team event – the football match. Conversely, the central aim of teachers is the interactions between themselves and the students in the classroom, which is *not* a team event.

D7k Team performance

Without naming people, programmes or departments, briefly discuss your experience of working in educational teams. Identify successes and those situations where agreement was difficult. Say how problems were resolved.

You may have had experience of tutors who are unwilling to contribute to a team activity (an example would be reluctance to part with material which they have developed, seeing it as their property). However, the incorporation of further education colleges has created the necessity for greater collaboration between staff because of the range of new pressures affecting colleagues. In order to survive within this highly pressured environment, the willingness to share all aspects of work with colleagues (including material preparation) is crucial. If you are willing to share responsibilities, you will often find that others are more willing to be generous towards you. It is interesting to note that, following incorporation and the onset of the culture of Total Quality Management (TQM is discussed later in this chapter), management in colleges have leaned towards the formation of more formal teams.

D7l Team structures

Discuss how the management of your establishment is structured. Consider processes such as decision-making, the devolution of responsibility, the ability to be responsive, access to information, etc.

The establishment of teams to take responsibility for particular aspects of educational provision can be extremely useful and does appear to support the empowerment ideas of Freire, Deming and Revans (see Chapter 12). However, the increase in the number of teams can cause management structures and communication processes to become more rigid at a time when flexibility and responsiveness are extremely important. If a team has a clear mandate and the ability to change things, they can become a valuable asset to a college. It is when they are formed without a clearly defined, achievable purpose and are given responsibility without authority that problems often arise.

189

> ### D7m   *Evidence of working with others*
>
> Collect relevant examples of memorandums, letters, emails and meeting minutes to show your involvement with colleagues and your membership of teams. Obtain witness statements from colleagues and/or line managers regarding the contribution you make to these teams. (Your organization's performance management process and documentation may also be useful here.)

So far this section has dealt with forming and working within teams internal to the organization. Now it is necessary to move on to look at the wider picture and include all contacts with whom you may come into association. This may include internal colleagues with whom you do not necessarily come in contact through team meetings. These may be support staff (i.e. administrators, reprographics staff, guidance workers, caretakers, housekeepers, librarians, counsellors, etc.). All these individuals are central to the smooth running of the organization and have a huge impact on the students' total learning experience.

You will also be involved with links with external agencies, some of direct importance to your learners, and others more of a support to you as a tutor. Another consequence of the 1993 incorporation of colleges of further education with its deliberate creation of a competitive culture was the gradual movement away from collaboration with colleagues in similar local institutions. This has created a greater need for teachers to belong to professional support agencies in order to maintain some contact with other practitioners, possibly in the form of subject-based associations. More recently in the 2000s, there has been a move to return to some collaboration and you may find yourself involved with contemporary initiatives in liaison with other local colleges.

A more direct connection with the students' experiences are the qualification awarding bodies, with whom you will need to keep close contact. As these award providers have responsibility for validating courses (which includes quality assurance of provision) you will be required to provide them with relevant information from time to time. Regular visits will be made from external assessors and verifiers, and you may be required to attend some awarding body training in order to run certain courses. There will be a similar relationship with higher education institutions as colleges often franchise courses from their local universities.

Add to this list your local employers, who are very important contacts for three main reasons. Firstly, your students may be on a course paid for by an employer. If you work for a business unit they will be your main source of students and you may tailor courses especially to suit certain employees. Secondly, you may have vocational students who require periods of placement within industry. Employers can provide this experience and often furnish you with feedback on your students' progress. Lastly, it is becoming more common for tutors in further education to take up industrial experience themselves to keep them up to date with the outside world and hence give their courses more credibility.

Government agencies have an enormous impact on the day-to-day running of further education, although you may not necessarily have direct contact with them yourself. The most important one to mention here is the Learning and Skills Council. This is made up of a variety of people who represent local business and communities, learners who are disadvantaged, employees, young people, students with special learning needs, adult learners and individuals who face discrimination. This agency controls the funding of post-16 education and the quality assurance process.

Other external contacts may include visiting speakers, suppliers of materials and resources, local secondary schools (for marketing and recruitment), advice agencies such as the careers service, centres used for outreach provision and prison education departments. Lengthy though it may be, the above is not intended to be an exhaustive list!

Organizations often describe internal and external contacts as 'stakeholders', in other words those who have an unquestionable interest in its success. For example, students, staff, suppliers, franchise partners, parents, funding bodies and so on.

In order to help you decipher the maze of possible contacts, the following activity may help you to identify those of most importance to you at this time:

D7n   Stakeholder contact

Identify the stakeholders who have a direct interest in the continuing success of your organization. Compile a list of your own internal and external contacts. (An organizational chart may help you here, or you may wish to draw up your own diagram to show the network of contacts which you maintain.) Critically analyse how these contacts directly or indirectly benefit your learners.

7.4 | COMMUNICATION WITH COLLEAGUES

Now that you are aware of your internal and external contacts, it is important to consider how you communicate with them. Within Chapter 6 we touched on communication with learners here we will be considering complex systems or channels of communication which need to exist to promote the smooth working of the organization.

You may have already formed some views of how communication works within your own teaching environment. In Bush and West-Bunham (1994), a chapter by Riches makes the point that unsatisfactory communication is a common complaint within organizations when he claims that:

> Mistakes are often made because communication is not seen as a two-way exchange, but as a directive from above, without any consideration of those for whom the communication is intended, or of their views.

Within education, communication is made more critical due to the speed and frequency of change. In recent times educational establishments have simultaneously had to become more efficient, complex and aware of market forces and government legislation. Riches (ibid.) gives a useful classification of different spheres of communication that can be related to the educational setting:

- *Interpersonal communication* concerns the behaviour of individual people when transferring information verbally and non-verbally

- *Organizational communication* appreciates the fact that all members of an organization may be sending and receiving signals simultaneously (a network)
- *Basic mechanical aspects of communication* identifies the use of mechanical or electronic devices to transmit and receive messages

Person-to-person communication is obviously important in all aspects of education, but other means of communication have taken on a more significant role. While memorandums and telephones used to be the main methods of communication between colleagues in different workrooms and on different sites, the popularity of electronic mail has taken over. The reasons for this are fairly obvious, and include speed of response, facility to mail more than one person at once and the ability to file and store messages for future reference. One can however argue that it has also removed or reduced the quality of an important aspect, i.e. personal contact.

Riches (ibid.) also categorizes communication flow within typical organizations as *downward, upward* and *horizontal*. The strongest flow is usually *downward*, from top management down through formal layers of authority. This could be via more 'static' means such as organizational rules, job specifications or work manuals. On the other hand, it could be via more dynamic communication that changes more regularly, for example, briefings, advisory meetings, staff development sessions, in-house newsletters, etc. Communication can break down if individuals are isolated from line managers, for example, when they are on different sites. Formal meetings are then necessary, and within education the timing of these is extremely complicated due to individual timetables and different patterns of working, etc. Electronic mail has partly solved this problem, but personal contact is still needed.

Effective *upward* communication (from workers to managers) depends upon the trust built between the levels and culture of the organization. *Horizontal* communication is the most frequent type within an organization, as you will often talk to work colleagues both informally and formally throughout the day. This type of communication is strongly linked to teamwork. It is also important as it bridges the gap between departments and teams.

D7o   Presenting your viewpoint

Consider the processes available to you to make your voice heard. Say how your organization facilitates the participation of staff and the dissemination of views and opinions.

Barriers to organizational communication are many and varied. Inevitably there are formal and informal 'gatekeepers' who are either authorized to monitor messages or make it their business to intercept communications and to decide how much, if any, of the message to pass on. Such people are in powerful positions, which are sometimes deliberately established, but often are assumed without either full management knowledge or approval.

Another barrier can be the incorrect use of language and jargon – just as in the classroom. People who have different values can put different weight on different parts of a message as it progresses up and down the chain. A person's status can impede communication – you may not feel able to approach a senior manager for example. Failure to hear and/or interpret a message correctly could be a problem – you may hear what you want to hear.

The larger the organization, the more complex are the communication channels. Face-to-face contact may be less frequent, managers may be segregated from the staff. The further a message has to travel, the more likely it will become distorted. If you work closely together as a subject team, and are based within the same room, communication will be frequent and informal. You will keep each other up to date without the need for frequent meetings. However, with individuals increasingly having more diverse roles, teams can lose touch if care is not taken to sustain regular, formal contact. Evaluation and quality assurance can help to give your team a focus for interaction.

To help you to understand the communication networks that exist within your organization, you may like to try the following activity:

D7p Communication analysis

List all the methods of communication in your organization. Comment on the effectiveness of each one. Consider the direction of the communications – are they top down or vice versa? Suggest how you could improve the communication system to make it more effective. (You may find it helpful to draw out the communication channels in diagrammatical form.)

7.5 QUALITY ASSURANCE AND EVALUATION

Even if you have not been working in education for long, you will undoubtedly have heard talk of quality processes in relation to meeting the needs of learners. The concept of quality has always been within the education system, but it is only in the past two decades that it has been transformed based on models pertaining from industry.

Although you will most likely have your own understanding of quality, it is important that we establish a precise definition here. However, defining quality is not as straightforward as it may seem. For example, the word may be used as both a noun and an adjective. The Concise Oxford Dictionary (1990) defines quality as:

the degree of excellence of a thing
a distinctive attribute or faculty
a characteristic trait

The word is often used to signify excellence in something, for example, a product or service. Within education it can be defined as 'meeting the customer requirements and expectations', but in the current competitive climate it may also be used to describe 'exceeding customer expectations', as organizations compete for students and positions in league tables. Sallis (1996) states that 'Quality is what makes the difference between things being excellent or run of the mill. Increasingly in education, quality makes the difference between success and failure.'

When providing a rationale for why an educational establishment should be involved in quality assurance Sallis classified his results into four main areas:

1. The *moral imperative*, which implies that educational establishments should provide the very best possible educational opportunities for learners – and few people in education would argue with this.

2. The *professional imperative*, closely linked to the above, implies a professional commitment to the needs of learners, which includes a duty to improve the quality of education.

3. *Competition*. Institutions need differentiation from their competitors in order to maintain a healthy supply of students.

4. The final imperative is that of *accountability*, where organizations must prove the high standards of their services within the public domain. Institutions are measured via government inspection against strict performance criteria to verify their application for funding.

You may hear the terms 'Quality Control', 'Quality Assurance' and 'Total Quality Management' used within your workplace. It may be useful to differentiate between them here. *Quality Control* is the detection and elimination of things which are not up to standard, i.e. a checking process. Government inspection is a method of quality control. External verification or moderation by awarding bodies is another quality control measure. *Quality Assurance*, on the other hand, is a process with the aim of preventing faults before they occur. It is about consistency, getting things right first time. Quality assurance aims to reduce wasted resources and unhappy customers. Your organization will more than likely have a Quality Assurance System in place. *Total Quality Management* incorporates and further develops quality assurance. It involves everyone in an organization being devoted to satisfying the customers' needs and is based on a culture of continuous improvement. *Quality Circles* are a direct form of employee participation in TQM. Employees are encouraged to volunteer to form teams in order to solve problems which they themselves have identified. This gives the employee 'ownership' and as a result, greater motivation. This is in contrast to other forms of employee participation when suggestions are passed on to management for consideration, and therefore ownership lost.

The underpinning philosophy for this movement has its roots in industry, originating in the United States as far back as the 1920s. Recognized as the original quality 'guru', W. Edwards Deming, an American government statistician, demonstrated his theories as part of the revitalization of Japanese industry after the Second World War. Deming (1986) recognizes that 'Quality should be aimed at the needs of the consumer, present and future', and that 'it is customers that keep a company in business'. He states that people should 'work smarter, not harder' in order to achieve an increase in productivity. Working with fellow American Joseph Juran, Deming developed his notions of the elimination of waste and delay in production and established the first quality circles in Japan. These ideas were ignored by the United States until the late 1970s, by which stage Japan had a much larger share of the commercial market.

To the Japanese, the message has been simple – listen to customers and improve the methods of production and the quality of products to a high standard in order to meet their needs. Japan took on board Deming's suggestion that money should be invested in the 'front end' of the process to establish quality in the first place, rather than spend time and money 'checking and mending' at the end of the system.

These ideas were successful first in manufacturing and then in the service industries. In the meantime the United States continued with its emphasis on maximizing outputs and profits. Around 1980, the United States began to realize the importance of the quality message, the relationship between the customer and the organization and the need for longer-term planning.

It was not until the late 1980s that total quality began to be discussed in connection with education, beginning initially with community colleges in the United States and some United Kingdom further education colleges. This has spread to higher education and ultimately to schools.

During the 1990s there was a push for educational organizations to become accredited with a variety of quality awards. These include Investors in People, ISO 9000 and other national quality marks, some linked to specialist areas of provision, for example, Adult Basic Education. All these help in the marketing of the organization and in the competition between institutions. Organizations set up more rigorous quality assurance systems and trained staff in the quality ethos. We have been made more aware of our internal and external 'customers' and 'stakeholders' and the need for accountability through the inspection process. As quality assurance is pro-active, it has been necessary to write detailed policies and procedures to cover all aspects of the organization's work, for example, Student and Staff Charters, Equal Opportunity and Health and Safety Policies, Appeals Procedures, as well as detailed procedures for any important organizational process. Naturally, there will also be a Quality Policy. These may all be held within some type of Quality Manual, especially if the organization is aiming for the ISO 9000 international standard. The whole vision of the organization will be explained through a 'Mission Statement'.

D7q   Establishment mission

Read your establishment's 'Mission Statement' together with other policies written for your organization. See if you can identify where the principles articulated in the Mission Statement are evident in other policy statements.

Once an organization has these items in place, it is necessary to provide the means to ensure that these promises will be maintained. An example that will relate directly to you is that of schemes of work. You will need to identify the key processes such as when and how diagnostic assessment of individual needs will take place. You may also be required to show how you intend to induct students into your course, and how you will differentiate within lessons to meet all students' learning styles. Any contemporary initiatives will need to be incorporated, such as the inclusion of Information Technology into the curriculum. This is all in addition to the more traditional information such as ensuring that you cover the syllabus, what resources you will use and how you will assess the learners!

In order to measure whether an organization is achieving the ideals of its mission statement, it will usually draw up sets of 'Performance Indicators'. These are factors which can be used to help determine whether institutional strategic goals are being met. Examples of these indicators will be recruitment, retention and achievement targets. You may be involved with setting these for your area, but will almost certainly be involved with achieving these targets and will have key goals set via performance reviews with your line manager.

It is no accident that these targets are also closely linked to the funding of courses, so this information will be used by funding bodies such as the Learning Skills Council. Other indicators will be linked to student satisfaction and progression, as well as the financial strength of the organization. An institution may also compare its performance indicators with those of other providers (a form of benchmarking) to check that it is keeping up nationally.

All this information is required to be maintained for inspection purposes. Each organization will have its own preferred method for this, but you will obviously need to play a part. A course or team leader may have the responsibility for maintaining the records, and for reporting the information to management (upward communication). This may give you an insight into the reasons for the huge amount of administration in education today.

D7r Quality processes

Summarize the quality procedures that impinge on your particular work. Identify how the data you provide feeds back to inform internal and external quality monitoring.

There are a number of ways in which quality assurance data are used to inform quality control. Quality systems need this feedback loop. Outcomes must be analysed against the overall plan. Evaluation is a key element in strategic planning for any organization, and this process should focus on the customer (students, employers, parents, etc.) and should focus on two issues.

First, how far is the organization meeting the individual requirements of customers (internal and external); and second, how far is it meeting its strategic goals. Sallis (ibid.) categorizes these into immediate, short and long-term levels of evaluation

- *Immediate* is less formal and involves you checking how students are progressing on a daily or weekly basis (depending on regularity of contact). You may, for example, check that students have completed their homework or (by using questioning in class) that they can remember what was learned in the previous session.

- *Short-term* is more structured, and will involve the review process described earlier in the chapter. Attainment in assessments and progress with work experience are examples. This will require recording and involves some statistical data. Its aim is to highlight any problems and to prevent students from under-achieving.

- *Long-term* is an overview of progress towards strategic goals. It is mainly management-led and involves sampling of customer views on a large scale. Often this is through the use of questionnaires, but may also be via meetings with a representative sample of learners.

Data collected via this type of questionnaire will probably generate quantitative data, whereas the meetings with students may reveal qualitative information. The quantitative data will be put with other data on pass rates, retention, etc. to feed back against the performance indicators. Questionnaires will address the whole student experience as well as teaching and learning. There may well be questions linked to enrolment and recruitment as well as refreshment and library facilities and so on.

As well as these institutionally directed questionnaires, you may find it useful to carry out your own evaluations in class which are more specifically directed at whether students are satisfied with lesson content and your own teaching style. Closed or multiple-choice questions will give you quantitative information (i.e. the 'what'), open questions will generate qualitative replies (i.e. the 'why'). The latter is of more use to you when improving your courses, the former is of more interest to management towards measurement of strategic goals. Evaluation of your own performance is discussed in more detail in Chapter 10.

D7s Quantitative and qualitative data

Discuss the comparative value to you (when you are trying to understand your own performance as a teacher) of quantitative data (i.e. statistical information) as opposed to qualitative data (feedback on student attitudes, feelings and expectations, for example).

Quality control measures mentioned so far have concentrated on the performance of learners and the organization as a whole. However, you may be directly measured for performance, not only via any performance management system, but also via observation of your teaching. Checklists used will be linked to inspection criteria and possibly to the FENTO Standards. You may be observed by line management and/or by peers. Expect to be graded – this will be a new dimension to you as this observation is not purely developmental as it is on teacher training programmes, but must provide some statistical data to feed into the quality assurance system.

Organizational self-assessment is an important part of accountability. All these measures will be used as key evidence in the reporting process. It is not just necessary to 'do', but also essential to *prove* that you 'do'.

As a result of all this measuring, institutions have had to develop more comprehensive systems for recording, storing and reporting data. Management Information Systems have to be able to report accurately to funding bodies, administer examinations information and run the payroll as well as keep management generally informed of progress towards strategic goals. The process is further complicated by the increased flexibility of certain teaching programmes, the increased number of part-time staff, and the number of interested parties to whom the organization is accountable.

D7t The effect of quality information

Give some examples of improvements you have made to your course/subject (design, delivery and assessment) as a direct result of information gained during the quality processes. It may help to show these changes on a scheme of work. Include samples of the data used to inform the changes.

7.6 CONCLUSION

This chapter has aimed to show the wider aspects of the tutor's role and how factors external to the classroom can have an impact on the whole learner's experience. Whatever your initial role within the post-compulsory sector, you will not be able to escape the culture of constant change and accountability. We hope you can see the importance of maintaining systems of recording and evaluation, and the importance of maintaining a network of personal contacts through effective communication. Your communication skills need to be multifaceted, using different approaches with different people. You also need to respond to those within and external to your organization.

Quality assurance is important, as doing things right first time costs nothing but forward planning. Mistakes can be expensive – and there is nothing more expensive than a learner leaving education because of a bad experience – they may never feel able to return. However, as it is inevitable that you will make some mistakes, the important thing is that you learn from these.

Accept feedback on your skills willingly. Get involved, meet people, build up your own network of contacts. Say 'yes' to invitations to join new teams. Reflect on the roles you take and how the teams you are in perform. Reflect on communication channels in your organization – how easily do they flow? Reflect on the quality your students receive from you and the whole organization. Do you really listen to your students? Accept constant change as a challenge and it will not stress you – it is unlikely to go away. Rest assured, teaching in post-compulsory education will never be dull.

7.7 USEFUL SOURCES

If you wish to read about the introduction of quality assurance to the manufacturing and service industries – straight from the mouth of a quality guru – see Deming, W.E. (1986) *Out of the Crisis: Quality, Productivity and Competitive Position*. Cambridge: Cambridge University Press.

For a good, easy-to-read book on Total Quality Management, look at Sallis, E. (1996) *Total Quality Management in Education*. London: Kogan Page.

Morrison, K. (1998) *Management Theories for Educational Change*. London: Paul Chapman, talks about the quality gurus and quality awards. He also has a good chapter on teamwork.

If you want to reflect on some of the effects of incorporation of the FE sector, Elliott, G. (1996) *Crisis and Change in Vocational Education and Training*. London: Jessica Kingsley, has a chapter on Quality Assurance which looks at how lecturers have been affected.

If you require a practical book on organizational communication, see Katz, B. (1989) *Turning Practical Communication into Business Power*. London: Mercury Books.

Mullins, L.J. (1999) *Management and Organisational Behaviour* (5th edn). London: Pearson Education, has a good chapter on Group Processes and Behaviour (p.483) that relates to teams and communication within an organization. It is a good all-round book if you are interested in the structure of organizations.

To find out the roles that you may play within a team, try the questionnaire in Belbin, R. Meredith (1981) *Management Teams. Why they succeed or fail.* London: Butterworth Heinemann.

Try *tipcet.com* for a range of materials and suggested sources related to communication, evaluation and working in groups.

7.8 RATIONALE FOR MANAGING THE LEARNING PROCESS – KEY AREA D

FAQs	At Stage 1	At Stage 2	At Stage 3
Why do it?	You are not only responsible for managing the teaching but also the quality of the learning which results from your efforts. As we have said in earlier chapters, the nature of the learning is dependent upon many factors in addition to your input. The learning environment is one of these key influences and so you must ensure that it is not undermining all of your attempts to promote student progress.	In order to promote learning teachers must create an effective and productive learning environment where they are able to structure and monitor the learning process. An effective learning environment is not merely physical, but is also influenced by the participants, their levels of motivation, group dynamics, communication, etc. Teachers must be aware of the many variables within each situation that can affect the quality of the learning experience.	It is important to evaluate the structure of the learning environment, the learning activities, the effectiveness of the communication with the learners and their review of the learning process in order to manage learning effectively. This evaluation involves an analysis of the characteristics of the learning environment, the range of learning activities both formal and informal, the process of communication and results of the learners' review.

Where are we going?	Between you (yourself and the learners) there are a large number of variables, such as previous experience, needs, expectations, etc., which make the workings of the environment difficult to understand. It is your responsibility to get an insight into how these complex interactions work.	Your aim should be to understand the nature of your own particular teaching environment. Consider the influence of the learners and their characteristics, the demands of the subject you are teaching, the qualities and limitations of the setting you are working in, time and resource constraints. Most important of all, reflect on your own teaching style, methods of communication and their effects on learners.	Your aim is to gather data about the whole process of managing learning in order to be able to identify and rectify problematic areas and optimize the quality and productivity of the students' experience. The purpose of this process is to become a responsive and effective teacher who is aware of the range of specific influences on a particular learning context.
How do we get there?	Consider the dynamics of the group you are teaching and how it operates. Identify which of your methods works best. Try to communicate with the students as effectively as possible and be aware of those influences which change the relationship. Usually, learners will respond positively when they realize that a teacher has got their best interests at heart. Don't pretend to be what you are not, be yourself.	You need to consider what encourages learners to learn, as well as dealing with the practical organization of the environment, including the legal, health, safety and security requirements. You must also consider how to enhance the learning environment and communication process for which you are responsible. This will involve planning and developing appropriate resources and collaborating with students and teaching colleagues and collecting data as you review the process.	To be effective, a teacher must be aware of the interrelationship between the teaching environment, effective learning activities, and good learner communication and feedback. You should also be aware of the range of resources which are currently available to support learning and those which might be specifically produced. The teacher should also have a good understanding of learning theories, concepts relating to inclusion and the principles of good management and communication.
Is this the best way?	The best way for both novice and experts is to focus on the needs of the students and to find a way of meeting those needs as far as is possible. Let them know what you are trying to do, they may help.	Your involvement with the institution's quality systems will provide you with feedback on the success of the environment you have developed, but even given positive feedback you must be willing to be responsive to new demands, particularly from different groups of learners.	There are so many possible routes to a successful learning outcome that it is impossible to specify a route or guarantee its success. However, a good understanding of the learning context will enable a teacher to narrow the choices and make informed decisions.

When is the right time?	Seek a second opinion before you make any major changes. If you are thinking of changing things, try to anticipate the difficulties it might cause and consider how you may get around these problems. Explain the intended changes and seek help from both the students and from colleagues. Remember, curriculum innovations work better when they are planned.	Often learners will resent changes in teaching approaches or more demanding assessment, etc at a time when they are under pressure. Also, it is difficult to be innovative in isolation when other teachers are committed to other, more conventional approaches. Minor changes to teaching strategies can be introduced at any time and quick responses to learner needs is good management. However, major curriculum development needs to be planned well in advance to obtain collegial support and to let students know the changes.	The management of the learning process is an ongoing commitment as problems can occur at any during the academic year. However, there are obviously key times, such as enrolment, assesment or progression, when difficulties are more likely to be evident. The collection of data on the various responses to these 'difficulties' can be very valuable in terms of the insight provided into the internal processes of the department concerned. The usefulness of data is often dependent upon its availability at crucial stages.
Who needs to know?	The students need to know about any changes you are making and obviously any colleagues who will be affected need to be informed. Although you are responsible for managing what goes on during your sessions, the methods that you use can have implications elsewhere.	Obviously your learners and colleagues need to know when you are involved in innovation and development. It is also wise to let support staff, such as those from the library and learning resource service and student support, have advanced notice of changes. Always take the opportunity to review the learning process with students prior to, during and after any changes and developments.	The evaluation of the learning process will, most likely, already be an ongoing process in your particular workplace. It is also likely that there are formal data-collection pro forma and management information systems where you can obtain previous data. You need to let the quality managers, your department colleagues and the students know if you are using this data for other purposes.

How do we know when we've got there?	You will know straight away when your group of learners are working productively. Their interest and involvement will be easy to identify and once you have achieved this level of commitment, you will have the confidence and information which will allow you to do it again. Make notes on the process and get informal feedback from the learners about their perceptions of why they enjoyed it.	It does take time for changes to have effect and often the initial feedback can be disappointing. So don't be too hasty in condemning your innovation, but allow everyone time to get used to it. In the long term you will be looking for better motivated, more effective and productive learners but you should build up to this gradually. Look for small examples of more positive responses at first, such as verbal confirmation that the developments are 'interesting', 'helpful' etc.	You are looking for a data-collection system which provides both formative and summative data at times when it is needed. You should have a clear idea of what an optimum learning environment would consist of in relation to your particular learners and your curriculum subject. You should have the data and be able to make informed judgements at a time when changes and developments are financially and organizationally possible. Useful data should emerge from the curriculum processes.
Has everyone had a fair chance?	Don't expect everyone to respond positively. Remember that those who are reluctant may have good reasons. Try to find out what those are and plan for these differences when you organize your next session.	A good manager of learning will be as aware of those students who are having difficulties as those who are succeeding well. Ensure that no learner is being excluded even though it may seem to be at a fairly trivial level. Learning materials and processes often need minor modifications to ensure the optimum inclusion of learners with specific needs.	Reflect on the range of influences on the management of the learning process and the devices, materials and resources that enhance learning, and its management. Consider also those procedures which inhibit student learning and effective communication.

7.8 KEY AREA D – MANAGING THE LEARNING PROCESS

Purpose: Teachers and teaching teams need to be effective in establishing a productive learning environment and in working with learners and colleagues to structure and monitor the learning process. Central to these activities is the teachers' capacity to communicate effectively with learners and colleagues. Teachers must consider what encourages learners to learn as well as dealing with the practical organization of the environment, including the legal requirements relating to health, safety and security. They must also consider how to resource the varied approaches to teaching and learning and recognize, by forming effective working relationships with others, that successful management of teaching and learning requires collaboration. Finally, teachers should evaluate teaching and learning and play their part in contributing to the organization's quality assurance system. For an analysis of this process at FENTO Stages 1, 2 and 3, see the Rationale on pp. 199–201.

Please note: The FENTO Standards listed below are relevant to the following three levels of award – Stage 1 (Introduction), Stage 2 (Intermediate) and Stage 3 (Full Certification). All the standards are required at Stage 3, only those in italic and bold are required at Stage 2 and only those in italic are required at Stage 1.

UNIT D3. COMMUNICATE EFFECTIVELY WITH LEARNERS *In order to do this teachers should:*

	Demonstrate that they are able to:	*and have specific knowledge and critical understanding of:*	*plus generic knowledge of:*		*Summary of appropriate evidence in this Key Area*	*Relevant Chapter Activities*
a	*Criteria:* *select and organize relevant information clearly and concisely*	● How to select and organize information effectively	● Theories concerning motivation and ways of motivating learners ● Ways of structuring and presenting information and ideas	a	Schemes of Work, Session Plans, Learning Materials	B4g, B4h,C5j, D7n. D7o. D7p
b	*present information to learners clearly and in an appropriate format*	● Ways of presenting information and ideas	● Appropriate media and language forms for presenting information	b	Schemes of Work, Session Plans, Learning Materials	D7p, E8b
c	*use a range of communication skills and methods appropriate to specific learners and to the subject being studied*	● The appropriate forms and registers of language	● Different teaching techniques ● Different ways of learning	c	Schemes of Work, Session Plans, Learning Materials	D7p, E8b

d	maintain and encourage effective communication with and between all learners	● The conventions of grammar and spelling ● The audio-visual aids which are appropriate and how to use them effectively ● Developments in information learning technology and how these can support and promote learning	d	Schemes of Work, Session Plans, Learning Materials, Learning Contracts	D7p, E8b
e	foster learners' enjoyment of learning	● Their personal responsibilities for health and safety ● The organization's learning programmes and available resources ● Good practice in catering for the needs of all students including learners who require additional support	e	Schemes of Work, Session Plans, Learning Materials, Learning Contracts	A3g, A3q, A3r, A3w, B4c, D4s, C5g, C5m, C5u, E8j
f	listen to and respond to learners' ideas	● The role of information and learning technology in supporting learning and teaching ● The importance of pacing teaching and learning appropriately	f	Action Plans, Diagnostic Tests, Schemes of Work, Session Plans, Learning Materials, Learning Contracts	A3g, A3q, A3r, A3w, B4c, D4s, C5g, C5m, C5u, E8j
				Plus commentary in PDJ on the purpose and value of communicating effectively with learners, together with records in PF of Teaching Observations, Lesson Plans, Rationales, Self-Evaluations and Progress Summary	

Key to above standards required at each FENTO Stage:

Introduction Stage – italic
Intermediate Stage + bold
Certification Stage – all

UNIT D4. REVIEW THE LEARNING PROCESS WITH LEARNERS *In order to do this teachers should:*

	Demonstrate that they are able to:	*and have specific knowledge and critical understanding of:*	*plus generic knowledge of:*		*Summary of appropriate evidence in this Key Area*	*Relevant Chapter Activities*
a	create opportunities for discussion and conduct regular reviews with learners	**Criteria:** • Criteria for evaluating learners' experience and progress	• Theories concerning motivation and ways of motivating learners • Ways of structuring and presenting information and ideas • Appropriate media and language forms for presenting information • Different teaching techniques	a	Learning Reviews, Action Plans, Student-Centred Evaluations	A3c, A3j; A3m, A3r, B4v, C5b, C5c, C5m, C5p, D6d, D6i, D7a, D7b, D7c, D7d, D7f, D7g, D7h, D7i; E8b, E8j; E8m
b	*give constructive and positive feedback to learners which values their efforts*	• Ways of seeking, responding to and giving feedback • Action planning techniques and recording procedures	• Different ways of learning • Their personal responsibilities for health and safety • The organization's learning programmes and available resources • Good practice in catering for the needs of all students including learners who require additional support • The role of information and learning technology in supporting learning and teaching	b	Learning Review, Action Plans, Assessment Feedback	A3c, A3j; A3m, A3r, B4v, C5b, C5c, C5m, C5p, D6d, D6i, D7a, D7b, D7c, D7d, D7f, D7g, D7h, D7i; E8b, E8j; E8m, G10k
c	seek and respond appropriately to feedback from learners on their learning	• The limits of teachers' own competence to deal with learners' concerns and appropriate sources for teachers' own support	• The importance of pacing teaching and learning appropriately	c	Learning Review, Action Plans, Curriculum Development, Schemes of Work	B4c, B4e, D7a, D7b, D7c, D7d, D7f, D7g, D7h, D7i, E8b, E8j, E8m, G10k

d	identify areas of concern and need in relation to the learning programme	• The specific communication needs of individual students, including those with learning difficulties and disabilities	Learning Review, Action Plans, Curriculum Development, Schemes of Work	D7a, D7b, D7c, D7d, D7f, D7g, D7h, D7i, E8b, E8j, E8m
e	agree appropriate actions with learners	disabilities	Learning Review, Action Plans	D7a, D7b, D7c, D7d, D7f, D7g, D7h, D7i, E8b, E8j, E8m
f	consider referral and alternative support networks to assist learners	• Source of additional learner support, guidance and counselling • The organization's referral procedures	Review and referral records, Learning Support Audit	D7e, D7d, D7e, D7f, E8g, E8h, E8i, E8m, E8o
g	record the outcomes of reviews in accordance with organizational procedures	• Distinctions between learning support and pastoral care functions	Learning Review, Action Plans	E8h, D7e, D7d, D7e, D7h

Plus commentary in PDJ on the purpose and value of reviewing the learning process with learners, together with records in your Practitioner File of Teaching Observations, Lesson Plans, Rationales, Self-Evaluations and Progress Summary

Key to above standards required at each FENTO Stage:

Introduction Stage – italic

Intermediate Stage + bold

Certification Stage – all

	Demonstrate that they will be able to:	and will have specific knowledge and critical understanding of:	plus generic knowledge of:		Summary of appropriate evidence in this Key Area	Relevant Chapter Activities

UNIT D6. ESTABLISH AND MAINTAIN EFFECTIVE WORKING RELATIONSHIPS *In order to do this teachers should:*

	Demonstrate that they will be able to:	and will have specific knowledge and critical understanding of:	plus generic knowledge of:		Summary of appropriate evidence in this Key Area	Relevant Chapter Activities
a	Criteria: contribute to the design, development and validation of learning programmes	The requirements for learning programme design, implementation and review	• Theories concerning motivation and ways of motivating learners • Ways of structuring and presenting information and ideas • Appropriate media and language forms for presenting information	a	Schemes of Work, Programme Specifications, Module Descriptions	B4c, B4d, B4e, B4l, D6f, D6i, D7d, D7i, D7k, D7l, D7m, D7t
b	liaise with external learning providers, where appropriate	Additional or alternative opportunities for learning, including on-site learning, franchised provision and distance learning	• Different teaching techniques • Different ways of learning	b	Minutes of meetings, Action Plans, External Verifier's Visits	B4c, B4d, B4f, B4l
c	contribute to and maintain an effective internal communication network that includes technical, administrative and academic support for colleagues	The organization's tracking and recording systems • Administrative policies and procedures • The information needs of others	• Their personal responsibilities for health and safety • The organization's learning programmes and available resources • Good practice in catering for the needs of all students including learners who require additional support	c	Tracking and recording records, Learning Reviews, Action Plans, Annual Reports	A3j, B4f, D6i, D7a, D7b, D7c, D7d, D7e, D7h, D7m, D7n, D7s
d	establish appropriate links and liaise with external stakeholders, as required	Appropriate channels of communication with external stakeholders	• The role of information and learning technology in supporting learning and teaching	d	Communications with awarding bodies, universities, LSCs, Basic Skills Agency, Ofsted, etc.	D7d, D7e, D7i, D7r
e	work with other organizations and services to promote learners' participation, retention and achievement	The nature of local networks and how to access them	• The importance of pacing teaching and learning appropriately	e	External Awarding Body, LEA, LSC, FENTO, Ofsted communication	D6i, D6l, D7i, D7j, D7k, D7l, D7m, D7n, D7o, E8g, E8h, E8k

	Competence	Knowledge		Examples	Codes
f	work collaboratively with colleagues to deliver the learning programme	• Ways of integrating one's own teaching with that of others within a team	f	Team teaching plans and records, Schemes of Work, Library Support, etc.	D6i, D6l, D7i, D7j, D7k, D7l, D7m, D7n, D7o, E8g, E8h, E8k
g	negotiate with colleagues outside the immediate programme on behalf of the learners	• Appropriate methods of advocating for, and mediating on behalf of learners	g	Library & Learning Resources, Student Support, External Awarding Body reports, National Meetings, Secondment	B4c, B4d, D7a D7b, D7d, D7e, D7m, E8f, E8g, E8k, E8m, E8o
h	share expertise with colleagues and respond to their needs, for the benefit of learners and the learning programme	• Collaborative and collegiate styles of working	h	Collaborative developments, Moderation	D6l, D6m, D7m, D7n
i	contribute to the programme review and evaluation	• Relevant external stakeholders who need to be kept informed including parents, carers, schools, employers, local authorities, TECs, inspectors, other agencies and other professionals	i	Programme review documentation, annual reports, etc.	D7h, D7i, G10d to G10i
j	contribute to the management information systems and ensure that colleagues are given all necessary information at the correct time and in the agreed organizational format		j	Learning Reviews, Action Plans, Cohort details, Student profiles, APL records, Assessment Boards	D7d, D7e, D7i, D7r, D7s, D7t

k	*respond positively and constructively to feedback*	
k	Student evaluations, Action Plans, curriculum development	D7h, D7i, G10d to G10i
	Plus commentary in PDJ on the purpose and value of establishing effective working relationships, together with records in your Practitioner File of Teaching Observations, Lesson Plans, Rationales, Self-Evaluations and Progress Summary	

Key to above standards required at each FENTO Stage:

Introduction Stage – italic

Intermediate Stage + bold

Certification Stage – all

UNIT D7. CONTRIBUTE TO THE ORGANIZATION'S QUALITY ASSURANCE SYSTEM *In order to do this teachers should:*

	Demonstrate that they will be able to:	and will have specific knowledge and critical understanding of:	plus generic knowledge of:		Summary of appropriate evidence in this Key Area	Relevant Chapter Activities
a	*Criteria: take responsibility for the quality of the service they provide*	• The purposes of quality-assurance systems and their role within FE and within the organization	• Theories concerning motivation and ways of motivating learners • Ways of structuring and presenting information and ideas • Appropriate media and language forms for presenting information • Different teaching techniques • Different ways of learning • Their personal responsibilities for health and safety • The organization's learning programmes and available resources • Good practice in catering for the needs of all students including learners who require additional support • The role of information and learning technology in supporting learning and teaching • The importance of pacing teaching and learning appropriately	a	Quality procedures, evaluations, Action Plans	D7q, D7r, D7s, D7t, G10d to G10i
b	contribute to quality assurance systems as individuals and in teams	• The purpose of the methods used to respond to change and ensure quality development • Ways of using new technologies to monitor, evaluate and improve the quality of delivery		b	Evaluation responses, Value-added analysis, Action Plans, Annual Reports	D7q, D7r, D7s, D7t, F9n, F9n, G10d to G10i
c	*provide feedback in a form suitable to help measure the quality of learning and teaching*	• Ways of acknowledging and responding to continuous states of change • How to be effective within the FE culture of quality improvement		c	Moderation Reports, Action on External reports, Quantitative and Qualitative cohort data	D7q, D7r, D7s, D7t, E8h, F9m, F9n, G10d to G10i
d	contribute to the development of the organization's practice on inclusive learning	• the organization's quality assurance policy and its relationship to the organization's mission and values		d	Student Progress records, SoW, Session Plans, showing differentiated learning, etc.	E8j to E8m
e	identify appropriate data with which to evaluate the quality of the services provided	• internal and external criteria by which to evaluate the effectiveness and efficiency of the organization		e	Performance Criteria, Learning Outcomes, etc.	D7q, D7r, D7s, D7t, E8h, F9m, F9n, G10d to G10i

			Reports on data received	
f	analyse the information gathered from the evaluation data	• procedures for gathering and assessing relevant information		G10d to G10i
g	adapt and develop learning programmes, teaching strategies and materials in the light of the evaluation	• resource constraints and allocation procedures	Course Development Committee minutes, etc.	B4c to B4l, D7i, E8m
h	use feedback from sources within and outside the organization in the promotion of continuous improvement	• The different quality assurance indicators used by the organization, awarding bodies, FEFC funding and inspection regimes and external service users • Local and national performance indicators and their relevance to continuous improvement	Various evaluations from internal and external sources	B4c to B4l, D7i, E8m

Plus commentary in PDJ on the purposes and value of contributing to the organization's quality assurance system, together with records in your Practitioner File of Teaching Observations, Lesson Plans, Rationales, Self-Evaluations and Progress Summary

Key to above standards required at each FENTO Stage:

Introduction Stage – italic

Intermediate **Stage + bold**

Certification Stage – all

Providing learners with support

Alison Barton

Key Area E Inducting learners, ensuring access to guidance opportunities and providing effective learning and personal support

Key concepts in this chapter

Access, Active response, Advice, APEL, Contractual Boundaries, Diagnostic Testing, Effective, Efficient, Empathy, Enrolment with Integrity, Formalized Induction, Funding Driven, Genuineness, Inclusive Facilitation, Inclusive Learning, Information and Guidance, Learner Need, Learner Support, Listening Skills, Passive Acceptance, Progression, Respect, Responsibility, Review Ownership, Safe Zone, SENDA, Support Audit, Widening Participation

Before you begin this chapter you may wish to check the FAQs on pages 233–5

Index to Chapter 8

Chapter 8 Activities designed to generate evidence against the Standards

8.1 | INTRODUCTION

We will explore in this chapter the many ways in which we can provide support for our learners in post-compulsory education. This support differs as we, as well as our learners, move through the continuum from 'novice' to 'expert' and as we progress our perceptions of our role and the influences that affect us begin to change.

Initially, at the introductory phase of our own learning (FENTO Stage 1 – see Chapter 1) it is likely that we will focus on ourselves and the skills we require to pass our subject-specific knowledge on to our learners. During this stage we will be establishing our own technical efficiency at achieving predetermined teaching and learning goals. Much of our energy and planning time will be taken up in preparing for the teaching process and creating resources to achieve the goals of the sessions we are teaching. It is also likely that, during this stage, our focus on 'supporting' learners will be based around the very personal relationship we are building between the learners in our classroom and ourselves. We may even feel *responsible* for our learners and attempt to 'sort out' and 'solve' many of their needs for them.

Stage 2 may well correspond to a developing maturity as a teacher and, with our fundamental teaching skills in place, we begin to explore and become aware of the situational context in which we teach and how this impacts upon our teaching approach.

As we have stressed in earlier chapters, this 'situation' will embrace a range of influences, including our values and beliefs about teaching and learning, the culture and structure of the organization in which we work, the characteristics of learners and our growing awareness of the teaching process. During this stage, we may well refocus our ideas about 'supporting learners' and look more widely into the type of support offered within our establishment as a whole. We may be involved in processes that help to match the support offered to the needs of individual students. We may begin to see support as part of the learning process and engage in recording that process for each learner and ourselves. We may also come to recognize the areas of support for which we are responsible and the associated skills we require to carry out these functions.

Later, at some point in our own development, our knowledge of teaching increases in sophistication, depth and breadth. Also moral and ethical considerations of teaching and education begin to formulate. We may start to focus more on the 'external influences' that impact on the teaching process in which we are engaged, and relate these to contemporary educational issues in government policy and our own growing awareness of our varied teaching roles and our students' learning processes.

Such developing awareness approximates to Stage 3 and helps us to see support in a much wider way. We may start by looking at where the instigation for the support came from, how it is funded, ethical issues, points of focus and how we, as teachers, play a part in its provision to learners.

Wherever you are in your own development now, providing learners with support will be relevant to you. During this chapter we will explore aspects of support and the effect this has on both teacher and learner. As a starting point, we are going to consider two notional case studies that identify two separate approaches which provide completely different experiences for the 'giver' and the 'receiver' of learning support.

8.2 | APPROACHES TO LEARNER SUPPORT

In educational establishment A the management team, in line with government initiatives, have set up learning support for all students to access. The establishment has lots of 'support' systems in place and has them ready for the learner should they be required. This institution 'sees' itself as making support available to those who need it and 'gives' support through its staff and services to identified learners as they progress through the establishment. Emerging at the other end with all their qualificatory aims met, the learners have 'taken' all they need to achieve their set goals.

In this establishment its teaching and support staff 'give' and the learner 'receives'. The responsibility for the support process sits firmly with the institution and its staff and the learner expects the right to 'purchase' support along with access to their programme. As with any situation where one side is always giving and the other taking, sometimes in this establishment support 'runs out'. Teachers get tired and exhausted with carrying the weight of the support; resources and services get used up and funding disappears, leaving support needs unmet. When this happens (just as in any giver and receiver scenario) the receiver gets angry when what is perceived as a right and entitlement has gone and will demand that this be returned. At the same time, the giver is blamed for not 'managing the support' successfully and being unable to meet the learners' needs.

An alternative to this approach may be found in establishment B. Here also the management team have established support systems in line with government policy but, in this case, there is a subtle difference.

A central aim of the learning process in establishment B is the development of both independent and interdependent learners through the development of individual empowerment. This institution not only 'offers' learning experiences and support and takes responsibility for this provision, but also expects its learners to contribute to both aspects and take responsibility (with the help of the providers) for *supporting themselves*. However, in situation B the institution is not simply the 'provider' because here many learners become able to support themselves (a liberating experience) while those who require constant support for a range of personal reasons can have time and resources allocated to them to meet their needs.

Of course, establishments such as that in the second example are by no means perfect. Institution B will still run out of money, some learners will still get angry and the establishment will still get 'blamed' for not doing things better. Even so, teaching there will 'feel' different and it is this difference on which we focus for the first activity in this chapter:

E8a Differences in ethos

Consider the contrasting effects which the two different approaches to learner support may have in the two establishments in the case study above. Focus in particular on how the learners in A may react as compared to those in institution B.

In the first example, establishment A *takes* responsibility and *gives* the necessary support provision. As a consequence, their learners are encouraged to *surrender* responsibility and *accept* the support provided. This establishment is meeting its targets and appears 'efficient' in the way it offers support.

In the second example, establishment B also offers appropriate support, but their concept of the learner is different. This institution has a vision of the learner as being able, given the right conditions, to take responsibility for their own learning. The learner becomes an active player in the relationship and this more empowered role encourages them 'to do' for themselves. The establishment accepts that it has responsibility to learners, but it stops taking responsibility for them. By allowing them to become responsible for themselves, the institution is 'efficient' in the support it offers, but more importantly it is also 'effective'.

This difference between being 'efficient' and 'effective' is one of the most important within the whole teaching cycle. In establishment B we can see the initiation of a process which encourages learners to take responsibility for supporting themselves. As a consequence, the learners move from a position of passive acceptance (where they assume that they will be 'spoon-fed' throughout their course) to an active responsive stance, which views teachers and support staff as a valuable resource that enables them to learn to support themselves. In this way important lifelong skills are developed and the self-esteem and confidence of all participants is enhanced.

Learning Support means just that. Supporting learners does not mean doing it for them. It is about empowering someone to take action and assume responsibility for themselves by providing at the right time the appropriate human and material resources for this to happen.

E8b The nature of support

The above contrasting approaches to support raise some interesting questions for the teacher and the way they support learners. Discuss whether you feel that it is always necessary to support learners on a one-to-one basis, or can learners be supported in groups? What effect may group support have on the learning process? How will we know that learning has been effective? Will our learners always require the same support or will it change, and will the rate of change be different for each individual learner? How can we improve the support we offer? Will the time come to pass our learners on to a different type of support offered by other colleagues? How do we know when we are stretched to our own limits and when to stop and request 'expert' help? Finally, who is going to support us?

8.3 INDUCTING LEARNERS INTO THE ORGANIZATION

Within a 'funding-driven' culture such as ours, the financial security of educational establishments is dependent upon our learners accessing the appropriate course for their needs, remaining on that course and developing both subject-specific knowledge and 'lifelong learning skills' (key skills) while arriving at a successful outcome in terms of achievement. This does not happen by chance. It happens because considerable care is given to the recruitment, selection and placement of learners onto our programmes.

Formalized induction is very much a part of this process. Within our classrooms, we as teachers have a responsibility to enable all of our learners to maximize their learning experiences. This means that we need to ease them into the group with which they will share their learning, find out about them as 'learners', identify their individual learning needs and begin the process of establishing the 'boundaries' of the teaching and learning situation.

For most of our learners, induction will happen in two significantly different ways and, depending on the role you have as a teacher, you will be involved in these processes at differing levels.

Institutional induction usually happens at the very beginning of the learners' programme. Some establishments have induction programmes that span the first six weeks of the first term. During this time learners are encouraged to take part in a range of activities to enable them to find out about the organization, its facilities and services, programmes of study and the systems and procedures of which they will be a part. At the end of this period, learners should feel 'at home' in the establishment, be able to 'find their way around', feel 'safe' in their new environment and recognize that they are on the right programme and at the right level for them to be able to achieve a successful outcome.

E8c Learners at home

Obviously, the above outcomes are what we all desire for our learners. Briefly consider how you would make these things happen for a particular group of your own learners within your own educational establishment.

Just like any good teaching situation, the answer does not lie in simply 'telling' or 'showing' the learner what is available to them. Induction should not be an endless round of boring and tiring visits or talks where the learner sits and accepts information that may or may not be effectively received.

This becomes even more important when we consider some of the safety aspects of which most students will need to be aware as they enter a particular institution. It is not enough to be told about the Health and Safety at Work Act or Fire Regulations, First Aid Procedures or specific regulations that apply to some programmes. As with all learning the student needs to 'see' the importance and relevance of the information and be able to access it in a way that makes it 'real' for them. Planning a good induction programme is being 'efficient'. However, being 'effective' involves not only meeting the perceived needs of new learners, but also making induction alive, real, relevant and useful to the learner.

E8d   Induction analysis

Identify the induction programme which operates for all new students at your establishment. Include examples of student profiles, analysis sheets of their identified needs and evaluation sheets from students who have completed induction (remember to maintain confidentiality at all times). From this information, suggest what are the strengths and weaknesses of the current induction process.

The second type of induction will usually be directly under the control of a programme tutor and will have a different focus to the institution-wide induction discussed previously.

At programme level, tutors will identify different outcomes that they wish to achieve with a particular group of learners and the planning of this induction is no different to the preparation of any other educational session which we may provide. We will still require specific objectives that are achievable through a range of predetermined activities. These activities, as always, will need to address a range of learning styles and allow learners to work both independently and collegially during the session. The objectives will need to be assessed (informally and unobtrusively) and then the whole process evaluated.

The purpose of this induction is to initiate the learners' ownership process of future learning and to excite them regarding the content of future sessions. It is also a time to explore the expectations and hopes we have for ourselves (teachers and learners) and each other, to establish the working practice of the group and recognize accepted patterns of behaviour towards each other. It is a also a good time to look at equal opportunities and inclusive learning and to allow the group to establish their own 'rules' which ensures ownership for all members.

This is also a good time to identify how learners like to learn best. As we commence teaching, this knowledge will allow us to utilize this 'safe' zone before we start to develop the learners' ability to access learning through a wider range of styles (see also Chapter 3). Programme induction is both about getting to know each other and the programme. We will establish how we will interact together and anticipate what we are all aiming to achieve.

Quite often when teachers are working under pressure, they wish to 'get on' with the real teaching and never allow their groups to take part in this important process. This is very unfortunate because other tutors, who do manage to go through this familiarization procedure, usually find that it considerably enriches the overall group learning experience.

E8e   Induction design

Design an Induction Programme for one of your learner groups. The programme is to last for between one and two hours. You should set suitable objectives to allow the learners to discover information about their programme of study, the group they belong to and themselves as learners. Allow time to reflect with them on what has been learnt in the session. If possible complete the induction with a group, evaluate the session from both your own

---

and the learners' perspective and make suggestions on how to improve it for future groups.

During the induction period many different things are happening that allow us to ensure that the learner is on the right programme and that we can successfully meet their needs. Initial diagnostic testing may well take place, identifying a range of support needs (both personal and academic) while also exploring how learners like to learn and focusing on identifiable strengths and areas for development. At this stage formal support from experts can be requested and budgeted for, while your learners can be involved in both processes.

At the beginning of the learning programme, Learner Contracts can be established (see examples in Chapter 6) which can have a range of purposes. Some contracts or agreements are more formal arrangements between the learner and provider, which set out the terms and conditions of the relationship and the formal support the college will provide. Others can be more open arrangements established between the individual learners, their group and the teacher, which set out boundaries within which all parties will operate.

E8f   Contractual boundaries

Looking back at the learning contract you may have produced for activities D6h and D6i in Chapter 6, discuss where the various boundaries of such an agreement lie and how difficult these are to establish and maintain.

8.4 | PROVIDING EFFECTIVE LEARNING SUPPORT

In this section we will look at the range of facilities and services that may be available to learners and the role we may take as teachers to enable learners to be responsible for success in their own learning. We will also look at Inclusive Learning and how this approach influences the support offered to learners.

The use of that important word 'effective' within the subheading above implies that we are concerned that our learning support provision actually does work, and the role you play in the implementation of this support will inevitably differ from situation to situation. The term 'learning support' does encompass a wide range of services which learners may access and, although you may carry much of this out, some aspects will require specialist help.

The importance of learning support has been nationally emphasized since the FEFC Learning Difficulties/Disabilities Committee produced their report *Inclusive Learning* in 1996 under the chairmanship of Professor John Tomlinson. Although the central concern of the report is equality of opportunity, Tomlinson and his colleagues emphasized the importance of optimizing the learning of *all students*, rather than focusing on special needs provision in isolation Thus the proposals set out the improvements necessary to establish a policy of *inclusive learning* which would require all staff to make the needs of all their students their priority.

Total inclusion requires us to support learners in a variety of ways while sustaining the principles (discussed earlier) of empowering the learners, rather than 'doing it for them'. In relation to supporting learners, the key aspects of the report can be summarized as follows:

- colleges are to be encouraged to produce long-term strategies on inclusive learning
- colleges are to establish 'Inclusive Learning' managers
- funding councils to provide funds in order that the initial assessment of learner need can be established
- funding councils to provide ongoing financial support to ensure individual need is met
- colleges should measure their progress toward being inclusive providers by self assessment
- colleges to be inspected to ensure inclusive learning is taking place
- that all learners' achievements be recognized within a National Qualifications framework including pre-foundation level
- that a broad view of progression be taken to include transferring and maintaining knowledge and skills
- colleges to take account and provide for underrepresented groups of learners, including those with multiple difficulties, mental health difficulties and emotional and behavioural difficulties

The 'inclusive approach' moves away from leaving the difficulty or problem as a learner responsibility to developing a way of working which responds to each individual learner's requirements by providing a sensitive, responsive and supportive learning environment. This identification that the responsibility for implementing the new policy lies firmly with the learning organization is a radical new concept, which also ensures that it has to be applied to all learners in the establishment and not just those who have been previously labelled as having some identifiable difficulty. It means that initially we have to clearly identify who our learners are, what support needs they have and how we can design teaching, learning and assessment to enable learners to succeed while meeting these needs.

This is so different to previous approaches to integration which have focused on the learners being 'supported' within a group, in other words, accommodation without inclusion. The Tomlinson Report (1996) also tells us exactly what we should be aiming for with our support:

> by inclusive learning we mean the greatest degree of match or fit between the individual learners' requirements and the provision that is made for them.

More recently, the Special Educational Needs and Disability Act (2001) which came into force on the 1 September 2002 places responsibility on institutions to take reasonable steps to ensure that a disabled person is not placed at substantial disadvantage in pursuing a course of study. The problem now is for teachers and their educational organizations to bring about the recommendations of Tomlinson and the requirements of SENDA. One solution is to take a three-stage approach, which can be summarized as Identify, Review and Evaluate.

8.4.1 Identification of learner need

There are many ways of identifying learner need and some or all of them may exist within your workplace. Initial interviewing procedures can identify already existing needs that may have been documented previously, or be part of a formal statement of need issued by the Local Education Authority. Because of Tomlinson and SENDA, all establishments now ensure that initial diagnostic testing of learners takes place on commencement of their programme or during the important induction period. Teachers also have a key role to play in recognizing when learners are finding difficulty in achieving to their ability and to recognize any new needs as they arise. In addition, learners can be encouraged to identify specific needs themselves and request support. However these identification processes take place, it is important that both the need and the required support is documented and passed to appropriate specialists within the establishment in order that funding may be drawn upon and the correct provision be made. It is also essential that the learner is made a part of this process and is involved in a discussion about both the need and the suitability of the intended provision so that those important concepts of 'responsibility' and 'ownership' can be firmly established early in the proceedings. Diagnostic tests are often used at the beginning of a learner's programme and as well as the identification of support needs. This initial diagnosis can establish the learner's current abilities in specific areas and identify strengths and limitations. As we discussed in Chapter 3, diagnostic tests can also be used to identify individual learning styles. As a result of completing initial assessment, individual learner action plans can be established which form the basis of all decisions about the learner's programme.

E8g   Learning support audit

Identify the full range of support offered to learners within your organization. Remember to include physical support such as note takers, interpreters, transport, etc. Also include support that relates to customizing materials which students may access (computer-based documents, audio, enlarged text). When you have established your list find out which staff are responsible for providing the support you need. Identify the processes (including the associated paperwork), which both recognize and request the support.

You may find that a chart (with entries similar to the example below) will be useful in summarizing your audit outcomes and that this 'support picture' will act as a helpful reference to provision and processes within your organization.

Support audit summary				
Support identified	Contact name	Tel. no.	Process	Required paperwork
Note-taking for a dyslexic learner.	Jane Turner, Learner Support Unit.	Ex. 3478	Interview at induction. Complete forms, pass to LSU. Meet LSU support	Complete LSU Diagnostic Test. DT to LSU. Appraisal Report completed with

				worker with student for appraisal report. Action Plan with agreed times for note-taking completed. LSU actions request. Note-taker provided. Review date set	learner, tutor and LSU staff. Copy of agreed Action Plan to learner, tutor, and LSU.

8.4.2   Review of support provision

The review process is also critical to the creation of effective learning support. Learners require many opportunities to regularly review the need they have, to chart any changes, identify their successes and establish any alterations in support that have to take place. The review process will also need to be recorded, and the advantage of this is that learners and providers can see the progress they are making in small stages and adjust the support as they go along.

The importance of the documentation used for review purposes cannot be stressed enough. The learner needs to have ownership of this and complete it along with the teacher. The learner will need to identify for themselves the progress they have made, the level of support they still require, the value of the support to their own learning process and their requirements for the immediate future. If review is carried out in this manner the learner has a say in what is provided, values the provision and sees it as 'support', not as someone taking over and doing the work for them. The learner also is aware that the support is responsive rather than fixed. It is changing to meet current needs and not something regarded as a permanent feature. This is an important aspect of development towards learner independence.

E8h   Learner ownership of review

Look at your organization's paperwork that is used for reviewing provision with your learners. Analyse the paperwork and pay particular attention to how it enables your learners to *own* the process of review. Discuss how effective you feel this is in practice and, where appropriate, suggest how the process could be improved.

8.4.3   Evaluation of learner support

The evaluation of particular support that you have just carried out for activity E8g is extremely important to any organization. We all need to be willing to monitor constantly all aspects of our provision, particularly support for the learner, the teacher and the organization. Evaluation should be seen as part of the learning process by everyone involved. In this way, identified strengths and weaknesses will automatically be considered when planning future support.

There are likely to be three levels of evaluation relating to support needs and each has a different focus. Initial evaluation will check the support in relation to the learner and ask questions that relate to learner achievement. A second focus for evaluation could be the impact on the class teacher, the remainder of the learner group, the cost, time and staffing implications. A third focus should be the key aspects of current policy initiatives (such as the Tomlinson Report or SENDA) and identify if the establishment's management has achieved the outcomes recommended within these reports.

8.5	ESTABLISHING INCLUSIVENESS

As teachers in post-compulsory education it is important to look at the ways in which we can work towards an inclusive approach in our classrooms and identify the benefits this will bring to all of our learners.

For inclusion to be successful it needs to start at the beginning of the learning process, even before the learner has entered your establishment (remember the approaches of establishments A and B at the start of this chapter?). Successful organizations will be part of the wider social context that they represent and will have built a relationship with that community which allows them to meet their present and future needs.

E8i   Community responsiveness

Explore how your local community has influenced your provision by identifying particular programmes within your institution which have developed directly as a result of the needs of specific learning groups.

Learning provision is one measure of an institution's close identification with the needs of a community. A more obvious one is the actual design and structure of the buildings. Feeling included within an organization should be evident from first entering the door. Ask yourself whether access is easy for everyone concerned. Establish whether wheelchair users or mothers with prams are able to use the same entrance as everyone else. Could you reach the reception desk if you are sitting in a wheelchair, are doors automatic and do they open to the side? Check if there are sufficient notices (including symbols as well as text) at appropriate heights for all people to find their way around.

The thought that goes into an 'inclusive' building is considerable. At the planning stage we would need to consider ease of access, availability of all services to learners in wheelchairs, those who are physically and mentally challenged and learners who have visual and auditory difficulties. It is essential that the initial feeling for all learners on entering the building and using the facilities must be welcoming. If this fails and learners, for whatever reason, feel isolated and segregated, then the chance of turning this into a positive, inclusive experience will most certainly have been damaged, if not lost altogether.

E8j   Access to inclusion

Consider the frustration learners may feel if their physical entry to your establishment is made difficult for them. Explore the buildings and identify strengths and limitations in providing equality of access to all learners who use them. Identify groups of learners who you feel may be better provided for. Give reasons and possible solutions.

As equally important as the physical resources are the human ones, such as the teachers and the many different support workers. Inevitably, these human resources rapidly gain more value as they develop into *inclusive* facilitators of learning.

E8k   Inclusive facilitators

Consider just what makes an *inclusive* teacher or support worker. What are the particular characteristics of their relationship with their learners?

From the very beginning of the relationship we really need to recognize that all learners are valued and respected for what they bring with them into the classroom. Having identified their individual needs and learning styles, we then need to develop our teaching to allow the learners in our group to equally access the learning we provide. This process of managing diversity (rather than trying to make everyone the same) is at the heart of inclusive learning. In practical ways this may mean us developing teaching materials that are differentiated at a range of levels, appeal to different learners' learning styles and allow access to concepts and ideas in a range of ways (see also Chapter 3). In order to optimize our teaching, we will also need to consider the different approaches we may take with learners, using a range of methods, some practical and creative, some requiring individual and group involvement and some experiential and didactic. The most important aspect for us to deal with is to ensure that we teach in a way which enables our learners to access and enjoy the learning experience. This will inevitably be much more effective than merely falling back on methods which are comfortable and familiar for us. A humanistic approach (also see Chapter 5) when making choices about learning strategies should be to always put the student at the centre of the decision-making process.

While we are teaching we also need to confirm individual learner success and progress in a positive and critical way, in order to establish what it is they need to do in order to continue to succeed. Positive, constructive, regular feedback to all learners is therefore an important part of working inclusively in the classroom.

Being diverse and responsive when planning teaching and learning must also include the assessment of our learners. To ensure an inclusive approach, we need to carefully consider whether our choice of assessment *method* is as appropriate to the learners as the defined learning outcomes (see also Chapter 9). Offering a range of assessment opportunities does not imply a reduction in the quality of the assessment process. It is an attempt to ensure that the assessment process is 'fit for purpose' by making it appropriate to not only to the subject, but also the particular students.

223

Having assessed them in as valid a way as possible, our valuing of the learners will also be evident in the quality of feedback we provide. Rather than being concerned about their clearance of particular assessment 'obstacles' we will be focusing on their progression after the hurdle. This will be achieved through accurate, fair and informative feedback which promotes development and growth. Recognizing achievement in this way should be followed by the identification (with our learners) of where they want to move on to next. Understanding the progression routes, both across and up the qualification framework, is essential if we are to provide the motivation for lifelong learning that inclusion suggests.

In summary, at the heart of inclusiveness is the acceptance that all of our learners have equal access to fair and accurate initial assessment, informed advice and guidance, and appropriate support to meet their identified needs. At the same time this is enhanced by a classroom environment that encourages diversity and is responsive to our students' changing needs through the creation of learning situations which are challenging and varied in delivery and assessment.

Fundamental to all of this, however, is the belief that learners are valued as individuals and this valuing is expressed through the culture of the classroom. With these values in place, learners can grow in confidence and ability as they are enabled to maximize their potential. A philosophy of inclusion is therefore at the heart of both learning support and the humanistic approach to teaching and learning.

8.6 | GUIDANCE AND ACCESS

We focus now on methods of enabling access to learning for all potential participants in education and training and the provision of suitable and easily available guidance to make their entry to our establishments as trouble-free as possible.

Once again we are proposing not merely being efficient, but moving on to ensure effectiveness. In other words, it is routine to provide career guidance facilities. A more important prerequisite is to ensure that this guidance meets the varying needs and expectations of *all* of our learners and that they are able to access this information when they require it.

8.6.1 Enrolling with integrity

On the face of it, the provision of advice and guidance is a simple process. However, the reality is that we live in an era when quite often, despite the best intentions of the tutors concerned, the intense funding and policy pressures on the providers of education to the post-compulsory sector can lead to some erosion of the integrity of recruitment.

Ironically, the reasons for this additional stress on the advice and guidance processes lie in the quality measures that operate nationally. The imperative to achieve these externally set targets does mean that the measurement of our learners' success, together with ours as teachers and that of our organization, is compared with other educational providers both locally and nationally. Therefore, potential students and the inspection process will naturally use comparable achievement statistics relating to courses and institutional provision as a measure of the quality of what we are offering (see also Chapter 10).

Measurement of success will often be based on crude, output-related, quantitative statistics because these data are relatively easy to collect, understand and use as a basis for comparison. Despite what David Boyle (2000) calls this 'tyranny of numbers', as teachers we know full well that much of the 'value added' which we achieve with our learners is also related to personal and social development, learning about learning (meta-learning) and thinking about thinking (meta-cognition). Such important outcomes are much less visible, difficult to measure, subjective and qualitative. More importantly, if learners are to have the opportunity to develop not only the specified outcomes but also these overarching values, they need to be directed to programmes which are appropriate to their abilities and interests. If learners find themselves either out of their depth and struggling with too demanding a subject, or feel patronized and bored taking a route which is far below their capabilities, they will often adopt an instrumental, shallow approach that merely addresses the set targets. The important, difficult-to-measure values suggested above may be sacrificed.

E8l   The ethics of guidance

Consider how teachers' approaches to providing guidance may be influenced by their concerns. Think about how it may be affected if teachers have each of the following as their main priority: a) the success of their establishment or department; b) the local employment situation; c) the learners' needs and abilities.

This exercise illustrates how teachers can often be caught up in a very difficult ethical dilemma when providing guidance. The survival of the department or even the institution will depend upon getting in sufficient funding through enrolments and it is easy to rationalize that the learners have been dealt with efficiently. We can argue that, after all, the programme they are joining is well established and respected; they will be supported well and therefore will be successful in their outcomes. Promoting this programme will also meet both the college's and local employment needs.

When we are thinking in this 'efficient' way we are interpreting guidance in a very shallow way. It should not, of course, be about the institution or the department; it should be about the learner and their process of learning. They need to be at the centre of this process in exactly the same way that they are at the centre of all of the other decisions we make as teachers. When we move the focus to the learner in this way, we start to consider their needs in much more depth and, as a consequence, the advice, information and guidance we provide are liable to be more accurate and appropriate.

E8m   Advice, information and guidance

Reflect on how advice, information and guidance differ and their role within your support processes.

Advice is simply giving an opinion on what to do in a particular situation and it seems that it is something that many teachers and a lot of adults feel that they ought to do, even when it is not sought. Unfortunately, even if they have requested it, the advice often turns out to be not quite what that person wants to hear and so they will not accept or act upon it.

One strategy to avoid 'handing down' unwanted wisdom, is to ask the learner exactly what it is they would like to do. Then, rather than advising them, we can help them to develop whatever it is they need in order to achieve the action they desire. This may lead us into giving information to our learners to enable them to make considered choices. *Information* giving differs from offering advice in that, when we give information to the learner, it is not accompanied by suggestions as to the best way forward. We simply give the information requested and allow the learner the freedom to take everything we offer and make their own decision about what they do with it. This gives all of the responsibility for the action to the learner and could be uncomfortable for them as it may be that making the decision to act is the real challenge. However, when asked for information, beware of changing it to 'advice'. It sounds more straightforward and direct, but it is not helpful in developing learners who can trust their own judgments and act on their own decisions.

Offering *guidance* is different to both giving advice and information. Giving information offers the learner many views and alternative paths to follow and leaves the learner with the decision of which way to go. Guidance, on the other hand, seems to happen when a learner has already narrowed down the choices and wants some guidance about the final decision. Guidance feels a bit like gathering all of the information available when sailing a ship so that you can see well ahead and plot the best course. This is an apt analogy because, together, you and your learner view the alternatives, look at all of the factors that may influence the results and, from your combined viewpoints, evaluate the possible outcomes. This sort of guidance leaves the learner at the helm, with a teacher standing supportively alongside.

The advice, information and guidance we make available to our learners will be important in their decision-making processes regarding either access to the right programmes of study, future employment or progression. We have already discussed the importance of placing learners on suitable programmes in terms of content and level, and seen the relevance of induction in fine tuning that process and adapting provision to meet the learners' needs.

8.6.2 Progression

We need to move on now to look at the sort of advice, information and guidance we provide while learners are on our programmes and the relevance of 'exit guidance' to both the learner and the college. In anticipation, you may like to explore some of the relevant aspects in the following activity:

E8n *Marketing your programme*

Identify the materials used to market your programme within your establishment. Consider the content of the material and the information it gives to prospective learners and employers. Think in terms of wider frameworks like 'cost', 'widening participation', 'inclusive learning' and consider improvements you could make. Aim at not only giving factual information about the course, but also enabling the reader to get a real feel for the ethos of the programme.

Due to the diverse nature of learners entering post-compulsory education, initial advice and guidance may address many different areas. Young adults who are entering education or training will bring with them needs which are very different to those of mature adults. Sixteen-year-olds accessing college for the first time will carry with them previous experiences of learning within a school context, some of which may be positive and others negative. Their expectations of the post-compulsory sector may be that it will be the same as school, and so the focus of our support will be in clarifying these expectations to encompass their new world. As teachers we will need to support them as they become independent and interdependent learners, capable of managing themselves through the process of learning and developing lifelong learning skills.

This group will also be simultaneously achieving their own personal maturity, developing relationships with other adults, preparing for independent living and using us as a bridge to higher education and employment. We will therefore need to be sensitive to both their academic and personal needs.

Adults entering post-compulsory education will also have past experiences of learning and these may colour their perception of what they are about to engage in. In addition adults may bring the insecurity of entering education after a break and feel uncomfortable within a 14–19 learning environment. This group may also be looking for a bridge between their current situation and employment or HE and will bring with them the many pressures associated with being adult, including family and financial difficulties and perhaps, where they are no longer in work, a loss of status. Whatever the focus of our advice and guidance is, we need to support both groups in becoming confident and self-motivated learners who will achieve success.

Initial advice and guidance may be around suitable programmes of study. It could also include different pathways of study, suitable provision in terms of timing of sessions, and long-term action planning for progression We may also want to identify the accreditation of their prior experience, learning and achievement (APEL) and the provision of services that will support access including financial agreements and institutional facilities (see also Chapter 4).

While they are on our programmes, we will need to give advice and guidance in relation to individual learner progress. This is where the learner contracts and review procedures, discussed earlier, will enable learners to see how they are progressing towards their desired aims and be responsive to adjustment to ensure success.

On completion of programmes all learners will seek advice and guidance on what can be done next to ease transition to either employment or further education at a suitable level. Many establishments have created a depth and breadth of provision which enables learners to do this with ease. They usually recognize that success is not always about linear progression up the education framework, but can also be lateral movement into related areas at the same academic level.

> ### E8o   Progression advice
>
> Identify the Careers and Guidance service offered to all learners by your organization. Identify the main aspects of this service that your learners would use on completion of their current programme of study. Explore how well the service is used and how effectively it caters for the particular needs of your students.

8.7   PROVIDING PERSONAL SUPPORT TO LEARNERS

For the final unit of this chapter we will revisit some earlier ideas, including the concepts of an inclusive and humanistic student-centred approach to learners and learning.

As previously discussed in Chapter 5, the humanistic approach to teaching and learning which developed mainly from the work of Carl Rogers (1983) and Abraham Maslow (1970) has since been embraced by many other educators. At the heart of this approach is the belief that the learner is valued for who they are and is empowered to become the autonomous and self-actualizing individual they are capable of becoming. This philosophy embraces the values of inclusiveness because it applies to all learners, regardless of their characteristics or individual needs, and sees the diversity of all humans as strength on which to build. Rogers (ibid.) believed that in order to support learners to achieve to their maximum potential, three conditions needed to be in place within the learning environment. He called these conditions the 'Core Conditions' and recognized that they are special to any supporting or helping relationship. They come from Person-Centred Counselling Theory as developed by Rogers. Put simply, as a teacher you need to first *Respect* your learner, second have an *Empathy* for what they are experiencing and feeling, and third be real and *Genuine* when you are relating to them An examination of these concepts is, perhaps, an appropriate way to end this chapter.

8.7.1   Respect

Respect in the classroom will have real implications for both the teacher and learner. As a teacher you can demonstrate respect for learners in many different ways which will, in turn, encourage the learners to respect you. As you would expect, the key question is how do we show respect to the learners in our groups?

The strategies are very simple but, because of all of the current pressures in teaching, are not always so easy to achieve. Some simple ways in which we can show respect are to:

● always know our learners' names and use them when we are working with our groups, especially when giving feedback

● enable learners to have a voice in our classrooms and give them time to speak and develop their ideas. This can often be a challenge to the teacher, as we may want to move things on

● listen to our learners; this requires that the teacher and the group be silent when someone is speaking. This may be one of the 'rules' which you might like established during induction when the group is deciding how they will work together

- allow learners to work at their own pace and recognize that this may not always be our pace. This acknowledges where the learner is in their own learning process; again this may be difficult when we have a syllabus to cover within a particular time

- be on time. The use of time is an important way to show respect to others. For example, handing marked work back on time and valuing the time you spend together with your group

When we show respect for our learners, what usually happens is that we are modelling a process for them which makes them feel good about themselves in their learning situation. The result of this is that, given time, the learner starts to respect us and the group they work with and this gives us a real foundation on which to build very positive future learning experiences.

8.7.2 Empathy

Empathy is often described being 'as if you are walking in another person's shoes'. The important consideration here is the 'as if'. In empathy, we are not *being the other person* but are trying, through listening, to understand how they are experiencing events, and what their understanding of the situation is for themselves. We don't need to become the other person to be empathic with them, but we do need to recognize how they are feeling and (remembering 'respect') to accept that, for them, this is the truth and a real description of what it is like.

So if our learners tell us that they are frightened about writing an assignment, telling them to pull themselves together and get on with it, or that everyone feels frightened when they start an assignment so not to worry, is neither respecting how they feel nor empathizing with them. A much better response would be to take this feeling seriously and then check out what is 'frightening' for them and work through strategies to make the overall task become more achievable. This approach allows us to be really supportive of our learners and at the same time helps them to feel valued and respected, reinforcing that their feelings and perceptions matter.

Another important part of being empathic is to avoid the temptation to say, 'Oh yes, that's just how I feel too, and this is what I do to help me'. When we are being respectful and empathic and offering support, how *we* feel is not that important. Our aim in supporting the learner is to help them find ways, through us or other support agencies, to solve issues for themselves. Telling the learner what we would do in the same situation is like putting a plaster on both their problem and their feelings about it. It renders them helpless and will not promote self-respect or personal value. Enabling learners to work with you or others to find a suitable solution for themselves recognizes both how they feel and the action they want to take. This is empowering and promotes real feelings of achievement and personal worth.

8.7.3 Genuineness

Genuineness is simply about being the 'real' you – a real person listening to what your learner is saying as opposed to a 'teacher' or 'parent' or someone in authority over them. The reality of the teacher/learner relationship is that, unless your learners already perceive you as a genuine person they can relate to, respecting them for who they are and understanding their point of view, they will not ask for your help and support in the first place. This answers the obvious, age-old question many of us ask of colleagues who are involved in a difficult relationship:

Q. 'Why don't you go and talk this through with X?'

A. 'Because they won't understand, or they will make me do something I don't want to do.'

The first rule then, in providing personal support to learners, seems to be that we must offer all of our learners (no exceptions here, please) the three conditions identified as respect, empathy and genuineness, and then we can be effective in our relationships with our learner groups.

8.7.4   Listening skills

To help us create these conditions there are some very simple listening and non-verbal communication skills we can use in the classroom. We need to be aware of our bodily posture. The way we sit or stand when we are listening to and supporting our learners is often more significant than the things we say. Think of a time in the past when someone told you off, or made you feel uncomfortable. It is likely they stood or sat directly in front of you, looked you straight in the eye, and had a formal body language which communicated to you that they were in control. In a supporting relationship this is the opposite to what we want to achieve. If we stand or sit to the side of the person we are supporting, they will feel equal to us and we will not be able to stare them straight in the eyes. We can look relaxed and interested in them and, by giving space and time for them to do the talking, we will help them to have control. These very simple steps, when added to the tone of our voice plus really hearing what they are saying, will reinforce those valuable three conditions we discussed earlier. We can also use some very basic listening skills to demonstrate to our learners that we have heard what they have said. We can identify what is said by repeating to the learner their own words, reflecting back to them the main content of what is said to show our understanding. We can identify the content of the discussion and also a little of the feelings the learner is demonstrating. We can also clarify what we understand and check this out with the learner to make sure we have not got the wrong end of the stick. Doing all of the above, will help the learner to see that we understand exactly what is being conveyed to us and, rather than interpreting what we think the problems and issues are, we should allow the learner to tell us what they really are for themselves. If this happens, you can see for yourself that the learner and teacher will develop a trusting relationship, upon which a lot of support and learner empowerment can be built.

8.8 │ CONCLUSION

We have already discussed the Tomlinson Report and the inclusive learning approaches which have developed from it. We will conclude this chapter by considering a report launched by Helena Kennedy on 2 July 1997 entitled *Learning Works*. The main focus of the report was to call on the government to put further education at the heart of its post-16 agenda and it also recognized that the motivation of learners was central to widening participation and should recognize in its aims the responsibility to work with others to encourage and promote a demand for learning. The final paragraph of the report also stresses that a culture of innovative and collaborative practice should be established. The report went on to make other important recommendations that can be summarized as follows:

Key aspects of the Kennedy Report (1997)

- employers should establish learning centres, coordinated with the University for Industry (UfI)
- a national entitlement for information, advice and guidance should exist
- legislation should be put in place to make it a duty for TV channels to educate as well as inform and entertain
- a national system of local partnerships should be established to widen participation
- a credit accumulation of qualifications should be operative within five years

In the report Helena Kennedy declared that 'funding was the most important lever for change'. It has therefore come as no surprise that a lot of the developments in post-compulsory education over the last five years have been driven by changes in funding mechanisms.

These developments have included many responses to 'widening participation' which include changes that have had a very positive effect and others which have very definitely been disadvantageous to teachers and learners within PCET.

Education and training are now most definitely seen as a 'commodity' which we must sell as you would any other product. At an institutional level, we have been made to focus on current 'market groups' of learners who do not use our services. Having identified gaps in our current provision, we have been creative in designing programmes of study to meet their individual needs. In many institutions, a 'stepped curriculum' has been put into place, which allows learners to access at an appropriate level and progress.

This stepped curriculum notion also allows transfer across curriculum areas with initial programmes having such a broad perspective that they are almost a 'taster' menu of a range of courses, which can be used as a base to move on to more specialist programmes of study.

The impact on provision has been positive as it allows new curriculum combinations to be explored. To achieve this staff must be willing to teach on a range of associated programmes, from 'foundation' level through to HE, which are linked to a particular curriculum area.

As a result of these new initiatives, many of our learners at 'foundation' and 'introductory' levels often have no formal qualifications. Consequently, they need significant support to help them develop intrinsic motivation and to encourage confidence and personal growth, before they can develop the skills of independent study. As a result, we are involved with teaching both our subject content and also the processes of learning. Learners at this level can feel very dependent on us and do require our constant feedback, intervention and support. As we have discussed earlier (when looking at Maslow's hierarchy of needs) with correct teaching strategies and sufficient support, these learners can become self-motivated and independent.

In addition to these new 'clients', we may simultaneously be involved in the teaching of more traditional groups (for example A level students) who are already independent and equally demanding. This teaching requires a different type of support, possibly resource-based. With the provision of these wider resource bases, plus their greater depth of subject knowledge, these learners will have the opportunity and the means to research their subjects. However, the precise nature of the prescribed curricula and the pressures on time will inevitably demand that they also have close and expert support if they are to succeed.

From this simple picture we can identify the diverse teaching approaches required and the different levels of support needs which each type of learner will demand. Alongside this, we also need to be aware that the widening of participation has inevitably raised serious issues of 'age', 'social class', 'gender' and 'disability' which have forced institutions to address the equality of provision and access across their community.

In many post-compulsory establishments we are now enrolling learners between the ages of 14 and 80 on a range of programmes at many different levels. The qualification framework offers anything from pre-GCSE through to undergraduate study, 'taster' sessions for adult education programmes and residential and short course provision. There is also vocational training from initial access through to NVQs at Levels 3 and 4.

This massive framework also includes professional qualifications and tailor-made awards that are developed to meet the needs of individual businesses in the local area. The whole philosophy of 'widening participation' has encouraged educational providers in the post-compulsory sector to be proactive and responsive to the needs of an ever-growing range of 'customers'.

The effect of widening provision is also felt in the venues in which teaching and learning now takes place. To be able to meet more learners, we have expanded the institutional environment into areas that are no longer within our control. Some of these work well, but others less so. Teachers are now teaching in the community using school and church premises, in local business centres and public buildings. You may also find teaching in a prison or other regulated settings and even in the homes of learners. Although this has certainly widened the client group in PCET, it also places more stress upon the teacher. In the light of all these developments, you may find it useful to consider the points raised by our final chapter activity below:

E8p   The cost of widening participation

Are different skills required to teach learners of different age groups?

What are the implications for transporting yourself and materials out to the learner?

What are the implications for teaching 'off-site' without any of the usual support services?

What are the implications for learners when using off-site facilities – do they have equality of opportunity in comparison with on-site learners?

At what times of the day is there a demand for teaching in the community, and has this altered the times of day when you now teach?

When teaching in the evening to 'tired' adult learners who have been at work all day, how different are the teaching approaches you have to adopt to those you may normally use in the morning or afternoon?

As we explore the widening of participation we can see that it has had a profound effect on institutions, teachers and learners. The walls of our establishments have become invisible and teaching/training is no longer confined to a known space. The skills required to teach at a range of levels to a wide range of abilities with various personal needs may all be required of one teacher and learners may find themselves working in very mixed groups in terms of ability and experience. All of these factors place considerable stress on the organization, the teacher and the learner alike and the support that we can offer and is offered to us in this constantly changing situation is critical to our healthy survival.

Widening participation has also focused on groups previously under-represented in formal PCET environments. These may include learners who carry a statement of Special Educational Needs, those with learning or physical difficulties, learners from ethnic minority and disadvantaged groups, learners whose first language is not English and those who carry a learning impairment due to visual or auditory difficulties. In many cases this may mean that as teachers we are working in our classrooms, workshops and laboratories alongside support staff, interpreters and note-takers.

In summary, we have identified that a range of factors will influence the support offered to our learners. Some of these factors will be personal to us and some related to the organization in which we are working. We have recognized that our own development as teachers will relate to the type of support we can offer and the focus of that support. Support also relates to the journey our learners take with us, from recruitment to achievement. How we visualize that support places the learner as either a consumer of our services or the central player in an interdependent game of learning. Key factors in this process are two simple ideas of being 'efficient' in what we do and being 'effective' in how we perceive our purposes and values.

At the very heart of all the support we offer, be it inclusive learning or widening participation, there is a core, irreducible tenet. Give our learners respect, empathy and genuine people to relate to, plus appropriate support to meet their individual and changing needs and we will empower them to achieve to their highest potential. It allows us to be both very efficient and very effective at the same time.

Carl Rogers (1983) succinctly summarized this philosophy:

> Learning should involve the student as a whole person, at an emotional and personal as well as at an intellectual level, learning should be pleasurable and relevant.

8.9 | USEFUL SOURCES

Sanders, P. (1996) *First Steps in Counselling*. London: PCCS Books
An introduction to basic counselling and listening skills that will support you in working with both students and colleagues. This book also gives an overview of

behavioural, cognitive and humanistic theories and how these relate to approaches we may take. Although the discussion is centred around counselling it is directly transferable into the classroom.

Rogers, C. (1980) *A Way of Being*. New York: Houghton Mifflin.
Another classic from Carl Rogers which provides more insight into Humanistic theory.

Cotton, A. (ed.) (1998) *Thinking about Teaching*. London: Hodder & Stoughton.
Read and enjoy Tony Cotton's review of eight teachers reflecting on their development which provides great insight and advice on practice.
For up to date information and also past copies of papers in relation to:

- The Tomlinson Report (Inclusive Learning) www.lifelonglearning.co.uk
- The Kennedy Report (Widening Participation) www.lifelonglearning.co.uk
- 14–19 Green Paper and other topical papers for the FE Sector www.dfes.gov.uk

Try *tipcet.com* for a range of materials and suggested sources related to learner support, widening participation and inclusive education, etc.

8.10 RATIONALE FOR PROVIDING LEARNERS WITH SUPPORT – KEY AREA E

FAQs	At Stage 1	At Stage 2	At Stage 3
Why do it?	For one reason or another, many learners are anxious about their ability to meet the demands of formal educational situations. Our responsibility is to help them overcome these anxieties so that they can make the best of the learning opportunities we are providing. Assessing the range of differing learner needs is a firm foundation for a successful teacher/student relationship.	It is the teachers' responsibility to provide effective support for learners and give them guidance on current and future opportunities and requirements. This level of support will enable learners to maximize their learning potential and overcome problems, which could cause them to underachieve, fail or withdraw from a course.	Analysing the support received by your learners will allow you to evaluate its effectiveness. You may then find it necessary to enhance certain aspects or to reduce provision which is underused.
Where are we going?	You are developing a real understanding of the learners you are responsible for, i.e. those you teach for however many hours per week. These understandings will	You are attempting to ensure that all learners have equality of opportunity in the sense of access to learning support, appropriate teaching, and effective	To be effective, learner support must be responsive to the needs of particular groups of students. Reflecting on the nature and extent of support provision will

	be at many levels and across a wide variety of interests, aspirations, needs and concerns.	learning environment and supportive assessment feedback.	allow you to ensure that support addresses particular identified needs.
How do we get there?	You are in an ideal position to become an 'authority' on the characteristics of your particular groups of learners. Your role will encourage most of your class members to express their fears and their hopes because they will usually have come into education in order to succeed. However, there will be those who have difficulty articulating their needs and it will be your task to help them identify any problems.	The first requirement is to ensure that students are recruited with integrity. Secondly, you should encourage the learners to express any doubts or anxieties they may have about the learning process. You need to be aware of the range of facilities and opportunities that are available to support learners so that you can refer them to appropriate support processes if the problem exceeds your resources.	You will need to develop systems of evaluation and analysis which give you details of support provision and how this relates to identified needs. Obviously, the more clearly you understand student need, the more specific you can be about the type of support needed.
Is this the best way?	There are formal processes of needs analysis (see Chapter 3), but often the initial identification of student need is gained through informal discussion. The success of this process will depend on you adopting an appropriately confident manner, while remaining supportive and empathetic.	You need to monitor the progress of students so that you will receive an early indication of potential failure or withdrawal. Don't attempt counselling if you are not qualified or sufficiently experienced. If in doubt always refer to an experienced colleague.	Collect data on the effectiveness of support and confirm that it is available at the right time, in the right place and addresses the identified need.
When is the right time?	The most important times when learning support is needed often occur during the early days of a programme, when the new students are slowly coming to terms with their new environment and the demands of the programme and the institution. There will also be anxieties later as assessment or progression begins to loom on the horizon. We also need to be aware of small signs of	Learners need support at all times but there are key periods when there may be a greater potential for a crisis of confidence that may lead to problems. These more difficult times are often related to periods of stress for both students and staff such as during enrolment, assessment or progression. If you can gain the confidence of learners early in their programme they are more	Analyse how different needs occur at different stages of a student's programme. Consider how these differing needs are interrelated and whether there is a common cause (e.g. low confidence/self-esteem) which may itself be tackled.

	concern which may be initiated simply by a misunderstanding of the processes.	likely to give you some indication of problems before it is too late to act.	
Who needs to know?	If you have concerns about any aspect of your learning situation, you should discuss it in the first instance with your line manager. You may then decide between you to provide formal learning support. Or you may prefer initially to tackle the problem in a more low-key manner.	Obviously, this depends on how serious the need for support may be. Teacher colleagues and other students are an obvious choice but do not neglect to inform the support services and specialist professionals and where appropriate parents, employers and carers.	Reflect on the support services as a whole and whether information is disseminated effectively.
How do we know when we've got there?	Groups of learners, who are enjoying the experience, usually become self-supporting and will let you know when there are problems you hadn't been aware of. This collaborative ethos is the ideal situation, but be aware that it may take some considerable time to achieve. Until you get there, you must continue to promote a conducive learning environment which is supportive without being overly intrusive. A difficult balancing act at the best of times.	It is the nature of the work that you are never completely free of students requiring support, but there is considerable satisfaction when a less confident or difficult student achieves and progresses, particularly if this is contrary to expectations of the student themselves and other stakeholders.	It is difficult to analyse the ongoing effectiveness of such a responsive provision as student support. Obviously, each new learner brings different demands and in some cases the support given is excellent and in others, often because of shortage of resources, the support provided is only minimal. A crucial aspect is the collection of accurate feedback from the learners themselves.
Has everyone had a fair chance?	Inevitably, you will experience the disappointment of a learner who, for one reason or another, is unable to fulfil the potential you have identified. All you can do is leave the door open for them to return and learn something from the process.	This is a difficult question when applied to support because there is always a nagging doubt about whether or not a failing student could have been helped more. Consistent standards and professionalism will help to minimize these ever-present difficulties.	Carry out an evaluation of the support given to a group of learners and identify the strengths and weaknesses of provision.

8.11 | KEY AREA E – PROVIDING LEARNERS WITH SUPPORT

Purpose: Teachers and teaching teams need to be effective in providing learners with support for their learning, guidance on current and future opportunities and requirements and personal tutorial support. This involves meeting learners' entitlements and providing them with access to the full range of facilities and opportunities which will enable them to benefit from their programme of study. Teachers and teaching teams will need to know how to access and use a wide range of services to help meet learners' needs. See 8.10 for an analysis of these key processes at Stages 1, 2 and 3.

Please note: The FENTO Standards listed below are relevant to the following three levels of award: Stage 1 (Introduction), Stage 2 (Intermediate) and Stage 3 (Full Certification). All the standards are required at Stage 3, only those in italic and bold are required at Stage 2 and only those in italic are required at Stage 1.

UNIT E1. INDUCT LEARNERS INTO THE ORGANIZATION *In order to do this teachers should:*

Demonstrate that they are able to:	*and will have specific knowledge and critical understanding of:*	*plus generic knowledge of:*	*Summary of appropriate evidence in this Key Area*		*Relevant Chapter Activities*
a	Criteria: contribute to the design and implementation of induction procedures	• The organization's induction procedures	• Learning support and guidance within the post-compulsory context and the facilities and opportunities which exist within the organization • The professional network of specialist services available to learners and how to access them	a	Learner needs analysis, Session plans for induction, Action plans	A3c to A3m, B4c, D6g, D6i, D7a to D7i; E8b to E8h, G10d to G10i
b	**provide learners with appropriate information on the organization and its facilities**	• Funding mechanisms and fee arrangements, the organization and its facilities and arrangements for obtaining access to learning support services	• Learners' entitlement to educational and personal support services • National systems for recording achievement	b	New entrant information packs, Leaner needs analysis, Learning Contract/ Agreement	A3c to A3m, B4c, D6g, D6i, D7a to D7i; G10d to G10i

237

	Criterion	Knowledge		Evidence	Reference
c	**clarify the organization's expectations of and its obligations to learners, including its health and safety requirements**	• The nature of learning contracts • Organizational and personal responsibility under the Health and Safety at Work Act • The organization's recording procedures	c	Learning Contract/Agreement, Specific Guidance Documents	D6g, D6i, E8b to E8h
d	help learners to gain access to advice and guidance on financial arrangements and personal support	• The organization's procedures for recording learners' achievements • Ways of matching individual needs to available opportunities • The educational, vocational, and personal development opportunities available to learners locally and nationally, including employment opportunities • IT systems and how to use them to access information on guidance and support • Appropriate stakeholders, including colleagues, other specialist professionals (e.g. student counsellors), employers, parents, guardians and carers • Review procedures and action planning methods	d	Guidance documentation, Learner support audit	D6g, D6i, E8b to E8h
e	**ensure that learners receive appropriate initial guidance on opportunities for progression**		e	Learning Contract or Agreement, Needs Analysis, Support referral/initiation procedures	D6g, D6i, E8b to E8h
f	*record information using organisational procedures*		f	Learning Contract or Agreement, Needs Analysis, Support referral/initiation procedures	D6g, D6i, E8b to E8h
g	**evaluate the effectiveness of the induction process with learners**		g	Evaluation feedback	G10d to G10i

Plus commentary in PDJ on the purpose and value of inducting learners into the organization, together with records in Practitioner File of Teaching Observations, Lesson Plans, Rationales, Self-Evaluations and Progress Summary

Key to above standards required at each FENTO Stage:

Introduction Stage – italic
Intermediate Stage + bold
Certification Stage – all

UNIT E2. PROVIDE EFFECTIVE LEARNING SUPPORT *In order to do this teachers should:*

	Demonstrate that they are able to:	*and will have specific knowledge and critical understanding of:*	*plus generic knowledge of:*		*Summary of appropriate evidence in this Key Area*	*Relevant Chapter Activities*
a	Criteria: provide learners with a comprehensive and clear statement of their entitlements and how to access the full range of services available to them	• Learners' entitlements and the services available	• Learning support and guidance within the post-compulsory context and the facilities and opportunities which exist within the organization • The professional network of specialist services available to learners and how to access them	a	Learning Contract, entitlement statement, Induction evaluation	E8d, E8e, E8f, E8g, E8h, E8l
b	ensure that learners are aware of the information facilities and resources available and how to find and use them effectively	• The organization's information facilities and resources and how to find and use them	• Learners' entitlement to educational and personal support services • National systems for recording achievement	b	Learning Contract, entitlement statement, Induction evaluation	E8d, E8e, E8f, E8g, E8h, E8l
c	provide learners with regular and structured opportunities to review their chosen course of study	• Organizational review procedures and how they apply to individual learners	• The organization's procedures for recording learners' achievements • Ways of matching individual needs to available opportunities	c	Learning Reviews, Action Plans	A3j; D7a to D7i
d	enable learners to make the best use of additional learner support, as appropriate		• The educational, vocational, and personal development opportunities available to learners locally and nationally, including employment opportunities	d	Learning Reviews, Action Plans. Learning support audit	A3j; D7a to D7i; E8f and E8g
e	*promote the concept that learners have a responsibility for ensuring that their learning is successful*	• How learners' programmes can be amended within agreed organizational and national procedures		e	Learning agreements	B4u, B4v, E8a, E8b, Em8

f	provide learners with opportunities to consider the next steps after their current programme	● Opportunities for learners' progression	f	Progression opportunities	E8l to E8o
g	provide structured opportunities for learners to evaluate and provide feedback on their experience of the organisation	● IT systems and how to use them to access information on guidance and support ● Appropriate stakeholders including colleagues, other specialist professionals (eg student counsellors), employers, parents, guardians and carers ● Review procedures and action planning methods	g	Evaluation feedback and databases	D7a to D7i and G10d to G10j

Plus commentary in PDJ on the purpose and value of providing effective learning support, together with records in Practitioner File of Teaching Observations, Lesson Plans, Rationales, Self-Evaluations and Progress Summary

Key to above standards required at each FENTO Stage:

Introduction Stage – italic
Intermediate Stage + bold
Certification Stage – all

UNIT E3 ENSURE ACCESS AND GUIDANCE OPPORTUNITIES FOR LEARNERS *In order to do this teachers should:*

Demonstrate that they are able to:	*and will have specific knowledge and critical understanding of:*	*plus generic knowledge of:*		*Summary of appropriate evidence in this Key Area*	*Relevant Chapter Activities*
a Criteria: ensure that learners have access to impartial, comprehensive and current information about training, employment and educational opportunities relevant to their needs and aspirations	• The organization's facilities and resources and how to find and use them • Career advice provision and how to access it	• Learning support and guidance within the post-compulsory context and the facilities and opportunities which exist within the organization • The professional network of specialist services available to learners and how to access them	a	Advice and guidance documentation, Learning Reviews, Action Plans	D7a to D7i, E8b to E8h
b contribute to a planned programme of guidance for individual learners	• Career planning techniques	• Learners' entitlement to educational and personal support services • National systems for recording achievement	b	Advice and guidance documentation, Learning Reviews, Action Plans	D7a to D7i, E8b to E8h
c provide learners with access to additional specialist guidance and support, as required		• The organization's procedures for recording learners' achievements	c	Referral documentation, Learning support audit	D7a to D7i, E8b to E8h
d *liaise with colleagues and other professionals to provide the most effective guidance and support for learners*	• National targets, attainment levels and qualifications and their relevance to the needs of individual learners	• Ways of matching individual needs to available opportunities • The educational, vocational, and personal development	d	Minutes of group meetings, support documentation, learning support audit	D7j to D7t
e provide learners with an appropriate summative statement of their experiences and achievements when they leave their programmes		opportunities available to learners locally and nationally, including employment opportunities	e	Student profiles and summative statements	F9e and F9p

f	record and process career plans, exit decisions and information on destinations, using organization's procedures	● Opportunities for employment and work in the community and their potential for learning and personal development	f	Record of student progression decisions	E8o
g	ensure that guidance meets the personal development needs, as well as the educational and vocational needs, of the learner	● IT systems and how to use them to access information on guidance and support ● Appropriate stakeholders, including colleagues, other specialist professionals (e.g. student counsellors), employers, parents, guardians and carers ● Review procedures and action planning methods	g	Record of student progression decisions	E8o
			Plus commentary in PDJ on the purpose and value of providing access and guidance opportunities, together with records in Practitioner File of Teaching Observations, Lesson Plans, Rationales, Self-Evaluations and Progress Summary	

Key to above standards required at each FENTO Stage:

Introduction Stage – italic
Intermediate Stage + bold
Certification Stage – all

UNIT E4. PROVIDE PERSONAL SUPPORT TO LEARNERS *In order to do this teachers should:*				
Demonstrate that they are able to:	*and will have specific knowledge and critical understanding of:*	*plus generic knowledge of:*	*Summary of appropriate evidence in this Key Area*	*Relevant Chapter Activities*
a **Criteria:** provide opportunities for learners to raise personal issues affecting their learning	● Counselling skills ● Ways of networking with other professionals and stakeholders in order to help individual learners ● The potential to do harm if teachers exceed their own levels of competence	● Learning support and guidance within the post-compulsory context and the facilities and opportunities which exist within the organization ● The professional network of specialist services available to learners and how to access them	a Needs Analysis, Learning Reviews, Action Plans, Student Evaluations	A3a to A3k, B4c to B4f, D6i, D7a to D7i, E8a to E8h
b create formal and informal opportunities to listen and respond to the views and feelings of individual learners	● Sources of specialist counselling and other professional support and how to access them ● Opportunities for employment and work in the community and their potential for learning and personal development	● Learners' entitlement to educational and personal support services ● National systems for recording achievement	b Programme Review, Learning Reviews, Action Plans, Student Evaluations, Student representatives	A3a to A3k, B4c to B4f, D6i, D7a to D7i, E8a to E8h
c maximize opportunities for learners to have access to specialist support as necessary		● The organization's procedures for recording learners' achievements ● Ways of matching individual needs to available opportunities	c Learning Support Referral, Library and Learning Resources	A3a to A3k, B4c to B4f, D6i, D7a to D7i, E8a to E8h
d know the limits of their own competence to deal with personal issues in relation to the tutorial function		● The educational, vocational, and personal development opportunities available to learners locally and nationally, including employment opportunities	d Contractual Boundaries, Learning Support Audit	A3a to A3k, B4c to B4f, D6i, D7a to D7i, E8a to E8h

					Standards
e	maintain close and effective links with colleagues and other professionals in order to help individual learners resolve their personal problems	• IT systems and how to use them to access information on guidance and support • Appropriate stakeholders, including colleagues, other specialist professionals (e.g. student counsellors), employers, parents, guardians and carers • Review procedures and action planning methods	e	Evaluation reviews, Team Meetings, Quality Processes	A3a to A3k, B4f, to B4f, D6i, D7a to D7i, E8a to E8h, G10d to G10i
f	act as advocates for, and mediate on behalf of, individual learners when problems arise		f	Learning Review, Support referral, Progression meetings, Meetings with External Examiners/Verifiers Boards of Assessors	A3a to A3k, B4f, to B4f, D6i, D7a to D7i, E8a to E8h, G10d to G10i
g	provide appropriate mentoring to individual learners		g	Mentor support	G10j and G10k
Key to above standards required at each FENTO Stage: *Introduction Stage – italic* **Intermediate Stage + bold** Certification Stage – all				Plus commentary in PDJ on the purpose and value of providing personal support to learners, together with records in Practitioner File of Teaching Observations, Lesson Plans, Rationales, Self-Evaluations and Progress Summary	

Assessing the outcomes of learning and learners' achievements

Fred Fawbert

Key Area F Using appropriate assessment methods to measure learning and achievement and make use of assessment information

Key concepts in this chapter: Appraisal, Assessment, Balance, Choosing answers, Controlled Response, Convergent, Criterion referencing, Distractor, Divergent, Evaluation, Fit for purpose, Formal, Formative, Ipsative, Free Response, Giving Value, Informal, Key, Learning Outcomes, Making answers, Measuring performance, Methods, Moderation, Modes, Multiple choice, Normal referencing, Objective tests, Practical tests, Process, Product, Reliability, Scheme, Specifications, Stem, Sufficient and fair, Summative, Validity, Written answers

Before you begin this chapter you may wish to check the FAQs on pp. 272–4.

Index to Chapter 9

Chapter 9 Activities designed to generate evidence against the Standards

9.1 INTRODUCTION

The assessment of learners' achievement has such a high profile within our present quality procedures that it has become, in effect, also an assessment of organizations, departments, teachers, trainers and support staff. However, despite its undoubted significance in the life of teachers and their students there is, ironically, a temptation mentally to relegate assessment to the status of a demanding end of term chore, which will get done when the time comes. It can easily be seen as something to be considered after all the hard work of teaching and learning has been completed.

In fact, the opposite is true. Assessment is not only a core activity, which impinges on all other aspects of teaching and learning; it is also a means of promoting or denying learner achievement and autonomy. As mentioned in Chapter 4, when planning teaching and learning, assessment should be one of the *first* things we consider, not the last. We need to understand not only the associated concepts and principles, but also the intended and unintended consequences of assessment practices. In order to achieve this, during this chapter we will discuss approaches to assessment and the conditions in which it may be used to promote learning and the situations where it may have the undesired opposite effect.

9.2 THE CHARACTERISTICS OF ASSESSMENT

A good starting point for this discussion is the *educational* meaning of the word 'assessment'. As you know, in conventional conversation, the terms evaluation, appraisal and assessment seem to be interchangeable and basically mean 'to make a judgement about the worth of something'. However, within education these words seem to be used almost exclusively to distinguish between three different forms of judgement-making:

- assessment – judge a learner's performance against identified criteria
- appraisal – judge a member of staff's contribution towards achieving the organization's mission
- evaluation – judge the success of a unit of teaching (i.e. session, programme or course) in achieving its aims and objectives

Of course, we are concerned here with the first of these definitions, 'assessment'. Evaluation is discussed in more detail in Chapters 8 and 10.

These days assessment in one form or another has become familiar to us all. Most members of our society have become used to having their performance measured and the ways in which data are collected about our abilities, are many and various. For example, we are assessed if we wish to drive on public roads, get a job or obtain a prescription for a pair of glasses. As a starting point for this chapter try the following activity:

F9a Approaches to assessment

Discuss how each of the three assessments below are carried out and what, in your view, are the strengths and weaknesses of these methods.

---

a) The practical 'driving' part of the driving test is based around learning outcomes and is a confirmation of practical skills within a real situation. The related theory paper checks out knowledge of the Highway Code and how it may be interpreted and these tests ensure that all qualified drivers on our roads have reached a national standard of acceptable performance. The actual driving is within an environment which cannot be controlled or predicted, and the driver's performance may be adversely affected by stress brought about by the test situation itself.

b) By testing the oral skills of applicants within an artificial situation, the job interview is used to select the most suitable candidate for employment. This interview allows the employer to probe the various levels of experience and ability of the applicant, but the amount of useful information gleaned may depend entirely on the verbal abilities of the candidate.

c) The eye test is a physiological examination against precisely defined criteria in order to establish a diagnosis as a basis for the technical prescription of a pair of spectacles or contact lenses. This close examination allows the optician to be aware of any eye defects or diseases and to use the prescribed lenses to correct any impairment in vision. Much of the test is based on the patient giving oral responses when comparing the effect of different lenses on each eye. These judgements can be very difficult and to some extent, are always subjective decisions.

The above brief review of a range of fairly familiar testing strategies does give us some indication of the general characteristics of assessment. We can confirm that effective assessment is:

1. concerned with measuring aspects of performance and attitude in a particular context (in other words, it has a clear purpose)

2.   a means of giving value

3.   carried out using appropriate modes and methods

4.   sufficient and fair

5.   valid and reliable

6.   fit for its purpose

We will use the above six key criteria to structure the debate which follows.

9.3   ASSESSMENT PURPOSES

Assessment will have differing goals. The above three examples which we have provided are designed to a) qualify a candidate to drive on our roads, b) reveal the characteristics of applicants for the same vacancy, promotion or course, so that judgements can be made and c) arrive at the specifications for glasses or contact lenses to meet the needs of a particular patient. These goals represent the three broad categories of all educational assessment, namely:

- *Qualification*
  The confirmation of achievement through certificated qualifications is now extremely important within PCET. It allows student progression to employment or other programmes of study where certificated credit transfer may be a means of accrediting earlier learning towards another award. It provides a 'transparent' public record of the institution's achievement, which may be used in national league tables to inform customer choice. We are concerned here with present attainment.

- *Selection*
  Most schools, colleges and universities will use assessment to select learners for admission and their criteria may not always be made public. Most employers will have devised criteria for joining their company and many professions have entry qualifications. The focus here is differentiation to provide data which will better inform judgements.

- *Diagnosis*
  When students are entering post-compulsory education, most establishments will use diagnostic appraisal in order to decide appropriate levels and programmes, be aware of learning characteristics, and understand support needs and student expectations (see also Chapters 4 and 8). We are concerned here as much with potential and aptitude as with previous achievement.

9.4   ASSESSMENT AIMS

The concept of 'giving value' introduced above is a good starting point for a discussion about the aims of assessment. In other words, the formal assessment process has added value to the recorded profile of abilities of each of the individuals involved. Compared to the popular perspective that assessment is a series of hurdles prepared by teachers to trip up unsuspecting students, the addition of value is much more positive and motivating perspective for those concerned. Even so, we shouldn't forget our discussion in Chapter 5, when we suggested that the same process which gives value to one group of learners, might be seen as a threat to others.

F9b   The threat of assessment

Discuss how a formal assessment process may seem threatening to some of your students and what you may do to counteract that.

Learners with low levels of self-esteem can manage to rationalize away the criticisms and jibes of family and friends, or may seek the security of a sub-cultural social group of like-minded peers. However, a systematic system of assessment where there is the potential that recorded data will be passed on to other teachers and assessors cannot be so easily dismissed. The support processes suggested previously in Chapter 9 must be in place to counter these fears before the burden of assessment becomes too great.

To return to our debate about adding value. As a result of the qualificatory, selection and diagnosis examples of assessment above, the following values can been attributed to the learners involved:

- *Driving test* – ability to drive a car safely on roads and motorway and the disposition to show respect to other road users

- *Job interview* – competence in work-related skills, working with others, meeting the company's employee regulations, self-motivation and ability to contribute to the mission statement

- *Eye test* – the comparative and combined performance of each of the patient's eyes

We have discussed briefly how the above assessments were carried out and their strengths and weaknesses. We now need to look beyond these to a range of other strategies.

9.5 | ASSESSMENT MODES

The *mode* or style of assessment is the overall approach. The choice of mode by the assessors will usually make their intentions clear, which in turn will provide an insight into their underpinning values. The *methods* used within these modes (see 9.6 below) will be more narrowly concerned with the range of techniques they employ and are not affected by the mode chosen.

The most familiar descriptors of *modes* that we use in assessment are *formal or informal*:

- **formal assessment** involves methods such as examinations, written tests, essays, multiple-choice questions, etc. It may also include situational tests, continuous assessment and student profiles.

- **informal assessment** is mainly concerned with observing and questioning the learner during course-related activities. Such unobtrusive techniques as consulting records and monitoring behaviour will often indicate not only what the student is able to do, but also what the student is *willing* to do.

At some time or another, we may all *informally* assess our learners. This may, for example, be based on the way they dress or talk or write.

> ### F9c Informal assessment
>
> Thinking about a group of your own students, discuss how you may *informally* assess them and consider the potential value of this and some of the problems with this technique.

As you would expect, the use of informal assessment *must be approached with caution*. Such approaches usually imply that the students will not know the criteria they are being assessed against or even that an assessment is taking place. Also, more often than not they will not be aware of the outcomes of the judgement or how it will affect their progress. In other words, informal assessment will often be ethically suspect, particularly if the results of that assessment may have a bearing on the student's final achievement. The possible implications of this type of 'labelling' and the self-fulfilling prophecy notion will be referred to again towards the end of the chapter.

However, despite the obvious dangers, there are situations where, when properly used, informal assessment may be helpful to a teacher or support worker who is concerned about how a particular student is coping with some of the more demanding aspects of their programme of study. This may take the form of observation or discreet questioning and may be indirectly related to time-keeping, personal hygiene, bullying, etc. Any information gained this way should be treated as a private means of confirming or rejecting specific concerns, and if any fears are aroused a more formal, recorded process should be undertaken.

9.5.1 Referencing assessment

Another important choice of modes, which either an assessor will make or will be prescribed by the awarding body, is between *norm, criterion* and *personal referencing*.

a) *Norm referencing* is simply a mode of assessment used when the assessor wishes to compare the performance of learners against a particular 'reference' group, which may be:

- fellow, class or group members
- local, regional or national groups of students taking the same assessment
- students in the same age group
- professional groups

This comparative approach to assessment is designed to facilitate forms of *selection* through the *ranking* of candidates and to promote internal and external quality procedures which demonstrate the *relative performance* of students, departments, institutions and local authorities over time.

b) *Criterion referencing*, in contrast, is concerned with the achievement of *defined objectives* and is *not* concerned with comparing student performances. To be effective, the criteria aimed at by the learners and referred to by the assessors must be as explicit as possible (see 9.6.6, Learning outcomes). Ideally, the information provided by such assessment will then make clear:

- the *level, range* and *type* of performance expected of the learners
- the specific details of the learners' achievement when they have satisfactorily completed the assessment
- to internal and external assessors and verifiers, the learners', teachers' and establishments' performance
- the relationship of the learners' achievements to other external, formal examinations and standards
- the effectiveness of the current curriculum design during any later evaluation processes

---

F9d   The implications of referencing

Discuss how the use of the above norm- and criterion-referenced modes may affect the achievement and progression of a group of your learners.

During the last decade there has been a gradual move at all levels of education from norm referencing towards the use of specific criteria. Learning outcomes are now so dominant within educational assessment that the remaining norm-referenced systems (such as those used in A level examinations and university degree classifications) are continually under fire. However, there are still pressures from employers, admissions tutors, etc., to have simple systems of grading, which facilitate selection. Such political pressures can lead to a less than satisfactory, hybrid assessment process. For example:

- In recent years within the traditionally norm-referenced higher education assessment practices, there has been a drive towards articulating assessment in terms of learning outcomes. In some situations, the specificity of these assessment targets does allow students to meet targets in such an unambiguous way that norm-referencing criteria are compromised. This process has the effect of apparently driving up student performance levels.

- The opposite situation exists in some further education programmes where there have been attempts to provide simple graded outcomes to facilitate various selection procedures. As a consequence, the familiar, criterion-referenced, competence-based systems may now also include norm-referenced grading, often based on portfolios or written examinations.

We include overleaf a simple representation of the mark distribution typical of each system. The vertical line on the left of each graph would represent the number of assessment candidates and the horizontal line shows the mark distribution, with the marks increasing from left to right in each example:

Many lecturers in higher education will defend the traditional norm-referenced approach shown in our example on the left. Their view is that only a minority

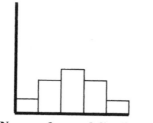

Norm-referenced distribution

Criterion-referenced distribution

should gain a first-class degree and the majority will lie in the 2:1 or 2:2 classification categories. These attitudes and their preferred processes usually result in assessment scores being grouped together in the central range (i.e. few candidates receive a mark below 40 per cent or above 70 per cent). However, because of the development in HE of a criterion-referenced approach through the imposition of precise learning outcomes, the curve of distribution should be moving towards the example on the right.

In contrast, the criterion-reference systems pioneered within post-compulsory education by NVQs should produce a distribution similar to the one on the right, because the majority of learners will achieve the defined learning outcomes. However, in an attempt to facilitate selection through the use of a simple grade, some assessment processes are now incorporating a norm-referenced system (shown on the left above) within a criterion-based, learning outcome framework.

c) *Personal referencing* has previously been used primarily in Adult and Community Education, and *ipsative* or self-referenced assessment is now being used in both post-compulsory and higher education. This personal referencing may be based on the students' previous attainment or simply the outcomes that the students identify for themselves (or negotiate with a tutor) within say, a student-initiated module or within a dissertation. Strictly speaking this is a form of criterion-based assessment, but again, it may well lie within a norm-referenced system.

These examples taken from contemporary educational situations may show that, across education, assessment processes are gradually moving to a position where the best use is made of both the norm and criterion-referenced approaches. However, an alternative view could be that, despite attempts to achieve 'transparency' of assessment through the use of defined learning outcomes (see 9.8 below), the difficulties involved in achieving the unambiguous specification of outcomes, plus political pressures for simple, often crude, quality and selection procedures, will always leave us in situations where we have to cope with difficult methodological compromises.

9.5.2 Formative and summative assessment

Assessment information may also be gathered in different ways. Using different techniques we may wish to collect data during a course, so that we are continuously assessing our learners, or we may wish to use a final assessment, which summarizes their achievement. Obviously, we need to make a decision about which of these two systems to use.

F9e Formative or summative?

Summarize the advantages and disadvantages for you *and your learners* of using either the formative or summative modes of assessment. Think not only about when you need information about learners' ability, but also of the effect of assessment on their performance.

a) *Formative assessment* is essentially an integral part of the learning process, which takes place throughout learning. Used in this way, the chosen assessment methods not only provide us with information about our learners' progress, they may also be used to encourage and motivate them. Most teachers also value the regular feedback on their learners' progress as this enables them to adjust programmes to address any shortfall they may discover in student achievement.

b) *Summative assessment*, as the name suggests, provides a final summary of the learner's achievement, and this traditional approach to assessment in the form of end of year examinations was the norm in most areas of education up until the 1970s. Although the advent of continuous assessment procedures has reduced reliance on the summative approach, it is still used in many areas of education and training because it meets the needs of stakeholders other than the students. Quality managers, parents, employers and the public in general attach great importance to summative results and, as we indicated in Chapter 4, often the assessment stipulated by external awarding bodies will effectively define the curriculum that is followed.

F9f Assessment focus

Consider some assessment for which you are responsible and analyse which aspects of student performance are given priority. Discuss how important you feel the process is, when compared to the product: in other words, the manner in which students approach the task (planning, organizing, designing) as compared to what they produce (assignment, action plan, artefact or performance).

9.5.3 Process or product

Another mode decision when planning assessment is the relative importance of *process* as compared to *product* when writing or interpreting criteria. In some cases, the end product may only be a relatively small part of the whole assessment process. In other cases, the final product is a good basis on which to base the majority of the assessment

9.5.4 Convergent or divergent

Our final mode decision will be to identify whether it is appropriate for our assessment to focus on *one* correct answer or for there to be range of possible solutions. A typical *convergent* approach would be the use of multi-choice questions (see 9.6.1 Objective tests below), which have only one correct answer.

Specific, competence-based assessments are also looking for a limited range of answers within a particular context.

However, it may be important, when assessing the creative abilities of your students, to encourage a range of solutions to a given problem.

F9g   Divergent mode

In relation to your own learners, consider those situations where it may be necessary to encourage a more divergent response to assessment problems.

Assessment which is designed to assess divergent thinking will be appropriate in those situations where there is no unique, correct solution. Obviously this will occur frequently within creative subjects such as fine art or drama, but it is also valuable within other subjects where it is important that students look at a range of alternatives.

9.6 | METHODS

There are many *methods* of assessment available to teachers and, although their value will not usually be affected by the mode, these methods may well reflect some of the mode's characteristics. For example, a simple way of defining our methods is whether or not they encourage a *free* response or a *controlled* response.

A *controlled* assessment task is one where a one-word answer or a short sentence is appropriate and this would be congruent with the convergent mode where the assessor is concerned to achieve a precise outcome. A *free* response may well be an essay question that, although encouraging some specific content in the answer, is also expecting the students to be creative in their interpretation.

Of course, in many vocational education situations, assessment will be a combination of both *written answers* and *practical tests*. We list below the various techniques used within these two approaches:

9.6.1   Objective tests

We have called our first *Written test* category 'Choosing and constructing answers', which, in effect, is an objective test. These items are written so that there is only one right answer and this facilitates objective marking, as they do not require the assessor to make subjective interpretations of the candidate response. The advantages of objective tests are that:

● the marking is consistent regardless of who is marking the test and is not affected by the 'halo' effect produced by the candidate's ability in written expression (i.e. the marking is reliable)

● answers are restricted to the questions asked and this enables quicker marking and more speedy feedback of the results

● they are able to test a wide range of knowledge and comprehension

Table 9.1 Assessment methods

Written tests		Practical tests	
Choosing and constructing 'answers'	Making answers	Active – hands on (knowing and doing) focusing on:	Passive – hands off (knowing only) focusing on:
Recall/Completion	Sentence completion	Process being tested	Recognition (use of photographs, diagrams, etc.)
Matching	Explanatory paragraph	Product of the process	Interview
Multiple choice	Essay/Assignment/ Dissertation (open)	Process and product (job observation)	Tape-recording answers
True/False	Essay writing (structured)	On-the-job fault diagnosis (problem-solving)	Separate from job fault diagnosis (problem-solving)
Sequencing	Summary paragraph	Situational role play	Imaginary role play
Multiple response	Listing Advantages/ disadvantages Process application (e.g. calculations) Project Open-book Seen paper exam Self-assessment	Games and simulations	ICT
ICT based self-assessment		Project	Profile/portfolio

F9h Objective test development and evaluation

Focusing on an area of subject assessment with which you are familiar, design an objective test consisting of 10 questions and then check your design against some of the criteria discussed below.

For objective tests and other types of assessment, it is important first to produce an assessment specification (see 9.7 below) which indicates syllabus coverage, abilities and skills to be tested, etc. Before writing the items, it is important to decide which format you are using. Obviously, it is easier to produce short answer/ sentence completion questions than those involving multiple choice. A multiple-choice question will consist of three components:

- *The stem* which is the part that *asks* the question
- *The key* which is the *correct answer*, chosen from several possibilities
- *The distractors* which are the remaining possible answers

Stems may be direct questions or incomplete statements. Keys must be posed in such a way that students with knowledge can see it. Distractors are incorrect answers, which appear correct to those who do not have the knowledge.

Table 9.2 Examples of objective test types:

Recall/ completion	a) What is the capital city of Spain? b) Who invented the telephone? c) The chemical symbol for water is …?
Matching	d) For each of the national dishes in List B, select from List A its area of origin: **List A** **List B** Austria North Africa Paella Pecan pie Denmark North America Apple strudel Shish kebab France Russia Sauerkraut Tagliatelle Germany Spain Borsch Fondue Greece Switzerland Moussaka Italy Turkey Bouillabaisse
Multiple choice	e) Which of the following is the world's longest river? 1. Nile 2. Amazon 3. Mississippi 4. Zambesi.

True/False	f) The mean of a set of scores is:
	    (i) The same as the average. True/False
	    (ii) Calculated by dividing the sum of the scores by the True/False
	        number of scores.
	    (iii) The score of the person halfway down the rank order. True/False

Sequencing	g) Place the following in the correct sequence: 1. depress the accelerator and move away 2. turn the ignition key 3. check the rear view mirror 4. adjust seat and mirrors 5. release handbrake 6. lift clutch 7. place in correct gear 8. depress clutch 9. depress brake
Multiple response	h) Which of the following are thought to be factors involved in heart disease? (i) smoking (ii) high blood pressure (iii) intake of surplus vitamins (iv) high cholesterol level in the blood (v) stress

When writing items:

1. the stem should be presented clearly and unambiguously
2. the stem should be correct in all respects
3. there should be no clues to the key
4. options should be grammatically consistent with the stem
5. items should be as concise as possible
6. negatives are not recommended as distractors (e.g. 'none of these')
7. negatives in the stem should be used sparingly (e.g. 'not,' 'never')
8. items should focus on important content not trivia
9. items should be set out clearly

After writing an objective test, it should be reviewed and then pre-tested/piloted. There are many formulae for evaluating the effectiveness of an objective test and a good example is a method of checking on the difficulty of the test:

Facility (difficulty) Index

$$\frac{CSAQ}{TC} \times \frac{100}{1} = \text{facility value} \quad \text{example:} \frac{40}{50} \times \frac{100}{1} = 80 \text{ per cent facility value}$$

CASQ = Candidates successfully answering question, TC = Total candidates. Over 70 per cent = fairly easy, 30–70 per cent moderately difficult, below 30 per cent = fairly difficult.

The Facility index can be used to check if the distractors within multiple choice items are appropriate or too distracting. A distractor should normally attract about 5 per cent; any less and it is not successful. If a distractor is gaining more responses than the key, it is too successful and is too close to the right answer.

9.6.2 Free response assessment

One of the most popular assessment methods is the free-response type of work, which is encouraged through essays, assignments and dissertations. We have called these 'Making answers' in our Assessment methods table above. An effectively designed free-response assessment will allow the 'high-flyers' to express a range of views and carry out an in-depth analysis of situations and processes. It will also allow the less able students to demonstrate their particular interests and strengths. When compared to the objective test, a free-response assessment will be high on validity and low on reliability (see 9.7 below). In other words, even though they are subject experts, the different interpretations of the assessors marking the work will often produce quite different marks.

This is why it is important to *moderate* the marking of essays, assignments and (especially) dissertations. Moderation involves a number of markers reviewing each other's assessments and (where there are differences) presenting a justification for their own interpretation/mark.

F9i   Moderation

Consider the methods you use to ensure that there is a consistency of marking within your team. Discuss the advantages of the chosen approach and also the difficulties in arriving at a process which ensures that assessment is not only consistent but also addresses the identified criteria.

It is very common for different markers of free response types of assessment (essays or assignments for example) to assess student answers differently and it is essential that the moderation process moves the team of markers towards an accepted consensus where a particular interpretation is agreed as acceptable.

Using a 'meeting halfway' approach to moderation is *not good practice* because it is often the result of one or more of the assessors marking less efficiently than the others and, because the difference in their values and views is not discussed, the markers do not have the opportunity to develop their practice through debate and comparison. The values of teachers which become evident during marking, will undoubtedly also be present in their teaching and so it is probable that the students will have understood one thing and will be marked against another.

Although there is an example of an objective test style of *sentence completion* in

257

the table above a free response use of this device would be something like '*My three reasons for and against capital punishment are...*'

A *structured essay* is a halfway house between objective and subjective approaches, where the learners will be asked to write about a particular subject but their answer will be constrained by detailed instructions about what must be included in their work. In considered examples of structured essays candidates are required to address particular issues, processes or periods, whereas in more crude examples the students may be asked to incorporate particular words, which can be ticked off by the assessor.

9.6.3 Practical tests

The assessment of practical skills within vocational areas does inevitably present the assessor with particular problems, which need to be addressed in order to sustain reliability and validity.

What is to be tested?

As we suggested early, the first step is to achieve an appropriate balance between process and product. This isn't always easy, because in many cases that vocational area is defined by the quality of its product (catering for example) and, in focusing on the product, some important requirements in the process of production could be overlooked. A good starting point would be to clarify the:

- *objectives* to be achieved and *key skills* to be demonstrated
- *quality* of performance (i.e. what criteria will be used to ensure that the candidate has reached the required standard)
- *relative importance* (i.e. weighting) of each task/skill/objective

The next consideration is at what stage should the assessment take place. Every process has a key period when the learner has to *manage important events* and this crucial time is not necessarily at the end.

When to test?

Sometimes, particularly when measuring value added, it is important to be aware of the levels of skill, understanding and experience which the learner brings to the programme. We need to decide:

- whether or not to measure the abilities of learners on entry to the programme (i.e. *pre-tests*)
- if it will be useful to use a series of *formative* assessment strategies during the programme or just use *summative* assessment on completion

What assessment strategy to use for practical subjects?

Good assessment is a fusion of timing, modes, methods and marking processes (see also Motivating through assessment under 9.10 below). Often we develop an appropriate strategy through a series of adjustments and modifications to make what we are doing compatible with the environment in which we are working. We need to check:

- whether it is important to test understanding separately from the practical skills and if so decide how to do this (e.g. multiple choice, structured questions, problem-solving)
- what proportion of the total marks will be allocated to the testing of under-standing
- the best method of assessing the practical aspects (i.e. do you set one piece of work per task, or select a task which will show proficiency in a number of skills)
- what proportion of the total marks will be allocated to the testing of practical skills

How to assess performance?

Again the accurate marking of performance requires a fine balance between process and product. We should agree:

- how the practical aspects of performance will be marked, e.g. using checklists about stages in the process, rating scales applied to the finished product, or a comparison with other work
- how to identify satisfactory performance
- whether we need to moderate the marks as our judgements may be very subjective
- the way in which those who fail to meet the standards are able to recover

How to arrange assessments?

The implementation of assessment is always a stressful time for both the tutors and the learners. If there is a breakdown in communication between the responsible parties it can create a range of tensions which will continue well beyond the period of assessment. To reduce problems we should:

- confirm that the instructions about what the learners being assessed need to do is clear and that the time allocated is appropriate and that the arrangements (e.g. the mark allocation) is known to those being tested
- ensure that sufficient equipment and materials are available to those being assessed
- identify who will benefit from the information gained through assessment from among the learners, teachers, employers and others
- how the results will be presented – i.e. individual, aggregate, profile

9.6.4   Competence-based assessment

Since the launch of the National Council for Vocational Qualifications, the use of competences as indicators of practitioner skills and understandings has been accepted by more than 80 per cent of national vocational areas. Initially, the design and development of these standards was the responsibility of employer-led bodies, and their teams went through a labourious process of disaggregating each of the key vocational areas into units of competence, which were then broken down into

The NVQ functional analysis approach to defining competence

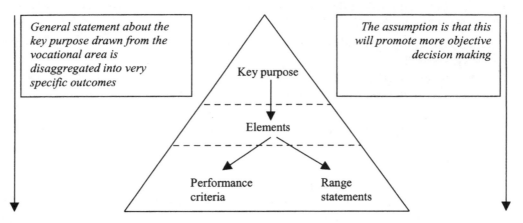

defined competence statements, with the related underpinning knowledge and range (extent and context of the performance) also clearly articulated.

  This process, which is shown in diagrammatic form below, had many critics (see for example Hodkinson and Issitt (1995), Ecclestone (1997), Hyland (1993, 1996) but there was a national governmental imperative to simplify vocational qualifications nationally and provide 'transparency' of assessment.

During the rapid developments which took place in the 1990s a generally accepted definition of competence was seen as *the ability to perform the activities within an occupation to the standards expected* which is everything a person should do at work if they are to be effective in their job, including skills, knowledge, understanding and the ability to transfer these to new situations, organize and plan work, coping with routine and non-routine task, the implementation of innovation and being personally effective.

Some of the strengths and weaknesses of using competences as the basis for assessment were voiced in a useful analysis by Auerbach (1986) which is summarized in the table opposite.

F9j   For and against competence approaches

Given the summary of the value of competence-based approaches (Table 9.3), analyse what you feel would be the positive and negative effects (or might be if you are not currently involved in CBET) in relation to your own learners.

9.6.5   Learner profiles and portfolios

The use of competences as an assessment vehicle is generally based around the development of a student profile or portfolio, the requirements of which will sometimes be closely prescribed by the awarding body and in other cases will be negotiated with the learner.

In those situations where a *prescribed profile* is in use, the defined learning outcomes (see also 9.6.6 below) will form the basis for discussion, negotiation and

Table 9.3   Strengths and weaknesses of competence-based vocational education

For – competences provide the learner with:	Against – competences create situations where:
explicit, predetermined outcomes	creative, divergent and critical thinking is limited
individualized, student-centred instruction	assessment-centred, group processes are subverted
the means of demonstrating skills and understandings	there is a lack of encouragement to synthesize and generate knowledge
a teacher who is a facilitator (humanist theory)	the measurable, observable imperative creates a positivist approach to learning (behaviourist theory)
flexible, modularized programmes	the reductionist disaggregation of learning can severely limit a more holistic view
continuous assessment	the over-concern with assessment and the necessary level of administration is restricting for teachers and learners
a forum to demonstrate the mastery of specific performance objectives	the demonstration of learning only through behaviour restricts the development of higher-level learning outcomes
a process where achievements are recorded in detail	some professional diagnostic activities cannot be expressed adequately enough

assessment and will provide a *formative* function, which allows the tutor to monitor development and identify and anticipate any problems. However, prescribed outcomes are essentially summative and in most cases, there will only be two possible outcomes. Either the assessment criteria associated with the learning outcome will have been achieved (i.e. satisfactory) or they will not yet have been achieved.

In some cases a *negotiated profile* may be used, which is similar to the one above, but differs in that the learners play a substantial part in defining their own learning outcomes at the beginning of the programme.

A further development of the use of profiles and outcomes (which may be incorporated into either of the above systems) could be a *personal development profile*, which is a vehicle for *formative* assessment. Often involving self-assessment, this process may be based on logs, journals and diaries and involves learner in reflecting on their own development against defined outcomes that have been negotiated with their tutor.

9.6.6   Learning outcomes

These days the ability to work with specific learning outcomes is a requirement at most levels of education. The awarding body may define these outcomes, or teachers involved in curriculum development may write them.

F9k Criterion referencing

Select a criterion-referenced scheme with which you are familiar and analyse the outcomes defined for it. If possible suggest how these might be improved.

We have discussed the relative merits of learning outcomes under 9.6.4 (above), but their additional value to the learning situation is that they help:

- to clarify the learning requirements of particular modules and pathways
- students to understand what they can expect to gain from a planned learning experience and what is expected of them
- determine appropriate learning strategies
- identify appropriate forms of assessment
- make possible the accreditation of prior learning

Structure

From a grammatical point of view, a learning outcome comprises of:

a) a subject
b) an active transitive verb or verb phrase
c) an 'object' of the verb
d) a qualifying clause or phrase which provides a context or condition

Criteria

Good learning outcomes should be:

- achievable
- measurable
- explicit
- and as succinct as possible

Examples would be:

Subject	Active verb or phrase	Object	Context/condition
The quantity surveyor will	be able to	accurately measure the	angle of the incline.
The drama student should	contribute effectively to	the production and performance	of at least 3 plays.
The trainee teacher	can	assess the work of her students	in a valid and reliable manner

Obviously, it is important to select verbs that are appropriate. Bloom (1956) and his colleagues suggested three taxonomies of educational objective and Gronlund (1985) gives examples of verbs which may be used to represent the increasing complexity of performance at each level of these domains (see also Chapter 4).

Table 9.4 Use of verbs within the three taxonomies of educational objectives

Cognitive		Affective		Psycho-motor	
General objective	Illustrative verbs	General objective	Illustrative verbs	General objective	Illustrative verbs
Knows specific facts	Defines, describes, identifies, labels	Attends closely	Follows, selects, locates, replies	Perceives and attends to source	Chooses, detects, isolates, relates
Understands the meaning of material	Explains, infers, predicts, summarizes	Willingness to respond	Discusses, labels, reports, selects	Develops a set for action	Begins, reacts, responds, starts
Applies concepts and principles	Changes, discovers, manipulates, solves	Commitment to a set of values	Initiates, justifies, selects, supports	Trial and error learning	Constructs, displays, measures
Analyses relationships	Differentiates, infers, selects, separates	Organizes according to values	Defends, orders, organizes, relates	Carries our physical processes with confidence	Assembles, builds, fastens, fixes, mends, organizes
Synthesizes to form a new whole	Combines, compiles, relates, revises	Develops a lifestyle congruent with own value system	Acts, discriminates, proposes, revises, serves, verifies	Skilful performance	Calibrates, manipulates, works
Evaluates materials and processes	Appraises, compares, justifies, supports			Adapts skills to particular needs	Adapts, alters, changes, revises
				Creates new skills to fit new needs	Combines, designs, originates

F9l Writing outcomes

Using the above guidance, try writing 10 learning outcomes for a programme with which you are familiar.

Obviously, a key requirement for a learning outcome is that it should be observable and measurable. Table 9.5 may help here:

Evaluate the purpose of your assessment and the defined outcomes against the following questions:

- Are the learning outcomes compatible with those of the scheme as a whole?
- Do the learning outcomes clearly specify those objectives required for success completion of the programme?
- Are the learning outcomes written as simple statements, comprehensive to both students and employers?

Table 9.5 The use of verbs when writing observable and measurable learning outcomes

AVOID WORDS LIKE:	USE WORDS LIKE:	AVOID WORDS LIKE:	USE WORDS LIKE:
Know	State	Be interested in	Outline
Understand	Describe	Acquire the feeling for	Summarize
Really know	Explain	Be aware of	Represent graphically
Really understand	List	Believe	Compare
Be familiar with	Evaluate	Have information about	Apply
Become acquainted with	Identify	Realize the significance of	Assess
Have a good grasp of	Distinguish between	Learn the basics of	Give examples of
Appreciate	Analyse	Have a working knowledge of	Suggest reasons why

- Have the learning outcomes been expressed in cognitive, affective and psycho-motor terms?
- Has the link between leaning outcomes, learning strategies and the mode and method of assessment been clearly articulated?
- Does the assessment strategy for each module indicate how a valid measurement will be made of the extent to which a student has achieved the learning outcomes?
- Has a wide variety of assessment methods been used?
- Is it clear who is responsible for carrying out the assessment (tutors/peers/students)?
- Is there an appropriate balance between formative and summative assessment?
- Has consideration been given as to the approaches of norm-referenced, criterion-referenced and personal-referenced methods of assessment?
- Are appropriate criteria used to describe the important features of expected student performance within the context of the module? Is student achievement recorded against agreed criteria, contributing to student feedback and final grading?

9.7 SUFFICIENT AND FAIR

The design and implementation of effective assessment has always placed great demands on both teacher and student and this burden has increased in recent years as the recording and justifying of learner achievement has increasingly become a priority. In such a climate, it is essential that assessment should be *sufficient*, but not over-demanding.

F9m Sufficiency in assessment

Considering your own teaching and learning situation, think about the assessment methods which are most appropriate for your learners and your subject. Then, bearing in mind the demands on your time, suggest how you might arrive at an assessment strategy which is 'sufficient'.

Some simple ways of achieving this sufficiency are by ensuring that:

- the specification is as clear and precise as possible to ensure that the assessment design may be focused clearly on only the defined outcomes and that there is no duplication of effort
- the time-consuming marking of 'free-response' assessment is kept to a minimum by deploying objective tests where only knowledge and comprehension require testing
- where possible *one task* is used as the basis for the assessment of *a number of defined outcomes*
- peer, group and self-assessment is used to lighten the load for both tutors and students where appropriate
- the timing of assessment is carefully considered in order to remove the frustrating bottleneck created by crowded assessment schedules

The establishment of sufficiency in assessment can also be confirmed by producing a grid of coverage. In the example in Table 9.6 using a notional NVQ Care Award, the individual assessment items (in all forms) have been calculated to give an idea of syllabus coverage in terms of level, domain and content. Obviously, other criteria could be introduced to make the audit more relevant to particular programmes.

In reality, the above distribution table may not be an accurate representation of how such a programme may be assessed; it is merely an illustration of how a balance grid (or a similar specification grid) can provide a useful audit to show if assessment is sufficient in comparison with other programmes. The important consideration is to ensure that each of the domains are included, but also that somewhere in our assessment processes we address each *level*. This means not just in terms of NVQ or National Qualifications Framework level, but also the *domain* level. For example, it is not sufficient for our learners to just 'know' and 'comprehend' at the lower end of Bloom's (ibid.) cognitive domain, when we can take them beyond to *analysing* and *evaluating*.

The establishment of *Fair assessment* is a little more difficult. On the face of it, you would think that if the assessment is valid and reliable (see 9.8 below) it will automatically be fair. However, as we have discussed in Chapters 5 and 8, less confident learners may feel intimidated by the very process of assessment. Although attempts may have been made to ensure that the assessment process is 'transparent' and the requirements are clear and unambiguous, some learners, who feel they are destined to failure, may not have the disposition to listen to or read the instructions

Table 9.6 Assessment coverage of NVQ Care Awards

NQF Level→	Level 1			Level 2			Level 3			Total items		
Domain→	Cog	Aff	P.mtr	Cog	Aff	P.mtr	Cog	Aff	P.mtr	Cog	Aff	P.mtr
Syllabus												
Equality	4	4	–	4	4	–	4	4	–	12	12	–
Management	3	2	–	3	2	–	4	2	–	10	6	–
Communication	3	3	2	3	3	2	4	3	1	10	9	5
Services and Information	2	–	–	2	–	–	3	–	–	7	–	–
Health and Safety	3	3	2	4	3	2	4	3	2	11	9	6
Care	6	5	8	6	5	8	7	5	4	19	15	20
Developmental activities	3	4	4	2	4	4	2	4	4	7	12	12
Therapeutic activities	4	4	5	4	4	5	6	4	4	14	12	14
Service delivery	3	2	2	3	2	2	3	2	2	9	6	6
	31	27	23	31	27	23	37	27	17	99	81	63

carefully enough. When you are nervous, it is sometimes difficult to interpret difficult words correctly or remember the sequence of processes, even though to others it seems straightforward. Ensure that you repeat instructions and reassure all learners before assessment. We have said that some learners will need more support than others during assessment and this was outlined in the previous chapter. However, inclusiveness also places great demands on the quality of *feedback* which learners are given.

9.7.1 Feedback

Jones and Bray (1986) confirmed that feedback does assist learners unless the material is too demanding; in which case, feedback becomes demoralizing. Feeding back merely the grades or confirming correct answers has *little effect* on subsequent performance, while detailed factual feedback, conceptual help or feedback on strategies used is more effective. Bennett (1974) also confirms that merely ticking or giving a mark is insufficient to optimize learning. We must indicate what the student can do to *improve performance*.

F9n *Improving performance*

Discuss some examples from the assessment feedback which you may have given your own students and say how you might have made this more useful in helping them to develop

Written feedback (on free-response essays and assignments) that is just confirmatory, i.e. 'you have achieved the learning outcome' is no more informative than a tick. The learner does not know from this feedback whether they have just achieved or whether they have gone well beyond the requirement. Similarly, a failure marked with a cross or a score below the required level, doesn't help the failing student to know what needs to be done to put things right. In the marking of written work, actual comments written in the margin close to the actual part of the learner's text being commented on, are probably the most valuable way to move a student forward. If you can also give them examples of how they might have expressed the point more effectively, so much the better.

In addition to giving you feedback on the success of your teaching, the purpose of formative assessment is not merely to confirm that students are at the right level, but to also help them realize how they can develop further. If the assessment and subsequent feedback doesn't achieve this, then it simply isn't formative.

9.8 | VALIDITY AND RELIABILITY

Two of the most important standards used to measure the methods used in assessment, evaluation and research are 'validity' and 'reliability'. Simply put, within assessment processes:

> *validity* is an indication of the extent to which teachers are assessing *what they say they are assessing*. *Reliability* is the *level of consistency* of the adopted assessment procedures

We will see later that these two measures have an important reciprocal relationship. First, though, we need to extend further our simple definitions.

9.8.1 Validity

Although, our first simple definition above, holds good for assessment generally the concept of validity may be broken down into several useful categories:

Face validity is the obvious first definition. This occurs when it is accepted that *on the face of it*, a chosen assessment methodology appears to have the necessary validity.

Ruth Currie (1986) goes on to present a conventional and what is generally viewed as an unproblematic summary of validity concepts:

> Validity really has two aspects. First, is what you expect your pupils to learn and do justifiable and reasonable? Second, do the methods of assessment achieve what they set out to do?

The first part of this definition is known as *curricular validity* and Currie (ibid.) goes on to emphasize that:

> unless you have a clear idea of what are the learning outcomes you expect – and feel reasonably confident that such learning outcomes are justifiable – you will not be able to make a valid assessment.

Next Currie turns to *construct validity* which represents a very common view of assessment validity in that it:

> means constructing a test or assessment ... that tests what it sets out to test and not something else.

To illustrate this Currie gives some useful examples of validity erosion, such as when (within an assessment of manual dexterity) listening skills or the ability to read engineering drawings (which are outside the purpose of the assessment) have a direct bearing on the result. Or, in another situation, using essay questions in a Physics or History examination when the pupils have not been taught how to write a good essay answer within the subject.

Currie also points out that under this heading norm-referenced assessment and criterion-referenced assessment (see 9.4.1 above) also have problems in relation to construct validity. The former because of the subtle influences of the discriminating processes present when we are comparing student with student and the latter because of the difficulties of devising clear, measurable criteria.

A further important consideration introduced by Currie is *retrospective and predictive validity*. *Retrospective validity* is mainly concerned with *content*, i.e. the teaching that has gone before and the objectives of the course. A test must ask only for what is expected and no more. For example, if a class has been taught three reasons for the First World War, it would then be invalid to ask for five reasons or give credit for them.

Predictive validity is often used in selection processes and yet, as Currie points out, 'these decisions are based on performances that may bear little resemblance to the course the student will embark upon'. A current example of this is the use of A level results as criteria for university places, when research has not established that there is a clear correlation between performance in these examinations and subsequent performance as an undergraduate.

9.8.2   Reliability

Currie then turns to *reliability* and again she considers two aspects of this concept. The first is that reliable assessment enables the assessor to

> make reliable comparisons. The comparisons may be between the performance of different pupils (norm-related reliability) or between the pupil's attainment and the course objectives (criterion-related reliability).

The second aspect is a more common perception of the term in that reliability is seen as *consistency*. 'How far would the same test give the same result if done by the same children under the same conditions?' Currie makes the point that this is an impossible situation to achieve absolutely as there will 'always be some variables'.

Examples of such variables given by Currie are human factors in relation to the assessed (such as memory, health, the affect of environmental conditions) and the assessors (such as tiredness, prejudice, subjectivity, etc).

At this stage then, a summary of these concepts could be that:

> Striving for *validity* s based on a concern to do what you *said* you intended to do and no more.

Establishing *reliability* is achieved through the use of a *replicable* and consistent process.

She also makes the point that the simplicity of the marking of **objective tests** will improve reliability but, where higher level cognitive performance is being tested, will usually lead to a reduction in validity.

These comments are apt at a time when at all levels of education there is a well-established process (through the National Curriculum, QCA and the NCVQ for example) where learning outcomes are externally devised and passed down to teachers and learners. Because such national specifications must be applicable in all relevant educational settings, the central concern is with reliability (i.e. consistency), often at the expense of validity. A reliability model may confirm that all learners are tested in the same way, but such a strategy does often involve the designers in ignoring important high-level outcomes, which are difficult to articulate and assess consistently.

Derek Rowntree (1981) summarizes this dilemma when he points out that, because of the inherent problems of language, the wording of precise and unambiguous definitions and their later interpretation will always make the achievement of precise reliability *elusive*. Perhaps more importantly, he emphasizes that it is assessment validity which is *essential*.

To summarize, despite our best efforts, the *reliability* of assessment is always difficult to achieve consistently. However, our central concern should constantly remain focused on achieving construct validity, i.e. we actually assess only what we intended to assess.

9.9 | FITNESS FOR PURPOSE – EVALUATING ASSESSMENT

As we have now considered all of the main concepts of educational assessment, this is a useful point at which we can check that our evolving design has addressed all the necessary aspects.

F9o   Fitness for purpose

What criteria *specific to your learning situation* would you use to decide if your assessment is fit for its purpose?

Obviously, your own assessment situation will have particular assessment demands and the characteristics of your learners will often mean that there are specific outcomes you wish to achieve with them in addition to those prescribed by the awarding body. We suggest that in order to ensure that our scheme is *fit for its purpose* we must confirm that the assessment has:

- *Coverage*
  that the important aspects of the curriculum will be assessed
- *Relevance*
  what we decide to assess has value and priority within the subject being studied

- *Intention*
  we are very clear about what it is we wish to assess, and establish clear criteria of achievement (objectives or outcomes)
- *Balance*
  our assessment achieves a balance between the different levels of the cognitive, affective and psycho-motor domains and the different parts of the syllabus
- *Integrity*
  we have let the students know the standard and criteria that they are expected to achieve
- *Reliability*
  our methods achieve consistent results with similar groups of learners
- *Validity*
  we are testing what we intended to test and no more
- *Objectivity*
  as far as possible we separate the interpretive process from personal feelings

---

F9p   *Assessment value*

Consider a group of your own learners, and summarize what you feel would be the general *purpose* of any assessment you may undertake relating to them. In other words, what overall *value* would you wish to be able to attribute to your learners as a result of the assessment?

9.10 | CONCLUSION

Obviously, the value that we want any assessment of our learners to provide will be related to the state of their current abilities and attitudes and how these have changed since they were last assessed. However, it is probably appropriate to bring this chapter to an end by emphasizing a point we made at the beginning. Formative assessment can be a central means of motivating students and encouraging them to develop independence and learner autonomy or, it can be used to encourage instrumental surface learning and learner dependence. Kathryn Ecclestone (2002) warns us about sacrificing this opportunity as we seek evidence of performance through imposed summative assessment regimes designed to provide data for quality processes. We should think about the long tradition of assessment as an accepted route to learner empowerment before we continue with this route. As Derek Rowntree (1977: 55) observes in his excellent analysis of the 'self-fulfilling prophecy' syndrome:

> For a few to emerge as outstandingly successful the majority must fail – to varying degrees. The failure may be only partial. Indeed, had the student been in a different (e.g. less selective) school or college, his performance might well have made him a success. But by comparison with those he has been led to emulate, he has fallen short .... Unfortunately, the ethos of competitive assessment often leads the student who has failed on a few tasks (e.g. learned more slowly than other people) to feel that he has failed as a person.

We started the chapter by saying that assessment should be our first consideration when planning learning. If we articulate at this early stage what we are preparing our learners for (whether as a result of our own assessment strategies or an external imposed policy) the values with which we wish to endow our learners on completion of the process will become very clear. One of those values should be to enhance the learners' view of their own self-worth and assessment should be used to encourage this learner independence, which identifies their abilities and indicates their strengths and how to build on them.

To complete this chapter, try the following activity bearing in mind the principles and concepts we have discussed:

F9q Summative statement

Prepare an A4 summative report on two of your learners that provides the reader with a good understanding of how they have developed during the programme. Consider their current abilities and understandings against not only the formal assessment criteria, but also such difficult assessment areas as their social skills, their willingness to contribute to group work, what they bring to class interactions, etc. Try to choose two contrasting students for this exercise.

The *summative statement* can be taken to represent any document, certificate, or diploma which a learner may take away from a programme to show what they have achieved. Naturally, they will want it to show not only what they have gained but also *how far they have travelled*. Some of these learning gains are easy to articulate, but other, perhaps more important achievements, will be difficult to express and may be specific to a particular context.

However, as we said at the beginning of the chapter (and at greater length in Chapter 5), the assessment process is only one aspect of the teaching and learning cycle, but because of our concern for accountability, for some learners it has taken on a whole new, more threatening dimension. In addition to measuring achievement against *externally* devised outcomes, we should also be concerned to confirm the achievement of targets, which our learners have *internally* identified for themselves. To them these attainments are an essential route to self-belief. To us they are indicators of the validity of our assessment processes.

Prescribed, observable, measurable outcomes have their place in establishing a reliable system of accreditation. However, they are only part of a complex portfolio of human attainment, which should be promoted by every worthwhile educational provision. Also, it is these very predictable, imperative qualities which cause precisely defined outcomes to become repetitive and tedious. Inevitably, our current systems place the highest value on that which we can measure, and yet equally, and perhaps more important qualities are ignored because they cannot be quantified. The following is a list (not definitive or in any particular order) of some of the qualities, which we should find a way of acknowledging, even though we cannot precisely define them:

Trust, empathy, respect, loyalty, love, dedication, humour, commitment, enthusiasm, tolerance, invention, intuition, creativity, responsiveness, inspiration, self-esteem

A truly learner-centred assessment system should be able to acknowledge the things that we value rather than valuing only the things we can measure.

9.11 USEFUL SOURCES

Ecclestone, K. (1996) *How to Assess the Vocational Curriculum*. London: Kogan Page
Kathryn Ecclestone presents a fine review of assessment processes within vocational education, including a valuable chapter on the development of professional expertise.

Gipps, C.V. (1994) *Beyond Testing*. London: The Falmer Press.
Caroline Gipps has captured the radical changes which occurred in the 1990s and their effect on assessment practices. She includes a welcome, insightful chapter on the ethics of assessment.

Lloyd Jones, R. and Bray, E. (1986) *Assessment from Principles to Action*. London: Macmillan.
An very useful review of assessment concepts and principles with some helpful illustrative examples from practice.

Rowntree, D. (1981) *Assessing Students: How shall we know them?* London: Harper & Row.
A classic of its kind from Derek Rowntree who is one of the acknowledged experts on assessment processes and their effects on learners. A tremendous reference book, obtainable in most libraries, but now unfortunately out of print.

Try *tipcet.com* for a range of materials and suggested sources related to a range of assessment processes.

9.12 RATIONALE FOR ASSESSING THE OUTCOMES OF LEARNING AND LEARNERS' ACHIEVEMENTS – KEY AREA F

FAQs	At Stage 1	At Stage 2	At Stage 3
Why do it?	Most students wish to know how successful their learning has been. It is our responsibility to ensure that the process of assessment sustains their desire to learn, rather than diminishing it. We can promote learning through assessment by ensuring that it is fair, reliable, encouraging and informative.	It is essential to establish that student learning has taken place. This knowledge helps us to establish the level that our students have achieved and to develop new learning to take them forward. We also need to establish that the learning has been understood and that they are capable of applying the knowledge gained.	There is a need to review continually the assessment process as reliability often remains elusive and validity can easily be undermined.

Where are we going?	A simple approach to assessment is first to prioritize those aspects of the subject we are teaching which we feel that the learner should be able to understand or do. Ask yourself which particular skills or knowledge could be said to represent the subject. Of course, we may be teaching on a programme where the learning outcomes have already been defined by an external body. Even so, we need to appreciate why the designers believe that the identified understandings and skills are important. This is essential for planning teaching.	In every learning situation we need to develop assessment strategies, which allow students to demonstrate their knowledge and understanding. Assessment processes must be reliable and allow for the collection of valid evidence. You will need to be able to describe a range of assessment opportunities that are appropriate to your own or other programmes. We must show evidence of planning, the selection of appropriate assessment methods, recording decisions and providing supportive and instructive feedback to our students.	We wish to move towards a situation where the assessment process encourages learner autonomy through the realization that knowledge creation is valued as much as knowledge replication. That there is room for learners to feel ownership of concepts and principles rather than automatically accepting that important knowledge lies with others. Rather than using assessment to establish conformity we should use the process to encourage the development of informed challenges to established views and values.
How do we get there?	We need to start with the key areas of learning which either we have prioritized or an external body has defined. Our next step is to decide what evidence we need to be sure that the necessary learning of these identified areas has been achieved. Of course, teachers are busy people and so we need to ensure (where possible) that the assessment process is not too demanding of our time.	Produce an assessment scheme for your area of work, matching the assessment methods and the stated learning outcomes and justifying the chosen strategy. Within this rationale consider the validity and reliability of the scheme. Assess your students and make and record your decisions appropriately. Explain how you might adapt your assessment methods to meet the needs of particular learners.	In these days of the dominance of centralized assessment procedures controlled by external awarding bodies, it is often difficult to develop ownership of the assessment process. However, it is important for both assessed and assessors to support a rigorous system that can withstand the pressures that funding related to student numbers, achievement and value added inevitably brings.
Is this the best way?	We need to be sure that we are assessing only what the learners have been told will be assessed. Efficient assessment will address several outcomes with one task.	Consider cost effectiveness, the resources available and how the assessment process may affect the learning experiences and attitudes of the students.	Evaluate the assessment process to discover not only the level of reliability and validity but also the robustness of the system in the face of external pressures.
When is the right time?	We may be constrained by dates set by external awarding bodies, external	Consider the purpose of the assessment and how it relates to the learning	Analyse the effect of the timing of assessment in relation to the

	verifier visits, assessment boards, etc. However, timing is important in assessment. It is essential that the learners have time to complete the assessment task and we have time to carry out careful marking.	experience. Check how the measurable learning outcomes relate to the key curriculum events. Confirm what the requirements are for the awarding body, the external examiners, the internal verifiers, etc.	development of student autonomy. Also reflect on the type of assessment – have you achieved an acceptable balance between formative and summative, formal and informal, reliability and validity?
Who needs to know?	Clear guidelines and accurate record keeping are essential features of effective assessment. We must ensure that the learners know what is expected of them, that we record attendance at exams, the handing in of assignments, extenuating circumstances, agreed marks, moderation, informative feedback, return dates, etc.	Confirm if the information on assessment has been recorded, stored securely and shared with colleagues and external agencies in an appropriate manner. Ensure feedback given to students is accurate and informative and will enable them to understand their performance better.	Evaluate how informed the students are in terms of their assessed performance. Have they sufficient information to know exactly why they did or didn't achieve and how to improve their performance? Alternatively, is the assessment so detailed and precise that it is encouraging student dependence?
How do we know when we've got there?	Most learners will be very aware of the strengths and weaknesses of their assessed performance and through any conventional evaluation process will let it be known if they feel that the assessment process has not been appropriate. Normal quality processes will also identify problems in terms of marking, feedback, etc.	When you have confidence that you are assessing what you intended to assess (validity) and have ensured consistency in the application of assessment processes (reliability). Moderation with colleagues, feedback from external examiners and internal verifiers and student evaluations and reviews will help in this.	You are looking for an robust, rigorous and independent assessment system which encourages the development of informed learner scepticism and student autonomy and is not compromised by the drive towards those levels of achievement or student retention which affect positions in league tables.
Has everyone had a fair chance?	We must ensure that those being assessed have been informed early in the teaching and learning process of how and when they will be assessed and that they have been prepared for it. They must know the process of informing tutors of extenuating circumstances and particular needs.	Confirm that the assessment is sufficiently flexible in design, sensitive in application and reliable in measurement to allow all students to demonstrate their current ability. Look out for ambiguity in expression, student misunderstandings and undue stress created by the assessment process.	Because assessment systems are notoriously difficult to manage and moderate consistently, an analysis of your own procedures will inevitably reveal some flaws even though they may be minor. Remember that validity is essential and reliability is always elusive.

9.13 KEY AREA F – ASSESSING THE OUTCOMES OF LEARNING AND LEARNERS' ACHIEVEMENT

Purpose: Teachers and teaching teams need to be effective in using an appropriate range of assessment methods to provide accurate information about learning and achievement. This involves ensuring that learners understand and are involved in the process, and that the timing of assessment and the monitoring and recording of achievement are appropriate. Teachers and teaching teams also need to be able to use assessment information for a variety of purposes. See 9.12 for an analysis of this process at FENTO Stages 1, 2 and 3.

Please note: The FENTO Standards listed below are relevant to the following three levels of award – Stage 1 (Introduction), Stage 2 (Intermediate) and Stage 3 (Full Certification). All the standards are required at Stage 3, only those in italic and bold are required at Stage 2 and only those in italic are required at Stage 1.

UNIT F1. USE APPROPRIATE ASSESSMENT METHODS TO MEASURE LEARNING AND ACHIEVEMENT *In order to do this teachers should:*

Demonstrate that they are able to:	*and will have specific knowledge and critical understanding of:*	*plus generic knowledge of:*		*Summary of appropriate evidence in this Key Area*	*Relevant Chapter Activities*
Criteria:					
a *identify an appropriate range of assessment methods which will deliver results which are fair, valid and reliable*	• Procedures for mapping assessment methods against syllabuses and standards • How to ensure that assessment is fit for the purpose	• The purposes of continuous and end-of programme assessment • Appropriate sources of information about assessment requirements	a	Assessment specifications	F9a to F9q
b *ensure equality of opportunity in the design of application of assessment procedures*	• Alternative assessment opportunities for learners with special assessment requirements	• The principles of assessment design as they relate to assessment at the required level and for particular kinds of learning	b	Assessment specifications and justifications	F9a, F9b, F9c, F9n, F9o, F9q
c *ensure that the assessment process, as a whole, is coherent*	• How to create a whole and balanced assessment process • Distinctions between formative and summative assessment procedures	• Concepts of validity, reliability, sufficiency, and their application to the assessment of learning and learners' achievements	c	Assessment specifications and justifications	F9a to F9q
d *ensure that learners understand the purpose and nature of the assessment process*			d	Assessment specifications and learner guidance doc urgently	F9n, F9o, F9p

	Practical skills	Knowledge and understanding			Reference
e	create realistic and relevant assessment activities which encourage learning as well as assessing specified outcomes which meet college and external requirements	• The purpose of self, peer and tutor assessments and how these methods of assessment relate to each other • Appropriate procedures for assessing knowledge • Competence and noncompetence based methods of assessment	• The role of assessment in relation to the learning cycle • Equity and inclusivity issues in relation to assessment • Ways of using assessment information to maintain standards and to reflect upon one's own teaching • The importance of equality of opportunity in the design and application of assessment systems	e — Assessment specifications and justifications	F9a to F9l
f	establish the required conditions for assessment and provide the necessary resources	• The appropriate timing and pace of assessment within a learning programme		f — Assessment specifications and justifications	F9a to F9q
g	use an appropriate variety of valid and reliable assessment procedures which are credible and compatible with the learning programme and the required learning outcomes	• Organizational procedures for recording assessment outcomes • Procedures for conducting and recording assessments, including the requirements of external awarding bodies		g — Assessment specifications and justifications	F9a to F9q
h	conduct assessments according to agreed procedures in a fair, consistent and equal manner	• Appropriate forms of feedback to learners		h — Assessment results, moderation details, assessment board decisions	F9a to F9q
i	record assessment results following the organization's procedures			i — Assessment results, moderation details, assessment board decisions	F9a to F9q
j	encourage learners to feel ownership of their assessment records in monitoring and reviewing their own progress			j — Assessment and evaluation feedback	D7a to D7i, F9a to F9q

k	ensure that learners are provided with clear and constructive feedback on assessment outcomes within an appropriate timescale	k	Individual student assessment feedback reports	F9n, D7d
l	ensure that assessment procedures conform to the organization's and national requirement, including those of external awarding bodies	l	Assessment specifications and justifications	F9o

Plus commentary in PDJ on the purposes and value of using appropriate assessment methods, together with records in your Practice File of Teaching Observations, Lesson Plans, Rationales, Self-Evaluations and Progress Summary

Key to above standards required at each FENTO Stage:

Introduction Stage – italic
Intermediate Stage + bold
Certification Stage – all

UNIT F2. MAKE USE OF ASSESSMENT INFORMATION *In order to do this teachers should:*

Demonstrate that they are able to:	have specific knowledge and critical understanding of:	have generic knowledge of:		Summary of appropriate evidence in this Key Area	Relevant Chapter Activities
a	**Criteria:** use continuous assessment to help individual learners assess their progress and identify learning issues	• Continuous assessment and end of programme (summative) assessment processes and when to use them	• The purposes of continuous and end-of programme assessment • Appropriate sources of information about assessment requirements	a	Assessment specifications and justifications	F9m, F9n, F9o
b	*use assessment information to assess how far learning objectives have been achieved*	• The role of assessment in the overall evaluation of learning programmes • Ways of using assessment information to monitor the effectiveness of the learning processes	• The principles of assessment design as they relate to assessment at the required level and for particular kinds of learning	b	Individual student assessment feedback reports and cohort results	F9m, F9n, F9o, F9q
c	*use assessment information in evaluating their own performance as teachers*	• Appropriate stakeholders, including parents, guardians, carers, employers, awarding bodies and other external institutions, and the nature of the assessment information they require	• Concepts of validity, reliability, sufficiency, and their application to the assessment of learning and learners' achievements	c	Individual student assessment feedback reports, analysis and external reports.	F9m, F9n, F9o, F9q
d	*make effective use of assessment information to identify the ways in which teaching might be improved*		• The role of assessment in relation to the learning cycle • Equity and inclusivity issues in relation to assessment	d	Individual student assessment feedback reports, analysis and external reports	F9m, F9n, F9o, F9q
e	provide assessment information to appropriate stakeholders		• Ways of using assessment information to maintain standards and to reflect upon one's own teaching	e	Individual student assessment feedback reports and cohort results	F9m, F9n, F9o, F9p, F9q
f	use assessment outcomes in modifying individual learning programmes as appropriate		• The importance of equality of opportunity in the design and application of assessment systems	f	Individual student assessment feedback reports, analysis and external reports	F9m, F9n, F9o, F9p, F9q

Key to above standards required at each FENTO Stage:

Introduction Stage – italic
Intermediate Stage + bold
Certification Stage – all

Plus commentary in PDJ on the purposes and value of making use of assessment information, together with records in your Practice File of Teaching Observations, Lesson Plans, Rationales, Self-Evaluations and Progress Summary

Reflecting upon and evaluating one's own performance and planning future practice

Yvonne Hutton

Key Area 'G' Evaluating your own practice as a means to plan for a better future practice

Key concepts in this chapter:

Adversarial, Controlled response, Critical incidents, Decision orientated, Educational evaluation, Fear factor, Formative Evaluation, Free response, Goal orientated, Goal-free, Illuminative, Learning spiral, Mentor, Questionnaire design, Rating scale, Reasoning, Re-constructing, Reflective paradox, Relating, Responding, Retelling, Self-evaluation, Situationalize, Student feedback, Summative Evaluation, Transactional

Before you begin this chapter you may wish to check the FAQs on pp. 303–6

Index to Chapter 10

Chapter 10 Activities designed to generate evidence against the Standards

10.1 INTRODUCTION

We have now moved through almost our entire teaching and training cycle. We have just this final evaluation stage to complete and we can then look back on the successful and less than successful learning experiences we have provided for our learners from a much better informed perspective. It is surprising how one run through a demanding routine does help not only to boost confidence, but also to open our eyes to the things we have misjudged, overlooked or just plain forgotten.

We have, of course, been encouraging you to reflect in your Personal Development Journal by using various activities as you have progressed through the earlier chapters, but now we wish to take more of an overview and develop evaluative reflections which may lead to a general improvement in practice. The theme of this chapter is evaluation and this will involve us in looking back at reflections and summarizing a way forward (i.e. reflecting about reflections or meta-reflection).

10.2 CRITICAL INCIDENTS AND EVALUATION

Most teachers have considerable pride in our profession and will point to examples of excellent teaching being carried out by colleagues, many of whom are involved in so many hours of face-to-face teaching each week that they have very little time for all the preparation, marking and administration expected in the present school, college and training environments.

Even so, fellow educational professionals have offered serious criticism of the professionalism of teachers and most of this is directed at our reluctance to analyse critical incidents within our practice from a theoretical and well as a pragmatic position. David Tripp (1993), made this pointed observation which still has much relevance today:

> in all the major professions there is another intellectual ingredient of practice: being able to explain and thereby justify what one does through a more knowledgeable, rigorous, and academic analysis. This does not appear to be necessary in teaching.

Tripp is referring to a characteristic, which other writers have also commented on, i.e. the resistance that many teachers, both experienced and novice, display towards the development of theory. Tripp too believes that teachers are reluctant to relate their experiences of teaching (and the critical incidents which happen everyday and which they deal with intuitively) to any underpinning concepts or principles, or to seek justification for their actions by reference to educational research. Tripp comments that:

> if they [the teachers] are not also able to articulate the specialist ... knowledge or the judgements that underlie what they do, they are ... craftspeople rather than professionals.

He argues that a more *evaluative reflection* of teaching processes would enable teachers to 'overcome their poor public image and achieve the status of a profession for their work'.

10.3 CRITICAL INCIDENT LOG

The purpose of your Personal Development Journal and Tripp's (ibid.) use of a *critical incident log* obviously have much in common. Based on his recording and analysis of critical incidents in teaching, Tripp (ibid.) states that teachers' work lacks public status because:

> they are seen to draw on the recall of 'right answers' rather than having to use their own judgements.

Tripp recommends that teachers apply reflective analysis to a series of critical incidents during their teaching practice and their professional teaching careers in order to develop what might be called 'diagnostic teaching'. Diagnostic teaching, as defined by Tripp, is the analysis of practice 'in a scholarly and academic fashion to produce expert interpretations upon which to base and justify ... professional judgements'.

Tripp (ibid.) recommends that teachers base their journal writing around such critical incidents and goes on to define critical incidents. They are not major events or 'things', because these may be few and far between. Teachers new to reflection can then use this as an excuse not to reflect because there have been no critical incidents today. Tripp believes that *critical incidents are created*. They are produced by the 'way we look at a situation'. The incident is made critical by the 'interpretation of the significance of an event'. So any lesson can be critically analysed and a particular event made critical by our reflection on it. We need to ask not only what happened but why it happened then and with that group and what it meant for the future teaching of that particular topic. We should 'situationalize' the event and apply the question 'why' to it and then generalize it in terms of professional practice and apply relevant theories to try to make sense of the event. This means challenging the comfortable and established habitual practices we rely on in everyday teaching. Take as an example, the following *critical incident* that happened to one of our teacher educators and caused her to look beyond her routine behaviour in class and consider a new technique.

Halfway through one of her lessons with a group of trainee teachers, a student who had missed her microteaching assessment the previous week, by arrangement presented her prepared session to the group. It was a good, creatively managed lesson during which she asked all the students to leave their desks and bring their chairs into a large circle. The tutor also joined that circle and later confirmed that everyone liked this new layout and found that it changed completely the interactive dynamics of the group.

The tutor reported later that:

We decided as a group to leave it that way for the rest of my session which became a much more discursive and student-led session thereafter. This layout is not something I use in my usual sessions with this group, or any other, mainly because I stick with the horseshoe layout of desks, which is in place in our teaching rooms.

The student had challenged this habitual practice and had made the tutor think about the position of authority she projected to the students with her at the front, and the students behind their desks. She confessed that:

I usually sit on my desk but had never thought to be radical enough to get rid of the desks completely. It challenged where I sit in the classroom and made me 'lead from the back' and let the students manage the discussion. It was a liberating experience for me and not really a major event, just one of those nice little 'happenings' we get everyday in our teaching.

G10a   Critical incident

Try to identify a recent critical incident (similar to the one described above) from your own practice. As our teacher says, not a 'major incident', but something that provided you with insights and probably some pleasure.

Tripp maintains that teachers need to cultivate the recording of such critical incidents because analysis of them makes the important link between instinctive practice and underpinning theory and then generalizes the event into continuing professional practice. They take us out of the ordinary and make us look at the things we do every day with fresh eyes. We are, in effect, observing ourselves.

10.3.1   The learning spiral

As we develop as teachers, it is inevitable that our critical reflections also mature and eventually we are able to see a whole range of implications from one small observation. This progressive development has been conceptualized as a learning spiral by some writers. Bain *et al.* (1999) have developed the notion of a *learning spiral* or a *spiral of reflection* which progresses in an upward direction, the lower loop representing early reflections on learning by a beginning teacher. The four points in the loop are an adaptation of Kolb's (1984) four learning styles (namely: Reflect, Plan, Act, Observe) and have been adapted to represent the stages a reflective teacher will pass through.

10.3.2   Spiral stages

The 'beginning' teacher will be reflecting at *level one* of the spiral and is merely reporting or 'retelling' the situation or incident to themselves 'with minimal transformation and no added observations or insights'. The spiral moves up to *level two* in which Bain says the student is now 'responding'. In addition to retelling they may 'ask a rhetorical question without attempting to answer it or consider alternatives'. They may also express feelings about the incident they are reflecting upon. Thus, to a limited degree, they are beginning to engage themselves in the process of reflection.

At *level three* of reflection the student-teacher is 'relating'. Bain explains that this involves the student identifying an aspect of data which:

> connect(s) with their prior or current experience.

The student is now reflecting back upon previous teaching and relating the present experience to earlier events. Thus they are beginning to develop a spiral of reflection, which draws positively on previous experiences.

Level four sees the beginning of the 'reasoning' process. The student seeks a 'deeper understanding of why something has happened' by relating it to underpinning theoretical concepts and personal experience. Bain believes this involves a 'high level of transformation'. The student is now relating theory to practice and attempting

> to explain their own or other's behaviour ... using their own insights.

The final, *fifth level* 'reconstructing' is the stage at which the student 'displays a high level of abstract thinking' to apply learning from this experience. They draw their own conclusions from their reflections and are able to 'generalize the experience'. They are now formulating their own *theory of teaching* and internalizing the *personal significance* of their learning. They are also beginning to plan future practice with the benefit of this deep reflection.

In terms of a beginning teacher, this spiral of learning may represent progress over the two years of the Certificate in Education course. From the position of a new reflector, i.e. a teacher new to the processes and challenges of teaching, reflections will necessarily be superficial because the knowledge and experience base is thin. However, through completion of course assignments and reflections on their own progress, the teacher develops a store of underpinning knowledge and theory from which reference can be made when analysing new experiences. Thus upward progress is made along the learning spiral.

G10b   Spiralling learning

Reflect on the ways in which your own reflective processes either do or do not accord with the theoretical stages in the learning spiral.

The spiral model implies that progress is always positively upwards but, of course, our reflections also deepen with the benefit of experience and hindsight. The upward direction of the spiral suggests that reflections become more meaningful as they build on earlier personal constructs. However, this does not automatically lead to improvements in teaching. For this to happen we need to be able to apply our reflections within teaching in order to make the important links between the theory and practice.

10.4 | PROFESSIONAL DEVELOPMENT JOURNAL

Continuing on the subject of recording and analysing teaching, let us now look at your progress with the Personal Development Journal. PDJs are used on a lot of courses, especially those that combine practical skills with underpinning theory. On many post-compulsory teacher-training programmes, they are used as a device to develop a *substantial narrative* based around the achievement of the FENTO standards.

Used in this way, the journal examines different aspects of our teaching and relates it to relevant theory by focusing it on an area of the FENTO standards. An example of this was perhaps during Chapter 3, when you were first asked to address the standards, i.e. those defined in Key Area A (Assessing Learner Needs). In order to develop an informed narrative around say 'action planning' (Activity A3j) it is possible that you first of all looked at the Key Area A FAQs (Frequently Asked Questions) at the end of Chapter 3. The guidance within the FAQs at Stages 1, 2 and 3 can help to get you in the frame of mind for reflecting on these particular processes at a particular level. They also indicate appropriate underpinning theory to support the analysis, which may have established for you the link between evidence from your teaching and general reflection on teaching processes and professional expertise, i.e. relevant theory.

Some trainee teachers, who have recently completed a degree course, find the Personal Development Journal challenging to write. This may be because it is written in the first person and that is considered a deadly sin in most academic writing. Most degree students are trained in objective, third-person writing and so the change to a first-person narrative is often difficult.

This style of writing is also very personal and so can be a challenge for students who are unused to writing about themselves. You will probably have found in responding to the first Activities in the early chapters you have managed to establish a link between the pen (or the word processor) and your inner thoughts and feelings about teaching. It is at this point that you begin reflective narrative writing.

You may have noticed that we have designed the Activities not only to address the various standards in relation to your own learning situation and learning groups, but also to allow your PDJ entries to build on each other in a cyclic fashion. Basing this process on your own practice should also ensure that you will be able, in later entries, to reflect upon previous ones and enhance the learning cycle/spiral.

10.4.1 Three reflective paradoxes

Gillie Bolton (2001), writing for student nurses who were approaching the writing of a Personal Development Journal for the first time, developed the concept of three paradoxes, which she believes lie at the heart of reflection – letting go of certainty, looking for something when you don't know what it is, beginning to act when you don't know how to act.

The first paradox Bolton (ibid.) considered 'in order to acquire confidence you have to let go of certainty' suggests that a confident person is more able to be flexible and creative in response to uncertain situations (see also self-concept in

Chapter 5). This, of course, applies equally to teaching as to nursing. Bolton claims that at some stage:

> a practitioner who knows all the right answers all the time is bound to be wrong.

The paradox of deliberately moving away from familiar certainty also highlights that reflective writing is about looking beneath the everyday, accepted conventions in teaching. In some situations where you are trying to promote learner autonomy and provide motivating, creative learning experiences, the constraining nature of such a convention as 'always state learning objectives at the beginning of a session' can undermine all your efforts to encourage your learners themselves to move beyond prescription towards the excitement of knowledge creation.

Bolton's second paradox, 'looking for something when you don't know what it is' captures a central difficulty that many learners encounter when engaging in critical reflection. The reason we usually decide to reflect on a critical incident is that we don't really understand why what we have experienced actually happened. We begin the reflective process believing that we can gain an insight into the unknown and, fortunately, our reflections often lead us to an understanding of the specifics of the situation and to a general understanding that can be applied to our teaching in the future.

The third paradox, 'beginning to act when you don't know how to act', refers to Donald Schon (1987) concepts of reflection-in as well as reflection-on action. Often when teaching we realize that some aspect of our session isn't being as effective as it should be and we stop, readjust and lead the students around a 'remedial learning loop' which we develop as we speak. This surprising aspect of skilled practice is, in part intuitive, but in the main it is our ability to trust our own reflections to come up with a course of action which is professional and considered, but when you begin the reflective process you have no idea what the course of action will be.

G10c Paradox

Reflect on the way in which Bolton's paradox theory has applied to you. Think about the processes described above under 'letting go', 'looking for something' and 'beginning to act' in relation to your own reflections.

These three paradoxes illustrate very well the different nature of journal writing, as compared to academic essay writing, and probably identify the main problems people have with beginning a reflective journal. The outcome and resulting action is unclear when you begin writing. It is the writing itself which clarifies the outcome for you, a kind of cathartic process. This is quite unlike writing a course assignment where you are certain of your outcomes before you begin to write.

10.4.2 Assembling the Personal Development Journal and the Practitioner File

Your entries in the PDJ will be of two quite different types.

- There will be written responses to chapter activities which are designed to address some of the many practical issues encountered in teaching and learning.

- On the other hand, instead of thinking about pragmatic implementation, you are encouraged to be involved in propositional thinking, i.e. theorizing about your teaching and the reason for actions and reactions you have observed from colleagues and learners.

Note: The chapter activities are optional and you may use them as a vehicle for reflection and evidence generation, or you may develop your own approach to meeting the standards.

Your Personal Development Journal should be written in the first person and should be a personal narrative account of how you have developed evidence for the areas of teaching practice covered by the journal entry. At the same time this commentary should be underpinned by references to relevant theories. This justifies your own reflections and gives you confidence in your own on-the-spot decisions and the conclusions you draw from them. At first this can be difficult, as it seems, particularly if you are used to academic writing, that the narrative style does not flow easily when written with accompanying quotations and references. The narrative style can seem self-conscious and not 'properly written', being subjective rather than objective. But, in fact, this is the basis of the best ground-breaking teacher research that is founded on teachers' personal reflections on their own practice.

A way to begin this kind of writing is to complete a reflective observation that looks at a *critical incident in your teaching from which you have learned*. The following, an actual reflection from a practitioner in post-compulsory education, may provide useful format for your entries:

Table 10.1   Format for a Reflective Log

1. Description of the event: (In here write, briefly, what happened in about 100 words)
Part way through teaching a particular topic some of the students said, 'we have already done this!' I felt a sick feeling in the pit of my stomach and the desire to turn around and come in again with an alternative lesson.
2. Your reflections on how you dealt with the incident: (This should be a longer account of what you did at the time to overcome the critical incident or to deal with it)
However, this being impossible, I relied on what I know best, which is talking in a direct but empathetic way to the students. I thus elicited from them when and how they had done the topic before and how much they remembered. I also apologised and made a note on my lesson plan. I then said we could use the session for revision. I did not exactly save face but demonstrated to students that I am human and that things can be covered more than once, in a different way, and still be useful. Later, when reflecting on the event, I resolved to record in detail the incident in my self-evaluation of the session and to ask students for feedback next session on how they felt the session went, thus finding out whether they felt disadvantaged by the incident.

Step 1. Although only brief, this is an important step as your description of how you remember the event may be quite different to the way other witnesses remember it. The way you develop your own perception or personal construct, will say a great deal about your expectations, values and purposes.

Step 2. The second half of the process is an analysis of your performance and whether you would have responded in the same way if you had been given more time to think about it. Probably, when you later look back on this section of your PDJ, you will be reassured to know that you can think 'on-your-feet'. It means you can do it again in another crucial situation. The second step in the process is partly narrative, but also it requires you to examine the incident again in hindsight. What might have been a gut reaction at the time (and may therefore seem to be unreliable) may seem now to have been absolutely the right thing to do. You know from this that you can rely on your instincts. It is useful to discuss with colleagues or fellow students, one of your critical incidents and ask for their comments on how you dealt with it, then do the same for them. Feedback like this usually reassures you that what you did was effective. Even if it was not, you survived it and with the benefit of reflective hindsight (recorded in your PDJ) will probably do it differently next time.

This kind of reflection encourages an open approach to teaching and reinforces that things do not always go according to plan. Eventually, you will feel confident with this uncertainty because it adds another element, that of creative practice, into your teaching. You may not always have the solution, either at the time or later on reflection, but that does not always matter. What matters is that you are not glossing over these incidents but are reflecting on and so learning from them.

10.4.3 Steps in a PDJ entry

You can now carry this style of writing into your Personal Development Journal and, if you haven't done it yet, start writing your first PDJ Entry. The following guidelines may help:

- a good place to begin is to have a look at the Frequently Asked Questions (FAQs) for the Key Area that you are writing the journal entry for. This will also put you in the correct mind-set for writing it

- next look at the various optional Activities suggested in the chapter which covers that particular Key Area (there are eight Key Areas (A to H) and they are covered in Chapters 3 to 10). The Activities can be identified by the clip-board graphic in the left-hand margin of the page. These activities are designed to generate evidence against the Standards

- then look at the FENTO Specifications at the end of the chapter to confirm what the suggested evidence is for that area

- you may wish to ignore the activity and find your own sources of evidence, which correspond to the suggestions in the specifications. This will give you confidence that you are covering the activities in your teaching required for this Key Area

- reflect on your evidence with or without the chapter activity

The whole process of developing critical thinking through the PDJ is centred around the notion of self-evaluation. Evaluation concepts have much in common with the assessment principles we discussed in the previous chapter. The national thrust towards TQM (discussed in Chapter 7) is centred around the promotion of institutional and individual evaluation processes. Systematic evaluation is obvious seen as the key to educational improvement and it is believed that it should include institutional, peer and self review.

Stufflebeam and Scriven (1985) gave us the three main purposes of evaluation: guiding decision making, providing records for accountability and promoting understanding of what is involved.

10.5 | APPROACHES TO EVALUATION

Over the last fifty or so years, the evaluation of education institutions has led to the development of a number of approaches or models. Six of these are summarized in the table below:

Table 10.2 Evaluation Models

Models	Focus	Characteristics
Goal-orientated	*The assessment of individual progress and the effectiveness of change.*	Developed by Ralph Tyler (1949) it advocated the objectives-orientated approach.
Summary:	Tyler argued that decisions about courses and programmes had to be based on the 'fit' between the objectives of the programme and its actual outcomes. If the objectives are achieved, decisions will have a particular focus; if they are not, a different focus will be taken.	
Decision-orientated	*One of the first alternatives to the objectives approach, focused on the context, input, process and product of the organization.*	Originators Daniel Stufflebeam and associates (1985) who focused on the four key criteria and their relationship within the organization.
Summary:	Using organizational documentation and meetings and interviews with staff, the evaluators collect data about whether the establishment is addressing the needs of the potential target audience, whether there are defects in the procedural design and if the outcomes meet their quality targets.	
Transactional	*A method of gaining a 'rounded' view of the organization through empirical data.*	Introduced by Robert Stake (1967) who advocated the analysis of processes and products over time.
Summary:	Stake believed that the boundaries between antecedents, transactions and outcomes which are unclear can produce useful data about intentions, influences and actual outcomes.	
Goal-free	*The identification of evaluation's goals and its internal roles.*	Set out by Michael Scriven (1973) who argued that the specific goals of evaluation can vary tremendously.
Summary:	Scriven proposed that evaluators too often, in trying to help the people involved to improve their programmes, become co-opted and fail to judge the programmes' merit accurately.	

Adversarial	Decision-making and the processes, which influence that within organizations.	Accessing the reasoning behind organizational decision-making.
Summary:	The approach adopts and modifies concepts from jury trials and administrative hearings as a means of focusing on particular issues, gathering testimony, exploring different perspectives and values and arriving at a reasoned judgement on the way forward for the organization	
Illuminative	Description and interpretation in an attempt to understand operational procedures and internal and external influences.	Developed by Parlett and Hamilton (1977), is concerned to understand processes rather than measure them.
Summary:	The purpose here is to discover what it is like to be participating as a learner or teacher on the particular programme and identify the practices and procedures which have had desirable results.	

G10d Approaches to evaluation

Using the table above, summarize what the different methods are focusing on and the sort of useful data they may produce which you feel could help to improve a programme or course you are involved in.

You will have noted that each of the models is a suggested way of trying to understand the range of very different processes and purposes, which you can find in most organizations, each of which are influenced by particular beliefs and purposes. Simply put, in turn the above evaluation processes attempt to address, setting objectives, making decisions, transmitting values, remaining objective, confronting issues and assembling a rich picture of the complex interactions taking place. Obviously, the purpose of all this analysis is to move to a more effective learning establishment.

Also, if we look beyond these sophisticated evaluation theories, it is very clear that the effectiveness of each of the above educational organizations depends entirely on the individuals who are the managers and staff. It is this *personal* level of responsibility that this chapter is designed to encourage and facilitate. Chapter 7 considered organizational quality procedures; here we are involved in something which, although incorporating the many purposes identified in the institutional models, is quite different. We wish to explore the ways in which we, as teachers, can further develop and apply the skills of analysis through the process of systematically evaluating our own practice.

We have said 'further develop' because, as you know, you have had many opportunities throughout the earlier chapters to reflect on many aspects of your own teaching. However, although you have made judgements along the way, you may not have critically analysed aspects of your own teaching in an attempt to improve your own practice progressively. Eventually, your Professional Development Journal should contain many interesting explorations of practice, which will provide evidence against the standards within each of the Key Areas as identified by the FENTO specifications at the end of each chapter. However, the next exercise below, may be better kept in your 'Practitioner File' as we are going to start with an evaluation of one of your teaching sessions:

G10e   Self-evaluation of a teaching session

This should be based, where possible, on a session where there has also been an observer/assessor present. The blank self-evaluation pro forma (I) is in the Appendix.

Most teacher education courses will provide a self-evaluation pro forma, which incorporates a series of criteria for the evaluation of a session. We include an example of a completed pro forma overleaf and there is a blank copy of this in the Appendix and on our website *tipcet.com*

Try to write a lengthy reflection for each section on the pro forma and do not avoid those areas which do not seem as significant as others in that particular session. These may just hold the key to why the session went as it did. You are reflecting on this session to complete the cycle of planning, teaching and reflection but this will also be something to which you can refer again and use as a basis for future evaluations of taught sessions.

G10f   Controlled response evaluation

Our example of a completed evaluation form below is supposedly from a Stage 2 teacher of catering (NVQ level 1). Consider the entries and say why she may have written the responses recorded there and how they might be improved.

TEACHER SELF-EVALUATION (I)

Programme Member: **Gladys Hepplethwaite**

College/Organisation **Northern College of Further Education**

Date: **10th January 2003**   Student Group: **Catering NVQ One**

Topic: **Prepare and cook egg and batter dishes – Scrambled and poached eggs**

Please record your observations in response to the criteria listed on the left:

ORGANIZATION AND SELECTION OF METHODS	
Please give your post-session insights in relation to:	
Meeting your perceived needs of the learners?	I think I met the needs of the group well. Everyone seemed happy in the class
Your preparation of the learning environment?	I made sure all of the resources were available and that there were sufficient so no one had to share.

Appropriateness of your defined learning outcomes?	The outcomes are defined in the NVQ element. They are clearly written so I needed to follow them exactly.
Relevance of lesson content?	The content (scrambled and poached eggs) allowed the learners to do 2 different methods – it is relevant to the NVQ Range.
Appropriateness of your methods in relation to student responses?	I did this well. First of all I did a demonstration and then I talked about the science of egg cookery. Then everyone had a go and I facilitated the session. Then we all evaluated eggs and looked at what we learnt.
Allocation of time to lesson phases?	No problem here.
How effective were your resources/ learning aids?	All of the pans and utensils are in a good condition. You need them to learn egg cookery. I did a handout with key points and recipes.
Teacher-student rapport?	We get on well and have a laugh. Just 2 students don't seem to enjoy the session. Always by themselves at the back.
How students developed their learning about learning?	We talked about what we learnt.
The level of challenge the learners experienced?	This was easy – everyone knows how to scramble eggs – the poaching is more tricky.
Adaptation to the changing demands of the session?	I didn't need to change a thing – it all went nicely to plan.
How you modified your strategies to differentiate between learners?	All of the learners are of the same standard – NVQ Level 1 – so we are working together from the beginning – they all have the same needs.
Assessment of learners?	I observed them making the egg dishes against the NCQ criteria.
ADDITIONAL COMMENTS	
Please give the name of the tutor who observed this session:	Mrs Barton

10.6 | SELF-EVALUATION

Obviously, a critical self-evaluation is difficult to carry out at the first attempt, especially when the event it is based on was also an observed, assessment session. The process of being observed is so stressful to student teachers that often, when they look back and try to remember the observed session, many areas are difficult to recall in detail. So inevitably, many of Gladys Hepplethwaite's reflections are vague and mostly descriptive rather than analytical. Also she has adopted a fairly defensive stance and, because of this, she has missed an opportunity to use the evaluation to demonstrate her clear understanding of the processes involved. Just three examples from the evaluation will help to illustrate this:

Relevance of lesson content: The content will have been included in Gladys's Session Plan, of which the observer has a copy – little is achieved by repeating this. It would have been more helpful if Gladys had said why, at this stage in their development, moving the students on to prepare scrambled eggs is appropriate progression.

Allocation of time to lesson phases: Gladys could have taken this opportunity to discuss why her time allocation to different periods of the session was made and how she might improve it in future sessions.

Additional Comments: As is the case with many programme members, Gladys avoided this opportunity to highlight significant events during the session and show how she understood the reason for them and what she would do about a similar events in future.

Let Gladys's experience prepare you to be as analytical as possible about your observed sessions, but don't be surprised if, when you look back on this in a year's time, your reflection seem naive. Remember, you were relatively new to self-evaluation when you wrote it and it is surprising the progress you can make in one year.

Having said that, let's now assume that a year has passed and Gladys Hepplethwaite is a much more experienced, Stage 3 student. Following a recent teaching observations she has completed the less structured evaluation form overleaf. This type of evaluation form assumes that the respondent is sufficiently analytical and aware of the context to be able to identify the criteria which best represents her own developing value system.

G10g *Free response evaluation*

Gladys Hepplethwaite has been observed carrying out a learning review with her catering students. She has selected the criteria to respond to with her Stage 3 self-evaluation. Consider these criteria and her responses and say what you feel about the issues she has chosen to highlight and her comments.

TEACHER SELF-EVALUATION (II)

Programme Member: Gladys Hepplethwaite

College: Northern College

Date: 12th February 2004   Class: Level 3 NVQ Catering

Subject: SM5.3 Provide feedback on work performance to teams and
individuals

Observer Name: MR Wilkinson

Criterion One:	ESTABLISH AN EFFECTIVE ENVIRONMENT FOR FEEDBACK
Response:	We used the staff lounge and I ensured that we would not be interrupted and the phone was disconnected.
Criterion Two:	ENCOURAGE A POSITIVE STUDENT ORIENTATION TO THE FEEDBACK
Response:	7 members of the student team attended and 5 of them were very positive and willing to receive feedback in an open and constructive manner
Criterion Three:	FOCUS ON SPECIFIC ISSUES
Response:	All members of the team were provided with an agenda and the first item was AOB to allow them to add issues they wished to discuss
Criterion Four:	GIVE CLEAR EXPLANATIONS OF BOTH NEGATIVE AND POSITIVE FEEDBACK
Response:	Most to the feedback was positive apart from the incident of a customer complaint because of dirty cutlery and a chipped plate.
Criterion Five:	BE CONSTRUCTIVE – SUGGEST WAYS OF IMPROVING
Response:	I asked the team to suggest how we could ensure that this did not happen again.
Criterion Six:	NEGOTIATE APPROPRIATE RESPONSES FROM TEAM
Response:	All the team agreed that the customer had every right to complain and that the problem was a group problem rather than an individual one.
Criterion Seven:	NEGOTIATE APPROPRIATE RESPONSES FROM INDIVIDUALS
Response:	The team themselves suggested that the solution was to check the cutlery and crockery to be used more carefully before we lay the tables and begin serving.
Criterion Eight:	GET TEAM AND INDIVIDUALS TO REFLECT BACK ADVICE GIVEN

Response:	Team and individuals took turns in explaining the customer complaints procedures and how we respond according to the level of complaint.
Criterion Nine:	PROVIDE STRUCTURE OF CHOICE OF ACTIONS
Response:	Team and individuals suggested how the procedures could be improved to anticipate problems rather than wait for them to happen.
Criterion Ten:	ROUND SESSION OFF IN A POSITIVE MANNER
Response:	The team were congratulated on a positive session and it was agreed that a minute of the meeting would be provided so that each of them could keep a copy in their Portfolio.

The above evaluation shows a young teacher of catering very much in control of her environment. She has thought through the practice of reviewing learning and the principles of managing people and has organized a very effective feedback session where issues were addressed and satisfactorily solved. This shows a considerable and positive development from her first year self-evaluations.

G10h Maturing evaluation

Given Gladys' development since the first evaluation in 2003, where would you place her on the Learning Spiral we discussed at the start of the chapter? Comment also on the value of the 'free response' type of evaluation.

Before we leave the issue of self-evaluation it is worth stressing that the process is designed to establish the habit of continuous self-evaluation. A habit which will be part of the continuous improvement and development cycle which Deming (1986) said is the basis for 'delighted' customers, in this case your students and so yourself.

When you have completed your pro forma you will probably see that it required a lengthy reflection of all that happened in the session including evaluation of how you planned it and whether this was appropriate for the students and the circumstances of the session. It will not have been enough for you to recapitulate on what went well, but to examine what *did not* go as planned and to try to figure out why this was so.

This takes us back to the critical incident review and brings up an important point in the process of reflection. It is never enough merely to reassure ourselves that it was OK. As reflective practitioners we must always engage in active reflection of all our lessons, picking out the exciting and challenging incidents that make us a teacher out of the ordinary. Any teaching session has the potential for such deep reflection and should be seen as such. We are our own best observers because we are always there when we are teaching, so we should make use of ourselves as reflective self-observers and thus be continuously improving and developing through our own teaching.

10.6.1 Establishing a reflective spiral of learning

Key area G is about reflecting on and evaluating your own performance and so journal entries for this key area are developed through reflecting on earlier evaluations of teaching processes. For example, in key area G2 you are encouraged to evaluate on your own practice by reflecting on student feedback and on your own previous personal development journal entries. The evidence for the journal entry for this key area is your own previous reflections in your PDJ. Ask yourself questions about your relationships with a particular group of learners, such as:

- What was in my mind when I wrote this particular journal entry?
- What were my apprehensions about my justifications for how and why I planned this session?
- How did I feel about the group at that time?
- What sort of critical incidents have I had with this group since and how can reflecting upon them help me reach a deeper understanding of their needs?
- Which activities have gone down particularly well and why?

You now have a starting point from which to evaluate your current practice with this group and have an open mind from which you can acknowledge both successes and failures. Without this openness you will never set the scene for your own improvement.

10.7 | DEVELOPING STUDENT FEEDBACK

Another important aspect of improving practice in educational settings is finding ways of getting accurate feedback from students about how they are experiencing your sessions, what works for them and what does not. Many student questionnaires seem to be designed to eliminate the possibility of any detailed student comments and these are therefore not very useful in getting your students' views. The sort of questionnaire we are referring to is one which gives a series of tick-box answers with one line at the end for a brief student comment. Typically, this would be given out while the teacher stands over the student and is collected in after a few minutes.

G10i Student evaluation

Reflect on the problems of the student-based evaluation described above. Think not only about the value of the feedback received but its effect on the student group themselves.

Naturally, the students will resent such a cynical approach to evaluation and will believe that all such evaluations in the institutions are just as contrived and meaningless. There will be a feeling that it is impossible to get their view heard in such a threatening culture. When seeking student feedback, the very first thing a teacher needs to do is to get over the *fear factor*. The students' fear of upsetting the tutor (which may influence their assessment results) and the tutors' fear that they are going to say something about the teaching which may hurt and which the tutor may not be prepared to deal with. We have tried to establish in this chapter the fact that reflection is not always a comfortable process and that it may bring up things which cause us extra work and some anxiety. The same is true of any evaluation process which has integrity, but what a wonderfully reassuring thing it is to have a culture which actively encourages openness and honesty.

10.7.1 Mentoring: getting beyond the fear factor in evaluation

For this exercise you need to seek out someone who is willing to act as your mentor. It can be anyone who is willing and in a position to take on a confidant, supportive role which is not allied to any assessment process. Such a person may be difficult to find, but if you succeed you will usually find that a mentor is a very useful ally who can help you with many difficult judgements during and beyond your teacher training programme.

This exercise is to help you establish an open approach to listening to your students. First, you need to practise listening with your mentor first. Start by asking your mentor to observe one of your teaching sessions and then complete a self-evaluation of that session (either of the above pro forma) before your receive the feedback. This will mean your mind-set is open to enquiry before you discuss the session with your mentor. Imagine that the session you are discussing is an exercise for your course, which it is, and this will help to detach you emotionally from the comments that your mentor makes.

Next, find a safe, neutral place where you will not be disturbed and ask your mentor to set aside about thirty minutes to give you your feedback. You should listen carefully to the critical as well as the reassuring comments. Remember too, that you can be an *active* listener. In other words, chip in with you own comments, not to contradict the mentor, but to help develop the discussion. For example, your mentor may say, 'I thought that the lesson went a bit dull at that point', and you could say (being an honest person) 'Yes, I felt that, but was not sure why'. Your mentor then has an opening to suggest, from his or her point of view, what you could have done differently. In this way you will benefit from a very detailed analysis of the lesson and a series of comments from a trusted colleague about how you could improve and develop it for the future. People who are really daring will ask their mentors to comment on aspects of the observed teaching technique that they think should be worked on. One example could be the way questions are presented to the group. This process with a mentor leaves the way open for your own future reflections and establishes a listening approach.

> ### G10j *Working with a mentor*
>
> Of course, if you do manage to get a colleague to work with you in the role of mentor, this relationship will be an excellent process to reflect on regularly within your PDJ.

So, having got over the fear factor, you may like to consider alternative means than a questionnaire for gathering useful student feedback. As we have stressed, the method we have found to be most effective is *listening* to students.

10.7.2   Listening to students

Obviously, you need first of all to set up a meeting with your students at which you can ask them about their experiences of your course. A good way to get this started is to ask them three basic questions, to which they can add if they wish. These questions are:

1. What are the most effective parts of the course for you and why?
2. What the least effective parts, and why?
3. What would you change about the course?

Ask the class to get into groups of about five students and leave them to discuss the questions and make notes for about 20 minutes. It is a good idea, if logistically possible, to leave the students for this time and ask one to come and get you when they have finished their discussions. Obviously, be aware of health and safety issues around leaving the group but at least give them some space to talk without your influencing them.

Then ask each group to feedback and make your own notes of their comments. Resist the temptation to justify any negative comments, just accept them and write them down. This demonstrates to the students that you really do want to listen and to develop the course in line with their experiences. Thank the students for their frankness. It is challenging for them to feedback honestly and they need to feel reassured that their honesty is appreciated. Such a 'listening' session is best done at the end of a module or programme and you could possibly arrange a social event to follow on directly after the session, where you join the students in a more relaxed atmosphere. This helps to dispel any lingering feelings of resentment or unease.

G10k   Listening evaluation

Develop and implement a student-centred evaluation using an approach similar to the one outlined above and then reflect on the data with which you have been provided by your students and how this may help to improve your programme.

10.7.3   Questionnaire design

Questionnaires are, in fact, interviews by correspondence. However, you do not have the opportunity to ask supplementary questions when the answer you receive does not respond as precisely or fully to the question as you intended. For these reasons, designing a useful evaluation questionnaire is tricky. You need to reach a balance between gathering student feedback from which you can develop the course and producing a questionnaire that is not to difficult or time-consuming to analyse. Also, most people prefer a questionnaire to be anonymous so they feel able to respond honestly, but this means if there are comments that you would like to explore further, you cannot go back to that student and discuss the comments.

One approach is to give out a questionnaire as a start to course development and then hold a meeting similar to the one described in the previous section. In this way you can start discussion with a statement such as 'you raised some important issues in the student evaluation questionnaire that we would like to explore further with you'.

There are many published guides to questionnaire design, which will usually contain the following simple principles:

- keep it anonymous
- keep it short – about 10–12 questions is enough
- keep longer, individual response questions to the end
- try to use tick-box questions
- do not use leading questions
- do not use ambiguous questions
- do not use any unnecessary questions – what exactly do you want to find out?

G10l Designing an evaluation questionnaire

Using the above guidance, design a questionnaire to obtain evaluatory, learner feedback for your own programme. Before you begin, think about how you are going to process and analyse the data. If you intend to do it manually, make sure that you leave room on the form for making notes relating to the responses received. Also think about how and when you will administer the questionnaire. It is most effective to give it out to the group yourself and then collect them in at the end of the lesson. Although this ensures a good response rate, anonymity can be undermined if the students feel that their responses can be linked to them through your observation or by you collecting them personally for each individual. Take steps to reassure them, such as letting them place their completed questionnaire on a pile as they leave the room.

You also need to consider the timing of the questionnaire implementation. Obviously, if you use it just before a student assessment, a possible misinterpretation by the students could be that, if they are critical, it will have a bearing on the marks they are given. It is also important to avoid administering a questionnaire in situations where the learners are feeling stressed by assessment deadlines or looming examinations. This may result in the student responses reflecting a jaded view determined by the emotional state of the students at the time.

10.8 CONCLUSION

As with the assessment modes discussed in the previous chapter, evaluation approaches will also adopt a particular focus depending on their purpose and the values that underpin the programme or course being evaluated. Some will be formative (i.e. where data is collected *during* the teaching) and some will be summative (data collected *after*). As we showed earlier (in Table 10.2) evaluations may be designed to gather information about *decisions* or about *goals*. Educational evaluations may be *organization-centred* (often collecting prescribed data which is required to support quality monitoring), *tutor-centred* (where the teachers identify the criteria – we provided an example in activity G10l), or student-centred.

Earlier we discussed two student self-evaluation examples in activities G10f and G10g. In the first the tutor provided the criteria (tutor-centred) and in the second the student wrote the criteria (student-centred). Again, where educational provision (session, module, course or programme) is being evaluated, the tutor or the student may define the criteria and, as you would expect, each focus will be different.

Finally, the data collected may be *quantitative* which provides mostly information about what has happened, or it may be *qualitative*, which would give an insight into why particular aspects did or did not find favour.

In the table overleaf we have provided examples of three evaluation questionnaires, each of which uses a very different approach. These examples have been simplified and condensed in order to provide an easy means of comparison.

G10m   Evaluating evaluations

Consider the characteristics of the three evaluations in Table 10.3 and in particular think about the information they are trying to elicit and how successful such styles might be, particularly in your educational context.

These pro forma are available on the *tipcet.com* website.

Our summary of the characteristics of these three examples would be:

1. *Summative evaluation*: this is partially teacher-led and partially student-centred. The format of this end of programme approach and the criteria 'worthwhile' have been defined by the tutor, but the responding student can identify the processes and issues on which to comment under either or both headings. The strengths of this approach are that it allows a response on general as well as specific issues and it is essentially qualitative, as it is looking to the respondent to explain why.

2. *Formative evaluation*: this teacher-led evaluation is in the form of a log and, if completed properly will provide a wealth of information about each session in a programme. However, it is obviously very demanding of the student and if completed, may very well not be done properly. Obviously, the descriptor for each session could be entered by the teacher before handing to the student.

3. *Rating scale*: this again is a mixed approach. It is an essentially controlled response and quantitative in nature, but the three added questions at the bottom of the pro forma would allow a limited amount of free response, qualitative information to be collected. As you would expect, the balance between these two approaches can be decided by the designer of the questionnaire.

Remember these are only three examples of different ways of collecting data. They will obviously be improved if they are applied to particular situations by modifying the criteria, etc.

Table 10.3 Examples of evaluation pro formas

1. Summative evaluation

In the table below please list on the left-hand side those aspects which you feel have made this project/module/course worthwhile and on the right-hand side list those which you feel have reduced its value. Would you please also add a brief explanation for your views:

1. Worthwhile qualities:	Less worthwhile qualities:
Explanation	Explanation

2. Formative evaluation

Would you please keep a log below of the various sessions which you have attended during the current programme and add your comments in the appropriate column. Try to do this concurrently while your recollections are still fresh in your memory.

Session no.	Description:	Relevance:	Comments:
1.			
2.			

3. Rating scale

Please indicate your satisfaction with each of the listed aspects of your programme by placing a cross in your chosen box and then add your comments against the three statements at the bottom of the page

The following ratings apply:
1=Very satisfied, 2=Satisfied, 3=Dissatisfied, 4=Very dissatisfied

Module qualities:		1	2	3	4
1	The teaching on the module				
2	The learning materials (e.g. handouts, case studies, exercises, etc.)				
3	The explanations of the learning objectives				
4	The match of the content to the syllabus outline in the handbook				
5	Relevance of content				
6	The appropriateness of the assignment topics				

7	The explanation of the assessment criteria		
8	The quality of support given by staff on assignments		
9	The preparation of teaching staff		
10	The approachability of teaching staff		
11	The organizational arrangements for the module		
12	Your overall satisfaction with the module		
(a)	I found the best features of the programme to be:		
(b)	I did not like the following:		
(c)	I would like to see the following changes:		

2. *Worthwhile qualities:*

Less worthwhile qualities:

3.

Explanation:

Explanation:

4.

2. *Worthwhile qualities:*

Less worthwhile qualities:

Explanation:

Explanation:

You also need to consider the timing of the questionnaire implementation. Obviously, if you use it just before a student assessment, a possible misinterpretation by the students could be that, if they are critical, it will have a bearing on the marks they are given. It is also important to avoid situations where the learners are feeling stressed by assessment deadlines or looming examinations. This may result in the questionnaire responses reflecting a jaded view determined by the emotional state of the students at the time.

Finally, the approaches to self and programme evaluation described within this chapter have one important quality in common, they are each an attempt to *improve* provision within post-compulsory education. The collection of information which is *relevant* to both the decision and development process, is difficult and time-consuming. It is easy to identify that something is wrong, but finding our way through the complex of variables towards improvement is much more demanding and ultimately richly rewarding.

10.9 | USEFUL SOURCES

Cousins, J.B. and Earl, L.M. (eds) (1995) *Participatory Evaluation in Education*. London: The Falmer Press.
A useful introduction to the notion of a partnership between teachers and administrators to bring about educational improvement. Using several case studies by actual practitioners the book identifies principles for collaborative development.

Eisner, E.W. (1985) *The Art of Educational Evaluation*. London: The Falmer Press.
This is a well-known study by Elliot Eisner, in which he puts forward a strong case for focusing educational evaluation as much on the affective domain as the cognitive. His ideas have serious implications for assessment and curriculum planning.

Norris, N. (1990) *Understanding Educational Evaluation*. London: Kogan Page.
An effective overview of the range of evaluation models developed in both the USA and the UK and their relationship to applied research.

Try *tipcet.com* for a range of materials and suggested sources related to educational evaluation.

10.10 | REFLECTING UPON AND EVALUATING ONE'S OWN PERFORMANCE AND PLANNING FUTURE PRACTICE – KEY AREA G

FAQs	At Stage 1	At Stage 2	At Stage 3
Why do it?	In order to improve any complex process you have to collect information which will help you make decisions about what to change. Education is one	We reflect, analyse and evaluate in order to better understand the very complex range of relationships and influences which exist	Reflection, evaluation and analysis are a range of critical processes which teachers use to understand better the

	such process and as teachers we have the responsibility to collect data which will help us to put in place improvements. These changes are usually only small adjustments, but sometimes they are so radical that we are required to develop new courses and programmes. The same evaluation process is involved, only the scale is different.	within interactive situations. A reflective practitioner in the teaching context is someone who consciously examines a particular educational context in order to actively modify and improve the teaching and learning process. When analysing we theoretically break things down into their constituent parts in order to better understand the whole. We evaluate in order to measure the quality of the teaching and learning we are providing against identified criteria.	teaching and learning processes. Active reflection (praxis) is the process of identifying the various elements of the learning process while they are actually changing and developing; this enables us to modify our delivery as appropriate. When evaluating we are usually using given standards as a comparative measurement. Reflection is also often comparative but the emphasis may be on understanding rather than measuring.
Where are we going?	Continuous improvement is the goal of quality processes and evaluation strategies. To do this we collect the data we need, at times when we need it.	These critical processes lead us towards an optimum performance as teachers, which may lead to optimum achievement by the learners.	Because of the ever-changing variables within each teaching and learning situation, the reflective process is never ending. However, there is an end product, which is an autonomous, reflective learner and teacher.
How do we get there?	We arrive at a systematic improvement strategy by putting in place appropriate evaluations, which collect information on the effectiveness of all aspects of our provision. Individual teachers know their own learners and learning situations best, so it is up to us also to identify the best ways of generating the data, which will help us to optimize our provision.	Reflect before, during and after a session and record your intuitive feelings about the different processes. Analyse the range of relationships and influences operating within your teaching context. Evaluate at different stages of provision using a range of appropriate methods against well-defined criteria. Check on the development of study skills and independence as learners.	The more involved you become in trying to understand the complexities of teaching and learning, the more you become aware of the range of subtle influences operating within the process. It may help to analyse different aspects of provision in turn. For example learner needs, planning, delivery, assessment, etc. Look also at the less obvious aspects of learning such as student motivation and commitment, inclusion and the opportunity to interact with colleagues.

Is this the best way?	Standards are either continuously developed and sustained through internal evaluations or are decided externally and imposed. As professionals we must work towards re-establishing the former model.	Consider whether reflection is actually helpful or does it increase anxiety. Are you looking merely for right or wrong instead of developing your own criteria for good performance within this particular context. Check that the evaluation strategies are appropriate and relevant.	Use a reflective journal to record observations and insights and student-centred as well as teacher-initiated evaluations. Ensure that the evaluation process itself isn't affecting your teaching because you have become less holistic due to your concern to break everything down to allow analysis.
When is the right time?	The right time to evaluate is when things are able to be improved. In other words some form of evaluation (either formal or informal) should be continuously ongoing, because data which can help improve provision are constantly available.	Reflection is often more meaningful when you are less tired or stressed, however insights sometimes occur at surprising moments. Check the purpose of the evaluation and confirm whether it is designed to modify and correct while the teaching is in process (formative) or to use later to action-plan improvements (summative). Ensure that key events are not being overlooked or student experiences undervalued.	Consider whether the quality of your reflection is being affected by your own expectations within a teacher education process. Does reflection seem somehow like DIY teacher training? Did you expect/hope that the course would provide more positive answers to some of the problems facing teachers? Were you hoping for a 'science' of teaching with generic methods appropriate to all situations?
Who needs to know?	Evaluations help both learners and teachers, so both groups need to know about both the implementation and also the outcomes. Better still, both groups should be involved in the design, the implementation and the data analysis.	Within your particular context, you are the most important participant in the reflective process but it is wise to check out conclusions with colleagues. Share evaluations with managers, colleagues, students, support staff. Inspectors, governors and parents may require them.	Reflections are often extremely sensitive and you may not wish to share them. However, despite the personal nature of the process you were reflecting on, it may well be that from it you develop concepts which are generic and can be shared productively with others.
How do we know when we've got there?	The concept of continuous improvement does mean that the process never ends. However, there are obviously varying degrees of improvement which are possible and when serious problems have been	Reflection and evaluation should lead to improvement but they are *not* one and the same thing. Evaluative criteria are often externally devised and related to funding and need not necessarily reflect your	As discussed earlier, there is no final destination, but you will know when your reflections, evaluations and analysis are leading to important insights, which are confirmed by your reading and the experiences of others.

	eradicated, a level of optimum performance should be achievable which will then require periodic monitoring and adjustment.	particular values and purposes. Reflection may lead to insights into difficulties created by the standards process itself. Teachers must balance personal values with professional roles.	You will know when you have become the 'expert' in a particular teaching context where you understand the learners' characteristics and the range of contextual influences better than anyone else.
Has everyone had a fair chance?	Improvement in practice as a consequence of considered evaluation, will not necessarily benefit all of the learners in a given situation. We need to remain aware of the range of learner needs and ensure that we are catering for the minority as well as the majority.	Some teachers find active reflection difficult and need to develop the skill. When evaluating we must ensure that students have an opportunity to contribute and that teachers have a say in how and when it takes place. Confirm that staff and students know what evaluation criteria and data collection methods are being used.	Sometimes, one of the difficulties faced by reflective teachers is if their analysis reveals the fact that, for one reason or another, their learners are not getting the optimum possible learning experience. You must continue (on behalf of your learners) to strive for that provision, but you also need to know why this situation has occurred.

10.11 KEY AREA G – REFLECTING ON AND EVALUATING ONE'S OWN PERFORMANCE AND PLANNING FUTURE PRACTICE

Purpose: Teachers and teaching teams need to contribute effectively to the continuous improvement of quality by evaluating their own practice, by identifying opportunities for personal and professional development, and by participating in programmes of professional development. Teachers should recognize the importance of, and engage in, critical reflection on professional practice, within the context of the internal and external factors influencing post-compulsory education. *For an analysis of this process at FENTO Stages 1, 2 and 3 see 10.10.*

Please note: The FENTO Standards listed below are relevant to the following three levels of award – Stage 1 (Introduction), Stage 2 (Intermediate) and Stage 3 (Full Certification). All the standards are required at Stage 3. Only those in italic and bold are required at Stage 2 and only those in italic are required at Stage 1.

UNIT G1. EVALUATE ONE'S OWN PRACTICE *In order to do this teachers should:*

	Demonstrate that they are able to:	and will have specific knowledge and critical understanding of:	plus generic understanding of:		Summary of appropriate evidence in this Key Area:	Relevant Chapter Activities
a	Criteria: identify where and how their subject or vocational area fits within the organization and the wider post-compulsory sector	• Vocationalism and its role in post-compulsory education • Their current role and the knowledge and skills required to carry it out • What constitutes relevant evidence of teachers' own practice and how to interpret it	• The organization's aims, objectives and policies, and the nature of the service it provides • Appropriate sources of evidence from which to draw when evaluating their own work	a	Organization plan, Programme annual reports, National post-compulsory framework	B4d, B4f, D7r, D7s, D7t, H11a to H11d
b	consider their own professional practice in relation to the major influences upon further education	• Ways of addressing teachers, own development needs	• Methods of evaluating their own experience against the requirements of the job	b	Analysis of own teaching context and internal and external influences	1b, 2e, 2f, 2h, 2i, E8f
c	develop opportunities for good practice while recognizing the full range of factors and constraints operating within FE	• Methods of evaluating their own experience against the requirements of the job	• Ways of reflecting upon their own teaching experience and the experience of learners	c	Evaluations, Personal Action Plans, Contractual Boundaries	E8f, G10a to G10j

	Element	Knowledge and understanding		Evidence	Standards
d	identify the extent and nature of their current knowledge and skills in relation to the demands of the job	• The contribution which learners make to teachers' evaluation of their own teaching • The required skills and knowledge for working with learners, including teachers' own levels of competence in key skills • The limits of their own competence and responsibility • The impact of teachers' own values, beliefs and life experiences on learners and learning • The limits of teachers' own control over the evaluation of practice • Ways of analysing evaluation data • Current issues and trends within vocational educational training and development • Appropriate sources of professional support • The nature and role of the post-compulsory sector within the current vocational and educational structure and within the wider community • Likely future developments within PCE and their implications for teachers' own practice and that of the institution • The mission and aims of the organization and how to contribute to the decision-making processes within it	d	Self-Assessment Table, Subject updating, Teacher Profile	1a, H12a to H12g
e	conduct a critical evaluation of their own teaching by eliciting, valuing and using feedback from learners, other teachers, managers and external evaluators		e	Self-evaluations, Staff-appraisal, Teacher Profile	1a, G10e to G10g H12a to H12g
f	**evaluate their own Key Skills against what is required in their teaching**		f	Key Skills audit and accreditation	H12a to H12g
g	evaluate the quality of their relationships with learners, colleagues and other stakeholders		g	Student-centred evaluations, Teacher profiles, Appraisals	G10e to G10g H12a to H12g
h	assess their own contribution to the achievement of the organization's objectives		h	Quality audit, Teacher Profile	H12a to H12g
i	*create and use opportunities to question their own practice and to seek audits of their competence from others, as appropriate*		i	Mentor feedback, Staff Appraisals, Self-Assessment table, FENTO Standards accreditation	H12a to H12g
j	use evaluations to improve their own and their team's effectiveness		j	Subject and Student evaluations	G10e to G10g

Key to above standards required at each FENTO Stage: *Introduction Stage – italic* **Intermediate Stage + bold** Certification Stage – all		Plus commentary in PDJ on the purposes and value of evaluating one's own practice, together with records in your Practice File of Teaching Observations, Lesson Plans, Rationales, Self-Evaluations and Progress Summary

Unit G2. PLAN FOR FUTURE PRACTICE *In order to do this teachers should:*

Demonstrate that they are able to:	and will have specific knowledge and critical understanding of:	plus generic understanding of:		Summary of appropriate evidence in this Key Area:	Relevant Chapter Activities
Criteria:					
a. identify developments in vocational and educational fields relevant to their own areas of work and to FE in general	• current developments within teachers' own areas of professional competence and the relevance of these to teaching • changes in FE and the likely impact of these on teacher' practice	• The organization's aims, objectives and policies, and the nature of the service it provides • Appropriate sources of evidence from which to draw when evaluating their own work	a	Analysis of context, Teacher Profile	H12a to H12g
b. consider the relevance of current developments to their own practice within existing and potential roles	• how to plan teachers' own personal development and how personal development fits into wider organizational strategies	• Methods of evaluating their own experience against the requirements of the job	b	Analysis of context, Teacher Profile	H12a to H12g
c. monitor curriculum developments in their own subject and keep up-to-date with new topics and new areas of work	• ways of negotiating changes to current programmes of learning	• Ways of reflecting upon their own teaching experience and the experience of learners • Current issues and trends within vocational	c	Analysis of context, Teacher Profile, Subject Updating	H12a to H12g
d. take account of subject developments in the content of programmes and teaching	• the resource constraints applicable to personal and professional development	educational training and development • Appropriate sources of professional support	d	Analysis of context, Teacher Profile, Subject Updating	H12a to H12g
e. consider and implement appropriate changes in programme design and delivery that best reflect current vocational and educational developments	• the relevance of current developments to learning	• The nature and role of the post-compulsory sector within the current vocational and educational structure and within the wider community	e	Curriculum Development	B4a to B4v, H12a to H12g

f	take into account the resource constraints influencing intended developments and make the best use of the opportunities available		
	• Likely future developments within PCE and their implications for teachers' own practice and that of the institution • The mission and aims of the organization and how to contribute to the decision-making processes within it	f	Analysis of Context, Curriculum development
			B4a to B4v
		Plus commentary in PDJ on the purposes and value of planning for future practice, together with records in your Practice File of Teaching Observations, Lesson Plans, Rationales, Self-Evaluations and Progress Summary	

Key to above standards required at each FENTO Stage:

Introduction Stage – italic

Intermediate Stage + bold

Certification Stage – all

UNIT G3.   ENGAGE IN CONTINUING PROFESSIONAL DEVELOPMENT *In order to do this teachers should:*

	Demonstrate that they are able to:	and will have specific knowledge and critical understanding of:	plus generic understanding of:		Summary of appropriate evidence in this Key Area:	Relevant Chapter Activities
a	identify where their own knowledge and skills need to be updated	● The skills and knowledge required for working with learners, including key skills	● The organization's aims, objectives and policies, and the nature of the service it provides ● Appropriate sources of evidence from which to draw when evaluating their own work ● Methods of evaluating their own experience against the requirements of the job	a	Teacher Profile, CPD Action Plan	H12a to H12g
b	identify effective ways of maintaining their subject expertise and keeping it up-to-date	● Ways of addressing teachers' own development needs	● Ways of reflecting upon their own teaching experience and the experience of learners ● Current issues and trends within vocational educational training and development	b	Teacher Profile, CPD Action Plan	H12a to H12g
c	engage in research and study related to professional practice	● Theories of learning and the relevance of these to FE and to teachers' own work ● Relevant research in teachers' own specialist/ subject area	● Appropriate sources of professional support ● The nature and role of the post-compulsory sector within the current vocational and educational structure and within the wider community	c	Teacher Profile, CPD Action Plan	H12a to H12g
d	set realistic goals and targets for their own development	● Sources of information on professional development and how to access them		d	Teacher Profile, CPD Action Plan	H12a to H12g
e	Take up professional development opportunities relevant to their work and to institutional priorities			e	Teacher Profile, CPD Action Plan	H12a to H12g

Criteria:

| Key to above standards required at each FENTO Stage:

Introduction Stage – italic
Intermediate Stage + bold
Certification Stage – all | • What are appropriate opportunities for teachers' own training and development
• Sources of information for enhancing professional knowledge and how to access them | • Likely future developments within PCE and their implications for teachers' own practice and that of the institution
• The mission and aims of the organization and how to contribute to the decision-making processes within it | Plus commentary in PDJ on the purposes and value of engaging in Continuing Professional Development, together with records in your Practice File of Teaching Observations, Lesson Plans, Rationales, Self-Evaluations and Progress Summary |

Meeting professional requirements Part 1: values and policies in post-compulsory education

Fred Fawbert

Key Area H Working within a professional value base to agreed codes of professional practice – a review of the background to current policy and practice in the Post 16/FE Sector

Key concepts in this chapter:

Academic drift, Casualization, Collectivist consensus, Commodification, Crisis in capitalism, CTCs, De-professionalization, De-skilling, Economic Utility, Education Reform Act, Flexi-learning, Free-market, GNVQs, Great Debate, Hillgate group, HMI, Industrial Lead Body, Key Stage 4, Manpower Services Commission, Market economics, NCVQ, Neo-conservatism, Neo-liberal, New Right, Ofsted, Social Welfare, Structural unemployment, TEED, Training agency, Utopian planning, Vocationalism, Welfare state, YTS

Please note: Although we have set aside this and the following chapter (12) to consider the process of meeting professional requirements, the actual standards for Key Area H are designed to be met through the production of evidence for the other Key Areas discussed in our earlier chapters. The standards for Key Area H and the specifications for **H1 working within a professional value base** *and* **H2 conforming to agreed codes of practice** *can be found at the end of Chapter 12. However, the evidence will be generated through your response to the previous seven Key Areas in addition to the activities both within this chapter and finally, in Chapter 12.*

Index to Chapter 11

Chapter 11 Activities designed to generate evidence against the Standards

Ref	Activity	Page	Ref	Activity	Page
H11a	Neo-liberal influences	318	H11e	Education, the market and the economy	326
H11b	Rejection of collectivism	319			
H11c	Market responses	320	H11f	Changes in employment practice	327
H11d	Employer involvement in PCET	321	H11g	Reducing competition	328
			H11h	Accountability influences	331

11.1 | INTRODUCTION

An important aspect of being an informed professional in any field is having an awareness of not only current policies and practices, but also how these developments were brought about. Those of us in education and training also need to consider their potential effect on our colleagues, our learners and ourselves. However, before we provide a résumé of critical events in post-compulsory education, it is worth noting that the Post-16 Sector has arguably been, and continues to be, the focus for more radical change than any other area of British educational provision. Although we do hope that what we report here may be an illuminating backdrop, it will inevitably be superseded by other developments, almost before the print has dried.

11.2 | THE POLITICAL BACKGROUND TO PRESENT INITIATIVES IN POST-COMPULSORY EDUCATION

In her Foreword to this book Kathryn Ecclestone has captured exactly the turbulent nature of our area of education. The Sector has at various times been called Further Education, Post-16, Learning and Skills or Post-Compulsory, and this variety of titles does seem to sum up one of our major dilemmas: the sector has become a catch-all for the increasing areas of provision which fall outside of the compulsory schooling and higher education remit and sometimes it is difficult to comprehend completely the full extent of these college and private training provider responsibilities.

Whereas the next (final) chapter will address current policies, this chapter must consider how *previous* political pressures and their related policies have helped to establish our present climate and related institutional cultures. For many of us the seismic changes we have experienced in education and many other aspects of modern life were initiated by the world crisis in capitalism symbolized by the oil shortages of 1973. In Britain this led, among other things, to an alarming escalation in the number of young unemployed and was a period when Harold Wilson and his Labour government first publicly linked education directly to the failing economy. One of Labour's early initiatives (in response to the youth unemployment crisis) was particularly significant. In 1974, with trade union support, they established the Manpower Services Commission (MSC) under the aegis of the Department of Employment. This involvement of the DoE was, allegedly, justified because the rapidly worsening situation made it vital that urgent action should be taken and there were real fears that the then Department of Education and Science's Inspectorate (HMI) had the power to slow down or sabotage any vocational innovation. Thus began the years of progressive reduction in the power of the DES, which led to the eventual amalgamation of Employment and Education in 1995.

In retrospect, this Labour initiative set the tone for the policies of the succeeding Conservative regime, in that it marked the upsurge in government of a view that the type of general 'liberal' education being provided to the 'non-academic' stream in secondary and further education was largely inappropriate, costly and a consequence of what Martin Wiener (1985) called 'academic drift'. Although he was more concerned with undergraduate destinations, Wiener's attitude represented a perspective which found much favour with ministers who were concerned at that time about the combined power of the DES, universities and the LEAs. Wiener (ibid.) went on to point out that since the middle of the nineteenth century, each attempt to give greater emphasis to science and technology in schools and to install more practical and relevant curricula had been undermined by academic values which promoted education for its own sake and continually edged out vocationally aimed initiatives. Wiener believed that this process was continued in, and indeed was led by the universities, which encouraged their best products to carry out postgraduate work and pursue academic rather than industrial or business careers.

11.3 | RETURN TO VOCATIONALISM

However, nationally during the early 1970s, there was a consensus emerging which was radically different to the traditional academic preference for a broader, liberal approach to education. These changing values marked the emphatic return of government educational policy to a model that had been so dominant in Britain during late 1800s and which focused primarily on preparing students for employment. James Callaghan, the then Labour Prime Minister initiated what was called the 'Great Debate' with his 1976 Ruskin speech which echoed Wiener's concerns that vocational pathways within education were being undermined for selfish purposes by academics:

> I am concerned on my journeys to find complaints from industry that new recruits from the schools sometimes do not have the basic tools to do the job that is required. I have been concerned to find that many of our best trained students who have completed the higher levels of education at university or polytechnic have no desire or

intention of joining industry. Their preferences are to stay in academic life (very pleasant I know) or to find their way into the civil service. There seems to be a need for a more technological bias in science teaching that will lead towards practical applications in industry rather than towards academic studies ... . There is no virtue in producing socially well adjusted members of society who are unemployed because they do not have the skills.

Leslie Bash (1985), commenting on this 'fallacious and facile link between education and unemployment', was one of the many members of the academic establishment who responded to this attempt to lay at the door of education the blame for the huge problem of youth unemployment which was facing the Labour administration at that time. Bash went on to point out that unemployment was generated, not by failures of the state education system, but by shifts in the national and international economy:

> When the economy had been growing, industry had had no difficulty in providing training it considered appropriate. No matter how well educated or well trained UK school leavers had been, the 1970s and 1980s would still have been periods of massive structural unemployment ... the possible point of application of ameliorative measures would have been the economy itself, not the education system.

There were also present at that time, within both main political parties, those who could see that a potentially expensive problem of unemployed youth could, when given the right training, provide a low-paid, flexible workforce which would not only reduce the unemployment problem, but would also provide an effective economic device that could reduce pay levels nationally.

Margaret Thatcher's arrival as Prime Minister in 1979 rapidly confirmed a much more robust challenge to the post-war consensus that had existed for over thirty years between the two main parties in government and opposition. The liberal, equality of opportunity values enshrined in the 'One-Nation' approach was abandoned and replaced by a more ideologically driven neo-liberal mind-set, which has since dominated UK politics and policies for more than twenty years. This emerging political attitude was expressed in the field of education by successive Conservative Secretaries of State for Education who turned to the 'new right' ideas of privatization with their themes choice, market forces and improving quality through competition. New Right pressure groups such as the Centre for Policy Studies, the National Council for Educational Standards, the Adam Smith Institute and the Institute of Economic Affairs also heavily influenced government educational thinking.

Their concepts and principles are made clear by Lawton's (1994) review of Conservative education legislation from 1979 to 1994. He identifies six clear political value positions:

- the desire for more selection
- the wish to return to more traditional curricula and teaching methods
- the desire to reduce the influence of experts and educational theory by encouraging common-sense, traditional practices
- an appeal to parental choice as a means of encouraging market forces
- a wish to reduce educational expenditure
- a process of increased centralization which had the additional purpose of reducing the power and autonomy of the LEAs

Although there were other possible approaches to the problem of unemployment, the neo-liberal, free-market approach to economic decisions (as opposed to intervention through investment) led the Tories to target vocational training as a central solution. The Department of Employment through the MSC (later the Training Commission, then the Training Agency and then TEED) was used systematically during the following years as a conduit for the huge investment in the training of the young unemployed. As we will see, ultimately this elevation of the DoE and the MSC also had the effect of reducing the influence of the DES, the LEAs, the universities, polytechnics and the teachers.

This process of gradually eroding power as opposed to more direct action was probably selected because the type of aggressive legislation we saw towards the latter end of the most recent Conservative government (and since the advent in 1997 of New Labour) was just not politically viable in the early 1980s. One reason was that established power bases were too strong to be challenged, the Labour government's apprehension about HMI influence has been mentioned, but also the LEAs were sufficiently confident to challenge the DES as demonstrated by the example of Tameside which won its battle against comprehensivization in 1976. In addition, by using the MSC (on the outside) the process of destabilizing the existing system could be effected more easily. The assault was two-pronged, coming overtly from the government through pressure by politicians and less obviously through policy documents issued by the MSC.

In summary, the Conservative, neo-liberal view was that economic and political decision-making and social welfare should not be subject to central management, but left to respond naturally to market competition based upon economic individualism and the privatized provision of services. They believed that theories, utopian planning, abstract ideas, generalizsations and intellectuals should not be trusted as it was ideologies such as these which led to the damaging educational innovations propagated during the 1960s. In their view such initiatives as 'curriculum reform', 'relevance' and 'child-centred' education had helped to undermine traditional educational values without providing any obvious benefit to the student. They urged the government to learn the harsh lessons of this period and continue to support the principle of a strong paternalistic control promoting a disciplined society, social authoritarianism, hierarchy and subordination. They accepted that individual freedom is important, but stressed that it should be locked into acceptance of government authority.

H11a Neo-liberal influences

Reflect on your own experience of education during the last twenty years and comment on how the above neo-liberal views and policies have influenced provision within your own particular context.

11.4 | MARKET ECONOMICS

Although within the Conservative government the views of the neo-liberal and neo-conservative factions differed on several issues, their positions on education displayed many similarities. Both were determined to address the same key concerns, such as the purpose of education, the design of the curriculum and the control of the providers, e.g. schools, colleges and universities. Each agreed that powerful bureaucratic interest groups, particularly LEAs and teachers, had created a mediocre education system where under-achievement and declining standards were commonplace. The Hillgate group (1987) set out to counter this perceived deterioration in educational standards through an aggressive criticism of the progressive and egalitarian views of education and supporting parental choice as a fundamental ingredient in developing an effective education system.

It is important to note that, while neo-conservatism was a social doctrine, neo-liberalism was an economic one embedded in the writings of the eighteenth-century classical economist Adam Smith and the modern Austrian economist Friedrich Hayek (1960). The conversion of many Conservative politicians to the political and economic theories of Hayek was to be one of Margaret Thatcher's most significant achievements and ultimately was the driving force of much of the educational change that followed.

Hayek appealed to conservatives because he was critical of socialism, state involvement in social welfare and of economic and social decisions being taken from a collectivist, consensus basis. Hayek had a radical alternative view that the uninhibited workings of the market provided a superior mechanism through which to structure the workings of the state. In his view, economic and political decision-making and social welfare should not be subject to central management, but left to respond naturally to market competition based upon economic individualism and the privatized provision of services. Hayek considered collectivist ideas and practices as a threat to freedom and prosperity and these sentiments were subsequently wholly supported by Thatcher and her government's policies.

H11b   Rejection of collectivism

Thatcher believed that the Second World War had created an environment that encouraged the establishment of 'collectives' and that it took thirty years to reduce their influence. Obviously, she was talking primarily about trade unions, but her notions of 'individual striving' as opposed to collaborative approaches do have real implications for education. Reflect on how these political and economic views are evident within post-compulsory education today.

Another recurring theme of Hayek's work has been that collectivist social planning is doomed to failure because society is complex, that the 'facts' that planners deal with are not concrete, but are based on human behaviour and relationships, which are unpredictable. As a consequence, in Hayek's view the free market is superior to any kind of planning for such things as full employment, a welfare state, economic targets and redistribution of income. Although Hayek's theories are highly appealing to neo-liberals, they are also fundamentally incompatible with the interventionist tendencies of the neo-conservatives. However, Thatcher managed to unite her party behind Hayek's simple philosophy that:

> The market mechanism is superior to all planning because it works automatically with a beautiful simplicity – if you leave it alone.

Hayek's economic theories are based on a deceptively simple view that we should not interfere with social institutions that have been established over time. His central example of this would be the 'market', which (in Hayek's view) is a perfect mechanism because it responds automatically to the free decisions of individuals. Hayek and his followers were opposed to economic intervention to achieve 'social justice' through a redistribution of wealth. Their key principle was that the financial rewards given to people through the operation of the market are generally a good indicator of their contribution. In other words, the efficient will prosper, while others will not. These theories heavily influenced government policy, as the neo-liberals supported the importance of relying upon market forces to determine policies and provision and therefore were suspicious of the state and supported minimal government intervention.

H11c Market responses

Hayek's theories are based on a view that, as many of the variables within the economy are unpredictable and cannot be controlled, so market forces should be allowed to manage these influences. However, as we have discussed in earlier chapters, there it also a range of unpredictable variables within *every* educational situation.

Consider how Hayek's theories translate to the classroom and the appropriateness of educational policies based on these market principles.

One implication of the above policies was that education and other areas of public service were now seen as a *commodity* to be bought and sold in the marketplace. Another was that curricula within education should stress the importance of free-market ideas such as competition, choice and enterprise. Neo-conservatives, in particular those who belonged to the Hillgate group (1987), supported an agenda based on elitism, central control of education, a traditional curriculum and cultural heritage, all of which were viewed as crucial to social and economic well-being.

11.5 | THE RE-ORIENTATION OF FURTHER EDUCATION

Meanwhile, the extent of 'educational' initiatives relating to the young unemployed that were being delivered through the Department of Employment had grown rapidly since the creation of the MSC in 1974. By the mid–1980s much of the funding received by Further Education colleges was coming through the DoE. The training of the young was formalized in 1985, when the White Paper, *Education and Training for Young People* (DES 1985) recommended the establishment of the National Council for Vocational Qualifications (NCVQ) to tackle the issue of parity of esteem. The NCVQ's brief was to provide a more coherent and fair award system and they initiated the design of a national framework of vocational qualifications (NVQs). Using newly created Industrial Lead Bodies (which were heavily influenced by employers) the detailed specification of national standards of occupational competence to meet the needs of employees began in earnest (see also Chapter 9).

This framework was designed to support college, training agency and in-company based training as part of the strategy to reduce both youth unemployment and, perhaps more importantly, the burden on the taxpayer. To this end the use of private managing agents for YTS courses based in the employers' premises, rather than FE colleges, reflected the government's preference for private enterprise and its desire to use the private sector to encourage competition and make college provision more efficient and cost-effective. The use of short-term contracts by the MSC to fund the delivery of YTS courses in further education was also intended to promote efficiency.

H11d   Employer involvement in PCET

These mid-1980s' initiatives to pass more responsibility for vocational education to the employers (see also the ERA below) have had variable success during the last two decades. Comment on the employer influence on post-compulsory education and training within your particular educational setting.

The process of centralizing education was finally given full rein in the 1988 Education Reform Act, which gave an unprecedented amount of control (more than 400 additional powers) to the Secretary of State for Education. Speaking against the Bill (introduced by his own party) at its second reading in the Commons, former Prime Minister Edward Heath said:

> The Secretary of State has taken more powers under the Bill than any other member of the Cabinet, more than my right honourable friends the Chancellor of the Exchequer, the Secretary of State for Defence and the Secretary of State for Social Services.

The Act transferred polytechnics and major colleges of higher education out of LEA control, proposed financial delegation and self-government for LEA Colleges of Further Education and completely abolished the Inner London Education Authority.

To the government this was removing power from unrepresentative and over-bureaucratic local authorities to make services more responsive to the consumer. Many critics interpreted it as an attempt to increase the power of central government at the expense of democratically elected local councils that had dared to resist the worst excesses of Thatcherism.

The concept of City Technology Colleges (CTCs) 'responsive to the changing demands of adult and working life in an advanced industrial society' was supported. In the schools sector, the National Curriculum for the 5–16 age group was introduced with a core of maths, English and science with foundation subjects of history, geography, technology, music, art and physical education. The Secretary of State was also given the power to shape the foundation subjects by specifying attainment targets, programmes of study and assessment arrangements.

The Local Management of Schools arrangement included in the Act, removed decision-making from LEA members and officers and delegated it instead to governors and head teachers. In addition, the Act contained an 'opting out' clause which allowed governors of any maintained secondary school or primary school of over 300 pupils to apply to the Secretary of State to opt out of LEA control and become a centrally funded grant-maintained school. Also 'open enrolment' to secondary schools was introduced which did away with planned admission levels (PALs) and introduced a free-market philosophy allowing parents to seek out the better schools.

On the face of it the 1988 Education Act was dedicated to market philosophy in that it sought to move the control of education from those considered to be the producers (teachers and LEAs) to those considered to be the consumers (parents and employers). Thus the intended outcome was that education should be able to deliver what the customers demands. However, this free-market approach was initiated and controlled by centralist policies concerned with establishing a more coordinated system of education and training designed to meet the challenge of foreign competition. This contradiction subsequently fuelled criticism even from the right of the Conservative party. In particular, the Institute of Economic Affairs expressed concern about educational policies which restrict the freedom of the individual to pursue his or her own ends and which were introduced by a government acting in a restrictive, anti-market manner.

However, the Educational Reform Act, as radical as it was, didn't see an end to the centralist legislation imposed by the Conservatives. Further double-barrelled, radical legislation introduced in May 1991 marked an even more significant tightening of government control. Michael Howard, the Secretary of State for Employment presented the White Paper *Education and Training for the 21st Century* following Kenneth Clarke, the Secretary of Sate for Education and Science, who had earlier presented another White Paper *Higher Education: A New Framework*. The latter's proposed legislation abolished the binary line and established a single framework for higher education that contained universities, polytechnics and colleges of higher education, together with a common funding structure administered by a Higher Education Funding Council. This White Paper emphasized that:

> by the year 2000, the Government expects that approaching one in three of all 18–19 year olds will enter higher education.

Although this target was not achieved, the years since the Act have seen a massive expansion of the HE sector involving most HEIs in doubling their student numbers and some achieving three times the intake.

Education and Training for the 21st Century (Volumes 1 and 2) proposed the establishment of a 'new' sector of education comprising all colleges of further education and some sixth-form colleges which was to be under the aegis of a Central Council. Once sixth-form colleges, tertiary and FE colleges had been removed from LEA control by the Act, they went through a process of 'incorporation' that established them as self-managing institutions with a governing board (corporation) under the day-to-day control of a principal (chief executive). The majority of governors were drawn from the local business community and there was no statutory requirement for LEA involvement.

The legislation also proposed the introduction of the General National Vocational Qualification and the Further Education Funding Council was set up to finance the newly independent colleges. Their income was to be dependent on meeting set performance targets relating to recruitment, retention and achievement and, if these were not met, the college would face financial penalties. The Secretary of State was given reserve powers to ensure that colleges and schools offer only NVQs to students pursuing vocational options. Colleges within the sector were formula-funded using FTEs and performance indicators to arrive at the level of income.

The open enrolment provisions further promoted the notion of 'commodification' in an education 'market' by encouraging parental choice. The per capita funding arrangements meant that schools attracting more pupils received more funding, whereas those with fewer pupils got less. The creation of grant-maintained schools and city technology colleges also increased parental power, encouraged schools towards market competition and increased the influence of the business community in educational affairs.

Even after Margaret Thatcher was replaced as Prime Minister in November 1990, liberal views on education continued to be influential. Ken Clarke, Major's first Secretary of State, reiterated that choice and competition were necessary to raise standards, a view also supported in his successor's White Paper, *Choice and Diversity*, (DES, 1992). The Act established Ofsted, privatized inspection teams to replace the HMI system, and school league tables were introduced to aid parental choice.

It was also extremely significant that the above two 1991 White Papers were published under the logo of both the DES and the DoE and were presented jointly to the House of Commons by the Secretaries of State for Employment and Education. This strategy heralded the amalgamation of these two departments five years later and clearly confirmed that, in future, the key performance indicator for a successful education system will be *full employment*.

The 'education utility' principle, that was re-established by Callaghan in 1976 and which infers that there should be a direct correlation between investment in education and the performance of the national economy, now seems to have been firmly accepted by both major political parties.

However, these notions and the related market principles have received much opposition. Lawton (1994) argues that market choice has failed in improving educational standards and sees the market as inappropriate for the education service in principle as well as practice:

> as schooling is compulsory, 'perfect competition' is completely lacking, and there is not even a price mechanism available to regulate supply and demand. It is a rigged market non-market. We end up with the worst of both worlds – a confused mixture of compulsion and competition, with more demand for choice than can possibly be supplied. In education, the idea of a market is a non-starter; pretending that real choice exists for most parents is dishonest.

The Institute of Public Policy Research (1998) have also offered some very basic and fundamental criticisms of the prevailing view that Britain's future economic prosperity is dependent upon raising standards of reading, writing and arithmetic in schools. Although ministers have set ambitious targets to improve the literacy and numeracy of 11-year-olds in the belief that this would lay the groundwork for more effective competition with the tiger economies of the Pacific rim, the IPPR have said that there was no evidence that boosting national attainment in maths or literacy would have any effect on national economic performance:

> What could be a sober and informed debate about English education is in danger of being drowned out by the simplistic and often shrill rhetoric which seems to dominate policy-making in education. Ministers are misled by the 'tyranny' of international league tables ... but there was no correlation between positions in the international

maths league and economic prosperity as measured by GNP per head. Former Eastern bloc countries such as the Czech and Slovak Republics and Bulgaria performed well in maths without reaping an economic dividend.

The report went on to state that although the United States and Germany were more economically prosperous, their students were close to England's in maths results and that Britain's growth rate compared reasonably well with other countries at a similar stage of economic development.

Charles Bailey (1989), investigated many aspects of economic utility and identified characteristics of burgeoning 'new vocationalism' which were contradictory and undemocratic and, although not always articulated, were nevertheless implicit within the criteria used in the criticism of education. In his view these criticisms are, more often than not, based on invalid conceptions of the role of education and the implicit view that there is a universally accepted consensus:

> For a pupil to complain that his education is not relevant to the job he wants to do, or fails to equip him to face unemployment, is to assume that education has a proper instrumental purpose that it has failed to fulfil.

> For a prime minister to chide the system for failing to produce the scientists and technologists the country needs is to assume that the education system has manpower provision responsibilities that it is neglecting.

> For a politician to complain that the education system allows pupils to leave school with unfavourable attitudes towards wealth creation or technological growth or competition is to suggest that there are proper attitudes for an education system to foster.

Bailey believes that running through all the discussion of the economic utility model of education is an unspoken assumption that there is consensus about society, values and education. As an example he quotes a 1982 DES report, which stated:

> It has in recent years become a 'truth universally acknowledged' that education should be more closely linked with the world of work and with the country's economic performance; and there has been increasing pressure on schools to assess the relevance of their curriculum to their pupils' future working lives.

In Bailey's view, this assumed consensus is that of

> Continually accepted technological change and development, strangely related to nineteenth-century conceptions of the undoubted good of 'progress', all taking place in the context of a competitive free market economy, and in a wider context of international competitive trade.

Bailey's key point is that these objectives (wealth, competition, technological change, etc.) are perceived as ends in themselves and not as a means to an end. He also challenges the notions that promotion of competition and technological advances are necessarily compatible or advantageous. Historically, technological advance has often led to the elimination of skills, and competition the elimination of collaborative development.

Bailey also points out that such is the pace of technological change that vocational training is often out of date by the time the trainee is admitted to the workplace. The more specific the skills, the shorter their useful life.

Also of concern is the shallow nature of the generic skills which are advocated within many vocational programmes. These are seen as often being either hopelessly vague or absolutely trivial. In Bailey's view not only is it impossible to teach skills outside of their particular context, but it is also impossible to define them in abstract or to generalize them. More importantly, Bailey sees the practice of disaggregating knowledge and understanding from the acquisition of skills as undemocratic because

> only knowledge and understanding on a wide base can liberate a person from the particular restrictions of birth, social class and geography. Without such a base any choices are bound to be restricted because of the limited perspective brought to bear on them.

Bailey finishes by making the point that only a liberal education will prepare a person for the necessarily unpredictable and problematic nature of work because such an education provides an introduction to a range of cognitive perspectives and practice in creative thinking and problem-solving. Finally, perhaps the most telling analysis of the incompatibility between the market model and education was made by a Canadian philosopher, John McMurtry (1991). Based around the goals, motivations, methods and quality processes of both education and the market, his detailed analysis of the underlying conflict between the *principles* of these two approaches, does provide us with some extremely valuable insights. His contrasting findings are summarized in Table 11.1 below:

Table 11.1 John McMurtry's summary of the incompatibility of educational and market principles

Process	Principles	
	The market is about:	Education is concerned to:
Goals	Maximizing private money profits	Advance and disseminate shared knowledge
Motivations	Satisfying whoever has the money to purchase the goods that are wanted	Develop sound understanding whether it is wanted or not
Methods	Buying and selling the goods it has to offer to anyone for whatever price that can be achieved	Never buy or sell the item it has to offer, but to require of all who would have it that they fulfill its requirements autonomously
Quality	Excellence which can be measured by a) *how well a product is made* b) *how problem-free the product is and remains*	Provide excellence which can be measured by a) *how disinterested and impartial its representations are* b) *how deep and broad the problems it poses are to the one who receives it*

H11e Education, the market and the economy

Reflect on the relevance of the above views on market approaches and the relationship of education to the national economy with particular reference to your own educational situation.

Of course, the crucial implication of McMurtry's analysis is that, although teaching may be treated as a 'commodity', you cannot buy or sell *learning* and the creation of knowledge and its dissemination (the traditional purpose of education) is in direct opposition to the market principle that success within a competitive environment is dependent upon the 'ownership' and restricted distribution of knowledge.

11.6 TENSIONS WITHIN POST-COMPULSORY EDUCATION

During the nineties, the government's strategy for Further Education has been designed to increase student numbers, while simultaneously lowering funding costs. Indeed, from 1993 to 1998 student numbers in FE did increase by a third and Smithers and Robinson (2000) note that during the same period funding in real terms fell by 21 per cent. As was inevitable under such a scenario, college managers were faced with extremely difficult decisions, some of which challenged their concepts of good professional practice, both in terms of educational processes and staff management. However, in order to survive within this demanding environment it has been necessary for college managers to respond quickly and effectively to the continuously imposed central control mechanisms that have been implemented by succeeding governments. As a consequence, most post-compulsory educational organizations have resorted to a more hierarchical management style, which has often been fairly aggressive in the way it has operated and in its relationship with staff.

As labour costs usually represent the largest outgoings of any service organization (especially in the public sector), a drive by management to promote 'greater efficiency' in order to minimize costs and maximize income, became inevitable. College managers, encouraged by the College Employers' Forum (CEF) sought to replace the 'silver book' conditions for staff with college contracts that would allow for the greater 'productivity' by increasing teaching hours, reducing holiday entitlement and removing reduced class contact (RCC). Some colleges have also introduced bars within their salary scales and have replaced lecturers with assessors and facilitators on lower levels of pay. 'Efficiency gains' have also been achieved through a general move across the sector towards 'casualization', which has seen a decrease in the number of full-time salaried teaching staff, accompanied by a commensurate increase in hourly paid staff. In some cases these staff are employed by 'agencies'.

The ways in which learning is delivered have also allowed managers to make savings, for example a greater use of 'flexi-learning' has made possible significant reductions in class contact hours. As you would expect, all of the above management initiatives designed to enable survival under incorporation, have inevitably led to claims of de-professionalization and de-skilling.

H11f   Changes in employment practice

Discuss the current relationship between management and teachers within your own situation and how this affects teaching and learner support.

Analysis by many writers including Longhurst (1996) confirmed that the market principles, together with incorporation processes had created antagonistic relationships between college teaching staff and managers:

> the relationship between senior management and teaching staff in colleges is now one of exploitation This is just as surely the case as in a business firm where the profits of shareholders and the large salaries of senior managers are obtained by paying other employees less than the value of the commodities they produce.

Bill Stubbs, then Chief Executive of the Further Education Funding Council (FEFC), warned that the incorporation process would provide further education college managers with the opportunity to either prosper or go bankrupt and the year on year reduction in the unit of funding has undoubtedly created severe hardship for many staff and extremely difficult decisions for the executive managers of most institutions.

11.7 THE ADVENT OF NEW LABOUR

Since their success in the 1997 general election, New Labour have continued with many of the market-led policies established by their Conservative predecessors. Their justification has been that the power of the global market and their pledge to stay within the previous government's spending plans have left them with little choice but to continue with many of the Tory policies. However, some identifiable 'New Labour' policies did also emerge during the early years of this government. Perhaps their most notable concern, which has immediate relevance for the post-compulsory sector, is their focus on the education of the less academic 14–19 year olds, which has been a significant educational issue with various governments since the 1960s.

While in opposition in 1996, David Blunkett, the new Labour minister, acknowledged and to some extent supported Dearing's (1996) report *Review of Qualifications for 16–19 year olds* which identified a number of themes (i.e. low participation and achievement rates, high drop-out rates, variable standards and limited scope for broadly based curriculum and study). Once in office, Labour published *Qualifying for Success* (DfEE, 1997) that built on the agenda established by Dearing and aimed to raise and widen levels of participation, retention and achievement.

However, New Labour's social democratic values were evident here in their expressed intent to combat social exclusion and disaffection. Other New Labour themes, which became evident towards the millennium, were:

- social cohesion
- economic competitiveness
- up-skilling
- partnership
- widening participation
- lifelong learning

Within three months of taking office, the £3.5 billion New Deal scheme was launched to address the continuing problem of young unemployed (i.e. 18 to 24 year-olds) with the Investing in Young People Strategy (IiYP) outlined in *The Learning Age: a Renaissance for a New Britain* (DfEE, 1998a). This Green Paper is aimed at increasing the number of young people achieving at qualification framework level 2 and to ensure that all young people have the skills necessary for lifelong learning and employability.

The above paper makes clear New Labour's emphasis on the use of education and training to get people off welfare and into work and it is also evident that further education has a major role to play in helping to deliver the new government's intentions. High profile is given to Labour's twin aims of tackling *social exclusion and up-skilling* (in order to make Britain more competitive) in the significant White Paper *Further Education for the New Millennium* (DfEE, 1998b):

> The report sets out a radical vision to engage and draw back into learning those who have traditionally not taken advantage of educational opportunities – in particular, those with no or inadequate qualifications. For these people, continuing or returning to learning offers the prospect of breaking out of the cycle of economic and social exclusion.

It is also clear that the government are unhappy with the level of petty competition which existed between many colleges when they took office. Within the above paper they are urging the re-development of partnerships in order to achieve its defined goals and offering an implicit criticism of the wasteful Conservative reliance on competitive, market-led strategies as a means of deliberately deterring any collaboration between providers:

> We are also placing a new emphasis on partnerships within the sector, to reduce waste caused by unnecessary competition and to ensure that the sector is better placed to meet future challenges. (DfEE, 1998b)

H11g Reducing competition

Reflect on the levels of competition and cooperation which you have experienced in your particular post-compulsory educational context and the effect these influences might have on the development and provision of teaching and learning.

However, despite New Labour's criticism of the aggressive managerialist approaches which had been encouraged by the previous administration, there has been no hint of them moving away from the outcomes-based funding and inspection procedures which have caused so much stress within colleges. Although the FE funding has increased since 1997, additional money has to be 'something for something'. For example links have to be made to raising standards, widening participation, etc. and, as Smithers and Robinson (ibid) have pointed out, even where improved funding is based on anticipated increases in student numbers, an efficiency gain of 1–2 percentage per year is still expected.

In order to promote further social cohesion, Labour have established a Social Exclusion Unit directly accountable to the Prime Minister. The unit published their report *Bridging the Gap: New Opportunities for 16–18 year olds not in Education, Employment or Training* (July 1999) which reported that the most potent indicator of unemployment at 21 is non-participation for six months or more between 16 and 18 years old. A White Paper published the same year, *Learning to Siucceed: A New Framework for Post–16 Learning* (DfEE, 1999) follows up this aim of persuading young people to stay in education or training until at least 18 years of age.

Tackling low education levels has always been a concern for the political left in its quest for a more egalitarian society. New Labour recognize that a lack of basic skills in numeracy and literacy have marginalized a section of society, reinforced social exclusion and have had a negative impact on the UK's competitiveness. Their policy and legislative output since coming to office has undoubtedly taken a different direction to the previous government, a change which has been positively welcomed even by some groups critical of New Labour inertia in post-compulsory education.

> NATFHE (2002) strongly support lifelong learning and the government's agenda for the new learning and skills sector – so vital to a thriving economy and inclusive and participative society.

The current government has moved away from the Tories' market-led policies to a more marked reliance on strategic planning, especially at the regional level through the Learning and Skills Councils. This more collaborative strategy, linked to a greater commitment to lifelong learning and social inclusion, represent the clearest departure from the Conservative approach. Even so, after almost six years in office, many commentators are wondering whether New Labour reforms within PCET have been sufficiently robust.

Colleges are still incorporated, there has not been a departure from the policy of funding convergence, there is still widespread casualization, there are no national conditions of service or agreed annual salary reviews for staff working in the sector. Although additional money has been provided (usually dependent on colleges meeting certain government targets) there has been little in terms of structural reform. The real challenge is to reform the funding system, provide a better infrastructure and significantly improve resources in the sector.

Supporters of the government's approach would point out that the pace of change has been slow because of the problems inherited from eighteen years of Tory rule, such as social exclusion and chronic under-funding. Also trying to effect cultural change in the drive to make lifelong learning an integral part of the education system is a long-term strategy rather than a short-term aim.

11.8 TOWARDS A 14 TO 19 FRAMEWORK

However, there is definite evidence within the DfES of a will to establish equivalence of salaries and transferability of staff between the post-compulsory and compulsory sectors. This development will, of course, be expensive (as currently, further education staff are paid much less than their primary and secondary counterparts) and will certainly depend on how well PCET responds to the current government proposals to reform education and training for 14 to 19 year olds.

In February 2002, Estelle Morris (then Secretary of State) pointed out in her introduction to Labour's consultation document, *14–19:Extending Opportunities, Raising Standards*, that at the end of 2000 only three out of four 16 to 18 year olds in England were in education and training, which was well below European and OECD average. Also, in 2001, around 5 per cent of young people did not get any GCSEs at all and, although the proportion of Year 11 students gaining five or more A to C grades at GCSE had risen dramatically since the early 1990s, it still remained at only around 50 per cent of the cohort. Perhaps what was more worrying was the fact that only 20 per cent of young people from the lower socio-economic groups go on to some form of higher education, as compared to 70 per cent from the higher socio-economic groups.

These figures are particularly significant, when set against New Labour's much-publicized intention to increase and broaden participation in higher education so that (by 2010) 50 per cent of young people aged between 18 and 30 will go on to university, with access widened in particular for those whose families have no previous experience of higher education.

The authors of the Green Paper point out that there are many conflicting pressures on young people aged between 14 and 19 and that the price of disengagement from learning is often lifelong failure. Young people may be more autonomous and independent than were their parents and grandparents and consequently seem to demand more from their education and training. There is much evidence that they are prepared to reject what they do not like and what does not meet their immediate requirements. However, they can also find the world and their role in it more complex and confusing.

As we have pointed out in earlier chapters, between the ages of 14 and 19, young people are striving to develop and make sense of their personal, sexual and social identities. They are often demanding and assertive, and yet, because they lack self-confidence, they need our support and guidance to help them take advantage of their educational opportunities (see Chapters 7 and 8).

In essence, these New Labour proposals outline a systematic restructuring of Key Stage 4 of the National Curriculum to order to provide 'progression and differentiation for all' as suggested in the 1994 Dearing Review. It is proposed that, from September 2004, the new Key Stage 4 will consist of mathematics, English, science and ICT alongside citizenship, religious education, careers education, sex education, physical education and work-related learning. Modern foreign languages and design and technology will no longer be 'required study' for all students; but they will join the arts and humanities as subjects where, in the words of the Green Paper, there will be 'a new statutory entitlement of access'.

Unfortunately, the Green Paper also promises that 'targets and performance tables will continue to play an important role in driving up standards'. Many believe that this continuation of the New Right accountability mindset is likely to undermine New Labour's espoused policy of tackling social exclusion and disadvantage, improving skills, partnership and lifelong learning with a group of learners (less academic 14 to 19 year olds) whose needs (according to the Green Paper) we have failed to address adequately for the last 50 years.

On the basis of past and present experience, by their very nature, accountability systems inevitably adopt a 'reliability' approach (see Chapter 9) where the need for replication and consistency across the sector does, unfortunately, lead to the use of simplified criteria as the measurable outcomes. However, such crude measures will be significantly more inappropriate when the outcomes, which teachers must define (during their attempts to motivate traditionally reluctant learners) will tend to be short-term and unique to particular students within a specific context. Such bespoke targets have an inherent validity because they are attempting to restructure in a particular way unique and previously damaged self-concepts.

In addition, performance tables inevitably lead to the identification of achievement (and underachievement) not only by the institution, but also by the department and the individual. Such strategies stimulate aggressive competition both at an institutional and an individual level, which will often have been one of the reasons why these learners withdrew from an active participation in education in the first place.

The need for a continuation of this accountability burden has not been justified and is simply not appropriate to the very difficult task that lies ahead for PCET and may well discourage both the learner and the teacher. This long-awaited restructured Key Stage 4 has the potential to achieve so much more. As Denis Lawton (2002) points out:

> The time has surely come for a clear policy on education based on co-operation not competition, social justice not selfish individualism, excellent schools for all not selection justified in terms of diversity and choice. Only then will it be possible to rely more on professional trust instead of technicist accountability.

H11h   Accountability influences

Consider the above points of view related to targets and performance tables and discuss how they have affected your own teaching and the experience of your learners.

11.9 | CONCLUSION

This chapter has been a brief résumé of changes, which have taken place within post-compulsory education during the last thirty years. We have stressed throughout this book that the sector is constantly evolving and that these changes have inevitably created particular stress for both teachers and learners within PCET.

The advent of the 14 to 19 curriculum promises to broaden the role of further education even more, but may also bring with it more stability and recognition for our sector. It is clear that the development of a diversified Key Stage 4 has the potential to provide appropriate progression routes for many different 14 to 19 learners. We will be faced with developing this diversified provision through the wide range of teaching, learning and support that such a complex and demanding innovation will require.

The early part of the twenty-first century promises a continuation of the hugely demanding process of change and innovation to which post-compulsory education has responded so well during the last thirty years. However, there is evidence that the important work of the sector will begin to be more appropriately recognized and rewarded. In the final chapter we will discuss some of the ways of gathering from our practice appropriate data, which may be used as evidence of continuing professional development. In this way, we will improve our chances of receiving the rewards we have earned.

11.10 | USEFUL SOURCES

Dale, R. (1989) *The State and Education Policy*. Milton Keynes. Open University Press.
Although this text is dated, Roger Dale's book remains a fine example of an analysis of the influence of government policies in shaping British educational provision. A critical introduction by Michael Apple provides an insight into how ideological stances affect objective decision-making and shape policy.

Lawton, D. (1994) *The Tory Mind on Education 1979–94*. London: The Falmer Press.
As the title implies, Denis Lawton examines the values and beliefs underpinning the educational policies of the Conservative government up until 1994. Although now somewhat dated, it is extremely valuable to be able to understand the origins of many of the policies which were developed by the Tories, but are still much in evidence within the present administration.

Matheson, C. and Matheson, D. (2000) *Educational Issues in the Learning Age*. London: Continuum. Catherine and David Matheson have edited a selection of papers which examine the role of education within a rapidly changing world. Education and its influence on culture, identity, society and power are considered within the context of postmodernism and globalization.

Whitty, G. (2002) *Making Sense of Educational Policy*. London: Paul Chapman. This excellent review by Geoff Whitty of education in relation to social theory places the policies of the New Right and New Labour within the context of significant, national educational issues and provides insightful analysis of how the different approaches to managing provision have evolved.

Hutton, W. (1995) *The State We're In* and (1997) *The State to Come*. London: Random House.
In these two examinations of Tory economic policy Will Hutton provides a searching indictment of the social effects of a free market and globalization and puts forward a strong argument for an alternative economic strategy as a basis for social justice.

Try *tipcet.com* for a range of materials and suggested sources related to post-compulsory educational policy and issues.

Meeting professional requirements Part 2: Codes of practice in post-compulsory education

Fred Fawbert

Key Area H Working within a professional value base to agreed codes of professional practice – standards and accountability within the Post 16/ FE Sector

Key concepts in this chapter

Code of Practice, Common Inspection Framework, GTC, Key Skills, Occupational Standards, Ofsted, Personal Code, Professional Value Base, QCA, Teacher Profile

*Please note: Although we have set aside this and the previous chapter (11) to consider the process of meeting professional requirements, the actual standards for Key Area H are designed to be met through the production of evidence for the other Key Areas discussed in our earlier chapters. The standards for Key Area H and the specifications for **H1 working within a professional value base** and **H2 conforming to agreed codes of practice** can be found at the end of this chapter. However, the evidence will be generated through your response to the previous seven Key Areas in addition to the activities both within Chapter 11 and in this chapter.*

Index to Chapter 12

12.10	Specification of Key Area 'H' FENTO Standards (Units H1 and H2) and the relevance of evidence generated through various chapter activities	359

Chapter 12 Activities designed to generate evidence against the Standards

Ref	Activity	Page	Ref	Activity	Page
H12a	Key Skills	336	H12d	Explicit values	352
H12b	Comparable codes	351	H12e	Value decisions	353
H12c	Difficult articulation	352	H12f	Profile entries	353

12.1 | INTRODUCTION

As we have mentioned many times in our earlier chapters, we all currently work within a culture of overt accountability. Although we have indicated our concerns about the effects that such regimes can have on teaching and learning, the very structure of this book does make clear that we have accepted these processes. On the whole, we feel that the various imposed standards have helped us move towards a more consistent and professional approach to post-compulsory education. We also believe that, although the externally devised criteria provided may sometimes seem constraining or irrelevant, their articulation does provide a valuable benchmark and a focus for debate and development.

However, ultimately the demands of our own professional development must take us beyond prescription. In order to become autonomous as teachers we should be able to set our own standards and also be willing to move beyond discretionary effort towards setting new and more demanding levels of performance. We must accept that these higher levels of teacher/learner interaction cannot be anticipated or articulated with any precision because, in such cases, the teacher will provide a unique, context-specific response to particular learner needs.

We hope that our earlier chapters may have helped to develop the insights and values that will bring about such a truly professional reaction. What we are doing is *building upon* familiar standards. Rather than slavishly meeting the learning outcomes, we are looking to interpret and extend them within each particular learning situation. Professional autonomy cannot be just about replicating knowledge; it must involve developing new knowledge to meet the needs of evolving situations.

12.2 | CODES OF PRACTICE

Our introductory discussion above indicates that when we are meeting professional requirements we are involved in two differing codes of practice. On the one hand there are the overt codes, which are made explicit by a professional regulating body. The FENTO occupational standards would be a good example of such a code, as we have shown within earlier chapters they have been carefully articulated to ensure that teachers within further education meet the agreed requirements at each of three different stages. In this chapter we will map the existing FENTO standards to other codes of practice. However, this process can only be indicative as we must expect any set of standards to change and develop over time. In addition to FENTO, in this chapter we will discuss other standards such as the Key

Skills requirements, the Ofsted implementation of the Common Inspection Framework and the General Teaching Council Code of Practice.

In contrast to these explicit standards, we will also consider more implicit codes which individual teachers and groups of academics accept but do not necessarily express in any tangible form. An example of this could be acceptable but covert codes of dress for themselves and their students. Another will be the language that is used between teacher and taught. Nowhere is acceptable language or the forms of dress defined and yet most members of staff subscribe to these agreed principles and the students also understand the implications of a particular tone or the use of a specific phrase. As with formal standards, these implicit requirements are based on and represent particular values and purposes. So, although much of this chapter will be concerned with explicit codes of practice, it is likely that the implicit, personal standards will be equally, if not more important to all teachers. At the forefront of such standards will be the teacher's own conception of what represents effective teaching, learning and learner support.

We will start with four examples of formal codes of practice and finish the chapter by considering some possible steps towards attempting an articulation of your own values and the collection of evidence, which demonstrates how these values are being sustained and promoted.

12.3 KEY SKILLS

The Qualifications and Curriculum Authority (QCA) developed Key Skills Qualifications and have established five levels, with levels 2 and 3 being those most relevant for teachers in post-compulsory education.

The six key skills are:

- communication
- application of number
- information technology
- working with others
- improving own learning and performance
- problem-solving

It is possible to integrate Key Skills within most programmes and to identify ways in which evidence can be generated at the appropriate level. Obviously, it is important that teachers not only develop evidence of their own Key Skills, but also identify ways in which they can encourage their own learners to develop theirs. Below you will find guidelines on the evidence required for each of the six Key Skills and, although these notes are not definitive, we feel that they should help you to identify the processes and activities in which you are involved, which can successfully be developed in order to apply for accreditation. To help this process we list in Table 12.1 below some of the Activities within each chapter that may be used as a basis for Key Skills evidence. In addition, you could draw on your commentaries in the Personal Development Journal together with records from your Practitioner File of Teaching Observations, Lesson Plans, Rationales, Self-Evaluations, etc.

H12a   Key Skills

Select one of the six Key Skills and consider the requirements detailed within the particular table below. Next check within Table 12.1 the recommended chapter activities, which should provide some evidence against the Key Skill. If you have completed the chapter activities or some similar form of evidence generation, you could write a linking commentary and check with your Key Skills coordinator what additional information may be needed.

Level 3   Key Skills in Communication

You will show that you can:

Contribute to discussions	Give a short talk/ presentation	Read and synthesize information	Write different types of documents
By achieving the following contributory sub-skills			
Vary how and when you participate to suit your purpose and the situation	Prepare the presentation to suit your purpose	Find and skim-read extended documents, such as textbooks, secondary sources, articles and reports, to identify relevant material	Select appropriate forms of presenting information to suit your purpose
Listen and respond sensitively and develop points and ideas	Match your language and style to suit the complexity of the subject, the formality of the situation and the needs of the audience	Scan and read the material to find the specific information you need	Select appropriate styles to suit the degree of formality required and nature of the subject
Make openings to encourage others to contribute	Structure what you say	Use appropriate sources of reference to help you to understand complex lines of reasoning and information from text and images	Organize material coherently
	Use techniques to engage the audience, including images	Compare accounts and recognize opinion and possible bias	Make meaning clear by writing, proof-reading and re-drafting documents so that spelling, punctuation and grammar are accurate
		Synthesize the information you have obtained for a purpose	

Level 2   Key Skills in Application of Number

You will show that you can:

Interpret information	Carry out calculations	Interpret results and present your findings
By achieving the following contributory sub-skills		
Obtain relevant information from different sources	Show clearly your methods of carrying out calculations and give the level of accuracy of your results	Select effective ways to present your findings
Read and understand graphs, tables, charts and diagrams	Carry out calculations involving two or more steps, with numbers of any size	Construct and use graphs, charts and diagrams and follow accepted conventions for labelling these
Read and understand numbers used in different ways, including negative numbers	Convert between fractions, decimals and percentages	Highlight the main points of your findings and describe your methods
Estimate amounts and proportions	Convert measurements between systems	Explain how the results of calculations meet the purpose of your activity
Read scales on a range of equipment to given levels of accuracy	Work out areas and volumes	
Select appropriate methods for obtaining the results you need, including grouping data when this is appropriate	Work out dimensions from scale drawings	
	Use proportion and calculate using ratios where appropriate	
	Compare sets of data with a minimum of 20 items	
	Use range to describe the spread within sets of data	
	Understand and use given formulae	
	Check your methods in ways that pick up faults and make sure your results make sense	

Level 3 Key Skills in Information Technology		
You will show that you can:		
Plan and select information	Develop information	Present information
By achieving the following contributory sub-skills		
Plan a substantial activity by breaking it down into a series of tasks	Enter and bring together information in a consistent form and use automated routines	Develop and structure your presentation and use the views of others to guide refinements
Compare the advantages and limitations of different sources of information and select those suitable for your purpose	Create and use structures and procedures for developing text, images and numbers	Develop and refine the presentation of text, images and numbers
Choose appropriate techniques for finding information and use them to carry out effective searches	Explore information	Present information so that it meets your purpose and the needs of the audience
Make selections based on relevance to your purpose and judgements on quality	Derive new information	Ensure work is accurate and makes sense
	Use methods of exchanging information to support your purpose	

You will also need to know:
The implications of using IT, comparing your use of IT with systems used elsewhere, when it is necessary to observe copyright or confidentiality, how to save your work for easy retrieval, how to manage versions and avoid loss, how to identify errors and their causes and minimize risk from viruses and how to work safely and minimize health risks.

Level 3 Key Skills in Working with others		
You will show that you can		
Work with others to plan complex work	Work with others to achieve agreed objectives	Review your work with others
By achieving the following contributory sub-skills		
Offer your own suggestions and show you are listening to others' views, in order to agree realistic objectives for working together	Obtain and make best use of resources, include support from others	Agree on the extent to which work with others has been successful and objectives have been met
Identify the resources, timescales and action needed to achieve the objectives	Organize and pace your work to meet deadlines and produce the quality of work required	Identify factors that have influenced the outcome

Agree responsibilities, including ways in which different roles could contribute to a successful outcome based on appropriate evidence	Work in a way that is safe for you and others	Agree ways of improving work with others in the future
Agree suitable working arrangements with those involved	Seek to establish and maintain cooperative working relationships over an extended period of time	
	Reach agreement on ways to overcome any difficulties, including how to resolve conflict in an amicable way	
	Exchange information on the extent to which your own work is meeting expected timescales and quality, and show initiative in obtaining progress reports from others	
	Agree and make changes that are necessary to achieve objectives	

Level 3 Key Skills in Improving own learning		
You will show that you can		
Agree targets	Develop an Action Plan	Review progress and achievement
By achieving the following contributory sub-skills		
Use various sources of information to identify ways to achieve what you want to do	Prioritize action to achieve your targets	Provide information on the quality of your learning and performance, including what you have learned and how you have learned it
Identify factors that might affect your plans	Deal with any difficulties in order to complete tasks and meet deadlines	Identify the factors that have affected the outcome
Agree targets which clearly say what you want to achieve, that are measurable and achievable over an extended period	Make revisions to your plan to take into account changed circumstances	Identify the targets you have met

Identify action points for each target, with timescales, and identify support you will need including arrangements for reviewing progress	Seek and actively use feedback and support from relevant sources to help you meet targets	Seek information from relevant sources to establish evidence of your achievements, including examples of how you have used your learning to meet new demands
Predict difficulties which may occur and identify alternative courses of action	Select and use different ways of learning, including studying a complex subject, learning through a complex practical activity, and independent learning	Present your own views and listen to the views of others to agree on ways to further improve your performance

Level 3   Key Skills in Problem Solving

You will show that you can

Explore problems and options	Plan and implement options	Check and describe results and review approach taken
By achieving the following contributory sub-skills		
Recognize when a problem exists	Plan how to carry out your chosen option and obtain agreement to go ahead from an appropriate person	Identify possible methods for checking if the problem has been solved
Select and use different methods for exploring the problem, including dividing it into sub-problems, and analysing its features	Implement your plan using support and feedback from others	Agree on the methods to use
Agree on how to show success in solving the problem	Review progress and revise your approach as necessary	Apply these methods and draw conclusions
Select and use a variety of methods to come up with different ways of tackling the problem		Describe the results
Compare the main features of each possible option, including risk factors		Review each stage of your approach to problem-solving
Justify the option you select to take forward		Identify alternative methods and options and predict if they would have been more effective

Table 12.1 Mapping Key Skills to the FENTO Standards

Eight Key Areas and related standards	Indicative chapter activities which generate appropriate evidence at Level 2/3					
	Communication	Application of Number	Information Technology	Working with others	Improving own learning	Problem solving
A **Assessing Learner Need**						
A1 Identify and plan for the needs of potential learners	A3g, A3h, A3m	A3c, A3d, A3e	A3j, A3k, A3l	A3f, A3q, A3h, A3j	A3p, A3q, A3r	A3l, A3m, A3n, A3s
A2 Make an initial assessment of learners' needs	A3c, A3j, A3r	A3c, A3d, A3e	A3j, A3k, A3l	A3m, A3t, A3w.	A3p, A3q, A3r	A3l, A3m, A3n, A3s
B **Planning and preparing teaching and learning programmes for groups and individuals:**						
B1 Identify the required outcomes of the learning programmes	B4c, B4e, B4g, B4j	N/A	B4l, B4r	B4c, B4f, B4m, B4n	B4h, B4o, B4r, B4t	B4b, B4e, B4f, B4g
B2 Identify appropriate teaching and learning techniques	B4c, B4e, B4g, B4j	N/A	B4l, B4r	B4c, B4f, B4m, B4n	B4h, B4o, B4r, B4t	B4b, B4e, B4f, B4g
B3 Enhance access to and provision of learning programmes	B4c, B4e, B4g, B4j	N/A	B4l, B4r	B4c, B4f, B4m, B4n	B4h, B4o, B4r, B4t	B4b, B4e, B4f, B4g
C **Developing and using a range of teaching and learning techniques**						
C1 Promote and encourage individual learning	C5g, C5j, C5k, C5q	N/A	C5b, C5m, C5p	C5c, C5g, C5m, C5n	C5q, C5s, C5v	C5a, C5h, C5j, C5s
C2 Facilitate learning in groups	C5g, C5j, C5k, C5q	N/A	C5b, C5m, C5p	C5c, C5g, C5m, C5n	C5q, C5s, C5v	C5a, C5h, C5j, C5s

		C5g, C5j, C5k, C5q	N/A	C5b, C5m, C5p	C5c, C5g, C5m, C5n	C5q, C5s, C5v	C5a, C5h, C5j, C5s
C3	Facilitate learning through experience	C5g, C5j, C5k, C5q	N/A	C5b, C5m, C5p	C5c, C5g, C5m, C5n	C5q, C5s, C5v	C5a, C5h, C5j, C5s
D	**Managing the Learning Process**						
D1	Establish and maintain an effective learning environment	D6a, D6b, D6e, D6l	N/A	D6i, D6n, D6o	D6b, D6d, D6e, D6i	D6g, D6k, D6m, D6o	D6c, D6e, D6f, D6o
D2	Plan and structure learning activities	D6a, D6b, D6e, D6l	N/A	D6i, D6n, D6o	D6b, D6d, D6e, D6i	D6g, D6k, D6m, D6o	D6c, D6e, D6f, D6o
D3	Communicate effectively with learners	D7a, D7c, D7f, D7p	N/A	D7h, D7i, D7r, D7s	D7d, D7e, D7j, D7m	D7d, D7g, D7m, D7p	D7d, D7g, D7j, D7o
D4	Review the learning process with learners	D7a, D7c, D7f, D7p	N/A	D7h, D7i, D7r, D7s	D7d, D7e, D7j, D7m	D7d, D7g, D7m, D7p	D7d, D7g, D7j, D7o
D5	Select and develop resources to support learning	D6a, D6b, D6e, D6l	N/A	D6i, D6n, D6o	D6b, D6d, D6e, D6i	D6g, D6k, D6m, D6o	D6c, D6e, D6f, D6o
D6	Establish and maintain effective working relationships	D7a, D7c, D7f, D7p	N/A	D7h, D7i, D7r, D7s	D7d, D7e, D7j. D7m	D7d, D7g, D7m, D7p	D7d, D7g, D7j, D7o
D7	Contribute to the organization's quality assurance systems	D7r, D7s, D7t	N/A	D7r, D7s, D7t	D7d, D7e, D7j. D7m	D7d, D7g, D7m, D7p	D7d, D7g, D7j, D7o
E	**Providing learners with support**						
E1	Induct learners into the organization	E8b, E8i, E8m, E8o	N/A	E8f, E8g, E8m, E8o	E8b, E8h, E8k, E8o	E8d, E8e, E8g, E8k	E8d, E8f, E8l, E8n
E2	Provide effective learning support	E8b, E8g, E8h, E8m	N/A	E8f, E8g, E8m, E8o	E8b, E8h, E8k, E8o	E8d, E8e, E8g, E8k	E8d, E8f, E8l, E8n
E3	Ensure access and guidance opportunities for learners	E8d, E8e, E8f, E8g	N/A	E8f, E8g, E8m, E8o	E8b, E8h, E8k, E8o	E8d, E8e, E8g, E8k	E8d, E8f, E8l, E8n

E4	Provide personal support to learners	E8d, E8f, E8l, E8n	E8d, E8e, E8g, E8k	E8b, E8h, E8k, E8o	E8f, E8g, E8m, E8o	N/A	E8e, E8f, E8k, E8m
F	Assessing the outcomes of learning and learners' achievements						
F1	Use appropriate assessment methods to measure learning and achievement	F9h, F9i, F9k, F9n	F9h, F9i, F9n, F9p	F9i, F9k, F9o, F9q	F9h, F9i, F9k, F9l	F9m, F9n, F9o, F9p	F9d, F9i, F9l, F9q
F2	Make use of assessment information	F9h, F9i, F9k, F9n	F9h, F9i, F9n, F9p	F9i, F9k, F9o, F9q	F9h, F9i, F9k, F9l	F9m, F9n, F9o, F9p	F9m, F9n, F9o, F9p
G	Reflecting on and evaluating one's own performance and planning future practice						
G1	Evaluate one's own practice	G10a, G10e, G10f	G10a, G10c, G10e	G10i, G10j, G10k	G10a, G10e, G10f	N/A	G10a, G10e, G10f
G2	Plan for future practice	G10g, G10h, G10i	G10f, G10g, G10h	G10i, G10j, G10k	G10g, G10h, G10i	N/A	G10g, G10h, G10i
G3	Engage in continuing professional development	G10j, G10k, G10l	G10i, G10j, G10l	G10i, G10j, G10k	G10j, G10k, G10l	N/A	G10j, G10k, G10l
H	Meeting professional requirements						
H1	Work within a professional value base	Above + H11 & H12	Above + H11 & H12	Above + H11 & H12	Above + H11 & H12	Above + H11 & H12	Above + H11 & H12
H2	Conform to agreed codes of professional practice	Above + H11 & H12	Above + H11 & H12	Above + H11 & H12	Above + H11 & H12	Above + H11 & H12	Above + H11 & H12

12.4 | OFSTED

Perhaps the key quality process currently undertaken by colleges is the Ofsted inspections under the Association of Colleges' Common Inspection Framework, which commenced within Further Education in April 2001. The CIF standards have much in common with the FENTO standards, but they differ in one major aspect. For Ofsted the focus is on the *experience of the learners* while for FENTO the criteria are related to the *performance of the teachers*. In Table 12.2 below we have attempted to show how these two perspectives are related. Although this correspondence cannot be precise, it does indicate how the same evidence may demonstrate how teachers respond to identified learner needs.

In the case of Ofsted, the key question that the inspectors will ask is:

> How effective and efficient is the provision of education and training in meeting the needs of learners, and why?

The above focus will be explored through seven sub-questions which will provide the focus for the inspection and twenty evaluation statements and quality criteria upon which the inspectors will base their judgements.

Seven key questions of the Common Inspection Framework:

- How well do learners achieve?
- How effective are teaching, training and learning?
- How are achievement and learning affected by resources?
- How effective are the assessment and monitoring of learning?
- How well do the programmes and courses meet the needs and interests of learners?
- How well are learners guided and supported
- How effective are leadership and management in raising achievement and supporting all learners?

The main purposes of the inspection will be to:

1. give an independent public account of the quality of education and training, the standards achieved and the efficiency with which resources are managed
2. help to bring about improvement by identifying strengths and weaknesses and highlighting good practice
3. keep the Secretary of State, the Learning and Skills Council (LSC) for England and the Employment Service informed about the quality and standards of education and training
4. promote a culture of self-assessment among providers, leading to the continuous improvement and maintenance of very high quality and standards

Although the above questions and the evaluation criteria do make the focus of inspections very clear, Ofsted have stressed that they wish to avoid being overly prescriptive. For example, colleges should not assume that lesson plans must be in a particular format, that exposition is undesirable, or that lessons must include a variety of activities at all cost. It is recognized that in different hands and with different students, different approaches can be equally effective.

Table 12.2 Mapping of Ofsted Standards to FENTO Key Areas

Eight FENTO Key Areas and related standards		OFSTED Evaluation and Quality criteria
A	Assessing Learner Need	
A1	Identify and plan for the needs of potential learners	Sec 2, Item 6 — Individual learning needs are accurately diagnosed and learners have access to effective additional support throughout their studies and training
A2	Make an initial assessment of learners' needs	Sec 2, Item 4 — Initial assessment provides an accurate basis on which to plan an appropriate programme of work
B	Planning and preparing teaching and learning programmes for groups and individuals	
B1	Identify the required outcomes of the learning programmes	Sec 2, Item 5 — The curriculum or an individual programme of work is planned and managed effectively to provide coherence and progression
B2	Identify appropriate teaching and learning techniques	Sec 2, Item 7 — Set, use and mark assignments and other tasks in a way that helps learners to progress
B3	Enhance access to and provision of learning programmes	Sec 2, Item 5 — The curriculum or programmes of work are socially inclusive, ensuring quality of access and opportunities for learners
C	Developing and using a range of teaching and learning techniques	
C1	Promote and encourage individual learning	Sec 2, Item 5 — Learners have the opportunity to broaden their experiences and enhance their personal development through a suitable variety of enrichment activities
C2	Facilitate learning in groups	Sec 2, Item 4 — Assessment information, including the analysis of performance of different groups of learners, is used to guide course and programme development

C3	Facilitate learning through experience	Sec 1, Item 1	Are prepared for effective participation in the workplace and the community
D	Managing the Learning Process		
D1	Establish and maintain an effective learning environment	Sec 2, Item 2	Show knowledge, technical competence and up-to-date expertise, at a level consistent with effective teaching, training and assessment of the course
D2	Plan and structure learning activities	Sec 1, Item 1	Make significant progress towards fulfilling their goals and potential
D3	Communicate effectively with learners	Sec 2, Item 2	Promote good working relationships that foster learning
D4	Review the learning process with learners	Sec 3, Item 7	The quality assurance arrangements are systematic and informed by the views of all interested parties
D5	Select and develop resources to support learning	Sec 2, Item 3	Learners have access to learning resources that are appropriate for effective independent study
D6	Establish and maintain effective working relationships	Sec 2, Item 3	There are enough qualified and experienced teaching, training and support staff
D7	Contribute to the organization's quality assurance systems	Sec 3, Item 7	Staff understand and are fully involved in the organization's quality assurance arrangements
E	Providing learners with support		
E1	Induct learners into the organization	Sec 2, Item 6	Induction programmes enable learners to settle into their course quickly, to understand their rights and responsibilities and the demands of the course
E2	Provide effective learning support	Sec 2, Item 6	Support arrangements are planned and managed coherently
E3	Ensure access and guidance opportunities for learners	Sec 2, Item 3	Accommodation provides a suitable setting for good teaching, training and learning and support for learners

E4	Provide personal support to learners	Sec 2, Item 6	Impartial guidance enables learners to choose the course or programme which is right for them;
F	Assessing the outcomes of learning and learners' achievements		
F1	Use appropriate assessment methods to measure learning and achievement	Sec 2, Item 4	Forms of assessment and recording are suitable for the courses and programmes being followed
		Sec 2, Item 4	Assessment is fair, accurate and carried out regularly
F2	Make use of assessment information	Sec 2, Item 4	Assessment is used to monitor progress and inform individual learners about how they are performing and how they might develop further
G	Reflecting on and evaluating one's own performance and planning future practice		
G1	Evaluate one's own practice	Sec 3, Item 7	Demanding targets for retention, achievement, progression and employment are set and met
G2	Plan for future practice	Sec 2, Item 4	Assessment information, including the analysis of performance of different groups of learners, is used to guide course and programme development
G3	Engage in continuing professional development	Sec 2, Item 3	The professional development of staff contributes to their effectiveness
H	Meeting professional requirements		
H1	Work within a professional value base	Sec 3, Item 7	Clear direction is given through strategic objectives, targets and values that are fully understood by staff, subcontractors and work placement providers
H2	Conform to agreed codes of professional practice	Sec 3, Item 7	There are explicit aims, values and strategies relating to equality for all that are reflected in the provider's work

In addition, although sessions will be observed, the inspectors will also be interested in the effective use of students' time outside of formal class teaching. Such provision is seen as essential if learners are to succeed and would include materials for students to work with on their own, IT facilities, libraries and other learning resources which make a major contribution to learning. The effectiveness of these facilities for learning will be evaluated.

Work experience also plays a significant part in many students' learning. Students who are employed, or who are based with an employer on a training programme, will undertake most of their learning away from college. The inspectors will wish to know how well students learn while at work, and will make judgements about how effectively their progress is monitored and recorded. This process may involve inspectors visiting students in their workplace and meeting with employers and work-based supervisors.

Inspection of work-based learning will assess whether the training process enables trainees to acquire the competence, skills and knowledge that comprise their learning objectives. Much training takes place at work, so workplace supervisors exercise a significant influence over trainees' learning. Work-based training is supplemented by off-the-job training that gives the trainees the background knowledge and skills that they apply in the workplace. Inspectors' judgements will take into account the extent to which teaching and training are suitable for adult learners, how they respond to teaching and whether they are capable of promoting their own learning.

The report on teaching and learning for the college as a whole will focus on the effectiveness of teaching, training and learning. It will draw out the strengths and weaknesses identified in curriculum areas. Lesson observation grades will be summarized under headings related to broad categories of qualifications. Overall attendance at lessons will be reported and compared with national benchmarks. Each curriculum section of the report will describe the quality of teaching on the courses inspected and include examples of lessons where teaching was particularly good or unsatisfactory.

During the inspection process judgements will be based mainly on:

- lesson observation
- discussions with learners, both individually and in groups
- discussions with teachers and managers
- scrutiny of students' marked work and practical work
- inspection of session plans and schemes of work
- analysis of students' feedback and surveys of their opinions
- analysis of attendance levels, which will be recorded and reported on in each curriculum section of the report

12.4.1 Observation of taught sessions

Inspectors will look for the following characteristics of good teaching (compare these with the criteria we developed in Chapter 5):

- use of clear objectives which are made known to the learners
- enthusiastic and interesting teaching that maintains the attention of all learners

- activities that are suitable for all learners, whatever their age and ability and which are suitably demanding
- awareness of different individual learner needs
- effective questioning of learners to check their understanding
- skilful leadership of discussions to ensure that learners' contributions are encouraged and valued
- clear explanations
- accurate and up-to-date technical knowledge
- sensitivity to issues relating to equality of opportunity and inclusivity
- clear writing on whiteboards and overhead projection acetates
- good-quality, well-produced handouts which are free from errors and which contain references where appropriate
- sufficient coverage of ground
- effective management of any transition between individual and group work
- a crisp end to the session, summarizing what has been learned and avoiding 'tailing off'

Session plans and Schemes of Work will be important documents during inspection and should contain the following detail:

Session plans should include	Schemes of Work should include
Basic information about the learner group	Basic information about the learner group
Details of course/programme, level, venue, etc.	Details of course/programme, level, venue, etc.
Clear statement of aims and objectives	Clear statement of overall aims and objectives
Main stages of session and proposed timings	Dates/week numbers and brief session details
Teacher input and activities	Teacher activity
Learner input and activities	Learner activity
Resources to be used	Resources to be used
Assessment methods	Assessment methods
Evaluation approach	Evaluation approach

Inspectors will focus on three main aspects while observing taught sessions. Their concerns with the quality of *teaching* will focus on the role of the teacher in preparing and delivering an effective lesson. Their judgements about *learning* will focus on the progress being made by learners during that session, taking into account their starting point. Their *attainment* concerns will focus on the standard of work produced by learners during that session, judged against the standards expected of learners at that point in their course, irrespective of their starting point.

The inspectors will produce summary judgements in the form of the grades indicated below which will be based on observations and other evidence collected during the inspection:

Observed sessions		Curriculum Areas and Leadership and Management	
Grade 1	Excellent	Grade 1	Outstanding
Grade 2	Very good	Grade 2	Good
Grade 3	Good	Grade 3	Satisfactory
Grade 4	Satisfactory	Grade 4	Unsatisfactory
Grade 5	Unsatisfactory	Grade 5	Very weak
Grade 6	Poor		
Grade 7	Very poor		

12.5 GTC CODE OF PRACTICE

The General Teaching Council for England (GTC) drew up their Code after extensive consultation with teachers from the compulsory sector in England. This Code sets out the beliefs, values and attitudes that make up teacher professionalism and recognizes that teachers work within a framework of legislation with many lines of accountability. It is the GTC belief that the complicated and varied roles that teachers need to fulfil make teaching one of the most demanding and rewarding of professions. The code was agreed in February 2002.

General Teaching Council Code of Professional Values and Practice for Teachers
Young people as pupils Teachers have insight into the learning needs of young people. They use professional judgement to meet those needs and to choose the best ways of motivating pupils to achieve success. They use assessment to inform and guide their work. Teachers have high expectations for all pupils, helping them to progress regardless of their personal circumstances and different needs and backgrounds. They work to make sure that pupils develop intellectually and personally, and to safeguard pupils' general health, safety and well-being. Teachers demonstrate the characteristics they are trying to inspire in pupils, including the spirit of intellectual enquiry, tolerance, honesty, fairness, patience, a genuine concern for other people and an appreciation of different backgrounds.
Teacher colleagues Teachers support their colleagues in achieving the highest professional standards. They are fully committed to sharing their own expertise and insights in the interests of the people they teach and are always open to learning from the effective practice of their colleagues. Teachers respect the rights of other people to equal opportunities and to dignity at work. They respect confidentiality where appropriate.
Other professionals, governors and interested people Teachers recognize that the well-being and development of pupils often depend on working in partnership with different professionals, the school governing body, support staff and other interested people within and beyond the school. They respect the skills,

expertise and contributions of these colleagues and partners and are concerned to build productive working relationships with them in the interests of pupils.

Parents and carers
Teachers respond sensitively to the differences in pupils' home backgrounds and circumstances and recognize the importance of working in partnership with parents and carers to understand and support their children's learning. They endeavour to communicate effectively and promote cooperation between the home and the school for the benefit of young people.

The school in context
Teachers support the place of the school in the community and appreciate the importance of their own professional status in society. They recognize that professionalism involves using judgement over appropriate standards of personal behaviour.

Learning and development
Teachers entering the teaching profession in England have been trained to a professional standard that has prepared them for the rigours and realities of the classroom. They understand that maintaining and developing their skills, knowledge and expertise is vital to achieving success. They take responsibility for their own continuing professional development, through the opportunities available to them, to make sure that pupils receive the best and most relevant education. Teachers continually reflect on their own practice, improve their skills and deepen their knowledge. They want to adapt their teaching appropriately to take account of new findings, ideas and techniques.

Conclusion
This code is intended to help make sure that the professional work of teachers helps their pupils to develop themselves fully and reach their highest potential in life. It is intended to be an evolving document, which will contribute to the definition of teacher professionalism and help in raising standards of achievement by pupils.

H12b   Comparable codes

Compare the above GTC Code with the FENTO occupational standards and the Ofsted Common Inspection Framework. Look particularly at the difference in tone and the specification of targets.

12.6   DEVELOPING A PERSONAL CODE OF PRACTICE

Throughout this book you have probably been using various chapter 'activities' and related work-based analysis to reflect on many aspects of your own teaching. Consequently, you have also been developing and expressing your own emerging 'code of practice'. As we have tried to say during our earlier chapters, for us this personal articulation represents the most important, defining steps in becoming a teacher. The establishment of your own value system is an ongoing process, which is more important than any externally imposed criteria. It is true that the various occupational and framework standards will have helped to guide you, but you will also have learnt much from colleagues and your own educational environment.

However, the crucial key to understanding will inevitably have been your relationship with your particular groups of learners. You may well have been influenced by some 'significant' experiences, but more probably it will have been the day-to-day, small interactions that have led to an awareness of the subtle ways in which you influence them and they affect you. Truly reflective practice is a sensitizing process, where the teacher's perceptual net gradually becomes so fine that it captures almost every nuance of learner reaction.

Even so, as important as sensitive awareness is, the progressive *development* of even an implicit code of practice must be dependent upon some explicit articulation. We often have a 'sense' of a particular aspect of practice, which could be called an intuitive grasp. Even though it remains unclear, this ill-defined feeling about a familiar situation or process may well influence our decision-making.

H12c Difficult articulation

Can you identify an aspect of your own practice of which you are aware, but which you haven't as yet thought through? It could be the way in which one or two students respond to some aspect of their learning, or it may be something a colleague has said about an individual or group, which you do not quite understand. Try to identify and analyse an example of a gut feeling, which is, so far, unexplained.

If you have tried this exercise, you may have found that a number of explanations, which you haven't previously considered, have now come to mind. The same may be true of the values you are developing in relation to teaching and learning. They may be as yet half-formed in your mind and yet, if you are going to make difficult decisions which will draw on your beliefs and attitudes, now would be a good time to begin to articulate them more clearly.

As we discussed in Chapter 10, a mentor is often a useful sounding board, who could help you to clarify your educational values. As Palmer (1998) observes:

> We should hold learning conversations to explore the mysteries of teaching and learning with the same respect as, say, a conversation about the mysteries of DNA.

H12d Explicit values

If you have already identified someone to act as your mentor you could begin a discussion around the aspects of teaching which you feel strongly about. If you do not wish to have such a formal relationship with a mentor, then perhaps you could hold a less formal discussion around the same topic with a colleague.

Obviously, the issues which are raised in the above conversation will be different for each practitioner, but you have made a start towards defining your own code of practice. It may be interesting to note that within Key Area H FENTO have identified some difficult tasks that many teachers would only tackle when they are more experienced. Three of these standards are listed below and you will notice that they require decisions, which depend very much on a well-established value system:

- H1a Encouraging learners to work effectively on their own

- H1c Remain open to different approaches and perspectives on teaching and learning
- H1d Develop conditions for learning which are based on mutual respect and trust

H12e   Value decisions

Develop a reflective response to one or more of the above criteria and discuss this with your mentor or a colleague.

Finally, now try to articulate your own important values and beliefs in relation to teaching and learning. Firstly, revisit the Ofsted, FENTO and GTC codes to identify the values that they have expressed which you feel strongly about (one way or another) and then add others of your own which may draw on your own reflections in your Personal Development Journal.

12.6.1   Teacher Profile

The articulation of a personal code of practice is useful because it identifies important aspects of practice that you value. However, you will be aware that job applications, promotion panels and the Teachers' Pay Initiative (TPI) all demand *evidence* that these beliefs find their way into practice and are valued by colleagues, managers and, most important of all, by your learners.

We suggest the development of a Teacher Profile, which would consist of documentary data that show the teachers' achievements in important areas of practice. Some of these are summarized in Table 12.3.

You can see that some data and evidence collected around the above themes will add substantially to your CV and will help you to begin to see the areas of practice that you value and expect others to value too.

H12f   Profile entries

Begin to collect entries for your profile using the above suggested categories as a starting point. However, don't forget that your own practice has many unique characteristics, which you should try to capture as well as the conventional values and beliefs.

12.7 | CONCLUSION

As expected, we are bringing the book to a close amidst continuing change and uncertainty! In addition to the 14–19 initiative discussed in the previous chapter, post-compulsory education in the coming years must face many new challenges. Learning Skills Councils will spearhead the government's drive for demand-led, employer-focused skills development to boost the economy.

Table 12.3 Suggested evidence for areas of practice in a Teacher Profile

Action research	Investigation of aspects of practice which may include a specific intervention (i.e. teaching in a different way) in order to generate useful data
Assessment	Specifications, variation of methods (e.g. controlled response/free response) marking schemes, feedback to students and cross-college moderation
Course development	Detail of the process of developing existing or new programmes, including consultation, curriculum design, course development committees, validation
Course evaluation	Student evaluation feedback both quantitative and qualitative
Cross-college innovations	Development of cross-college schemes, e.g. internal verification of Key Skills implementation
External examination	Extracts from external examiners' or verifiers' reports praising department or students
Journal articles	Publications of various kinds either individual or joint authorship
Research underpinning teaching	Curriculum research in the design of a programme or content supported by specific investigations
Seminar contribution	Contributions to in-house seminars or staff-development programmes, mentorship
Student learning	Evidence of excellent work, significant accomplishments, prizes, publications, mention in the press, exhibitions, selection for important roles
Student progression	Gaining places to study at a higher level, selected to represent the college or the county, employed in interesting posts, joining prestigious company
Subject contribution at a national level	Membership of national organizations, subject benchmarking, standards development, committee membership
Teaching development	Innovative approaches to teaching, mentorship, team-teaching, staff-development
Unsolicited written evidence	Letters from students who have successfully completed their studies giving reasons why they found the course/your support so valuable

Our new Learning and Skills Sector will be taken forward by a new broadly based, Sector Skills Council which will drive on the national Post-16 agenda led by four education Ministers in London, Edinburgh, Belfast and Cardiff.

It is very likely that present individual National Training Organizations such as FENTO, PAULO, ENTO, HESDA, ALI, etc. will gradually disappear as we move towards a single, coherent, accessible, set of occupational standards for an integrated Learning and Skills Sector.

The Adult Basic Skills Strategy Unit are involved in the development of a qualifications framework for teachers of adult literacy numeracy and ESOL, and this will have implications for all teachers within the new sector.

However, although the FENTO Occupational Standards for Teaching and Supporting Learning around which this book is based will also inevitably be developed and modified, the principles we have debated will remain. Hopefully, in the very near future the Institute for Learning will provide the same level of support for post-compulsory education, as the Institute for Learning and Teaching is providing for Higher Education. Perhaps the DfES may also finally find the money to turn into reality their long-standing proposal that there should be equivalence and transferability of teaching staff between the present post-compulsory and compulsory sectors. However, any hopes that we may have to be appropriately recognized and rewarded at last, will very much depend on how we respond to the initiative launched by Secretary of State Charles Clarke in November 2002 within 'Success for All', the DfES' vision for the future of the Learning and Skills Sector, which predictably has the 14–19 age group at the heart of its proposed policy developments:

> The sector must ensure that 14–19 learners have greater choice and higher standards, with a wide range of academic and vocational programmes providing clear opportunities to progress to higher education and skilled employment. It must also ensure that adult learners have greater access to excellent provision for basic skills, training for work and learning for personal development. And that employers have a productive engagement with a transformed and responsive network of providers committed to meeting regional and sub-regional skill needs. This is our challenge to you.

Clearly, there is within this document a concern that the old notions of competition between providers should quickly be replaced with a much more collaborative and comprehensive approach to provision which involves colleges, schools, private training providers and employers. Although there is still a very long way to go in the development of a coherent 14–19 Framework, it is very evident that the government envisage that post-compulsory education will play a significant part within a reformed KS4 and KS5. It is also safe to deduce from these proposals that during the next few years a great deal of money will be invested in PCET and in return, as you would expect, a great deal will be expected of us. Happily, there is much evidence available to show that we are very capable of meeting Charles Clarke's challenge.

One or two things are more certain. A great deal of money will be invested in PCET and a great deal will be expected of it in return. Our jobs will not get any easier, but we may at last start to be appropriately recognized and rewarded.

12.8 USEFUL SOURCES

Department of Education and Skills	*www.dfes.gov.uk*
FENTO	*www.fento.org.uk*
General Teaching Council	*www.gtce.org.uk*
Institute for Learning	*www.ifl.ac.uk*
Ofsted	*www.ofsted.gov.uk*
Research in Post-Compulsory Education	*www.triangle.co.uk*

Try *tipcet.com* for an update on policies and practices in post-compulsory education

12.9	RATIONALE FOR KEY AREA H – MEETING PROFESSIONAL REQUIREMENTS

FAQs	At Stage 1	At Stage 2	At Stage 3
Why do it?	Explicit standards provided by internal and external bodies will inform the development of your own values and purposes. By the very nature of their work, teachers must be self-regulating and self-motivated.	As a professional teacher and a reflective practitioner you have a responsibility to appraise your current abilities and experiences in relation to your own needs and ambitions and the needs and goals of your students, colleagues, department, faculty and college.	Beyond your immediate concern to improve your own practice will develop a concern to understand the wider context of education. You will gradually develop a set of educational values and purposes which you believe in and are prepared to support and defend.
Where are we going?	You are being guided by senior colleagues and by your own experiences of providing teaching and learning, towards the development of a personal value system in which you will believe sufficiently for you to be willing to defend whenever necessary and modify whenever it falls short of your own implicit standards. In other words, you are consciously developing towards becoming professional practitioner.	Your professional development will be wide-ranging, explicit and implicit and related to both personal enhancement and the needs of the college. Areas could include applications of ILT, the enhancement of student learning and the management of programmes. You may also consider relationship with colleagues, group membership and mutual support and subject updating to enable current and significant knowledge underpinned by experience to be shared with students. Reflect on experience, analyse your current role and evaluate your present contribution to the work of the department.	Reflect on the range of influences, both internal and external, which affect your own teaching context. Consider how departmental culture develops and is sustained and how, in comparison, other departments express their beliefs and values in relation to teaching, learning and assessment principles. Evaluate how your own particular skills and abilities may contribute to the department profile. Analyse the range of teaching and learning styles within your working context and the effect these may have on your learners.
How do we get there?	There are so many facets to your work in education that, inevitably, you will be developing in several	Before you consider who should be involved in your professional development plan, you need to identify	As an effective professional try to identify your strengths and the areas where you

	directions at once. However, if you put the students' needs first, the remainder will fall in place. A simple golden rule when working with learners is that, to be successful, you must find something about them to like.	the different forms of development you may become involved in. Consider your own basic key skills and related abilities and then consider your own specialism and possibilities of subject updating. Then reflect on a range of academic skills that you may develop, including research techniques. Finally, consider the many different approaches to teaching, which you could develop.	need to develop. Do you have a good understanding of the aims of the college as a whole? Do you understand how different courses are prioritized and how resources are allocated? Where does your programme stand in relation to national provision, are you conversant with current developments and anxieties?
Is this the best way?	As you would expect, there are many different roads to success and, usually, a teacher's personal qualities will indicate the route to be taken. Again, a sensitivity to the learners' needs will be a wonderful compass.	Consult with your line manager, staff-development officer, mentor, colleagues and students. Reflect on your developing areas of interest and the needs of the college. Are you aware of the effects of your teaching approach beyond the delivery of a particular syllabus?	Do your current methods help to develop student autonomy? Are you encouraging only individual striving or do your methods allow for the development of collaborative learning. Are you actively developing systems which support the dissemination of good practice?
When is the right time?	Often opportunities arrive at the wrong time, i.e. when you are so busy with other responsibilities that you are unable to recognize them, or take advantage of the opening presented. Knowing where you wish to go is a great help.	Professional development is an ongoing and continuous process, especially in organizational climates of change where you will be expected to be flexible and meet challenges as they arise. Reflective practice will help you to become more aware of these external needs.	Analyse your current range of commitments and identify the key periods in relation to your workload. Carry out an audit of your own particular qualities as a teacher and plan a process of development over the next two years. Consider the timing of the development in relation to your current commitments.
Who needs to know?	The more people who know about your areas of interest and particular skills the better. Use the profile guidance at the end of the chapter to start to collect evidence of your ability.	In order to initiate some of the identified developments you need to negotiate with colleagues involved in staff development, line management, human resource development and	Consider who you need to negotiate with in order to put the above further professional development plan into action.

		just as importantly with family, peers and students.	
How do we know when we've got there?	You will know that you have established yourself as a professional practitioner when you become concerned that standards are slipping. A well-established set of values is a sure sign that you have developed not only a commitment but also pride and some affection for what you do.	You will be aware of job satisfaction, raised standards, self-motivation, new job opportunities, new skills and knowledge and, perhaps, an increase in pay or status. However, you will inevitably wish to move on to a new destination fairly soon.	Reflect on accomplishments so far and begin to collect material evidence of professional achievement such as external examiners' reports, letters from students and employers. Collect examples of curriculum development, schemes of work, assessment schemes, and successful validations. (See profile development at end of this chapter.)
Has everyone had a fair chance?	Often taking advantage of career opportunities does mean that you have to become fairly selfish and decisions become difficult. Try to take a long-term perspective when making judgements.	Consider whether your development strategy will serve just your own needs or does it include your responsibility to your college. Reflect also on the opportunities that your employers provide and the barriers you are faced with (e.g. cost, time, resources, ability, etc.)	Consider how you may contribute to the professional development of other colleagues, how you might develop mentorship schemes to support students and induction processes to help new staff, etc.

12.10 KEY AREA H – MEETING PROFESSIONAL REQUIREMENTS

Purpose: Teachers and teaching teams need to be effective in applying the ethics and values of the teaching profession when working with learners and colleagues and in fulfilling their obligations and responsibilities as teachers. Among other things, teachers should recognize the diversity of students' needs and aspirations, understand and apply the concept of inclusive learning and encourage learner autonomy as well as reflecting the vocational and educational ethos of post-compulsory education. The actual standards for Key Area H are designed to be met through the production of evidence generated through your response to the previous seven Key Areas in addition to the activities both within Chapter 11 and in this chapter.

Please note: The FENTO Standards listed below are relevant to the following three levels of award – Stage 1 (Introduction), Stage 2 (Intermediate) and Stage 3 (Full Certification). All the standards are required at Stage 3, only those in italic and bold are required at Stage 2 and only those in italic are required at Stage 1.

UNIT H1. WORK WITHIN A PROFESSIONAL VALUE BASE *In order to do this teachers should*

Demonstrate that they are able to	and will have specific knowledge and critical understanding of	plus generic knowledge	Summary of appropriate evidence in this Key Area		Relevant Chapter Activities
Criteria a explore ways of encouraging learners to work effectively on their own and to take more responsibility for ensuring that their learning is successful		• The broad range of learning needs including the needs of those with learning difficulties and/or disabilities • Ways in which learners can work effectively on their own, and how to develop such learning	a	Learning Strategies, Developing Self-concept, Group Work, Learning Review, Inclusive Approaches	A3w, B4v,C5d, C5o, C5p, C5s, C5u, C5v, D7a,D7k, D7l,E8k, G10j
b *acknowledge the diversity of learners' experience and support the development needs of individuals*		• Alternative teaching styles and strategies • Equality of opportunity legislation, policies and best practice	b	Action Plans, Learning Agreements, Learning Reviews, Inclusive Approaches, Assessment Strategies	D7a, D7d, D7k, E8b, F9n, G10i, G10j

359

	Statement	Knowledge		Evidence	Standards
c	*remain open to different approaches and perspectives on teaching and learning*	• Their organization's equal opportunities policy and code of practice • The potential impact of their own values, beliefs and life experiences on learners and learning • Ways of ensuring that they meet the needs and aspirations of all learners • The organization's policies and practices for teaching and learning • Relevant national professional codes of practice • Key sources of information about potential markers and how to reach them	c	Subject updating, Innovative approaches, Collaborative teaching	H12a to H12f
d	*develop conditions for learning which are based on mutual respect and trust*	• How to create an environment conducive to learning	d	Assess needs, Accommodate learning styles, Emancipation, Developing Self-esteem, Facilitation, Motivational approaches, Inclusion	A3a, A3q, A3r, A3w, B4s, C5g, C5p, D6d, D7h, E8k, F9n, G10j
e	*evaluate how their own practice fosters a desire to learn and enables learners to work effectively on their own and to achieve to the best of their ability*		e	Personal Development Journal Commentary	G10a to G10m, H12a to H12f
f	*ensure that their own practice promotes equality of opportunity and addresses the needs of all learners*		f	Inclusive and Facilitative Approaches	E8a to E8p H12a to H12f
g	*recognize and respect the different values of all those with an interest in the learning process within the organization and the wider community*	• Ways of establishing and clarifying the limits of one's own authority in terms of legal responsibilities and lines of authority and communication	g	Personal Development Journal Commentary	A3r, A3w, B4v, C5v, D6k, D7t, E8o, F9pG10m H12a to H12f

h	use their own experiences of learning to inform their approach to teaching		Personal Development Journal Commentary	2a, 2e, 2h, 2i and 2j, *A3r, A3u, B4v,C5v, D6k, D7r, E8o, F9pG10m H12a to H12f*
i	work in a way which recognizes the needs of the institution and the values of the profession and reconciles potential conflicts between them		Personal Development Journal Commentary	A3r, A3w, B4v,C5v, D6k, D7r, E8o, F9pG10m H12a to H12f
j	work effectively with others to benefit learners	• Situations which provide opportunities to learn from others	Personal Development Journal Commentary	A3r, A3w, B4v, C5v, D6k, D7r, E8o, F9pG10m
k	exercise professional judgement and can justify their actions in terms of meeting learners' needs		Personal Development Journal Commentary	A3r, A3w, B4v, C5v, D6k, D7r, E8o, F9pG10m H12a to H12f

		Plus commentary in PDJ on the purposes and value of working within a professional value base, together with records in your Practice File of Teaching Observations, Lesson Plans, Rationales, Self-Evaluations and Progress Summary
Key to above standards required at each FENTO Stage: *Introduction Stage – italic* **Intermediate Stage + bold** Certification Stage – all		

UNIT H2. CONFORM TO AGREED CODES OF PROFESSIONAL PRACTICE *In order to do this teachers should:*

	Demonstrate that they are able to:	*and have specific knowledge and critical understanding of:*	*plus generic knowledge of:*	*Summary of appropriate evidence in this Key Area*		*Relevant Chapter Activities*
a	Criteria: identify an appropriate professional code of practices relevant to the vocational area and practice within post-compulsory education	Appropriate national codes of professional practice and their relevance to current practice within post-compulsory education	• The broad range of learning needs including the needs of those with learning difficulties and/or disabilities • Ways in which learners can work effectively on their own, and how to develop such learning	A	Personal Development Journal Commentary	H12a to H12f
b	adopt and maintain a professional form of behaviour towards learners and others		• Alternative teaching styles and strategies • Equality of opportunity legislation, policies and best practice • Their organization's equal opportunities policy and code of practice • The potential impact of their own values, beliefs and life experiences on learners and learning • Ways of ensuring that they meet the needs and aspirations of all learners • The organization's policies and practices for teaching and learning	b	Personal Development Journal Commentary	2i, A3r, B4u, B4v, 3ru, D6m, D7q, D7r, D7t, E8l, E8o, E8p, F9n, F9o, F9p, G10m, H11h, H12a to H12f

c	establish appropriate parameters for professional relationships and exercise judgement as to the best way to meet learners' needs	• Relevant national professional codes of practice • Key sources of information about potential markets and how to reach them	c	Personal Development Journal Commentary	2i, A3r, B4u, B4v, 3ru, D6m, D7q, D7r, D7t, E8l, E8o, E8p, F9n, F9o, F9p, G10m, H11h, H12a to H12f
d	demonstrate responsibility for the effectiveness of education and training and commitment to the well-being, progress and achievement of learners	Sources of specialist information and technical advice about one's responsibilities as a teacher and how to access such information	d	Personal Development Journal Commentary	2i, A3r, B4u, B4v, 3ru, D6m, D7q, D7r, D7t, E8l, E8o, E8p, F9n, F9o, F9p, G10m, H11h, H12a to H12f

	Statement	Detail		Evidence	Codes
e	*are aware of and meet their personal responsibilities towards learners and others within the framework of the organization's rules, regulations and duties of care towards learners and others*	• Legal responsibilities for learners including health and safety, data protection and copyright • The rights of learners and teachers' obligations to learners	e	Personal Development Journal Commentary	B4v, 3ru, D6m, D7q, D7r, D7t, E8l, E8o, E8p, F9n, F9o, F9p, G10m, H11h, H12a to H12f
f	**meet professional responsibilities in relation to organizational policies and practices**	• Contractual obligations • The limits of teachers' own authority and responsibility	f	Personal Development Journal Commentary	E8l, E8o, E8p, F9n, F9o, F9p, G10m, H11h, H12a to H12f
g	**represent the organization in a professional and appropriate manner**		g	Personal Development Journal Commentary	H11h, H12a to H12f
h	*respect the contribution of others to the learning process*		h	Personal Development Journal Commentary	H11h, H12a to H12f
i	*acknowledge the influence of resource constraints and make best professional use of resources and learning opportunities for the benefit of learners*		i	Personal Development Journal Commentary	H11h, H12a to H12f

Key to above standards required at each FENTO Stage: *Introduction Stage – italic* **Intermediate Stage + bold** Certification Stage – all		Plus commentary in PDJ on the purposes and value of conforming to agreed codes of professional practice, together with records in your Practice File of Teaching Observations, Lesson Plans, Rationales, Self-Evaluations and Progress Summary

BIBLIOGRAPHY

Armitage, A. *et al.* (1999) *Teaching and Training in Post-Compulsory Education*, Buckingham: Open University Press.

Asch, S.R. (1956) Studies of independence and conformity: A minority of one against a unanimous majority. *Psychological Monographs 9* (whole issue).

Auerbach, E.R. (1986) 'Competency-based ESL: One step forward or two steps back', *TESOL Quarterly*, Vol. 20, No. 3, (411–429)

Ausubel, D. and Andersson, R.C. (1965) *Readings in the Psychology of Cognition*, New York: Holt, Rinehart and Winston.

Bailey, C. (1989) 'The Challenge of Economic Utility', in Cosin, B., Flude, M. and Hales, M. (eds) *School, Work and Equality*, Buckingham: Open University Press.

Bain, D., Ballantyne R., Packer, J. and Mills, W. (1999) 'Understanding Journal Writing to Enhance Student Teachers' Reflectivity During Field Experience Placements' *Teachers and Teaching; theory and practice*, Vol. 5, No. 1, 23–32.

Ballantyne, R. & Packer, J. (1995) 'Making Connections: using student journals as a teaching/learning aid,' *HERDSA Gold Guide*, No. 2 (Canberra).

Bandura, A. and Walter, R.H. (1963) *Social learning and personality development*, New York: Holt, Rinehart & Winston.

Bash, L. (1985) *Urban Schooling: Theory and Practice*, Buckingham: Open University Press.

Belbin, M. (1993) 'Team Roles at Work' in Meredith, M. and Belbin, R. (1993) *Management Teams: Why they succeed or fail*, Butterworth: Heinemann.

Bennett, R. (1974) *First Class Answers in History*, London: Weidenfield and Nicolson.

Bigge, M.L. (1982) *Learning Theories for Teachers*, New York: Harper and Row.

Bloom, B.S. (ed) (1956) *Taxonomy of Educational Objectives: Handbook 1, Cognitive Domain*, London: Longman.

Bolton, G. (2001) *Reflective Practice: Writing and Professional Development*, London: Paul Chapman Publishing.

Boud, D., Keogh, R. and Walker, D. (1985) 'Promoting Reflection in Learning', in Boud, D. Keogh, R. and Walker, D. (1985), *Reflection: Turning Experience into Practice*, London: Kogan Page.

Boyle, D. (2000) *The Tyranny of Numbers*, London: Harper Collins.

Bruner, J. (1966) *Towards a Theory of Instruction*, Cambridge, Massachusetts: Harvard University Press.

Burns, R (1982) *Self-Concept Development and Education*, London: Holt, Rinehart and Winston.

Bush, T. and Middlewood, D. (eds) (1997) *Managing People in Education*, London: Paul Chapman Publishing.

Bush, T. & West-Burnham, J. (1994) *The Principles of Educational Management*, London: Longman Group UK Ltd.

Calderhead, J. and Gates, P. (eds) (1993) *Conceptualising Reflection in Teacher Development*, London: Falmer Press.

Calderhead, J. (1988) *Teachers' Professional Learning*, Philadelphia: Falmer Press.

Carr, W. (1995) *For Education – Towards Critical Educational Inquiry*, Buckingham: Open University Press.

Castling, A. (1996) *Competence based Teaching and Training*, City & Guilds: Macmillan.

Clement, D.E. and Sullivan, D.W. (1970) 'No risky shift effects with real groups and real risks' *Psychonomic Science*, Vol. 18, 243–5.

Cohen, L. and Manion, L. (1989) Research Methods in Education, London: Routledge.

Cooley, C.H. (1912) *Human Nature and Social Order*, New York, Scribners.

Crawford, M., Kydd, L. & Riches, C. (eds) (1997) *Leadership and Teams in Educational Management*, Buckingham: Open University Press.

Currie, R. (1986) 'Validity and Reliability' in Jones, R.L. and Bray, E. (1986) *Assessment from Principles to Action*. London: Macmillan.

Daines, J. and Graham, B. (1997) *Adult Learning, Adult Teaching*, Continuing Education Press: University of Nottingham

Dale, B.G. and Oakland, J.S. (1991) *Quality Improvement Through Standards*, Cheltenham: Stanley Thornes Ltd.

Dart, B. and Clarke, J. (1991) 'Helping students become better learners: a case study in teacher education', *Higher Education*, Vol. 22, 317–35.

Dearing, R. (1996) *Review of Qualifications for 16–19 year olds (Dearing II)*, Hayes: SCAA.

Deming, W.E. (1986) *Out of the Crisis: Quality, Productivity and Competitive Position*, Cambridge University Press.

Department of Employment (1984) *Training for Jobs*, London: HMSO

DES (1980) *A Framework for the School Curriculum*, London: HMSO.

DES (1985) *Education and Training for Young People*, London: HMSO.

DES/DOE (1991) *Education and Training for the 21st Century*, London: HMSO.

DES/DOE (1991) *Higher Education – A New Framework*, London: HMSO

Dewey, J. (1916) *Democracy and Education*, A Free Press Paperback

Dewey, J (1933) *How we think: A Restatement of the Relation of Reflective Thinking to the Educative Process* Chicago: Henry Regnery.

Dewey, J. (1938) *Experience and Education*, London: Collier Macmillan Publishers

DfEE (1997) *Qualifying for Success: A consultation paper on the future of post-16 qualifications* London: HMSO.

DfEE (1998a) *The Learning Age: A renaissance for a New Britain*, London: HMSO.

DfEE (1998b) *Further Education for the New Millennium: Response to the Kennedy Report*, London: HMSO.

DfEE (1999) *Learning to Succeed: A New Framework for Post-16 Learning*, London: HMSO.

DfEE (2002) *14–19: Extending Opportunities: Raising Standards*, London: HMSO.

DfES (2002) *Success For All: Reforming Further Education and Training*, London: HMSO.

DfES (2003) *14–19: Opportunity and Excellence* London: HMSO.

Douglas, S. (1992) 'Notes toward a history of media audiences', *Radical History Review*, 54 127–38.

Ecclestone, K. (2002) *Learning Autonomy in Post-16 Education*, London, Routledge Falmer.

Ecclestone, K. (1997) 'Energising or enervating: implications of NVQs in professional development' *Journal of Vocational Education and Training*, 49, No. 1, 65–79.

Ecclestone, K. (1996) *How to Assess the Vocational Curriculum*, London: Kogan Page.

Eldridge, W.D. (1983) 'The use of Personal Logs to assist Clinical Students in understanding and integrating theories of Counselling Intervention' *Instructional Science*, Vol. 12, 279–83.

Elliott, G. (1996) *Crisis and Change in Vocational Education and Training*, London: Jessica Kingsley Publishers.

Fawbert, F.P. (1987) *Using Video in Training*, Carnforth, UK: Parthenon Publishing.

FEU Development Officers (1994) *Tackling Targets*, London: Further Education Unit.

Freire, P. (2000) *Pedagogy of the Oppressed (30th Anniversary Edition)*, London: Continuum International Publishing.

Gagne, R.M. (1985) *The Conditions of Learning*, New York: Holt, Rinehart and Winston.

Gardner, H. (1993) *Multiple Intelligence's: The Theory in Practice*, New York: Basic Books.

Gibbs, G. (1988) Learning by Doing, London: Further Education Unit.

Gregoric, A. (1984) *An Adult's Guide to Style*, New York: Harper & Row.

Gronlund, N. (1985) *Stating Behavioural Objectives for Classroom Instruction, (3rd Edition)* New York: Macmillan.

Hackman, J.R. and Morris C.G. (1978) 'Group Process and group effectiveness: a reappraisal, in Berkowits, L. (ed.) *Group Processes*, New York: Academic Press.

Harper, H. (1997) *Management in Further Education*, David Fulton Publishers.

Harris, A., Bennett, N. and Preedy, M. (eds) (1997) *Organisational Effectiveness and Improvement in Education*, Buckingham: Open University Press.

Hayek, F. (1960) *The Constitution of Liberty*, London: Routledge and Kegan Paul.

Hettich, P. (1990) Journal writing: old fare or nouvelle cuisine? *Teaching of Psychology*, Vol. No. 17, 36–9.

Hillgate Group (1987) *The Reform of British Education*, London: Claridge Press.

Hodkinson, P. and Issitt, M. (1995) 'Competence, professionalism and vocational education and training,' in Hodkinson, P. and Issitt, M. (eds) *The challenge of competence*. London: Cassell.

Honey, P. and Mumford, A. (1982) *The Manual of Learning Styles Maidenhead: Peter Honey*.

Hyland, T. (1993) 'Professional development and competence-based education' *British Journal of Education Studies*, Vol. 19, No. 1, 123–32.

Hyland, T. (1996) 'Professionalism, ethics and work-based learning' *British Journal of Education Studies*, Vol. 44, No. 2, 168–180.

IPPR (1988) *Educational Attainment – A Comparative Study*, London: Institute for Public Policy Research.

James, W. (1890) *Principles of Psychology*, New York: Holt, Rinehart and Winston.

Johnson, D.W., and Johnson, R.T. (1979) 'Conflict in the classroom: Controversy in learning' *Review of Educational Research*, 49 (1), 51–70.

Johnson, D.W., and Johnson, R.T. (1990) *Cooperation and Competition: Theory and Research*, Edina, Minn.: Interaction Book Company.

Jones, R.L. and Bray, E. (1986) *Assessment: From Principles to Action*, London: Macmillan.

Katz, B. (1989) *Turning Practical Communication into Business Power*, London: Mercury Books.

Kelly, G (1955) *The Psychology of Personal Constructs, Vols. I and II*. New York: W.W. Norton.

Kemmis, S. (1985) 'Action research and the Politics of Reflection' in Boud, D., Keogh, R.

and Walker, D. (1985) *Reflection: Turning Experience into Practice*, London: Kogan Page.

Knowles, M. (1975) *Self-Directed Learning: A Guide for Learners and Teachers*, Chicago: Association Press.

Knowles, M. (1984) *The Adult Learner; A Neglected Species (3rd Edition)*, Houston: Gulf Publishing.

Kolb, D.A. (1984) *Experiential Learning – Experience as the source of learning and development*, Englewood Cliffs, New Jersey: Prentice Hall.

Krathwohl, D.R. (1964) *Taxonomy of Educational Objectives: Handbook II, Affective Domain*, New York: David McKay.

Landeen, J., Byrne, C. and Brown, B. (1992) 'Journal keeping as an educational strategy in teaching psychiatric nursing' *Journal of Advanced Nurnsing*, Vol. 17, 347–55.

Lawton, D. (1992) *Education and Politics in the 1990s*, London: The Falmer Press.

Lawton, D. (2002) 'Towards a 14 to 19 Framework' *Forum*, Vol. 44, No. 2.

Leary, M. (1981) 'Working with biography,' in Boydell, T. and Pedler, M. (eds) *Management Self-Development: Concepts and Practices*, Aldershot: Gower.

Lewin, K. (1951) *Field Theory in Social Sciences*, New York: Harper Row.

Longhurst, R.J. (1996) 'Education as a commodity: the political economy of the new further education' *Journal of Further and Higher Education*, Vol. 20, No. 2 49–66.

Martinez, P., Houghton, J. and Krupska, M. (1998) *Staff Development for Student Retention*, London: Further Education Development Agency.

Maslow, A.H. (1970) *Motivation and Personality*, New York: Harper and Row.

McAllister, M. (1996) 'Learning contracts: an Australian experience' *Nurse Education Today*, Vol. 16, 199–205.

McMurtry, J. (1991) 'Education and the Market Model' *Journal of Philosophy of Education*, Vol. 25, No. 2.

Mead, G.H. (1934) *Mind, Self and Society*, Chicago: University of Chicago Press

Meredith, M. and Belbin, R. (1981) *Management Teams: Why they Succeed or Fail*, Butterworth: Heinemann.

Minton D, (1991) *Teaching Skills in Further and Adult Education*, London: City and Guilds/Macmillan Publishing.

Moon, J. (1999) *Reflection in Learning and Professional Development: Theory and Practice*, London: Kogan Page.

Morrison, K. (1998) *Management Theories for Educational Change*, London: Paul Chapman Publishing Ltd.

Mullins, L.J. (1999) *Management and Organisational Behaviour (5th Edition)*, London: Pearson Education Limited.

Palmer, J.P. (1996) *The Courage to Teach*, New York: Jossey-Bass.

Parker, S. (1997) *Reflective Teaching in the Post-Modern World. A Manifesto for Education in Post-modernity*, Buckingham: Open University Press

Parlett, M and Hamilton, D (1977) 'Beyond the Numbers Game' in Hamilton, D. *et al.* (eds) *Beyond the Numbers Game*, London: Macmillan.

Pask, G (1976) 'Styles and strategies of learning' *British Journal of Educational Psychology*, Vol. 5, 128–48.

Perry, W.G. (1970) *Forms of Intellectual and Ethical Development in College Years*, New York: Holt, Rinehart and Winston.

Petty, G. (1998) *Teaching Today*, Cheltenham: Stanley Thornes.

Preedy, M., Glatter, R. and Levacic, R. (1997) *Educational Management: Strategy Quality and Resources*, Buckingham, Open University Press.

Reece, I., and Walker, S. (1997) *Teaching, Training and Learning – A Practical Approach (third edition)*, Sunderland: Business Education Publishers.

Reeves, F. (1995) *The Modernity of Further Education*, Wolverhampton: Bilston College Publications.

Revans, R. (1980) *Action Learning: New Techniques for Management*, London: Bland and Briggs.

Rogers, A. (1994) *Teaching Adults*, Buckingham: Open University Press.

Rogers, C. (1983) *Freedom to Learn for the 80s*, Columbus: Merrill.

Rowntree, D. (1977) *Assessing Students: How Shall we Know them?* London: Harper Row

Sallis, E. (1996) *Total Quality Management in Education*, London: Kogan Page.

Schon, D. (1987) *Educating the Reflective Practitioner*, San Francisco: Jossey-Bass.

Scriven, M (1973) 'The methodology of evaluation' in Worthen, B.R. and Sanders, J.R. (eds) *Educational Evaluation: Theory and Practice*, Belmont California: Wadsworth.

Shibutani, T. (1971) *Human Behaviour and Social Processes*, New York: Prentice-Hall.

Simpson, E.J. 'The Classification of Educational Objectives in the Psycho-motor Domain', *The Psychomotor Domain (Vol. 3)*, Washington: Gryphon.

Skinner, B.F. (1938) *The Behaviour of Organisms: an Experimental Analysis*, London: Routledge and Kegan Paul.

Smithers, A. and Robinson, P. (2000) *Changing Colleges: Further Education in the Market Place*, London: HMSO.

Social Exclusion Unit (1999) *Bridging the Gap: New Opportunities for 16–18 year olds not in Education, Employment or Training*, London: HMSO.

Stake, R.E. (1967) 'Towards a technology for the evaluation of educational programmes' in Tyler, R., *et al.*, *Perspectives on Curriculum Evaluation*, (AERA Monagraph Series) Chicago: Rand McNally.

Steiner, I.D. (1972) *Group Processes and Productivity*, New York: Academic Press.

Stenhouse, L. (1975) *An Introduction to Curriculum Research and Development*, London: Heinemann

Stoker, D. (1994) *Teaching and Learning in Practice* Nursing Times, Vol. 2, 65–73.

Stufflebeam, D.L. and Scriven, M.S. (eds) (1985) *Evaluation Models: Viewpoints on Educational and Human Services Evaluation*, Boston, Mass.: Kluwer-Nijhoff.

Thorndike, E.L. (1931) *Human Learning*, New York: Prentice-Hall.

Trevor, K. and Tollitt-Evans, J. (1992) *Teaching in Further Education*, London: Blackwell.

Tripp, D. (1993) *Critical Incidents in Teaching*, London: Routledge.

Tuckman, B.W. (1965) 'Developmental Sequence in Small Groups' *Psychological Bulletin*, Vol. 63, No. 6, 384–99.

Tyler, R. (1949) *Basic Principles of Curriculum and Instruction*, Chicago: University of Chicago Press.

Wagenaar, T.C. (1984) 'Using student journals in sociology courses' *Teaching Sociology*, Vol. 11, 419–37.

Walker, D. (1985) 'Writing and reflection' in Boud, D., Keogh, R. and Walker, D. (eds) *Reflection: Turning Experience into Learning*, London: Kogan Page.

Walkin, L. (1990) *Teaching and Learning in Further and Adult Education*, Cheltenham: Stanley Thornes.

Wiener, M. (1985) *English Culture and the Decline of the Industrial Spirit*, Harmondsworth: Penguin.

Yinger, R.J. and Clark, C.M. (1981) *Reflective Journal Writing: Theory and Practice*,

Occasional Paper No. 50, Michigan: The Institute for Research on Teaching, Michigan State University.

Zeichner, K.M. (1992) 'Conceptions of reflective teaching in contemporary US teacher education program reforms' in Valli, L. (ed), *Reflective Teacher Education*, Albany: New York State University Press.

INDEX